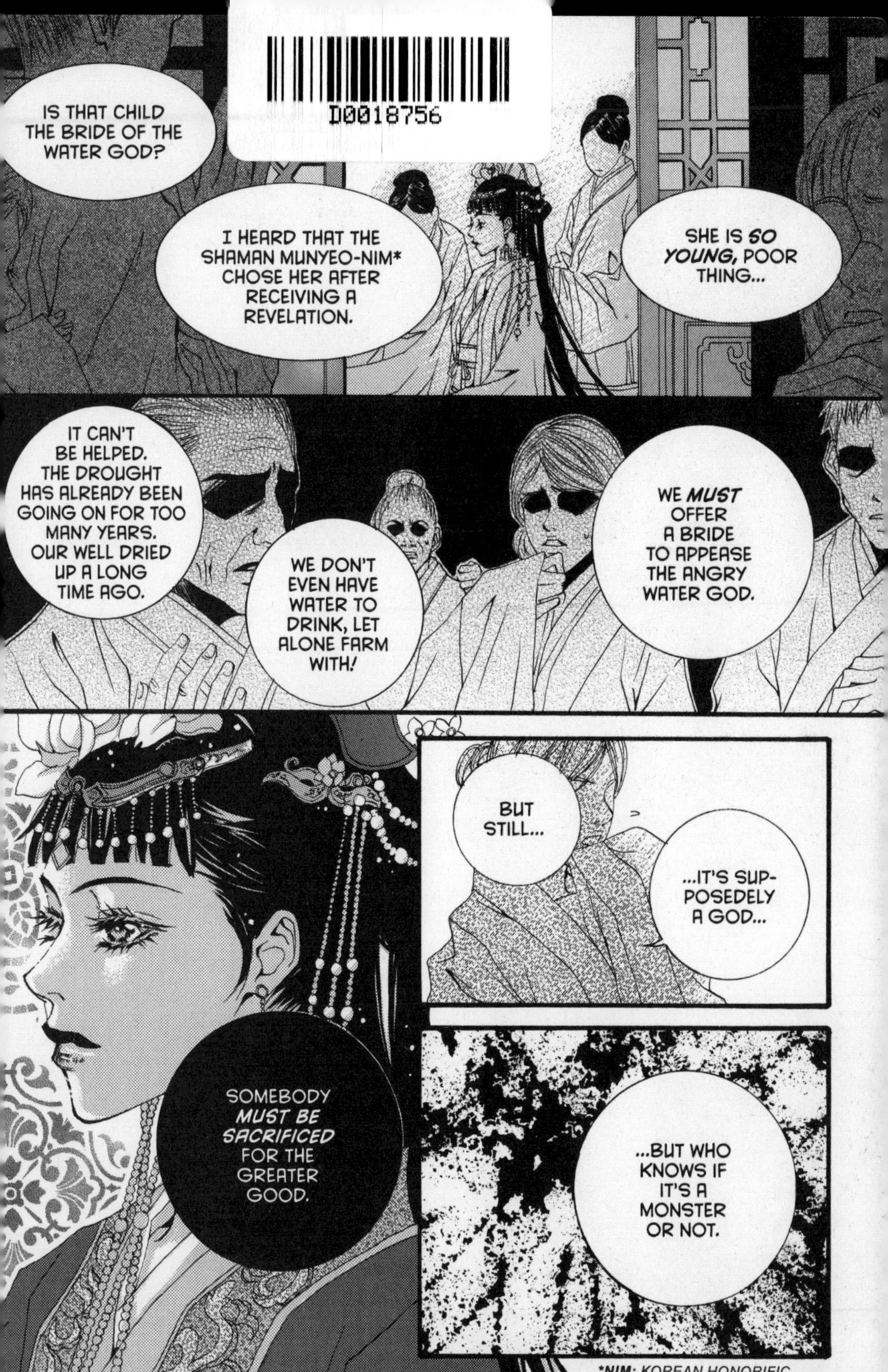
IS THAT CHILD THE BRIDE OF THE WATER GOD?
I HEARD THAT THE SHAMAN MUNYEO-NIM* CHOSE HER AFTER RECEIVING A REVELATION.
SHE IS *SO YOUNG,* POOR THING...
IT CAN'T BE HELPED. THE DROUGHT HAS ALREADY BEEN GOING ON FOR TOO MANY YEARS. OUR WELL DRIED UP A LONG TIME AGO.
WE DON'T EVEN HAVE WATER TO DRINK, LET ALONE FARM WITH!
WE *MUST* OFFER A BRIDE TO APPEASE THE ANGRY WATER GOD.
BUT STILL...
...IT'S SUP-POSEDELY A GOD...
SOMEBODY *MUST BE SACRIFICED* FOR THE GREATER GOOD.
...BUT WHO KNOWS IF IT'S A MONSTER OR NOT.

***NIM:** KOREAN HONORIFIC, SIMILAR TO "SIR" OR "MA'AM."

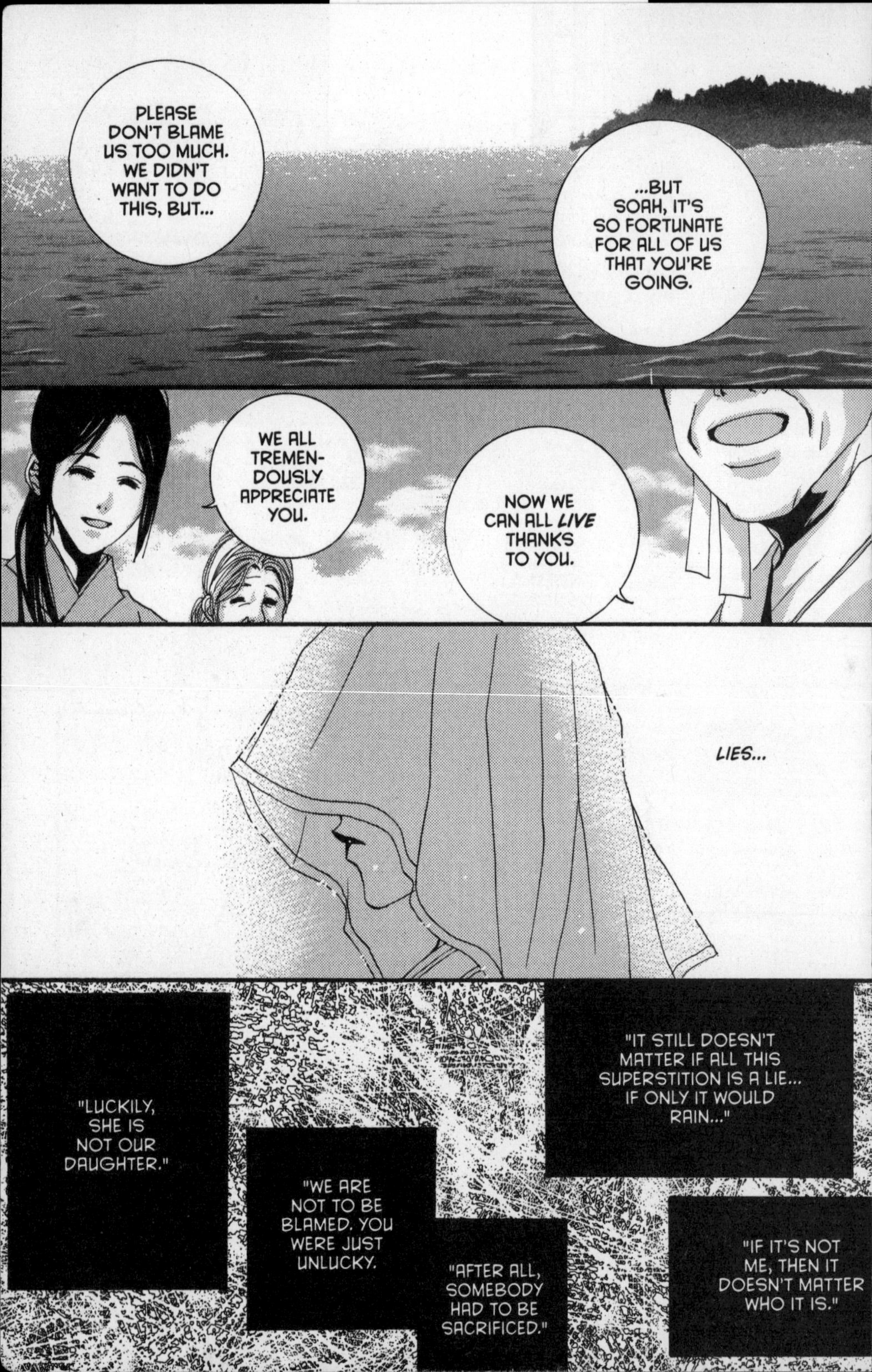
PLEASE DON'T BLAME US TOO MUCH. WE DIDN'T WANT TO DO THIS, BUT...
...BUT SOAH, IT'S SO FORTUNATE FOR ALL OF US THAT YOU'RE GOING.
WE ALL TREMEN-DOUSLY APPRECIATE YOU.
NOW WE CAN ALL *LIVE* THANKS TO YOU.
LIES...
"LUCKILY, SHE IS NOT OUR DAUGHTER."
"WE ARE NOT TO BE BLAMED. YOU WERE JUST UNLUCKY.
"AFTER ALL, SOMEBODY HAD TO BE SACRIFICED."
"IT STILL DOESN'T MATTER IF ALL THIS SUPERSTITION IS A LIE... IF ONLY IT WOULD RAIN..."
"IF IT'S NOT ME, THEN IT DOESN'T MATTER WHO IT IS."

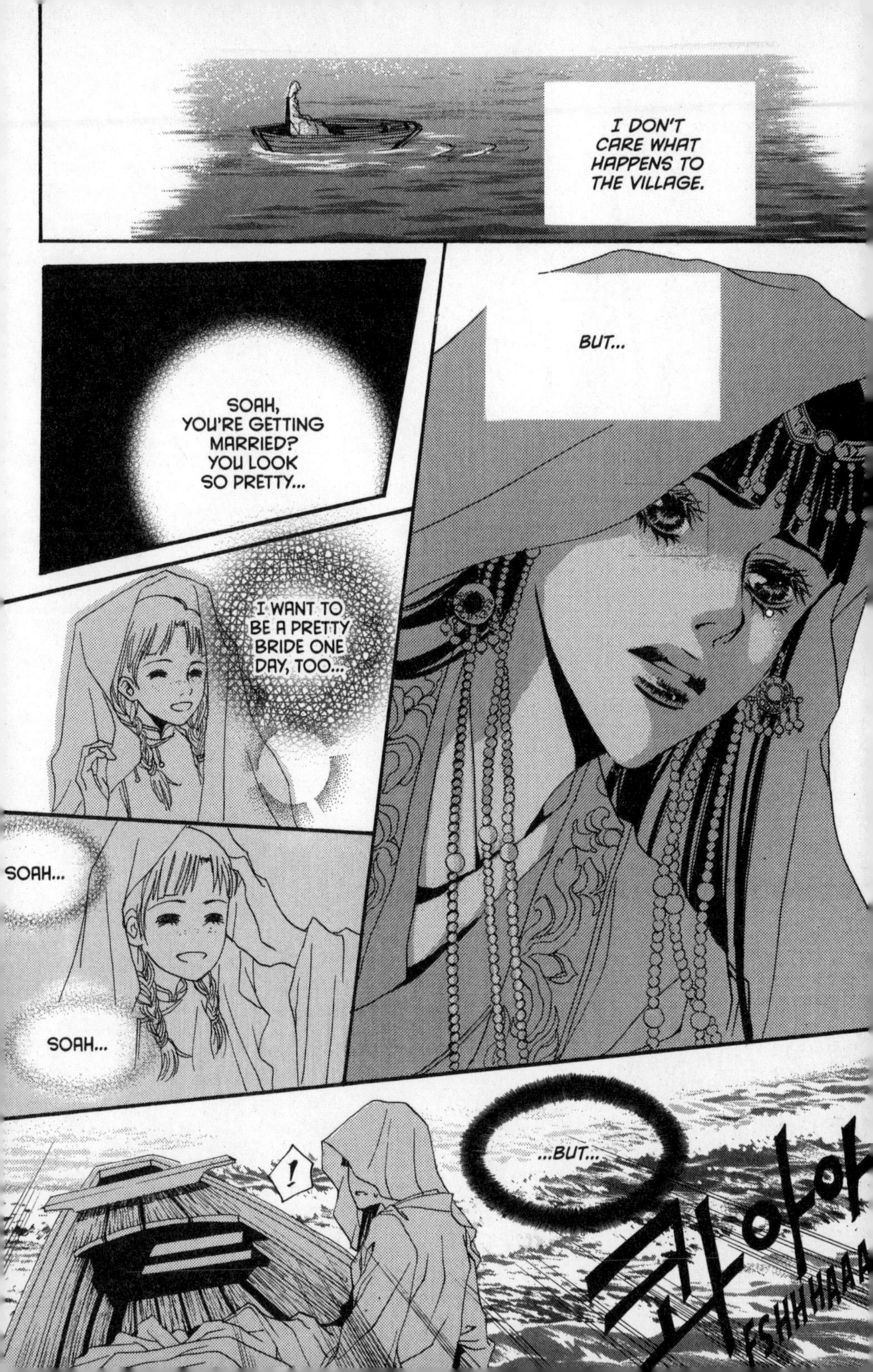
I DON'T CARE WHAT HAPPENS TO THE VILLAGE.
BUT...
SOAH, YOU'RE GETTING MARRIED? YOU LOOK SO PRETTY...
I WANT TO BE A PRETTY BRIDE ONE DAY, TOO...
SOAH...
SOAH...
...BUT...
!
FSHHHAAA

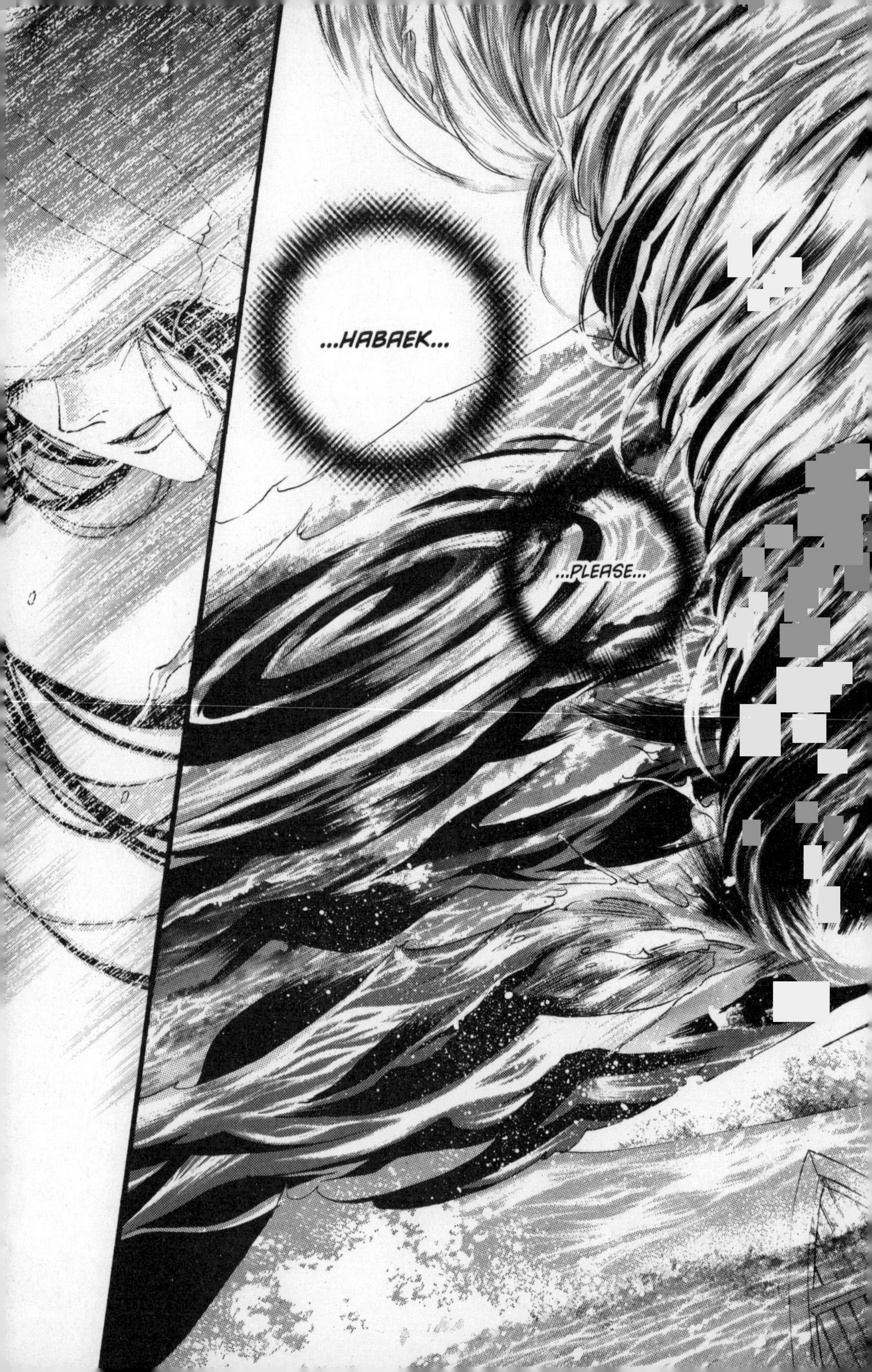
...HABAEK...
...PLEASE...

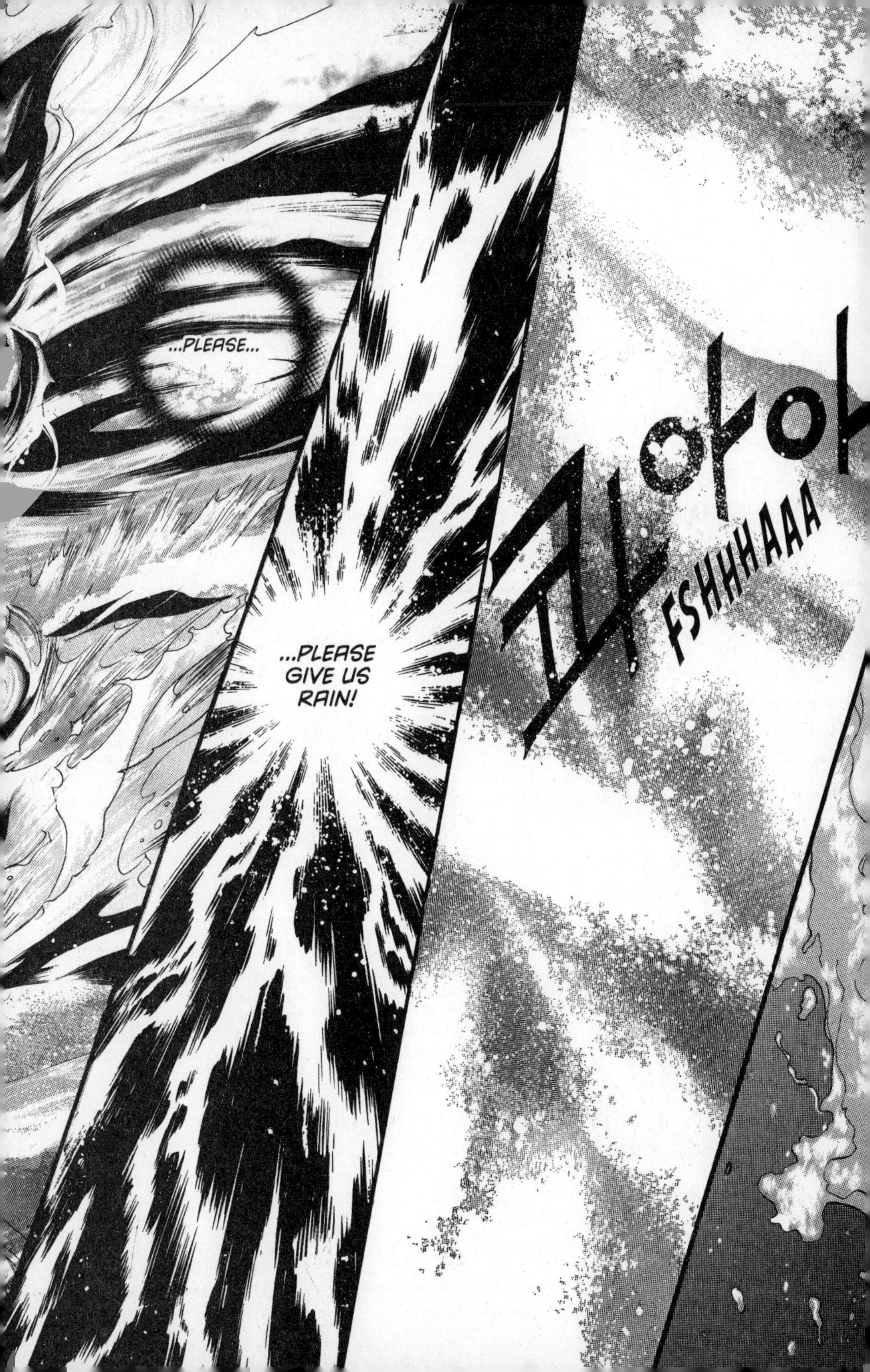
...PLEASE...
...PLEASE GIVE US RAIN!
FSHHHAAA

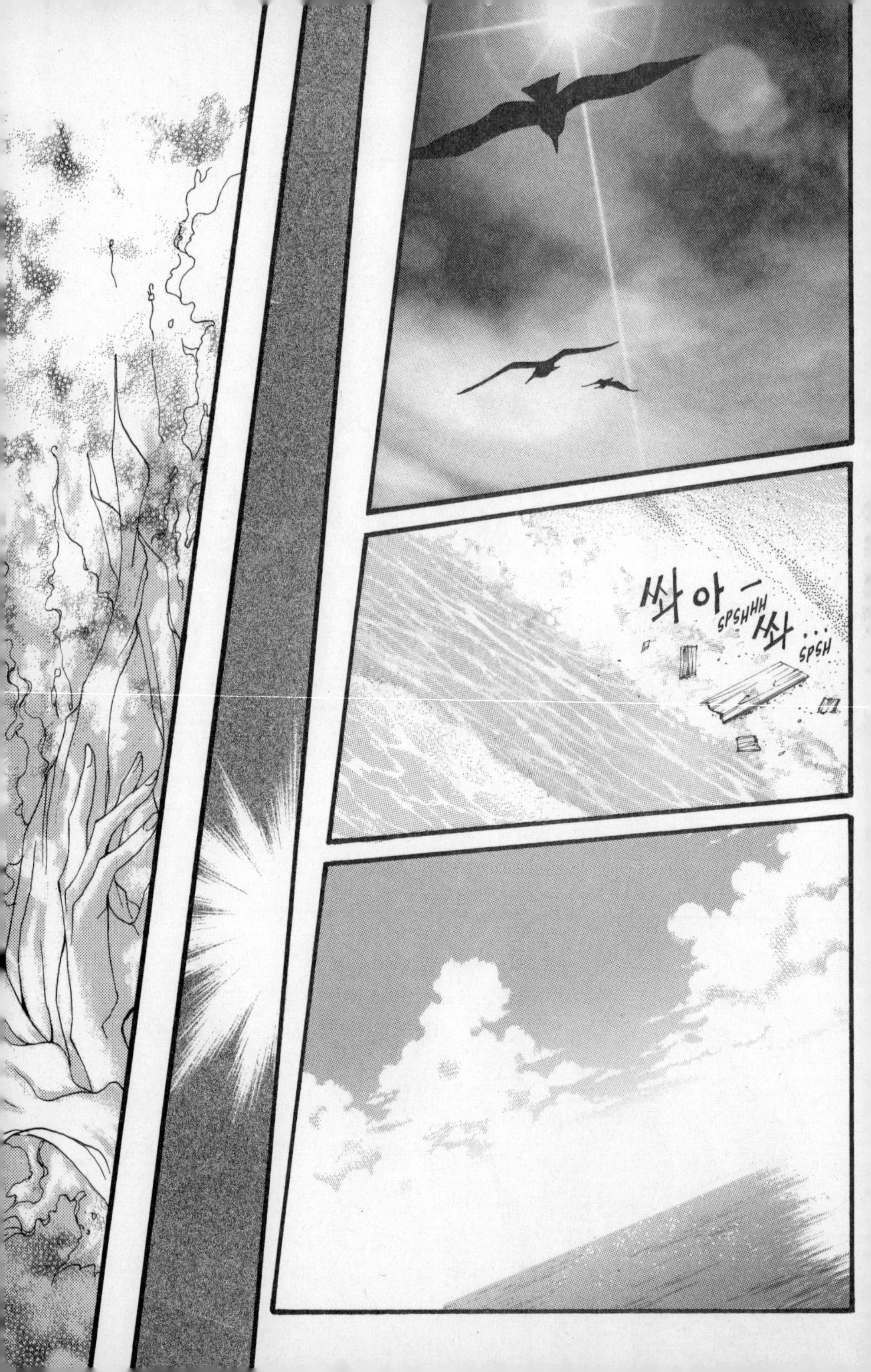

쏴아— 쏴…
SPSHHH
SPSH

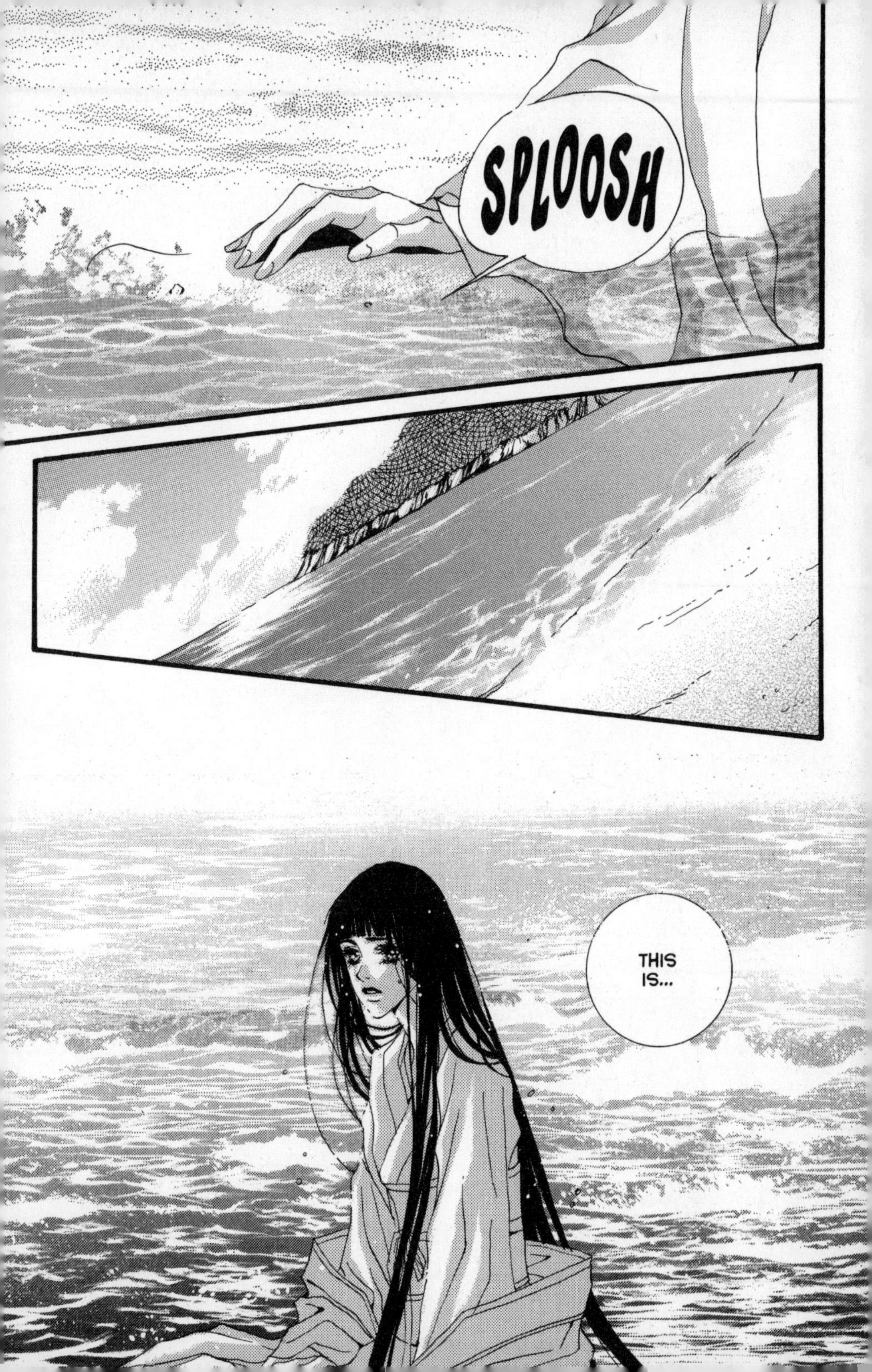
SPLOOSH
THIS IS...

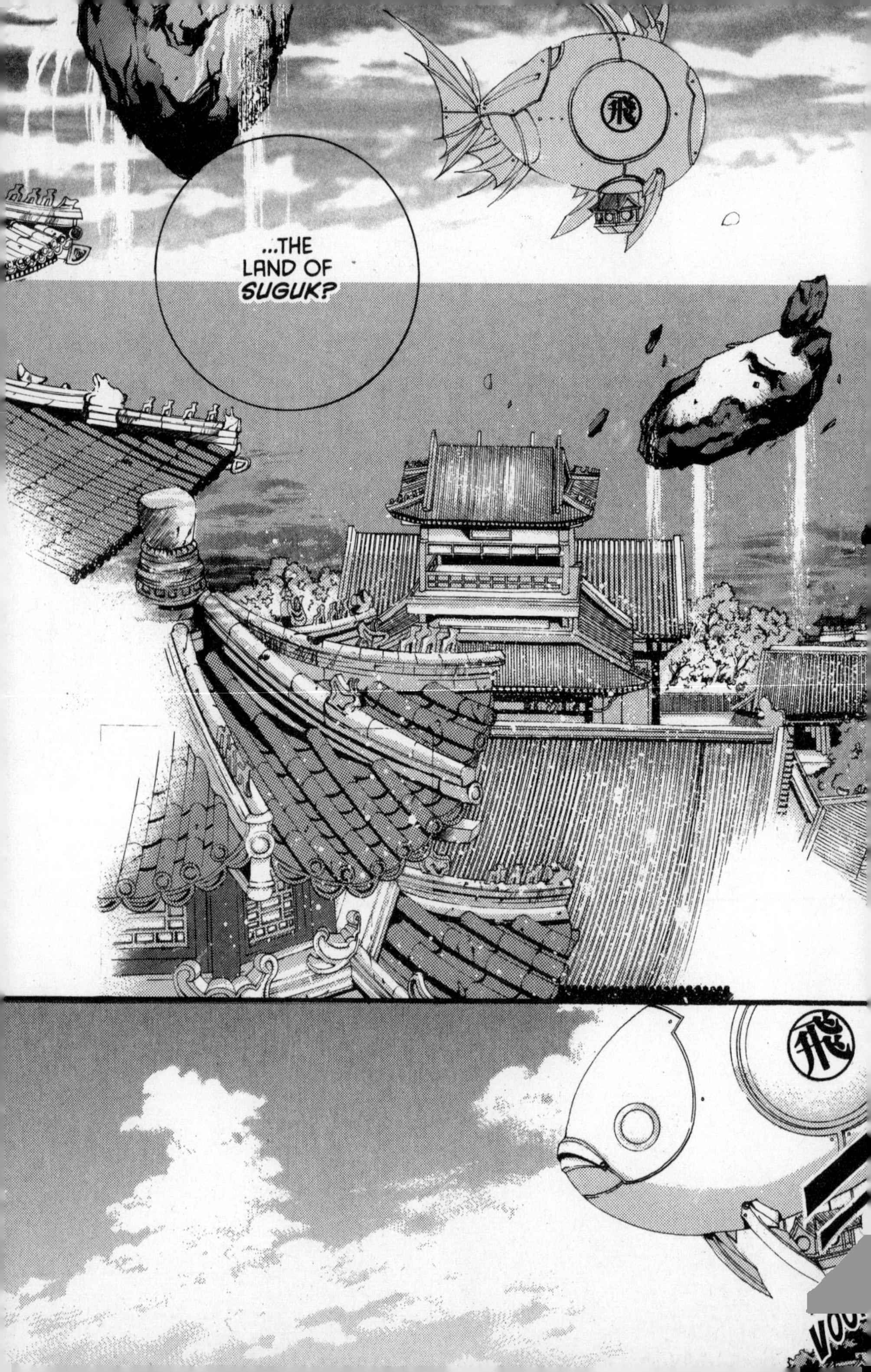
...THE LAND OF *SUGUK?*
飛
VOO

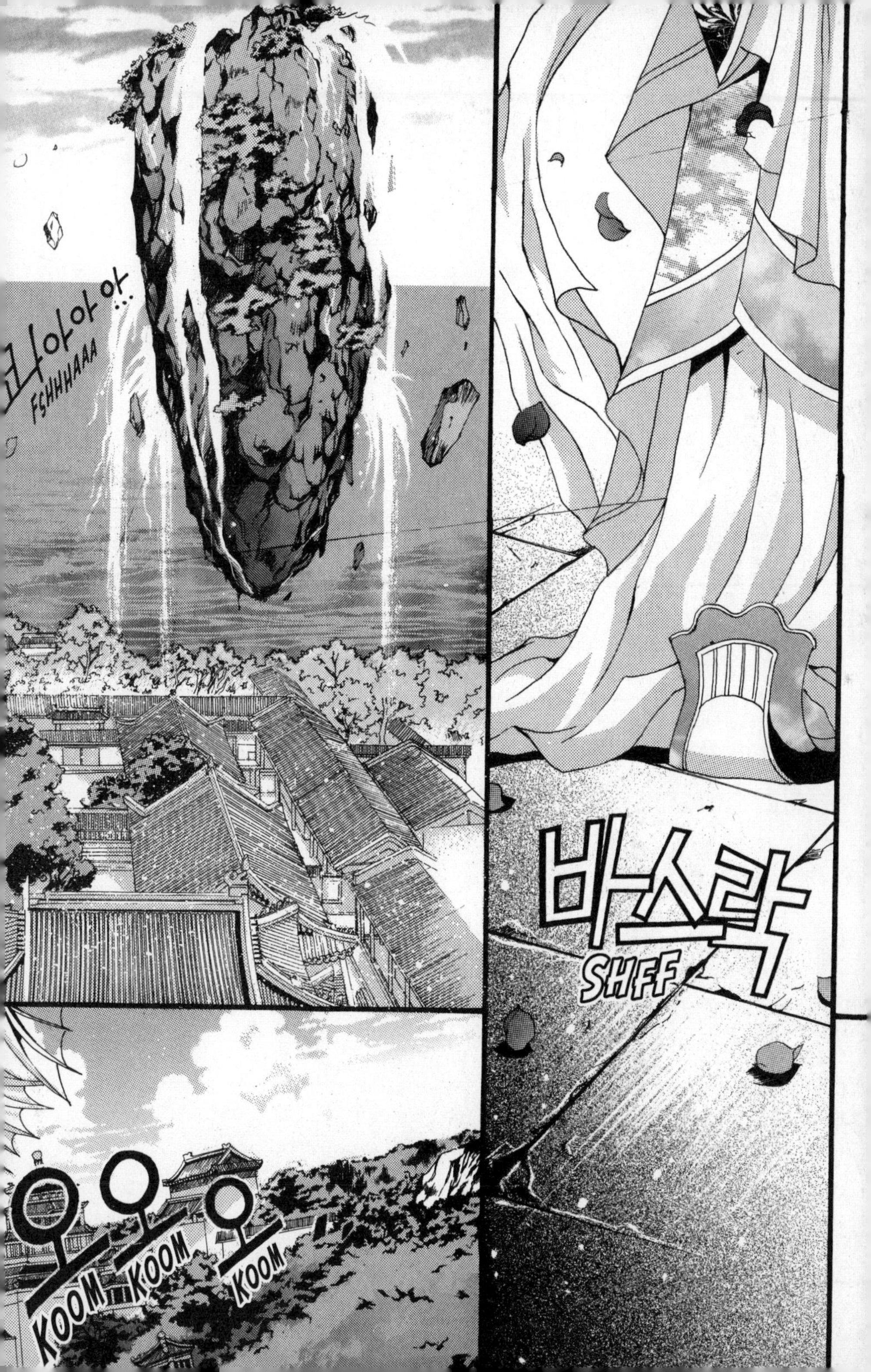

바스락
SHFF
파아아앗…
FSHHHAAA
오 오 오
KOOM KOOM KOOM

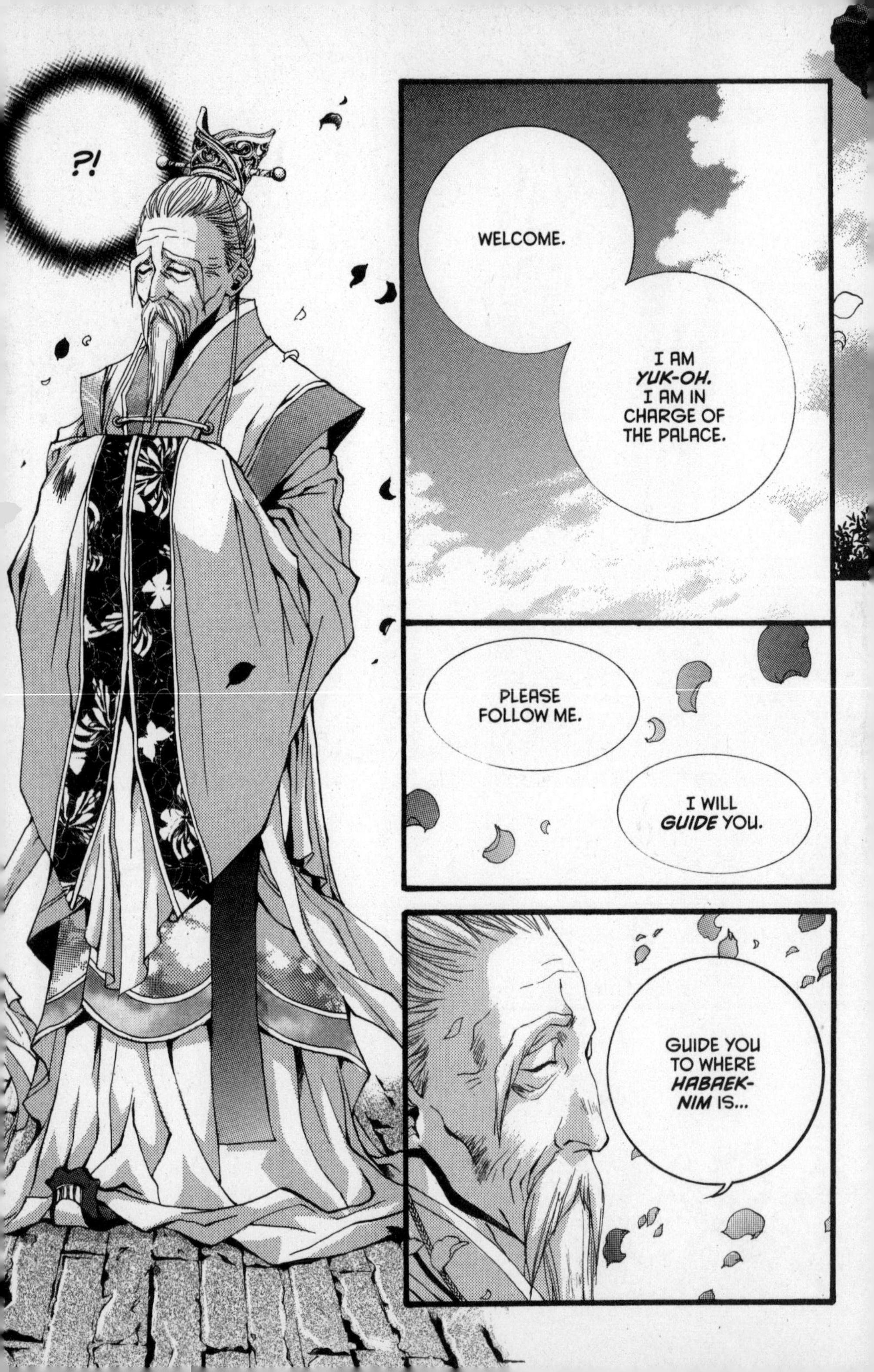
?!
WELCOME.
I AM *YUK-OH.* I AM IN CHARGE OF THE PALACE.
PLEASE FOLLOW ME.
I WILL *GUIDE* YOU.
GUIDE YOU TO WHERE *HABAEK-NIM* IS...

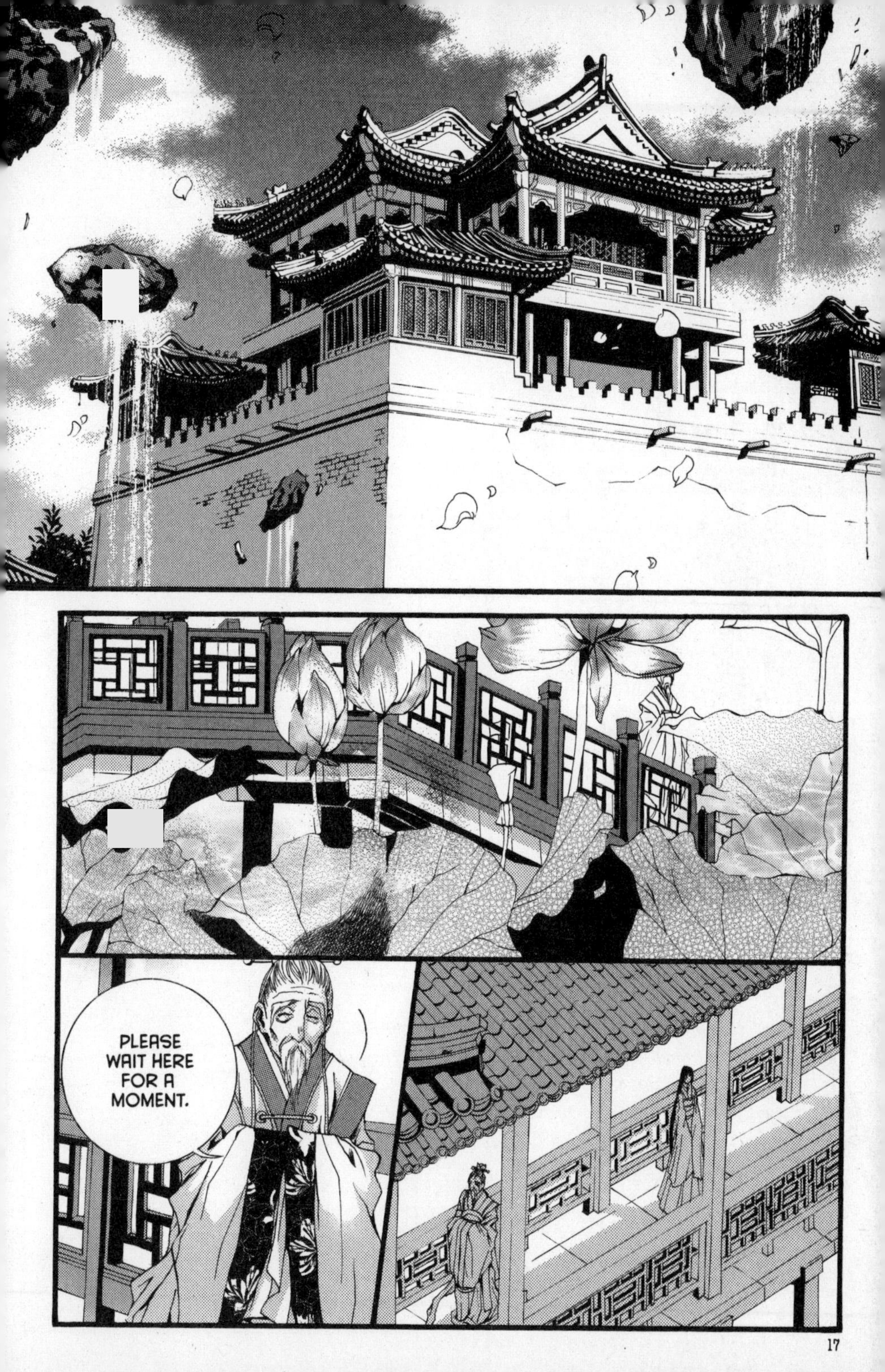
PLEASE WAIT HERE FOR A MOMENT.

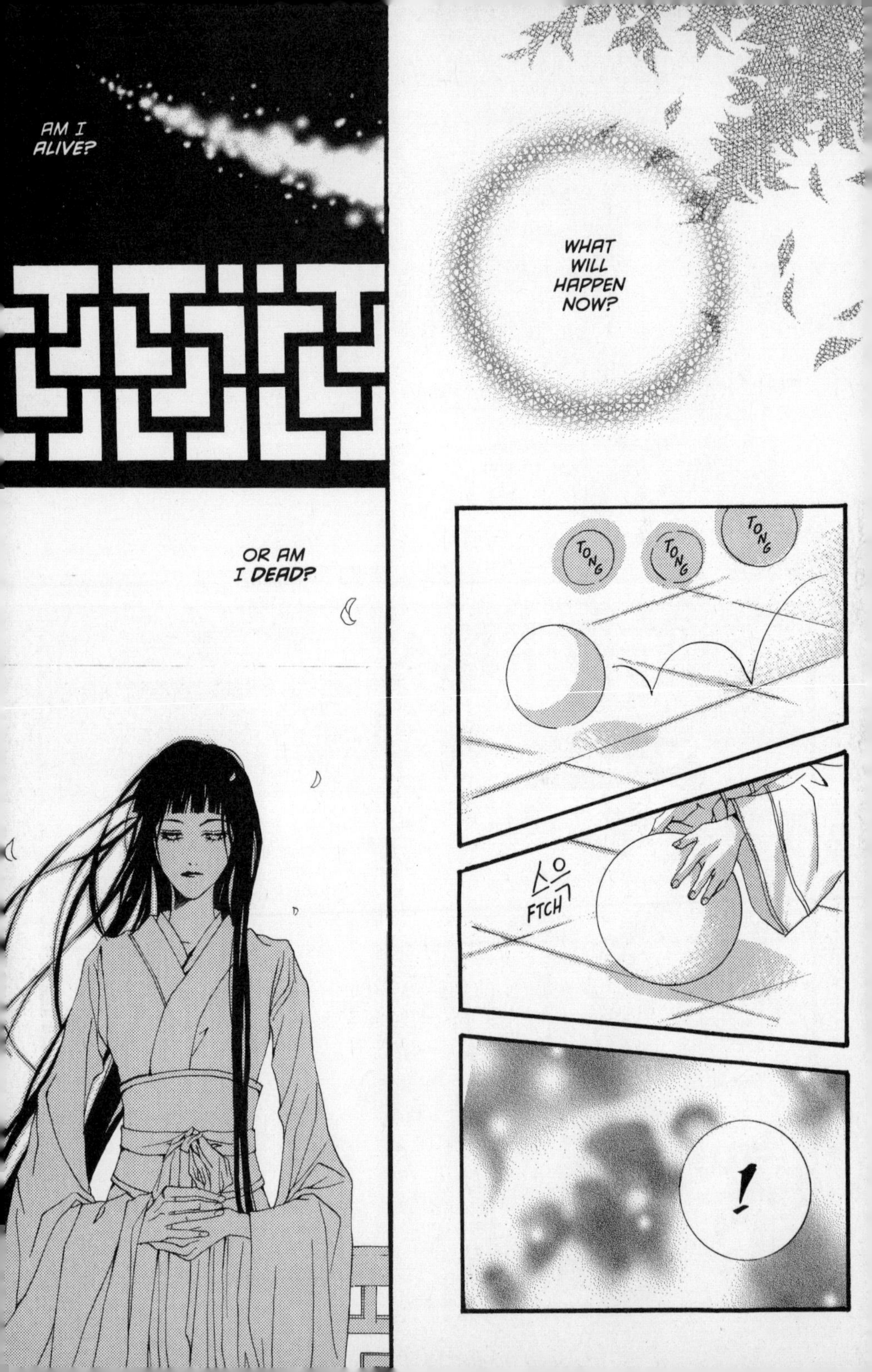
AM I ALIVE?
OR AM I DEAD?
WHAT WILL HAPPEN NOW?
TONG
TONG
TONG
스윽
FTCH
!

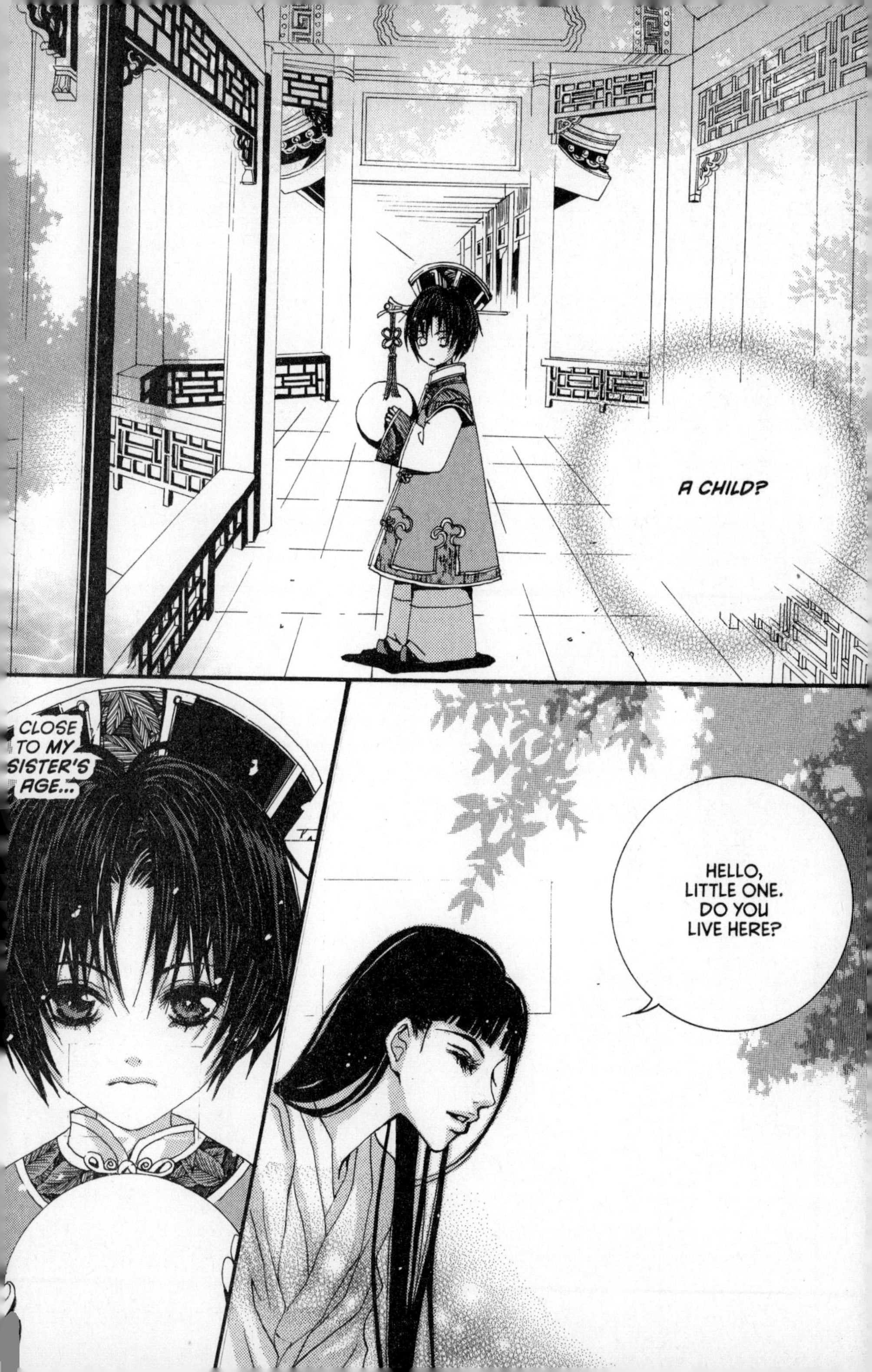
A CHILD?
HELLO, LITTLE ONE. DO YOU LIVE HERE?
CLOSE TO MY SISTER'S AGE...

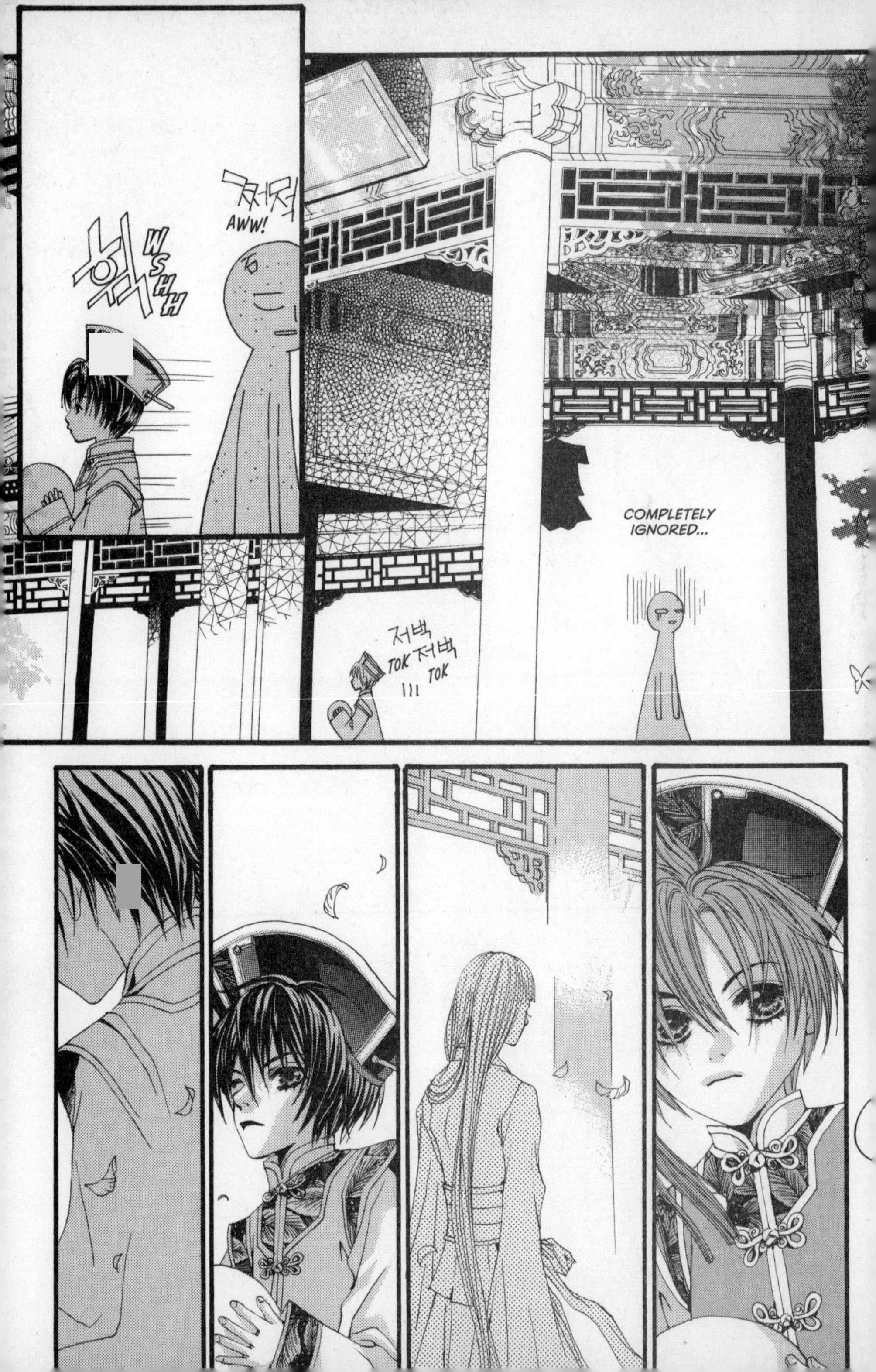
휙
WSHH
AWW!
저벅
TOK
저벅
TOK
COMPLETELY IGNORED...

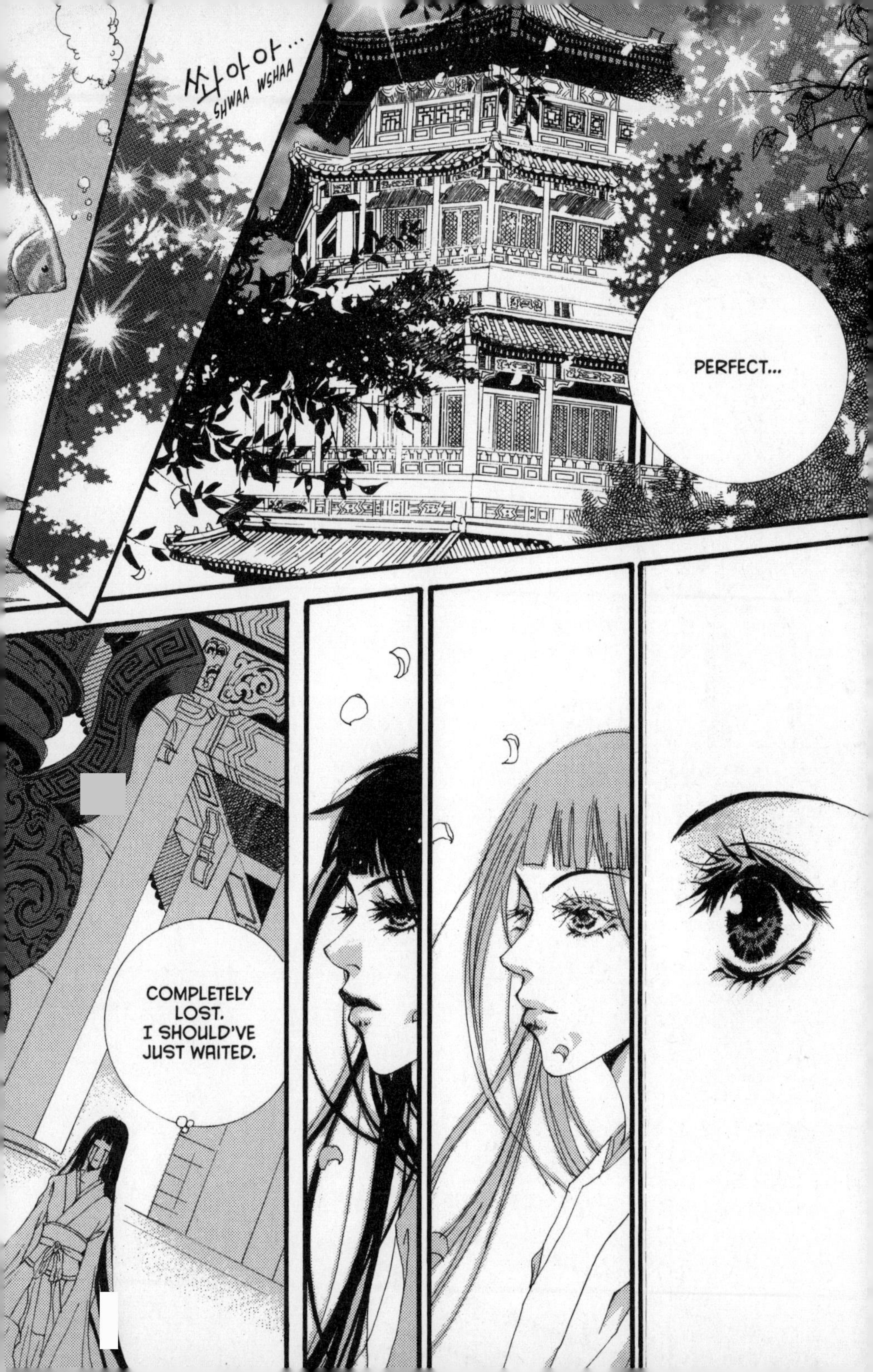

쏴아아...
SHWAA WSHAA
PERFECT...
COMPLETELY LOST. I SHOULD'VE JUST WAITED.

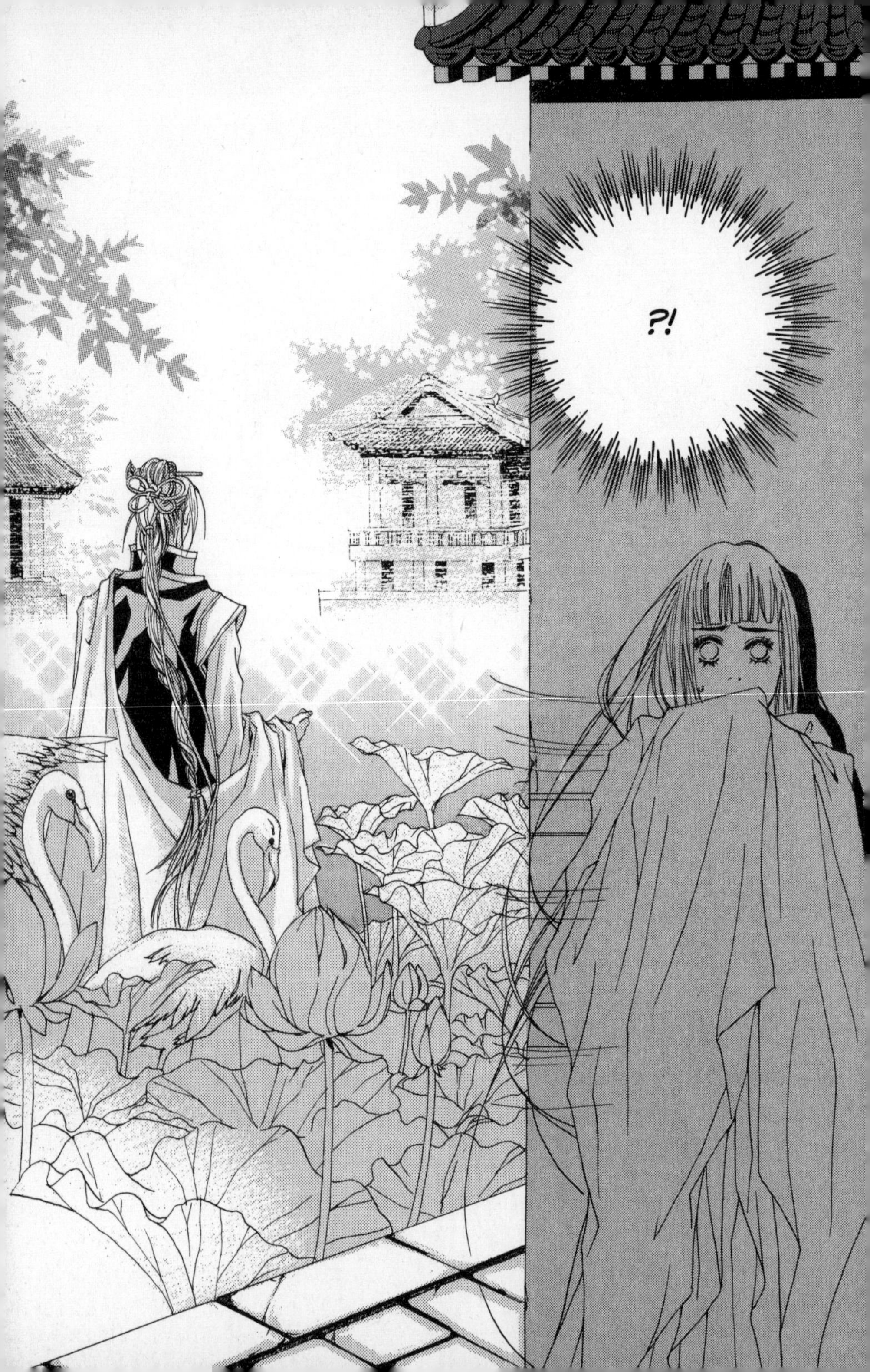
?!

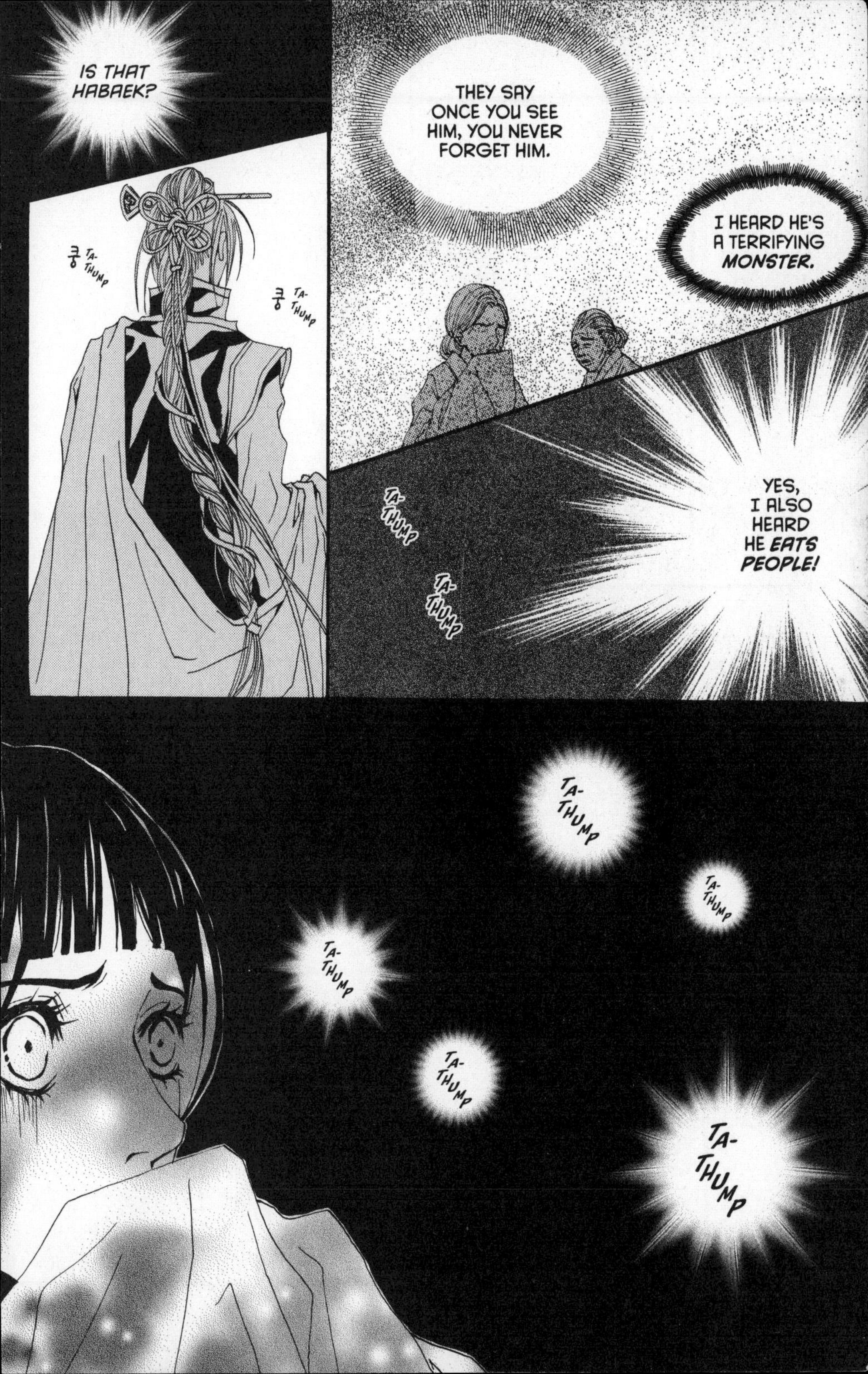

IS THAT HABAEK?
쿵 TA-THUMP
쿵 TA-THUMP
THEY SAY ONCE YOU SEE HIM, YOU NEVER FORGET HIM.
I HEARD HE'S A TERRIFYING MONSTER.
YES, I ALSO HEARD HE EATS PEOPLE!
TA-THUMP
TA-THUMP
TA-THUMP
TA-THUMP
TA-THUMP
TA-THUMP
TA-THUMP

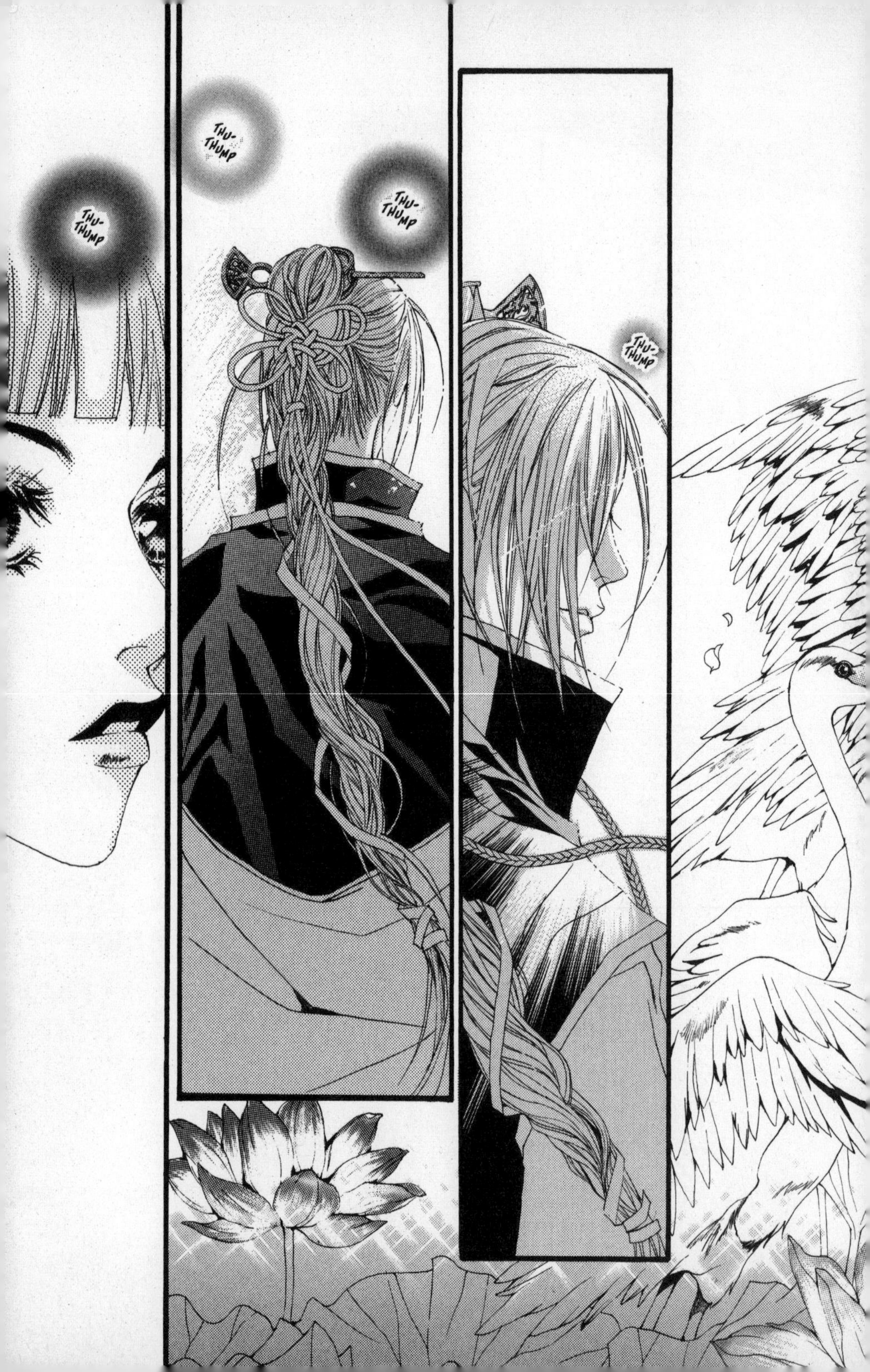
THU-
THUMP
THU-
THUMP
THU-
THUMP
THU-
THUMP

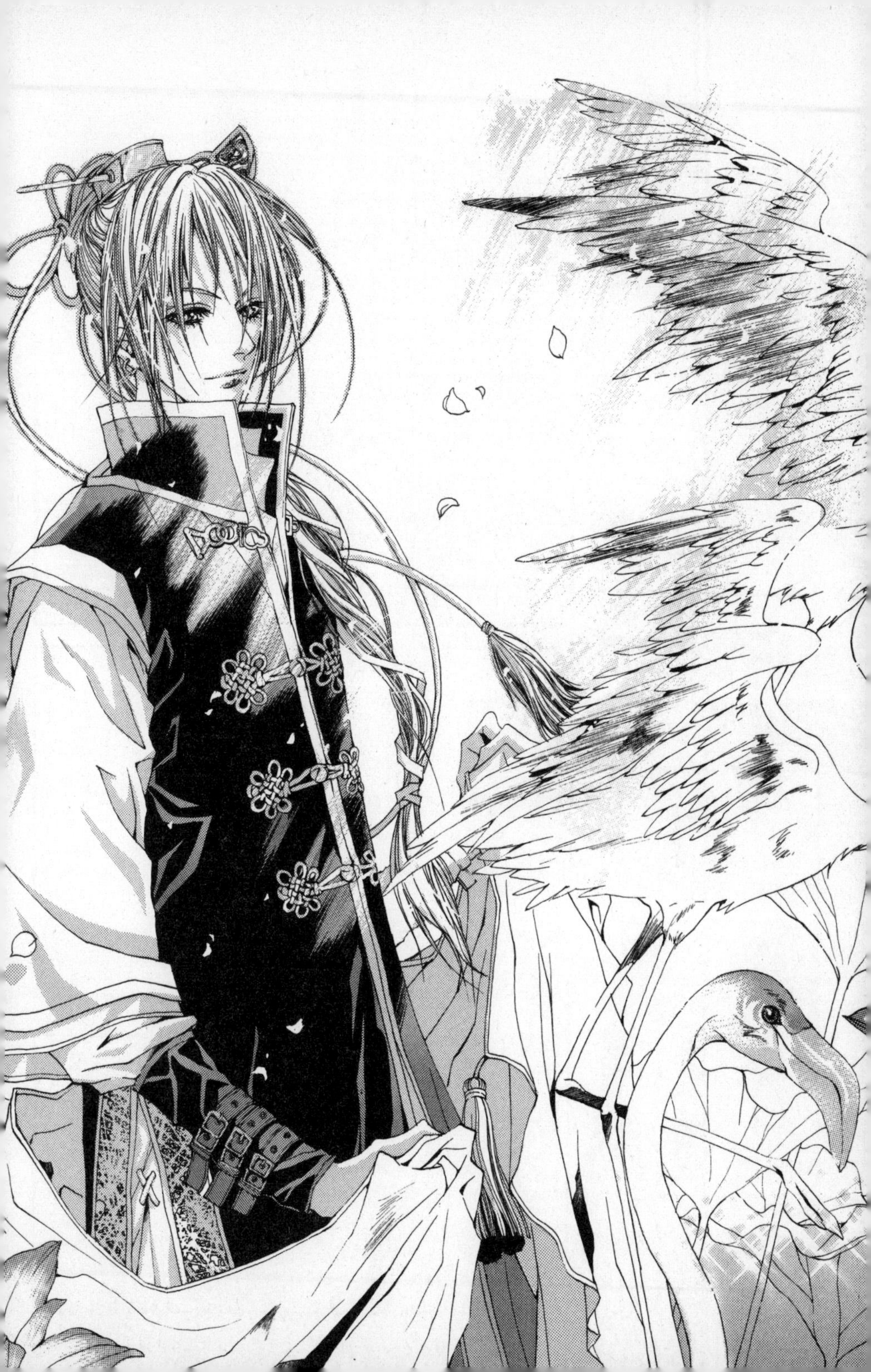

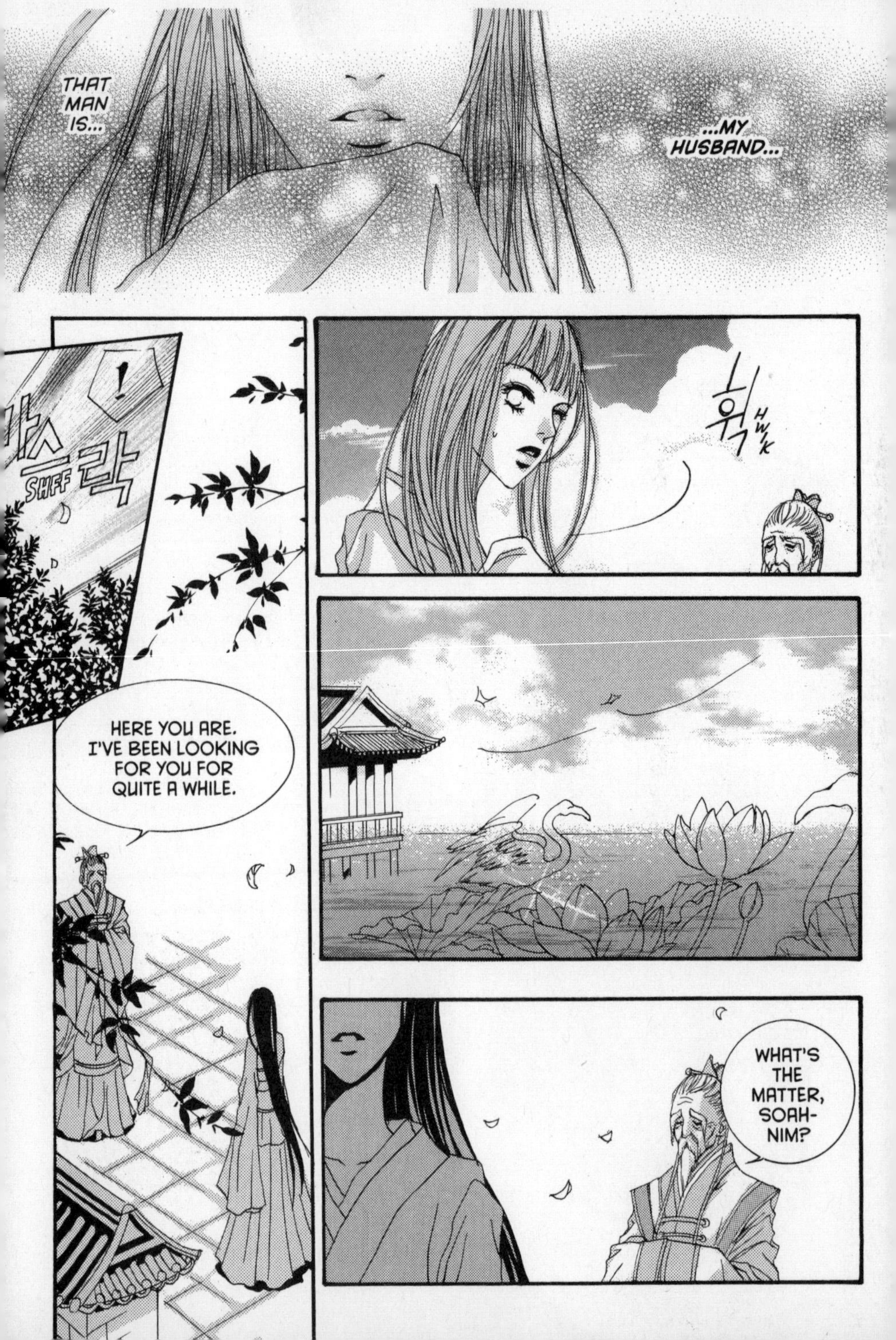
THAT MAN IS...
...MY HUSBAND...
휙 HWIK
파스락 SHFF
HERE YOU ARE. I'VE BEEN LOOKING FOR YOU FOR QUITE A WHILE.
WHAT'S THE MATTER, SOAH-NIM?

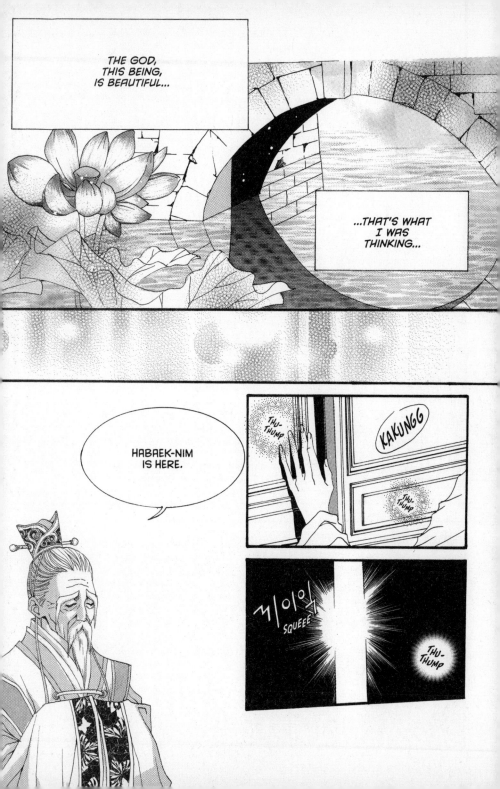

THE GOD,
THIS BEING,
IS BEAUTIFUL...

...THAT'S WHAT
I WAS
THINKING...

HABAEK-NIM
IS HERE.

THU-
THUMP

KAKUNGG

THU-
THUMP

시이익
SQUEEE

THU-
THUMP

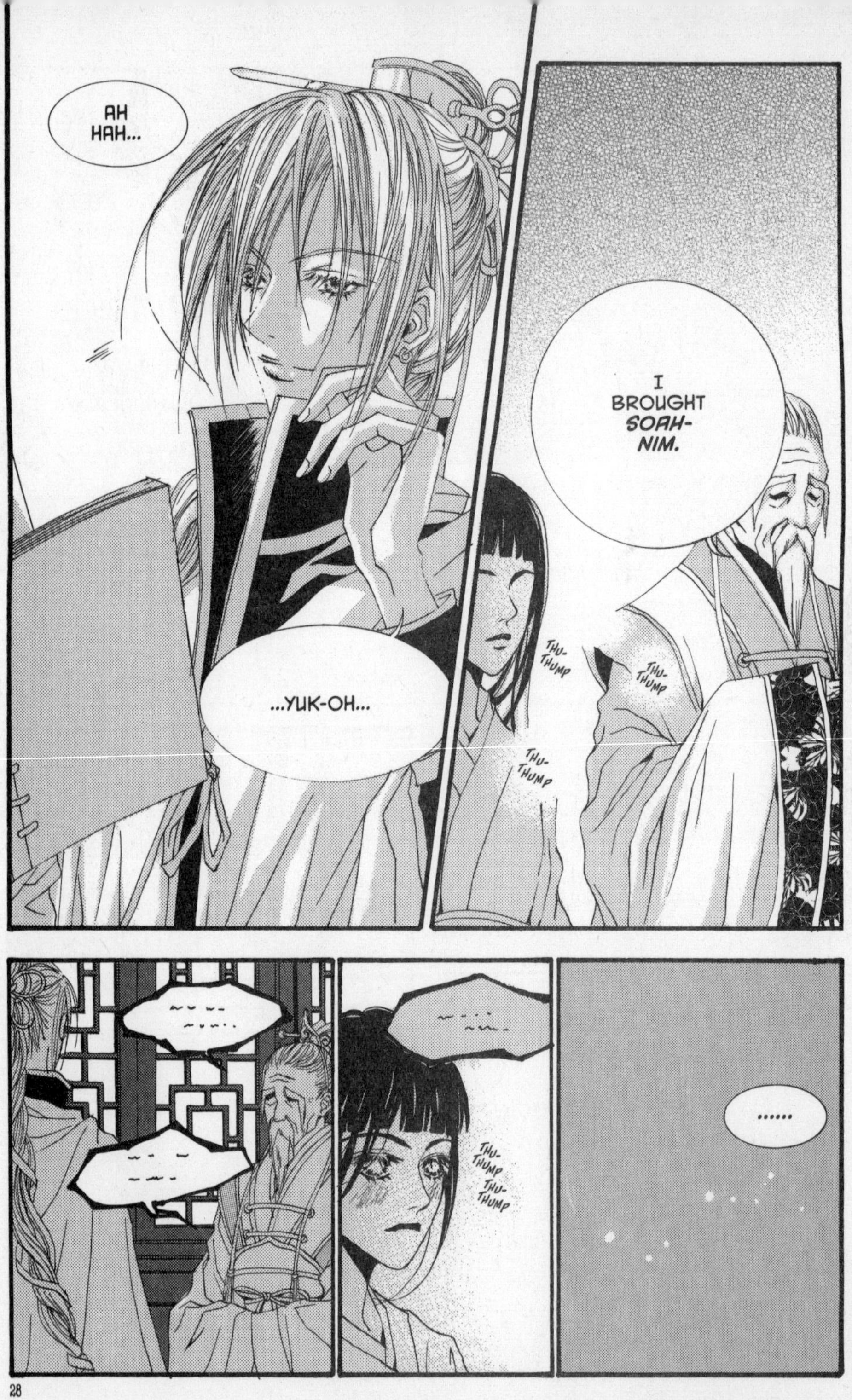
AH HAH...
I BROUGHT SOAH-NIM.
...YUK-OH...
THU-THUMP
THU-THUMP
THU-THUMP
THU-THUMP THU-THUMP
......

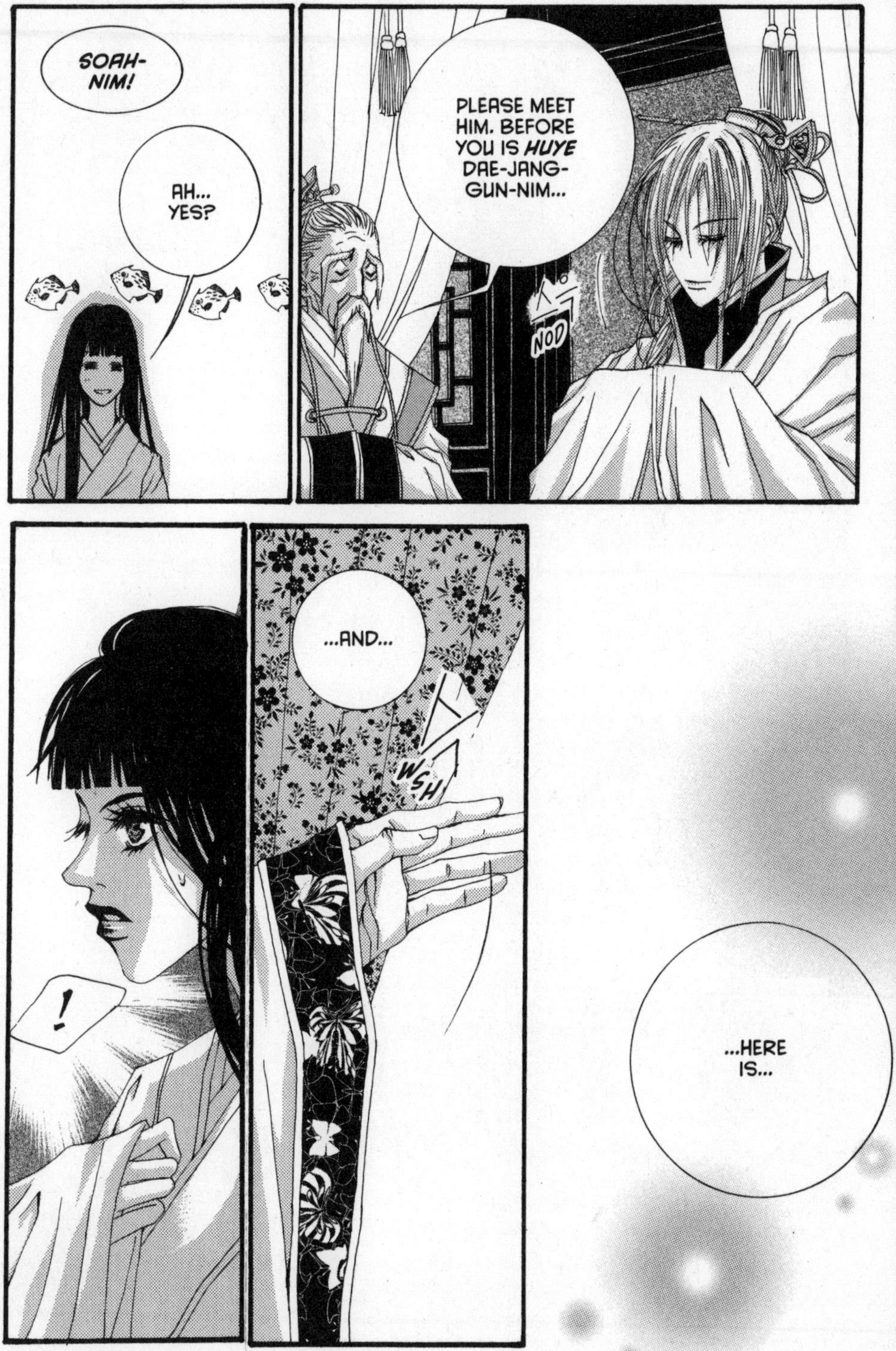
SOAH-NIM!
AH... YES?
PLEASE MEET HIM. BEFORE YOU IS HUYE DAE-JANG-GUN-NIM...
NOD
...AND...
WSH
!
...HERE IS...

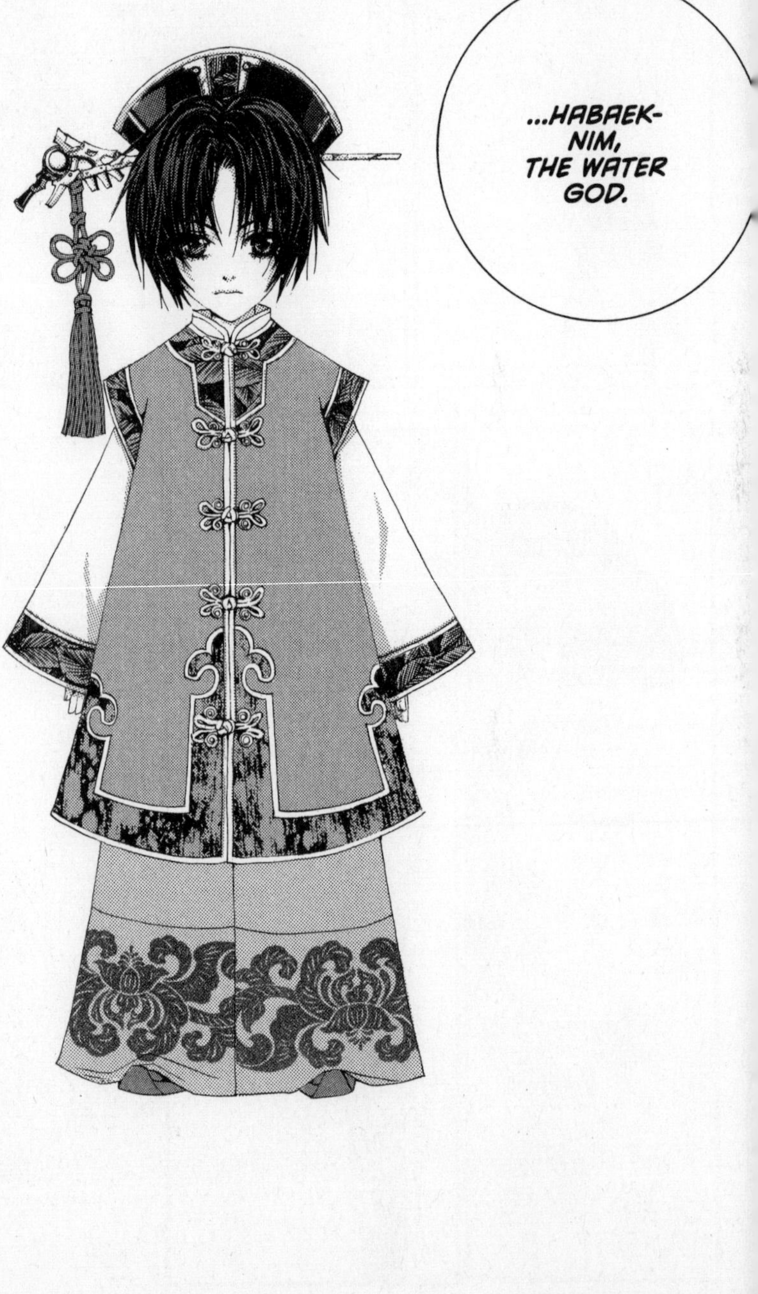
...HABAEK-NIM, THE WATER GOD.

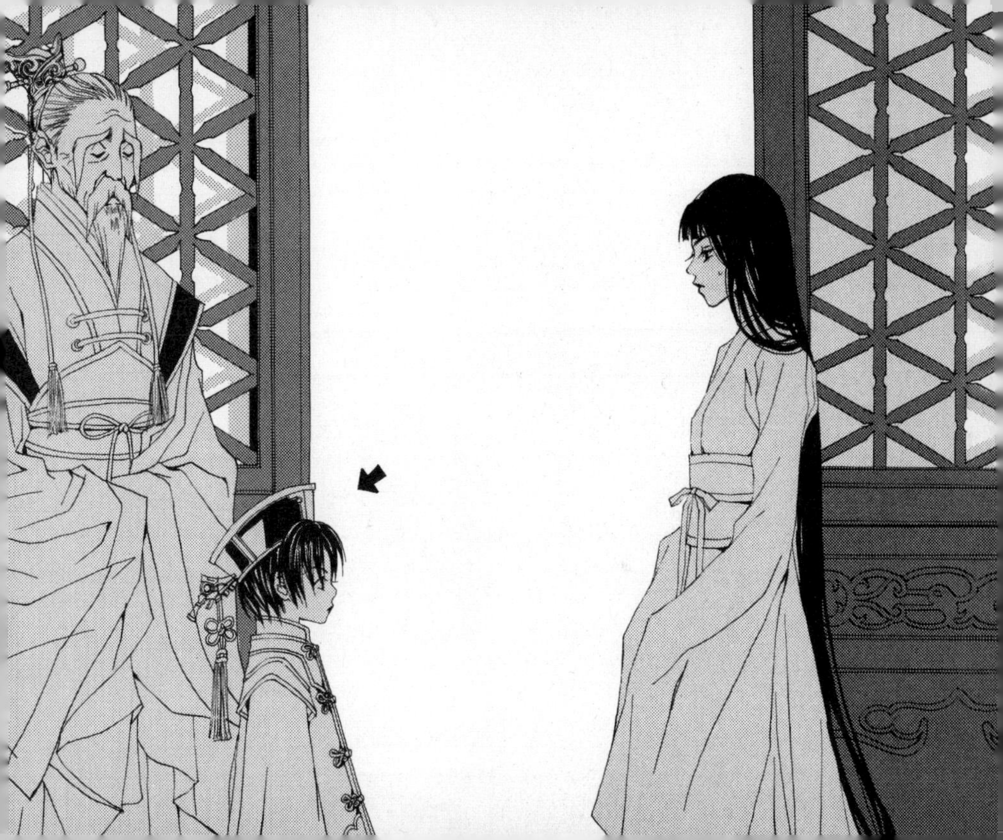

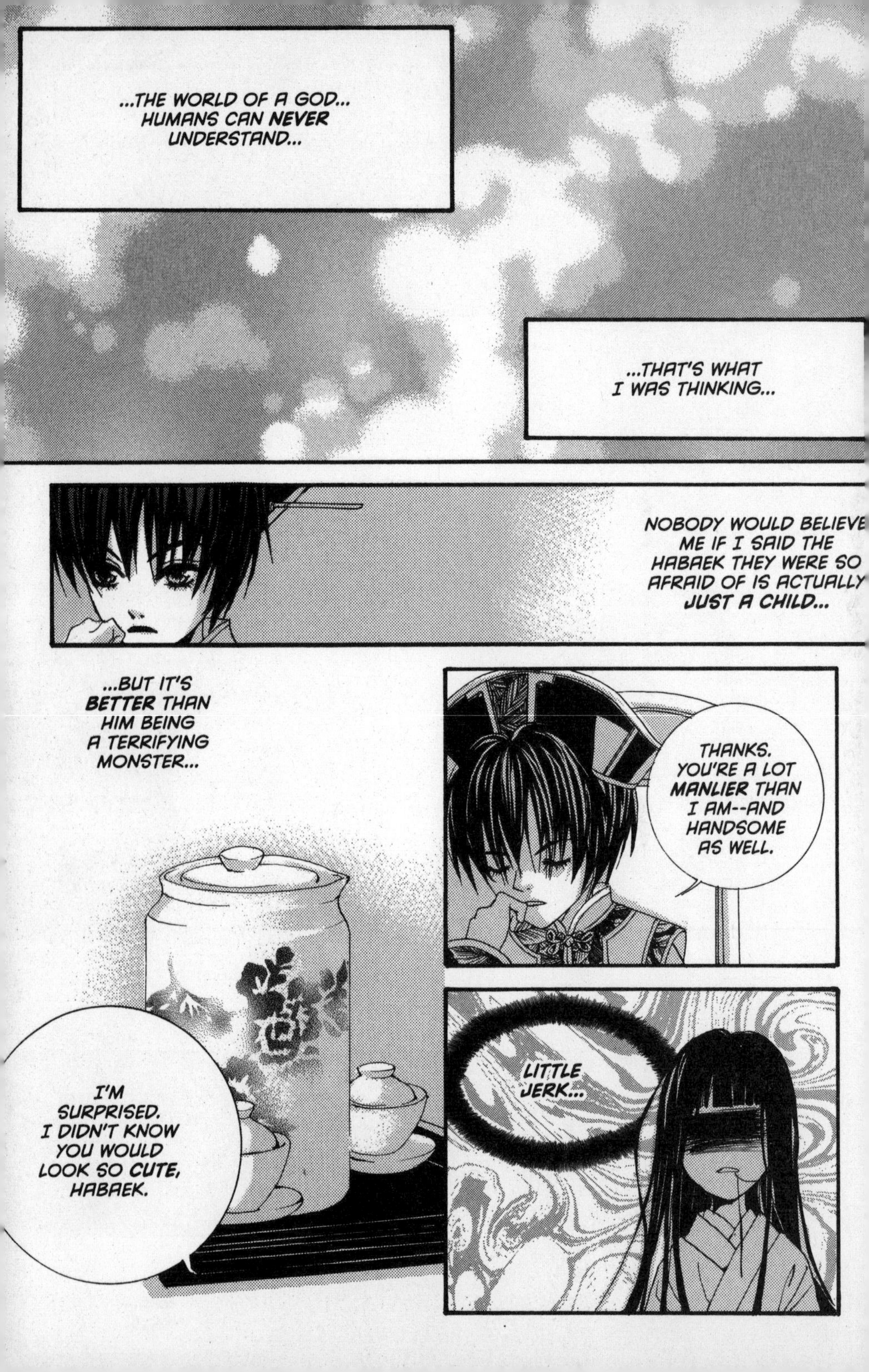
...THE WORLD OF A GOD... HUMANS CAN NEVER UNDERSTAND...
...THAT'S WHAT I WAS THINKING...
NOBODY WOULD BELIEVE ME IF I SAID THE HABAEK THEY WERE SO AFRAID OF IS ACTUALLY JUST A CHILD...
...BUT IT'S BETTER THAN HIM BEING A TERRIFYING MONSTER...
THANKS. YOU'RE A LOT MANLIER THAN I AM--AND HANDSOME AS WELL.
I'M SURPRISED. I DIDN'T KNOW YOU WOULD LOOK SO CUTE, HABAEK.
LITTLE JERK...

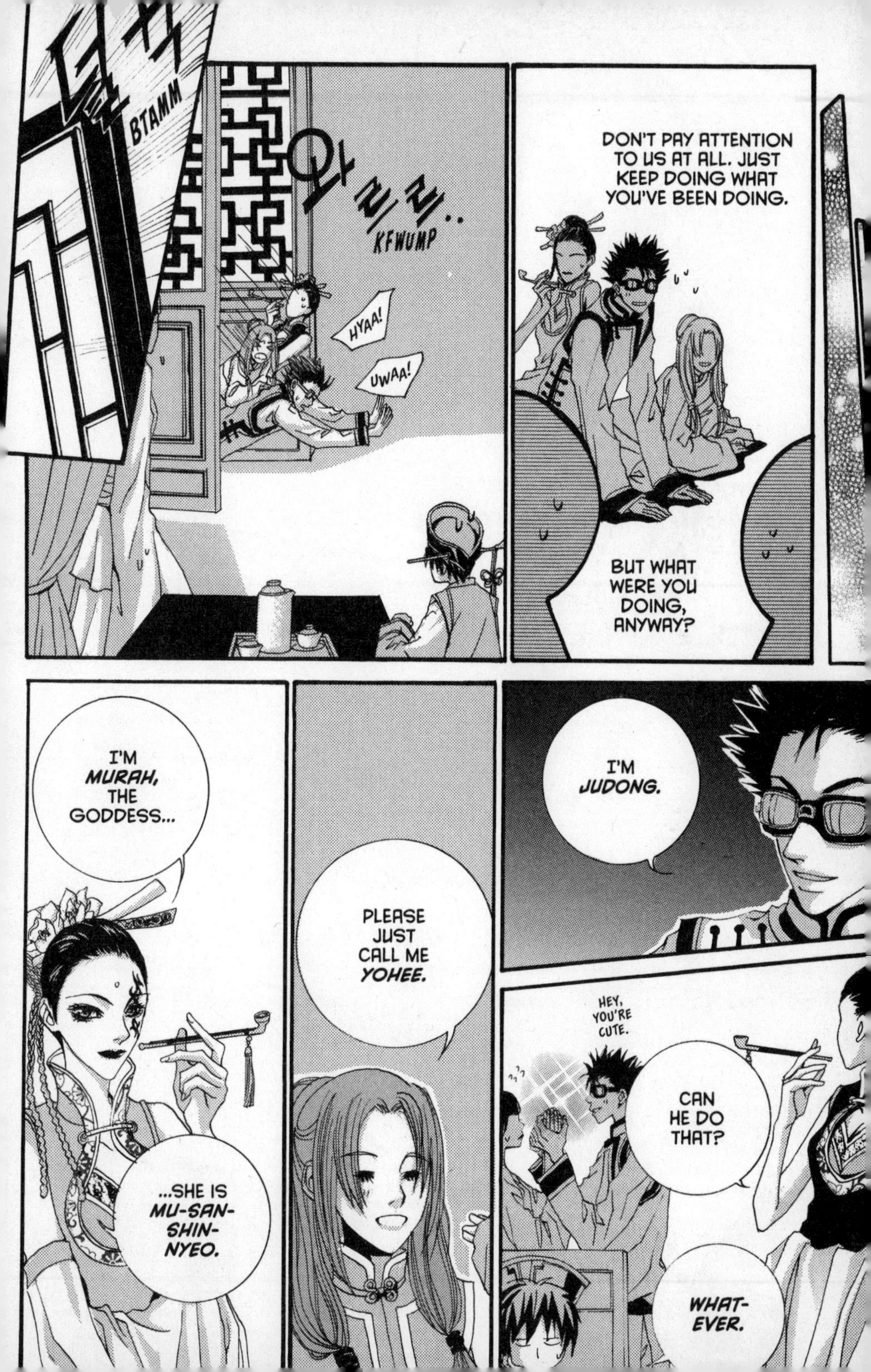
BTAMM
KFWUMP
HYAA!
UWAA!
DON'T PAY ATTENTION TO US AT ALL. JUST KEEP DOING WHAT YOU'VE BEEN DOING.
BUT WHAT WERE YOU DOING, ANYWAY?
I'M MURAH, THE GODDESS...
...SHE IS MU-SAN-SHIN-NYEO.
PLEASE JUST CALL ME YOHEE.
I'M JUDONG.
HEY, YOU'RE CUTE.
CAN HE DO THAT?
WHAT-EVER.

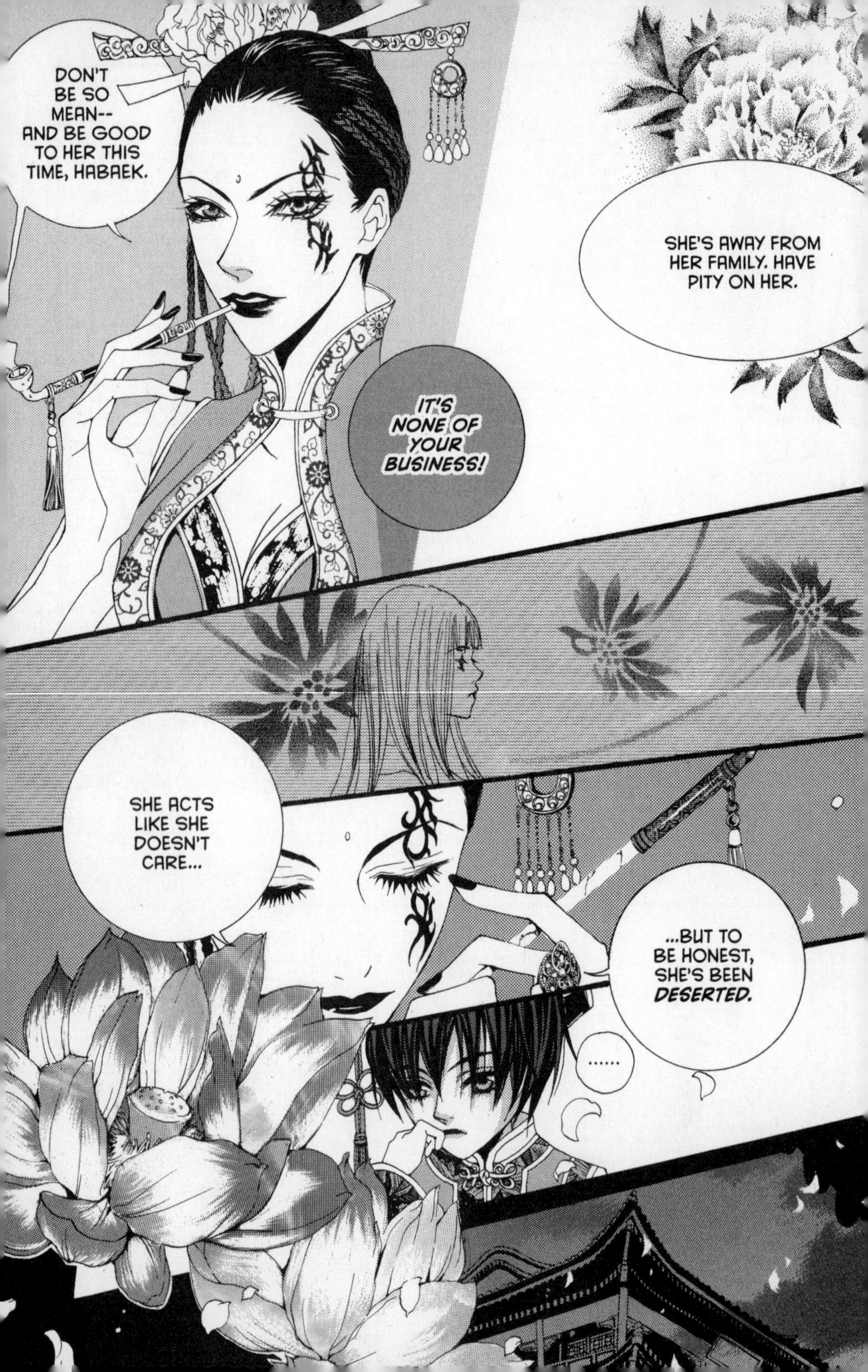
SHE'S AWAY FROM HER FAMILY. HAVE PITY ON HER.
DON'T BE SO MEAN-- AND BE GOOD TO HER THIS TIME, HABAEK.
IT'S NONE OF YOUR BUSINESS!
...BUT TO BE HONEST, SHE'S BEEN DESERTED.
SHE ACTS LIKE SHE DOESN'T CARE...
......

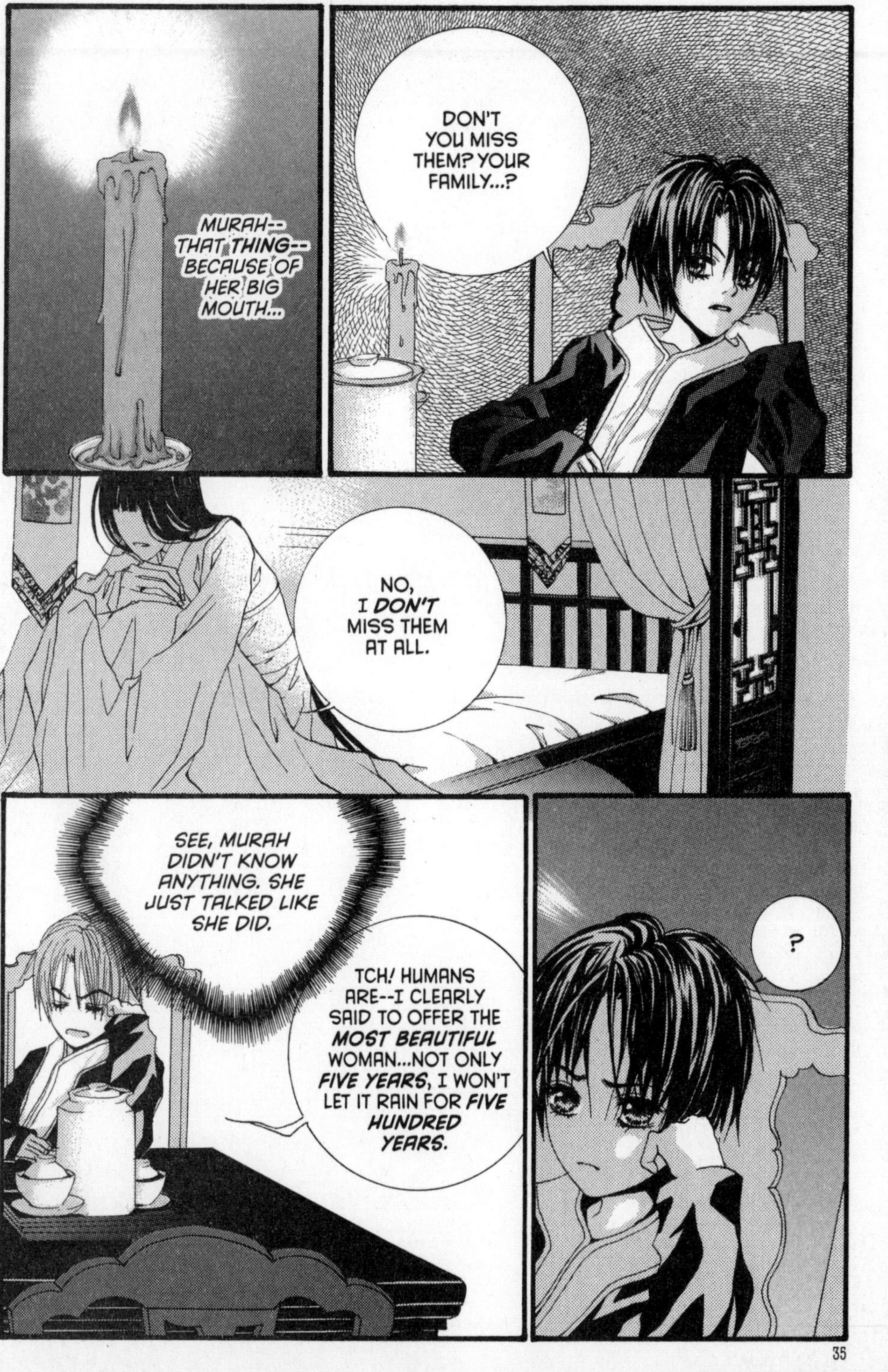
MURAH--
THAT THING--
BECAUSE OF
HER BIG
MOUTH...
DON'T YOU MISS THEM? YOUR FAMILY...?
NO, I DON'T MISS THEM AT ALL.
SEE, MURAH DIDN'T KNOW ANYTHING. SHE JUST TALKED LIKE SHE DID.
TCH! HUMANS ARE--I CLEARLY SAID TO OFFER THE MOST BEAUTIFUL WOMAN...NOT ONLY FIVE YEARS, I WON'T LET IT RAIN FOR FIVE HUNDRED YEARS.
?

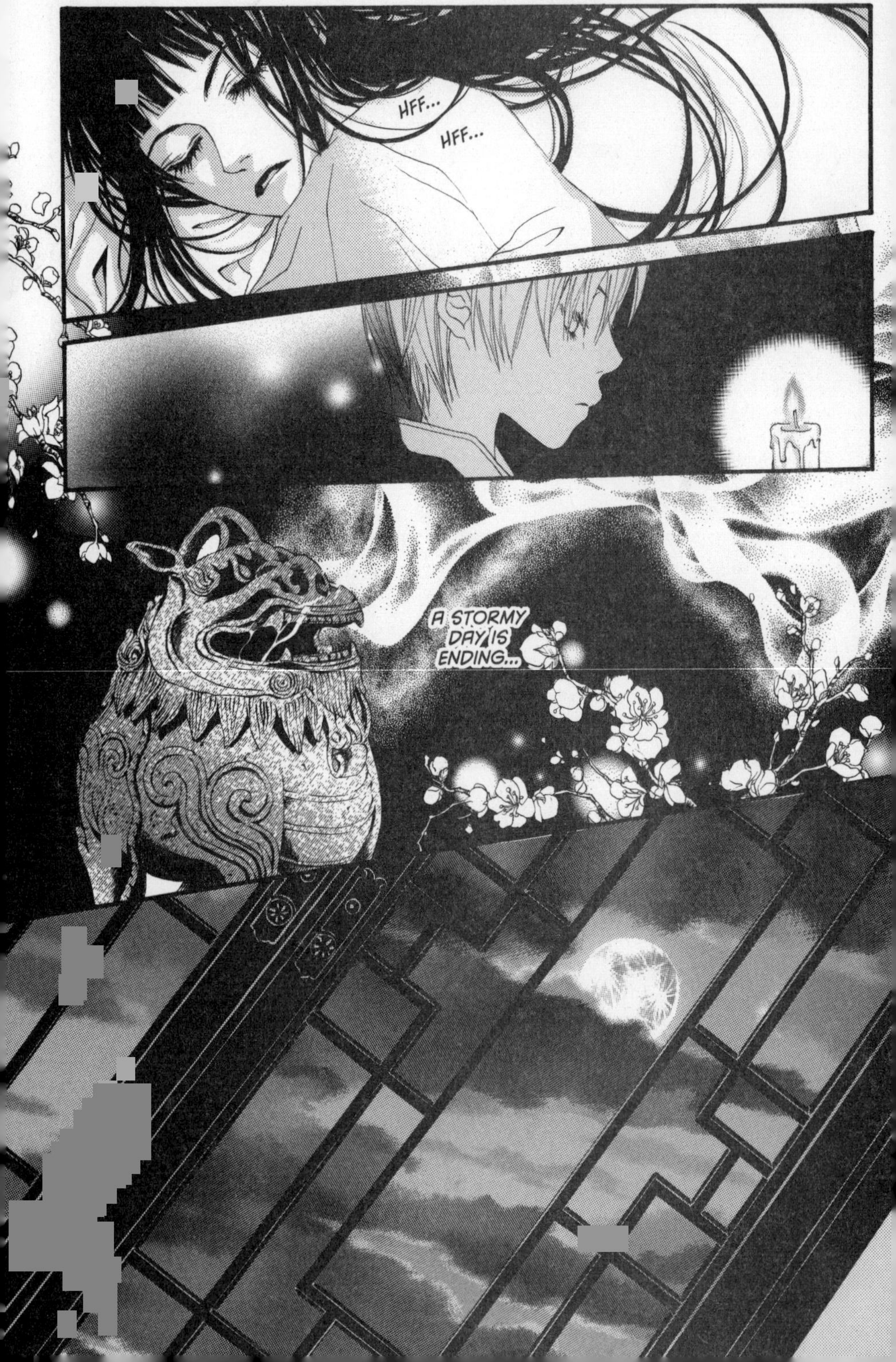
HFF...
HFF...
A STORMY DAY IS ENDING...

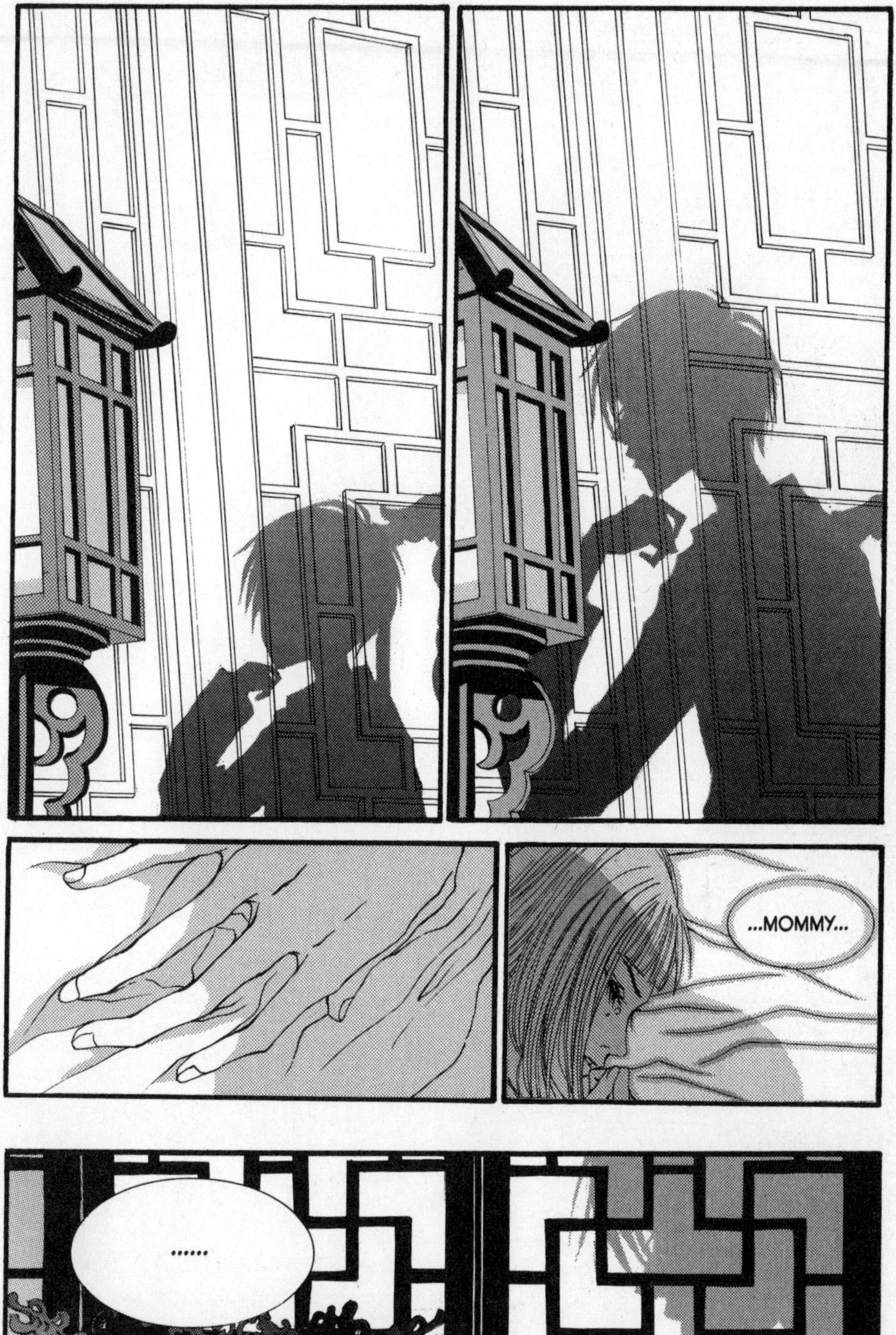
...MOMMY...
......

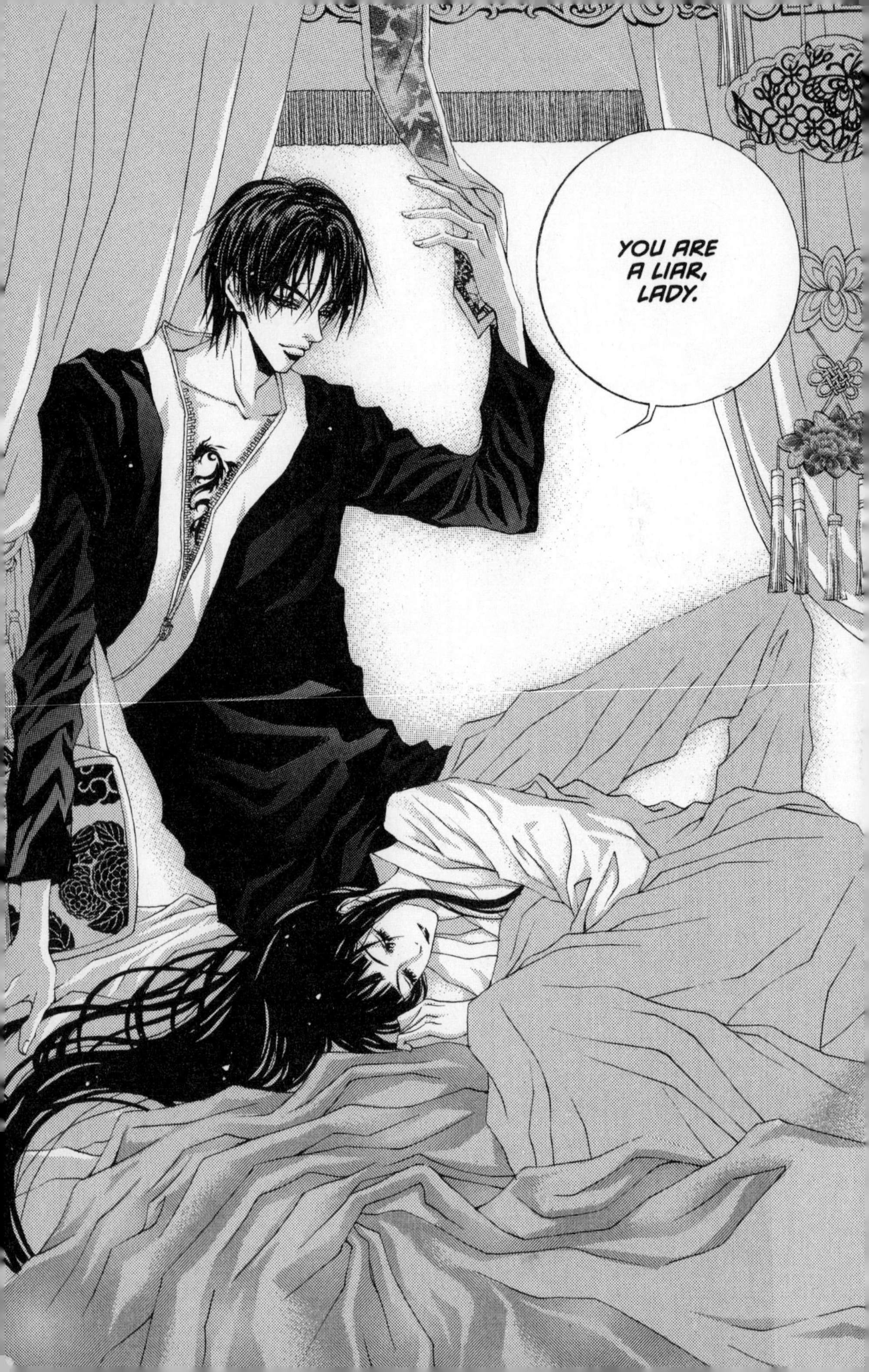
YOU ARE A LIAR, LADY.

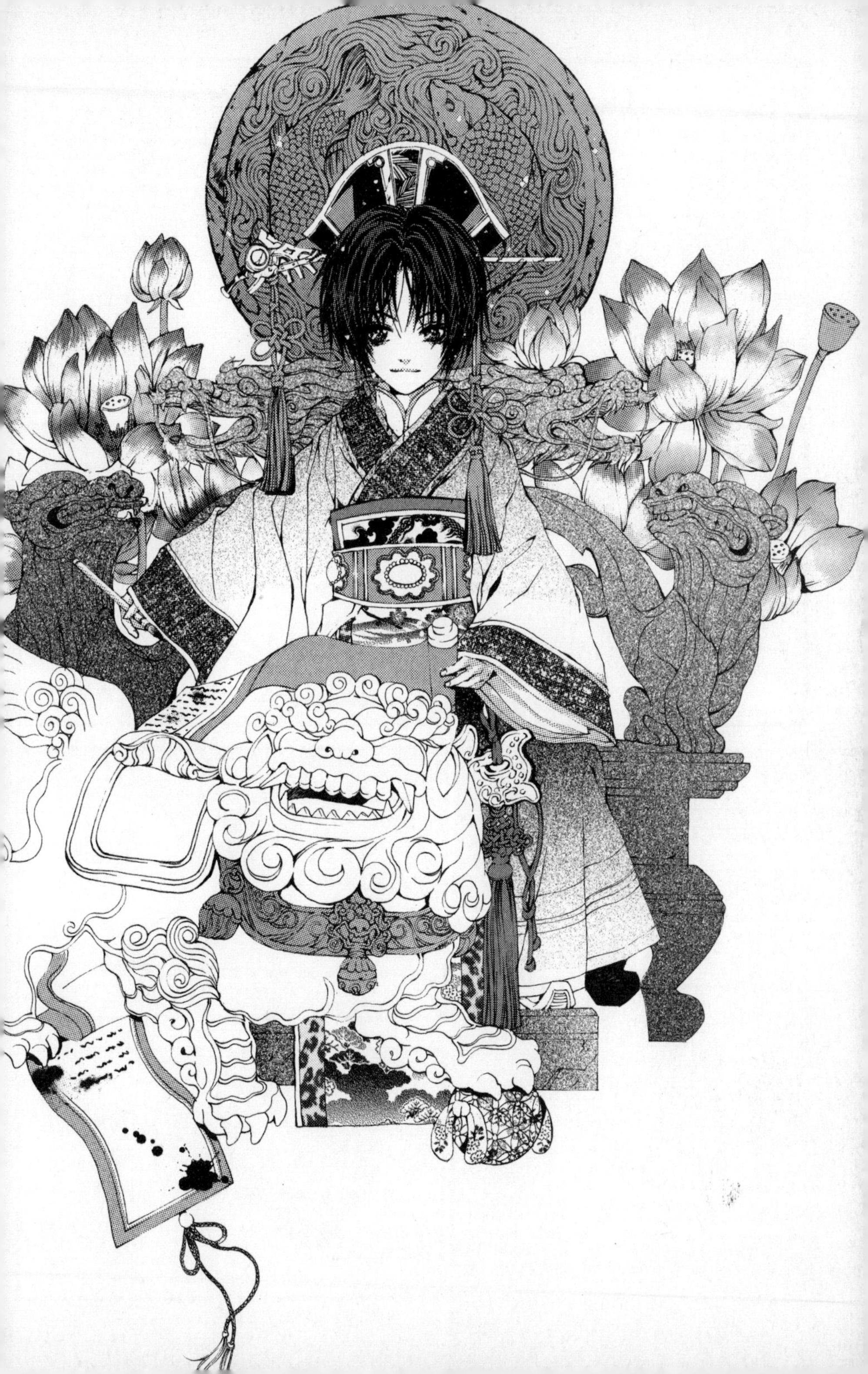

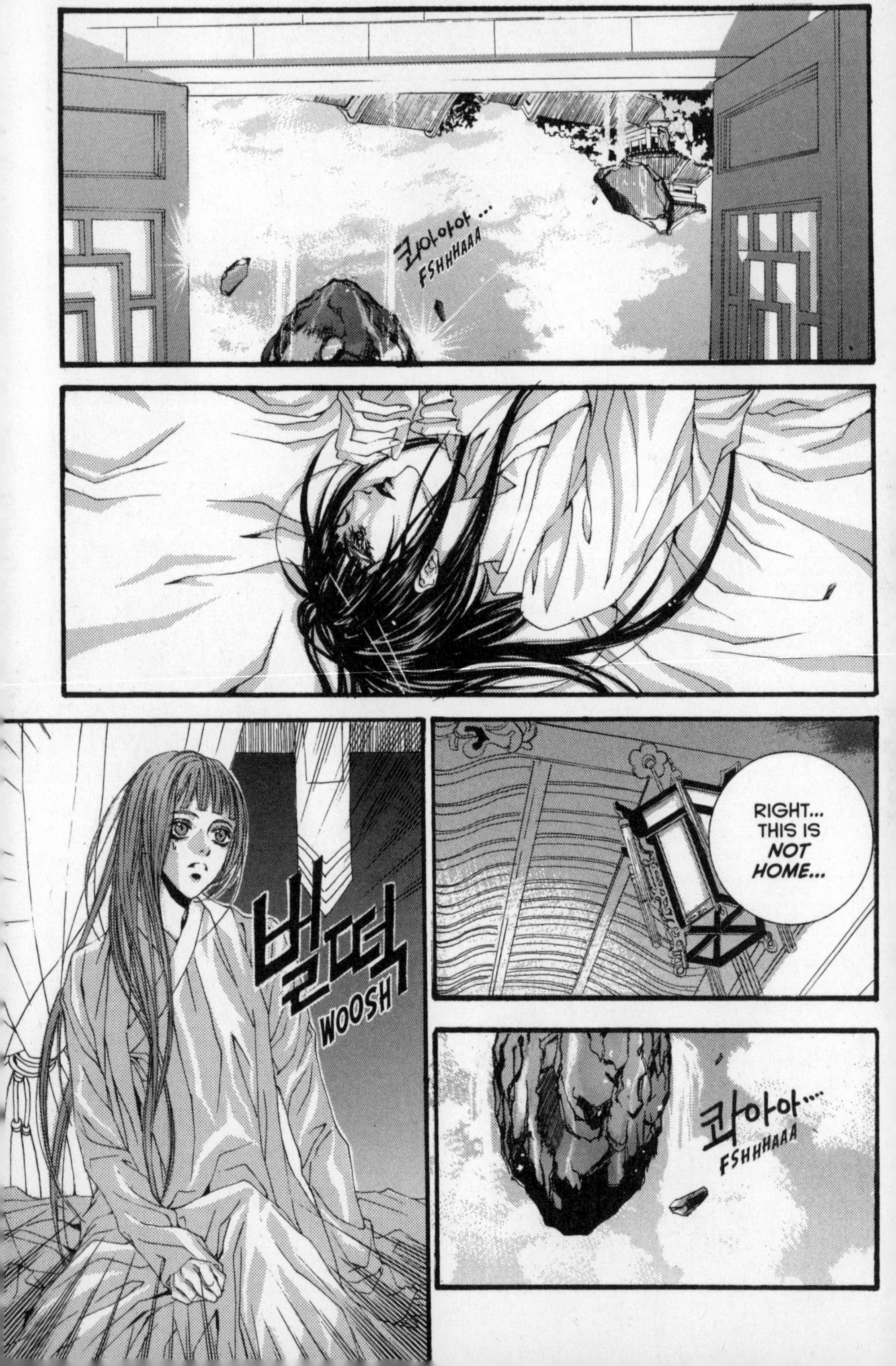

콰아아...
FSHHHAAA
벌떡
WOOSH
RIGHT... THIS IS NOT HOME...
콰아아...
FSHHHAAA

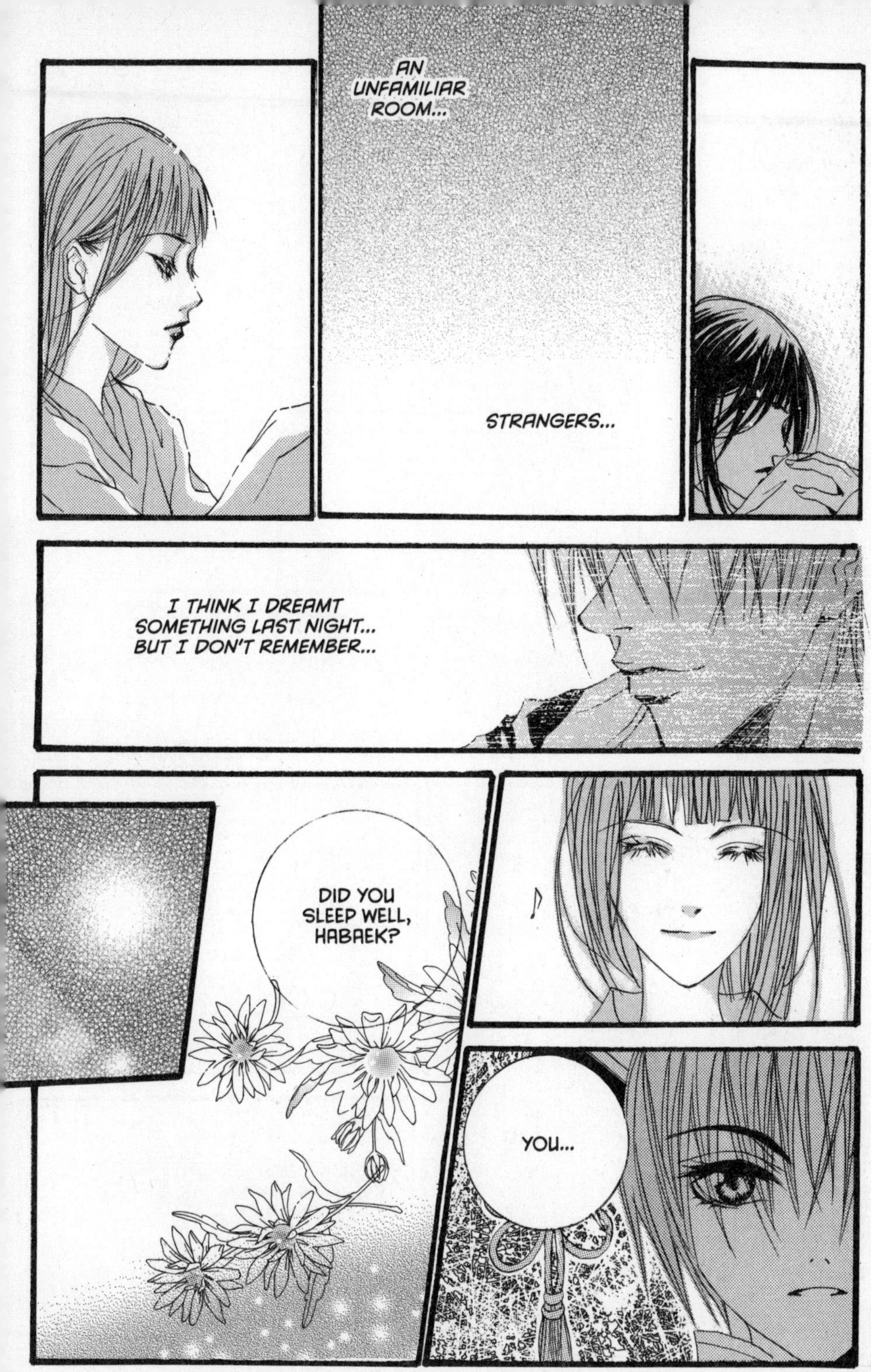
AN UNFAMILIAR ROOM...
STRANGERS...
I THINK I DREAMT SOMETHING LAST NIGHT... BUT I DON'T REMEMBER...
DID YOU SLEEP WELL, HABAEK?
YOU...

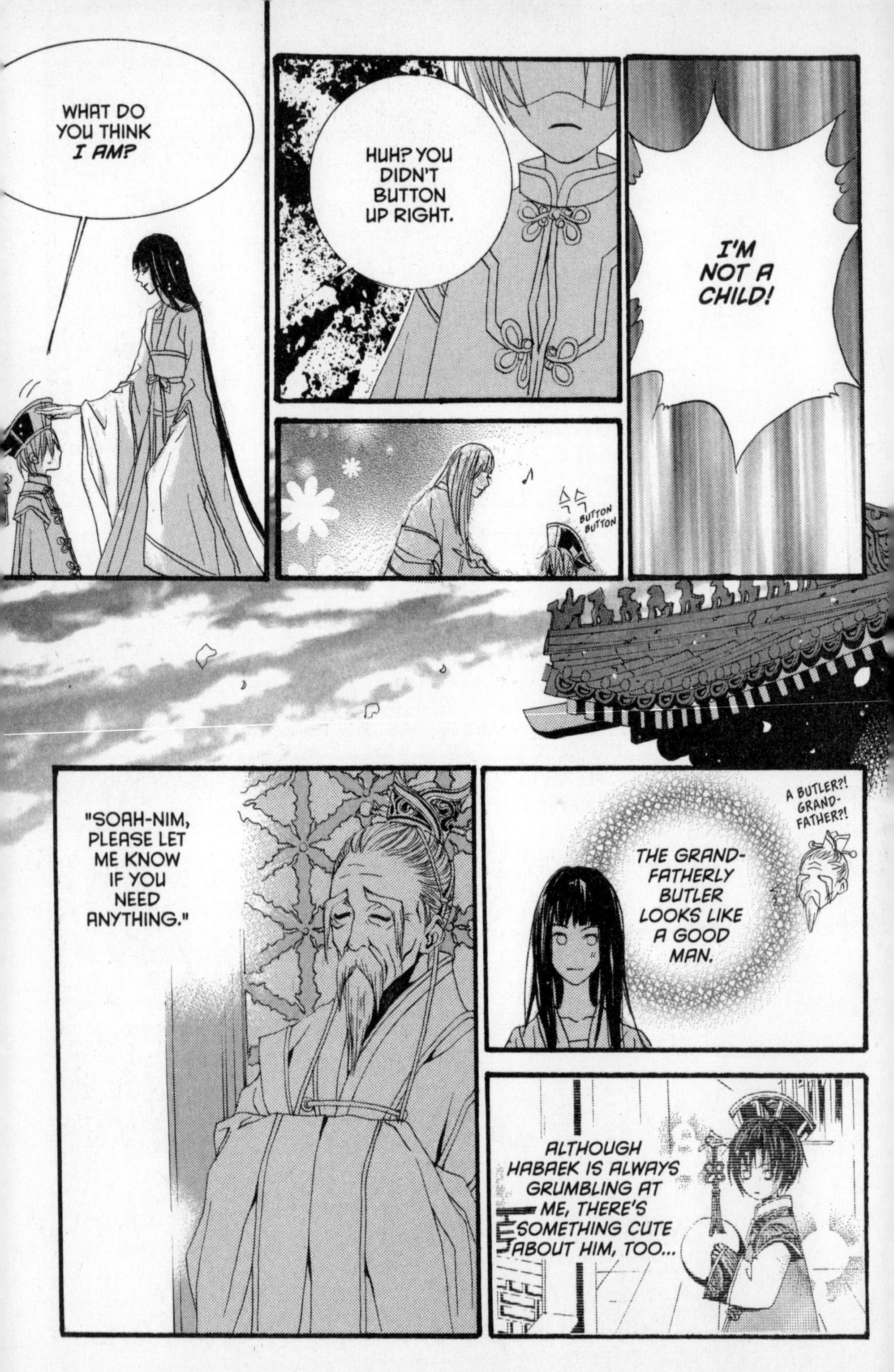
WHAT DO YOU THINK *I AM?*
HUH? YOU DIDN'T BUTTON UP RIGHT.
I'M NOT A CHILD!
BUTTON BUTTON
"SOAH-NIM, PLEASE LET ME KNOW IF YOU NEED ANYTHING."
THE GRAND-FATHERLY BUTLER LOOKS LIKE A GOOD MAN.
A BUTLER?! GRAND-FATHER?!
ALTHOUGH HABAEK IS ALWAYS GRUMBLING AT ME, THERE'S SOMETHING CUTE ABOUT HIM, TOO...

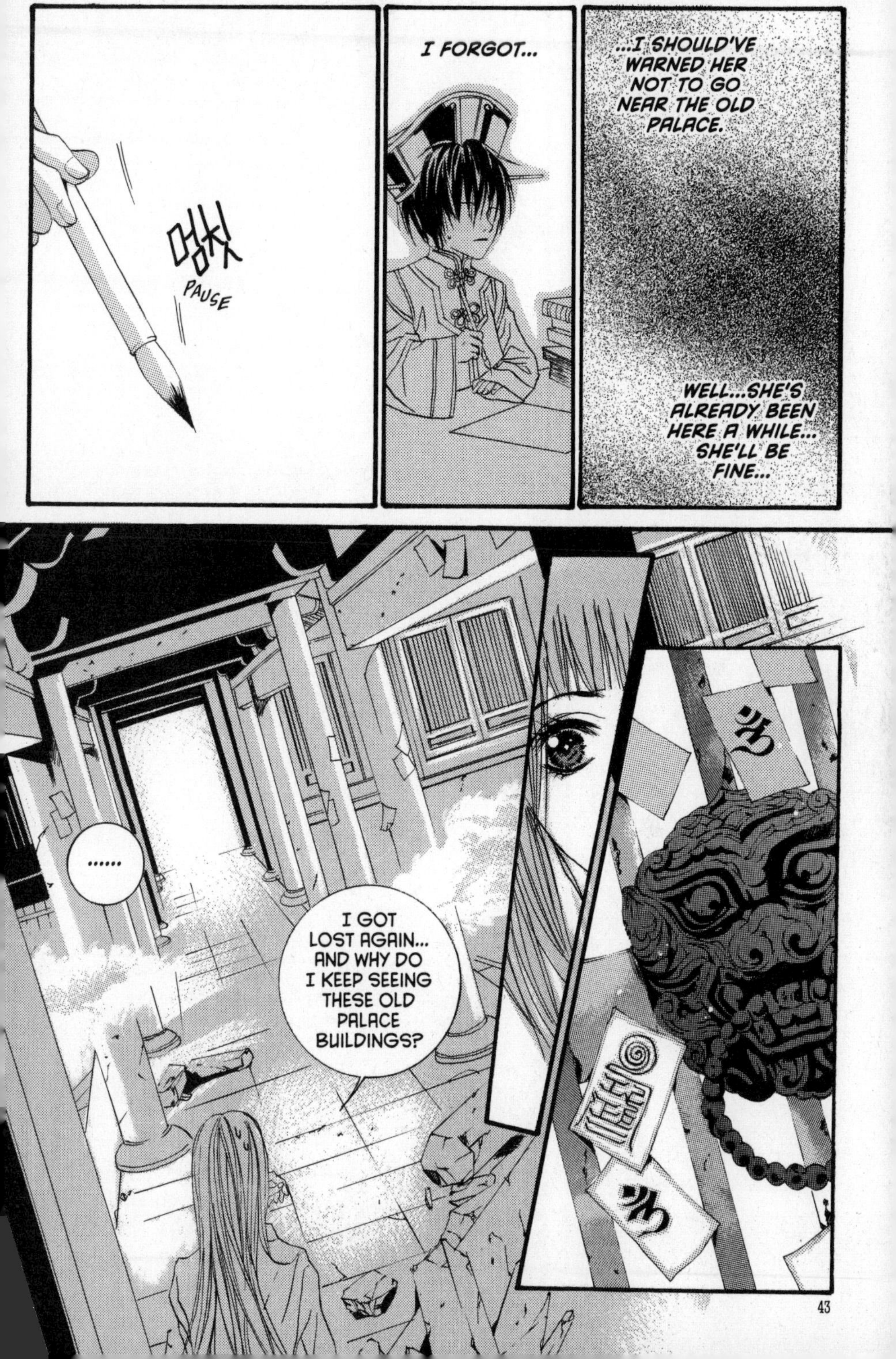
멈칫
PAUSE
I FORGOT...
...I SHOULD'VE WARNED HER NOT TO GO NEAR THE OLD PALACE.
WELL...SHE'S ALREADY BEEN HERE A WHILE... SHE'LL BE FINE...
......
I GOT LOST AGAIN... AND WHY DO I KEEP SEEING THESE OLD PALACE BUILDINGS?

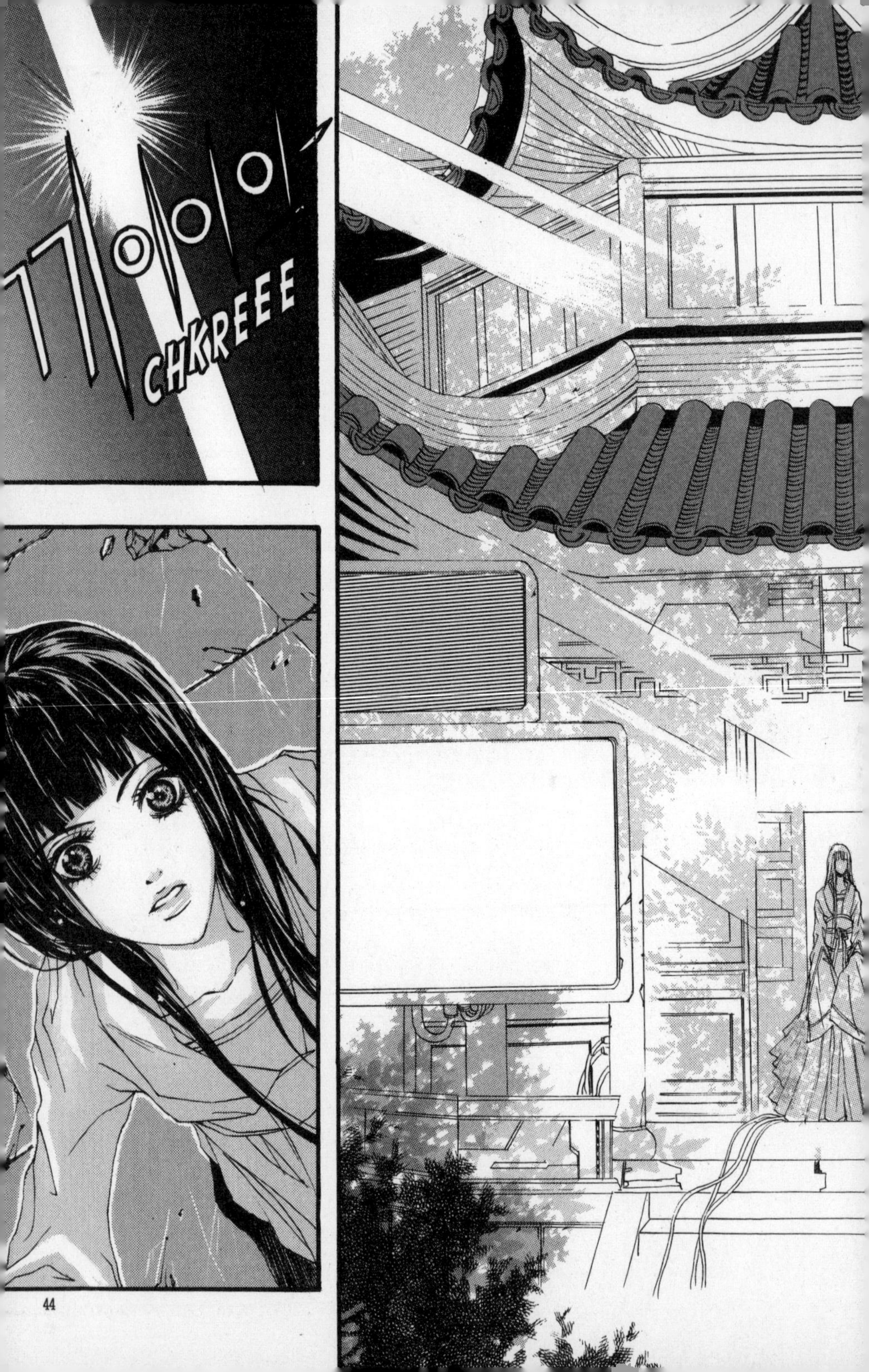
CHKREEE

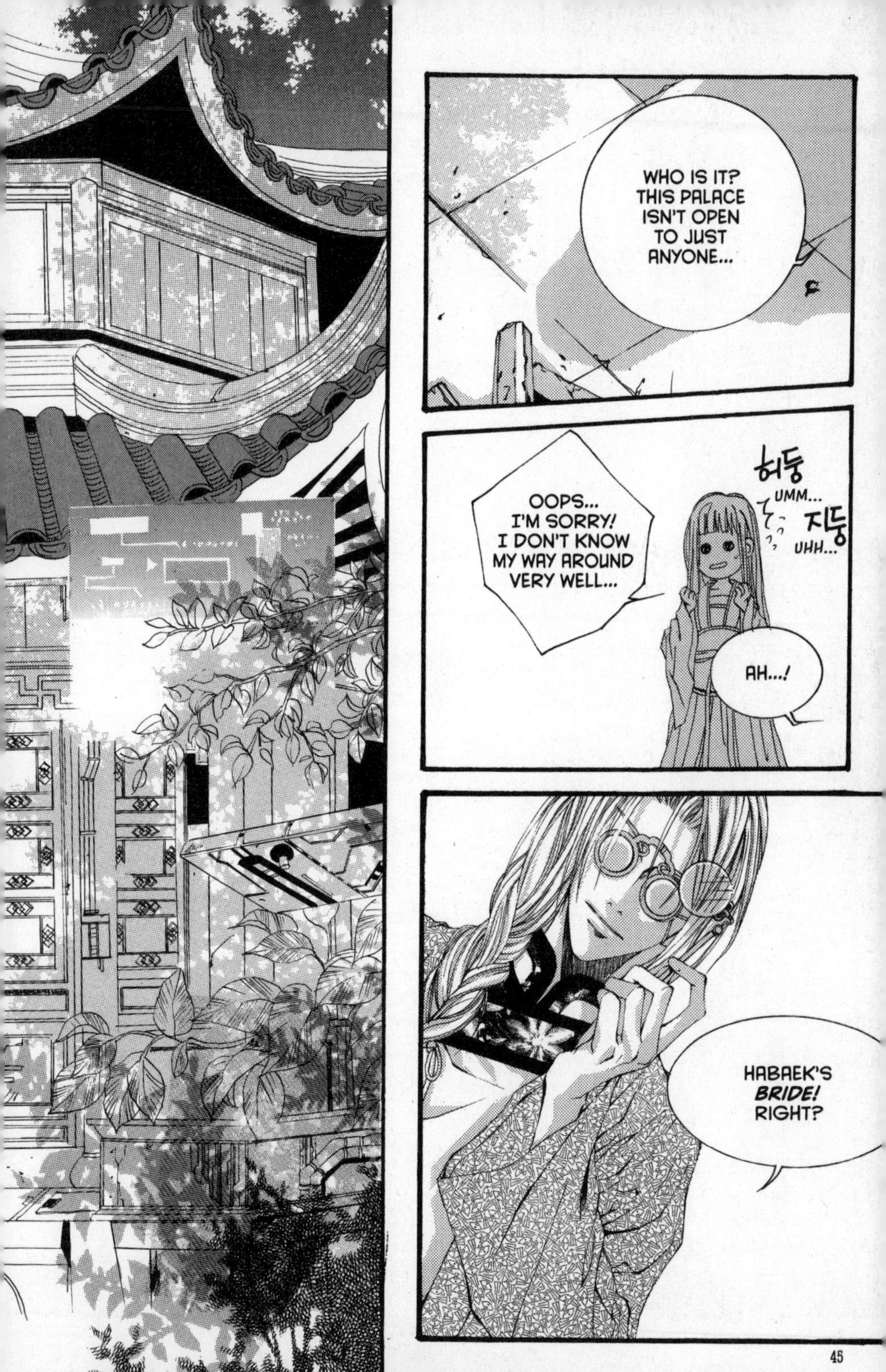
WHO IS IT? THIS PALACE ISN'T OPEN TO JUST ANYONE...
OOPS... I'M SORRY! I DON'T KNOW MY WAY AROUND VERY WELL...
허둥
UMM...
지둥
UHH...
AH...!
HABAEK'S *BRIDE!* RIGHT?

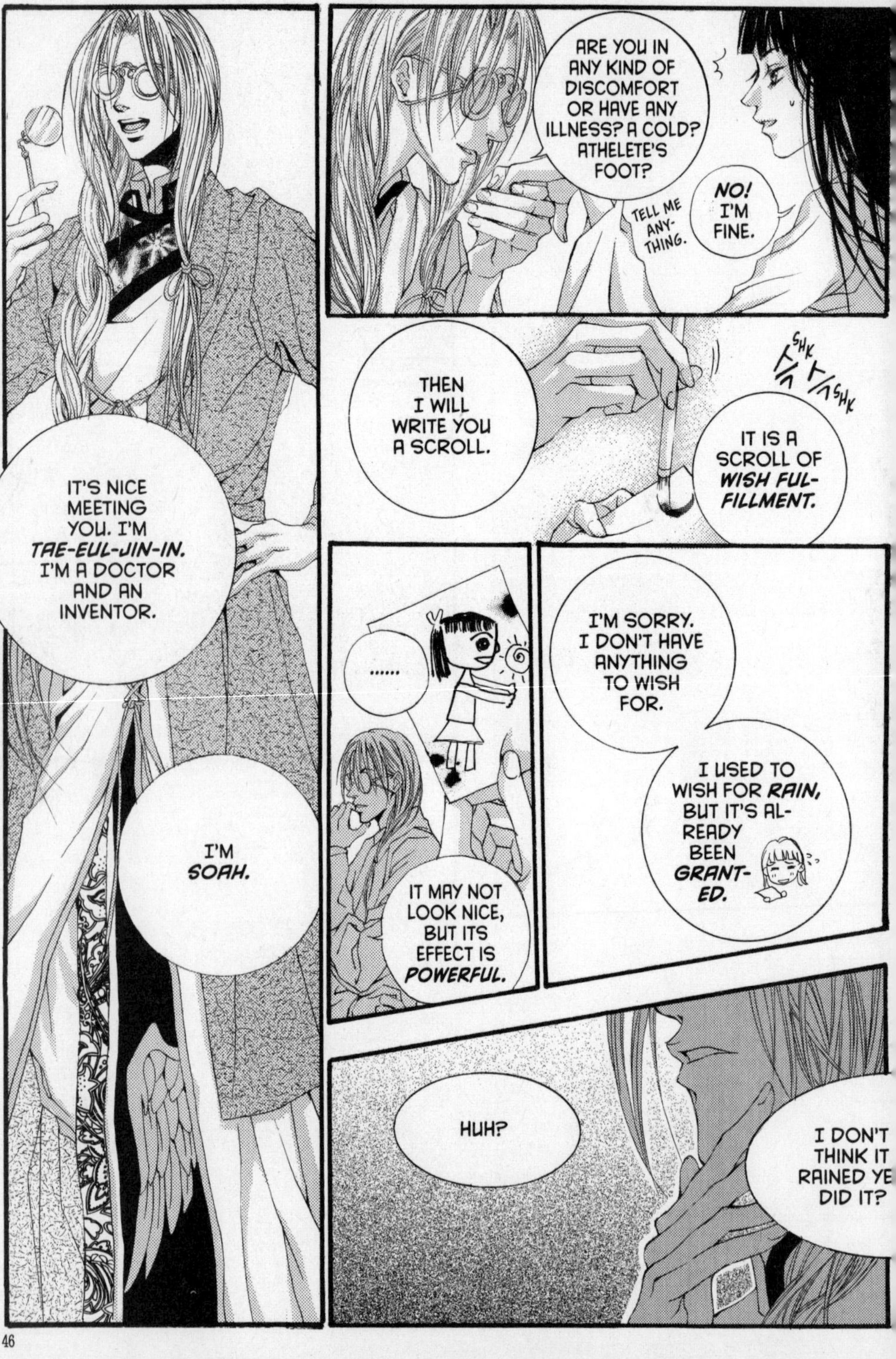
IT'S NICE MEETING YOU. I'M TAE-EUL-JIN-IN. I'M A DOCTOR AND AN INVENTOR.
I'M SOAH.
ARE YOU IN ANY KIND OF DISCOMFORT OR HAVE ANY ILLNESS? A COLD? ATHELETE'S FOOT?
TELL ME ANY-THING.
NO! I'M FINE.
THEN I WILL WRITE YOU A SCROLL.
SHK SHK
IT IS A SCROLL OF WISH FUL-FILLMENT.
......
IT MAY NOT LOOK NICE, BUT ITS EFFECT IS POWERFUL.
I'M SORRY. I DON'T HAVE ANYTHING TO WISH FOR.
I USED TO WISH FOR RAIN, BUT IT'S AL-READY BEEN GRANT-ED.
HUH?
I DON'T THINK IT RAINED YE DID IT?

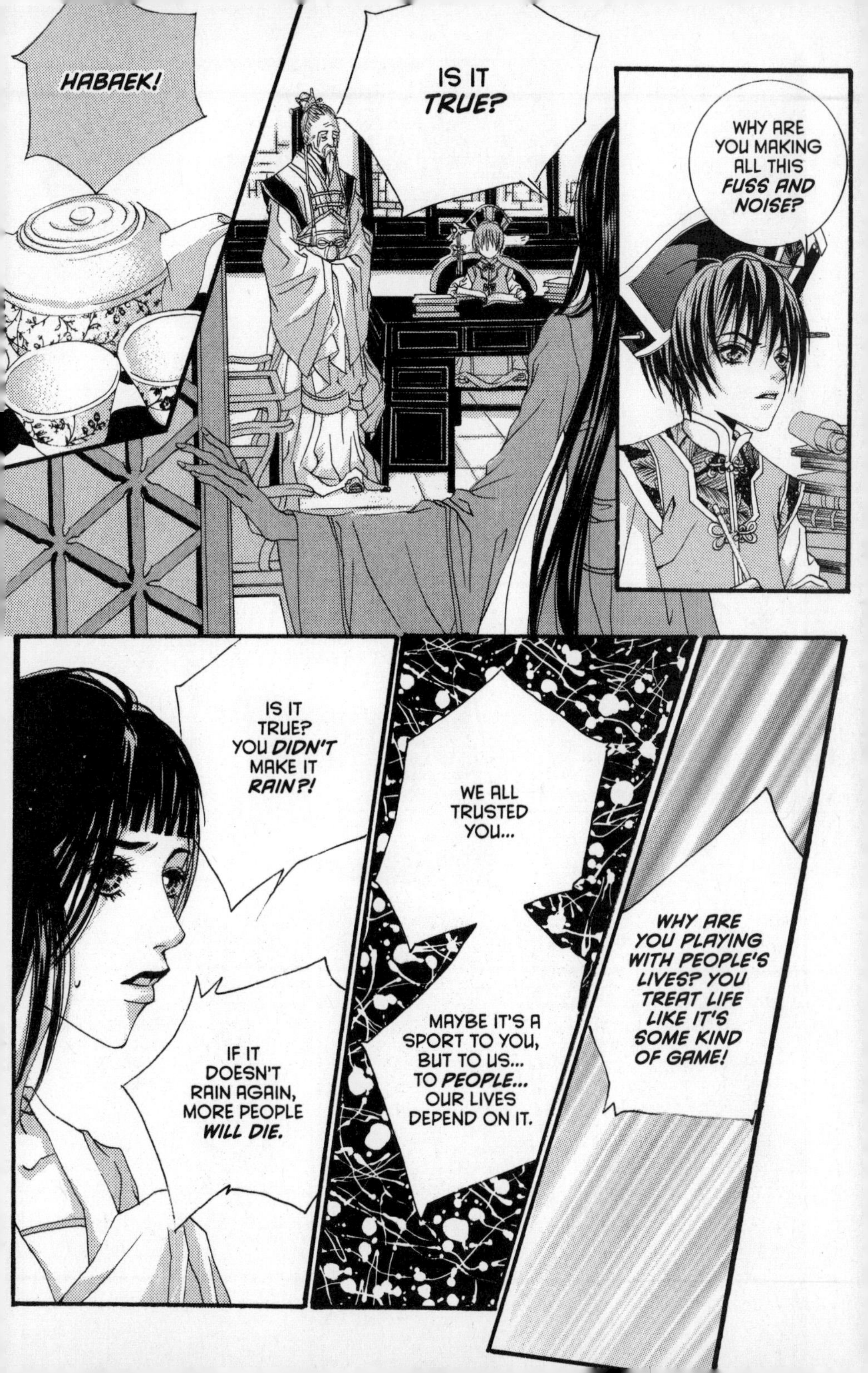
HABAEK!
IS IT TRUE?
WHY ARE YOU MAKING ALL THIS FUSS AND NOISE?
IS IT TRUE? YOU DIDN'T MAKE IT RAIN?!
IF IT DOESN'T RAIN AGAIN, MORE PEOPLE WILL DIE.
WE ALL TRUSTED YOU...
MAYBE IT'S A SPORT TO YOU, BUT TO US... TO PEOPLE... OUR LIVES DEPEND ON IT.
WHY ARE YOU PLAYING WITH PEOPLE'S LIVES? YOU TREAT LIFE LIKE IT'S SOME KIND OF GAME!

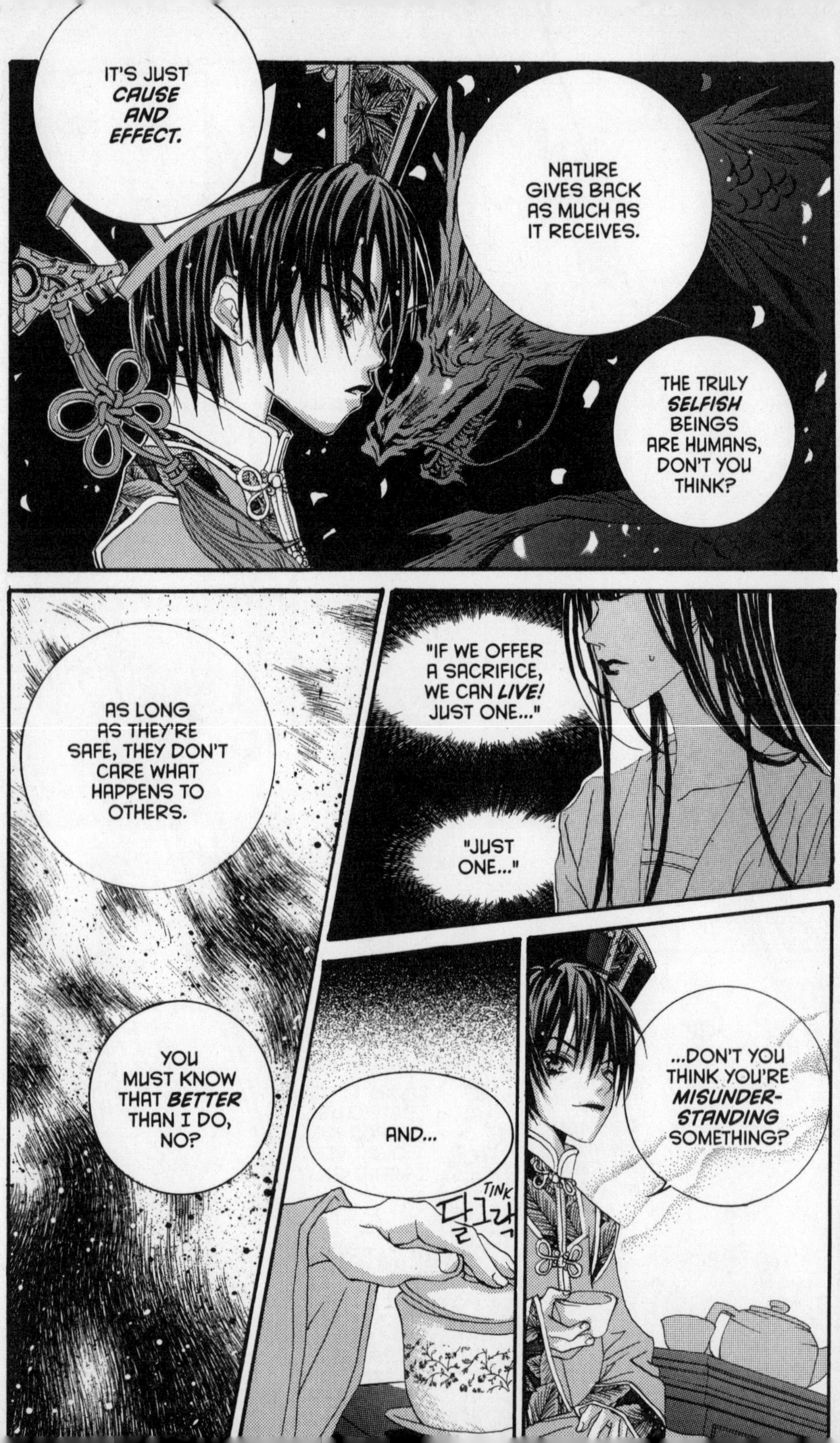
IT'S JUST *CAUSE AND EFFECT.*
NATURE GIVES BACK AS MUCH AS IT RECEIVES.
THE TRULY *SELFISH* BEINGS ARE HUMANS, DON'T YOU THINK?
"IF WE OFFER A SACRIFICE, WE CAN *LIVE!* JUST ONE..."
"JUST ONE..."
AS LONG AS THEY'RE SAFE, THEY DON'T CARE WHAT HAPPENS TO OTHERS.
...DON'T YOU THINK YOU'RE *MISUNDERSTANDING* SOMETHING?
TINK
달그락
AND...
YOU MUST KNOW THAT *BETTER* THAN I DO, NO?

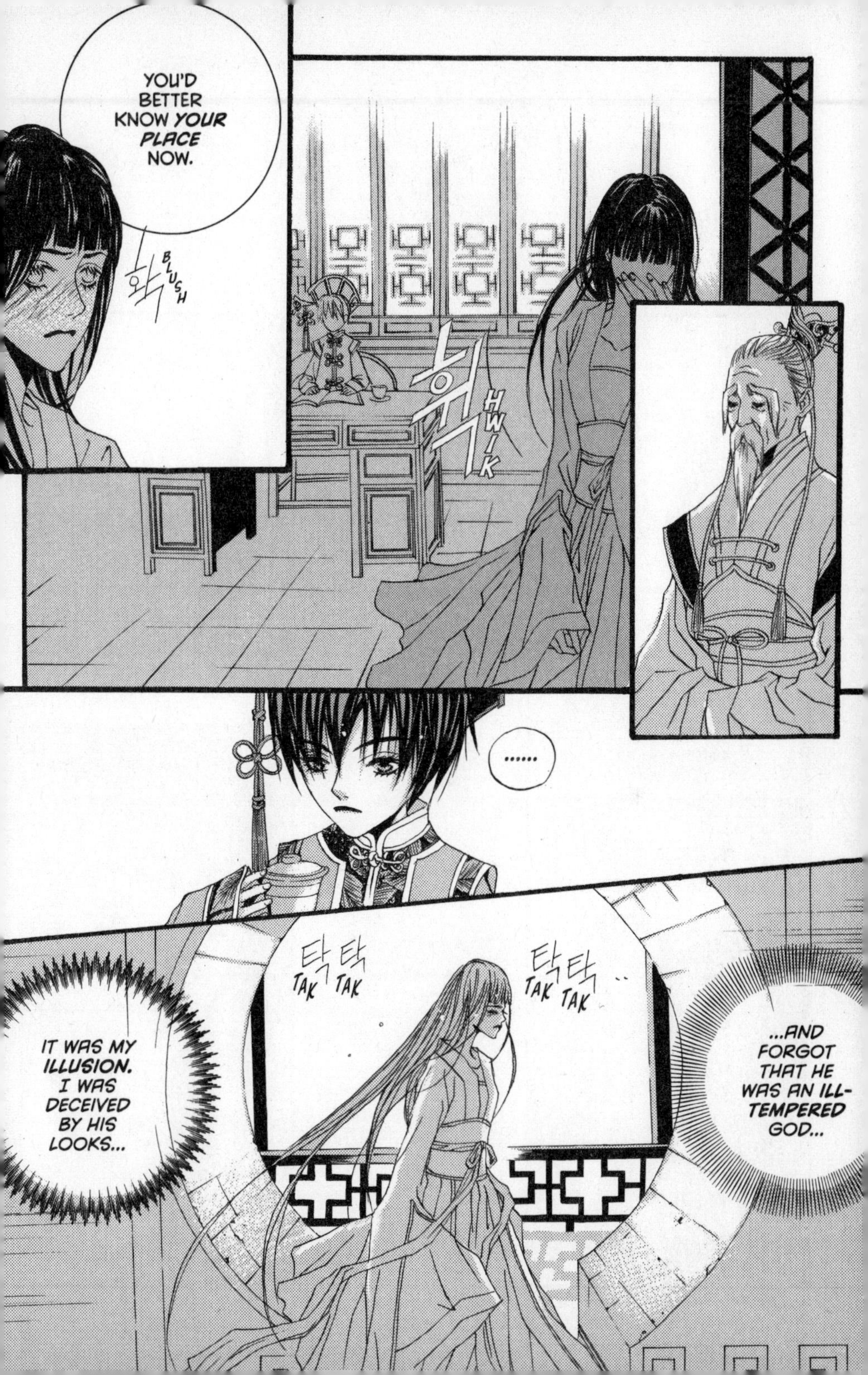
YOU'D BETTER KNOW YOUR PLACE NOW.
확 BLUSH
휙 HWIK
......
탁탁 TAK TAK
탁탁 TAK TAK ..
IT WAS MY ILLUSION. I WAS DECEIVED BY HIS LOOKS...
...AND FORGOT THAT HE WAS AN ILL-TEMPERED GOD...

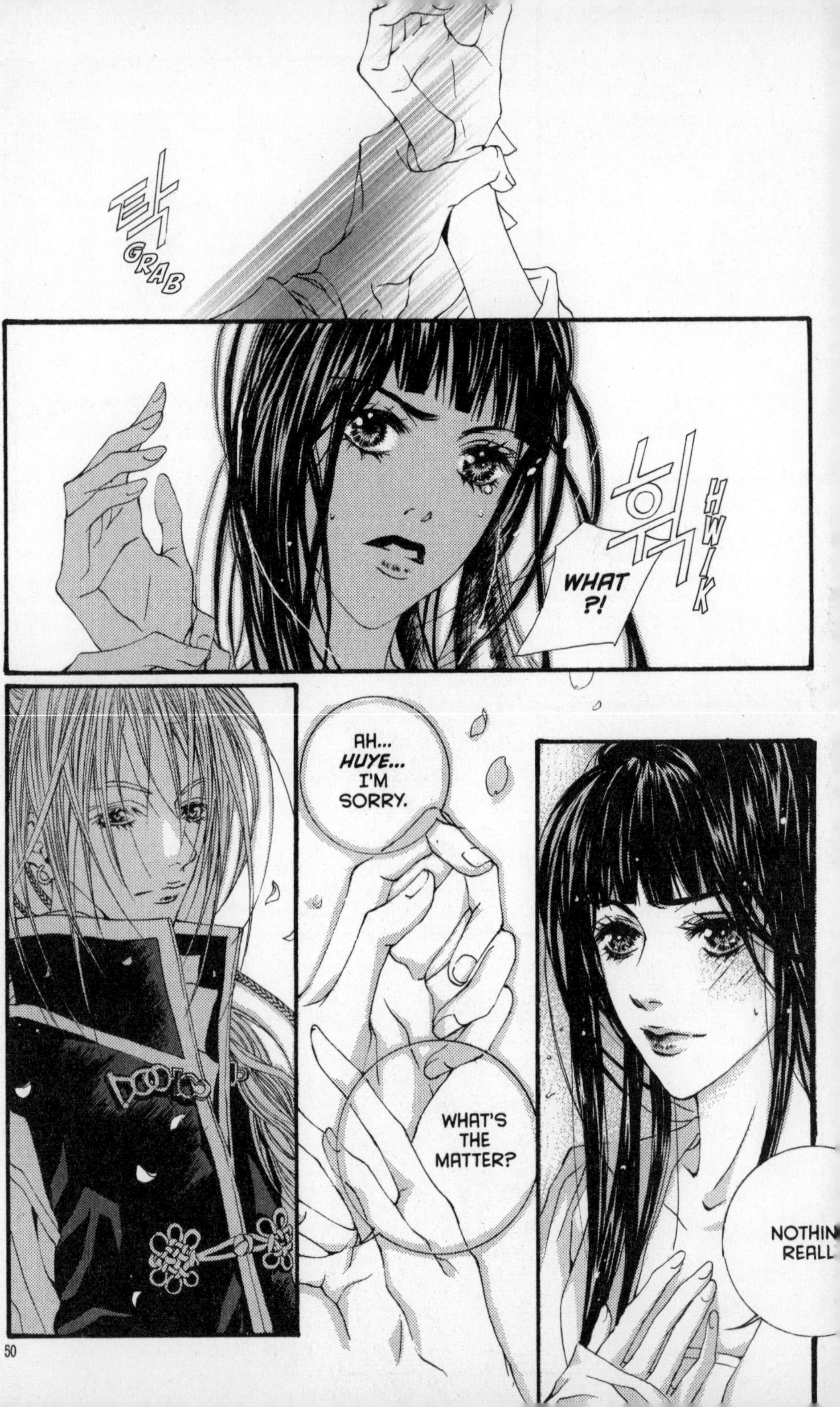
탁
GRAB
휙
HWIK
WHAT ?!
AH... HUYE... I'M SORRY.
WHAT'S THE MATTER?
NOTHIN REALL

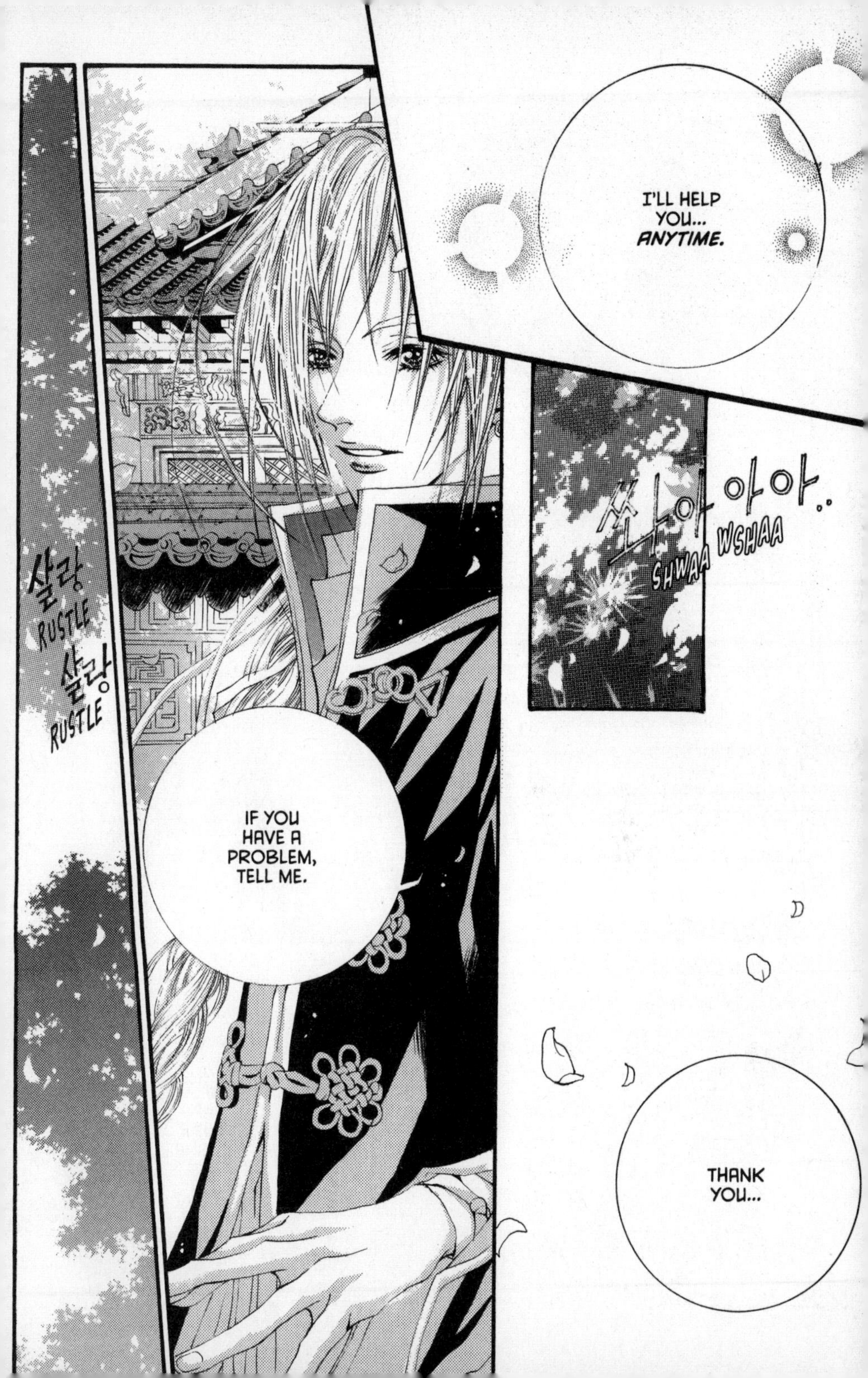
I'LL HELP YOU... ANYTIME.
쏴아아아..
SHWAA WSHAA
IF YOU HAVE A PROBLEM, TELL ME.
살랑 RUSTLE
살랑 RUSTLE
THANK YOU...

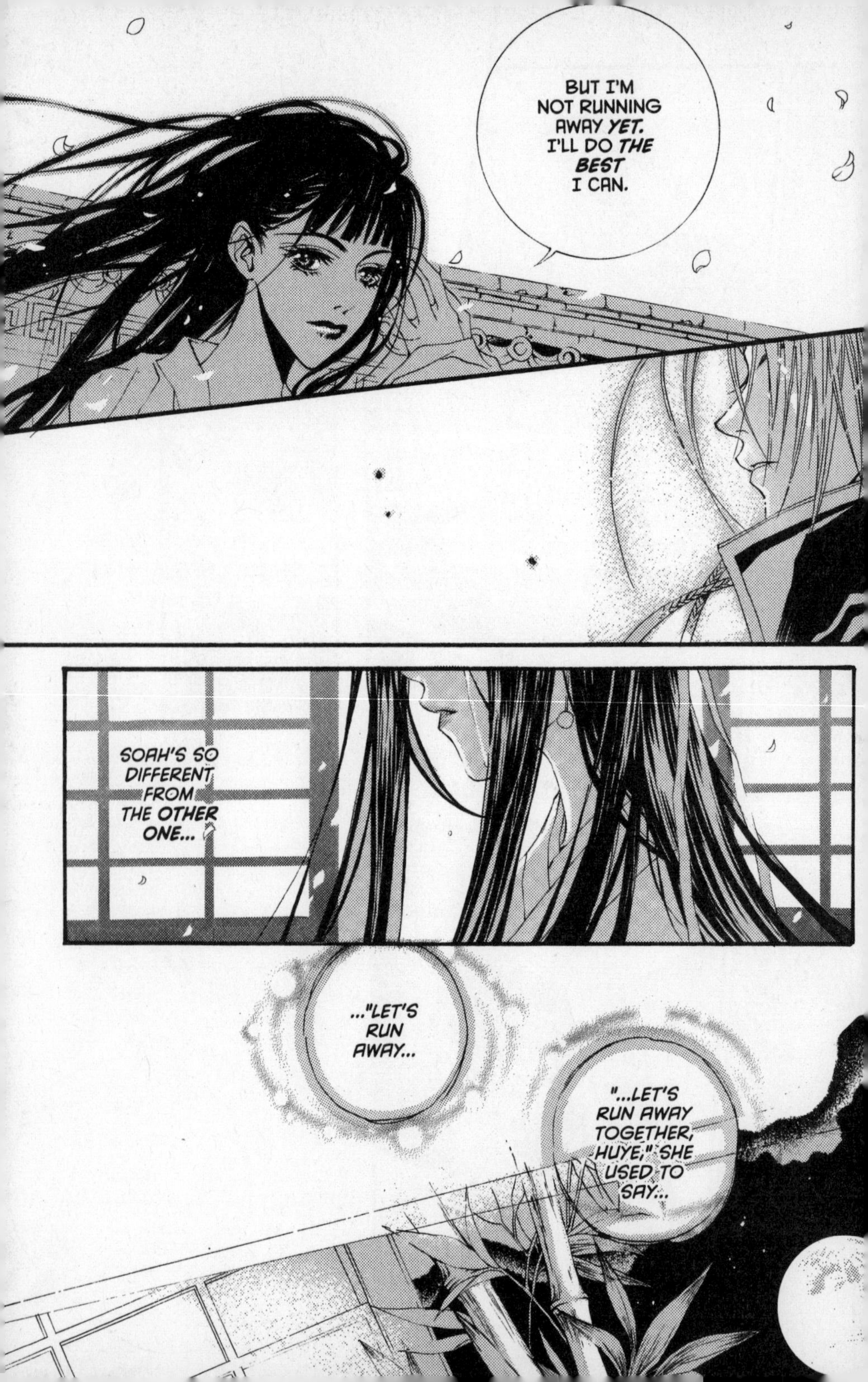
BUT I'M NOT RUNNING AWAY YET. I'LL DO THE BEST I CAN.
SOAH'S SO DIFFERENT FROM THE OTHER ONE...
..."LET'S RUN AWAY...
"...LET'S RUN AWAY TOGETHER, HUYE," SHE USED TO SAY...

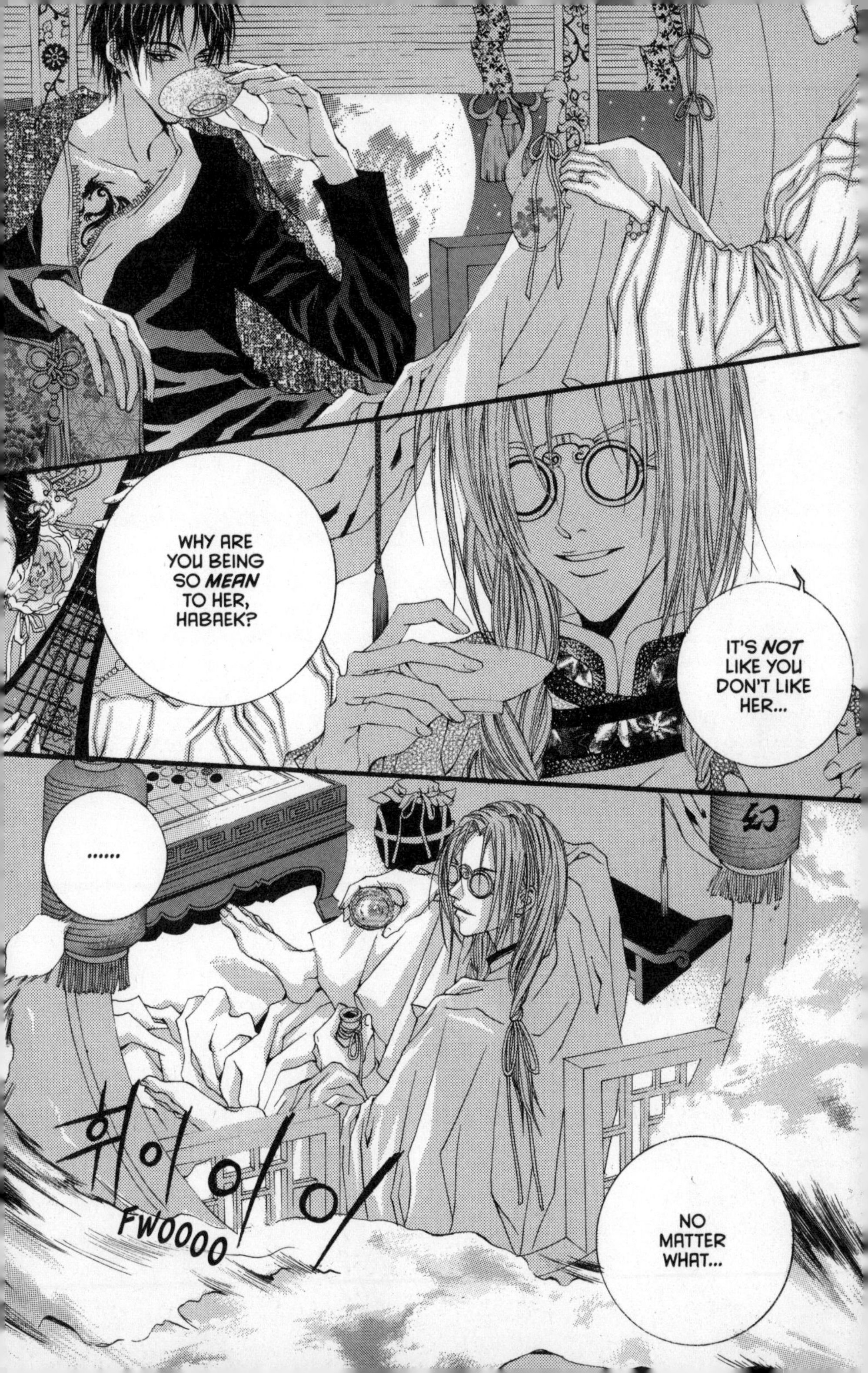
WHY ARE YOU BEING SO *MEAN* TO HER, HABAEK?
IT'S *NOT* LIKE YOU DON'T LIKE HER...
......
휘이이이
FWOOOO
NO MATTER WHAT...

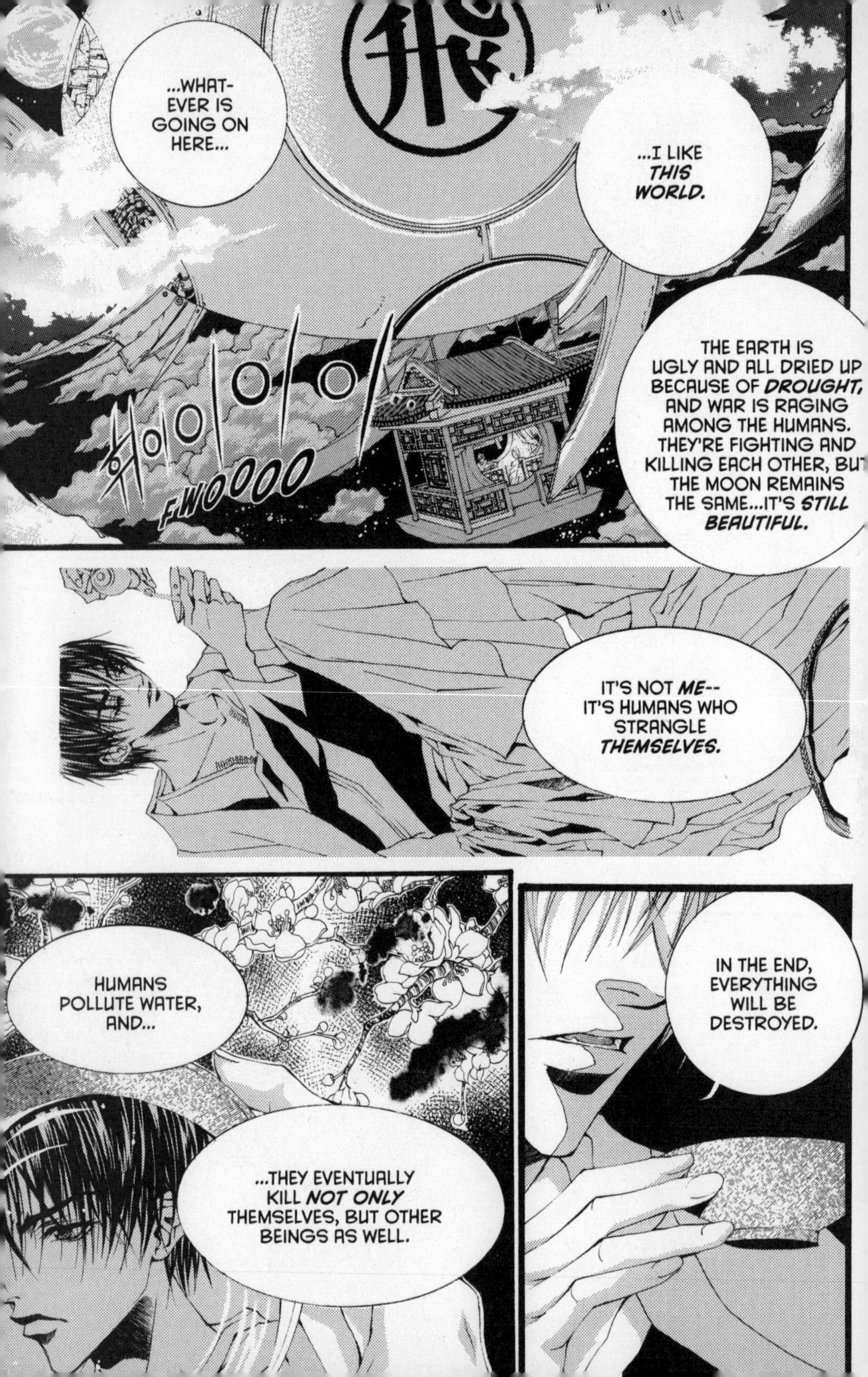
...I LIKE THIS WORLD.
...WHAT-EVER IS GOING ON HERE...
FWOOOO
THE EARTH IS UGLY AND ALL DRIED UP BECAUSE OF DROUGHT, AND WAR IS RAGING AMONG THE HUMANS. THEY'RE FIGHTING AND KILLING EACH OTHER, BUT THE MOON REMAINS THE SAME...IT'S STILL BEAUTIFUL.
IT'S NOT ME-- IT'S HUMANS WHO STRANGLE THEMSELVES.
IN THE END, EVERYTHING WILL BE DESTROYED.
HUMANS POLLUTE WATER, AND...
...THEY EVENTUALLY KILL NOT ONLY THEMSELVES, BUT OTHER BEINGS AS WELL.

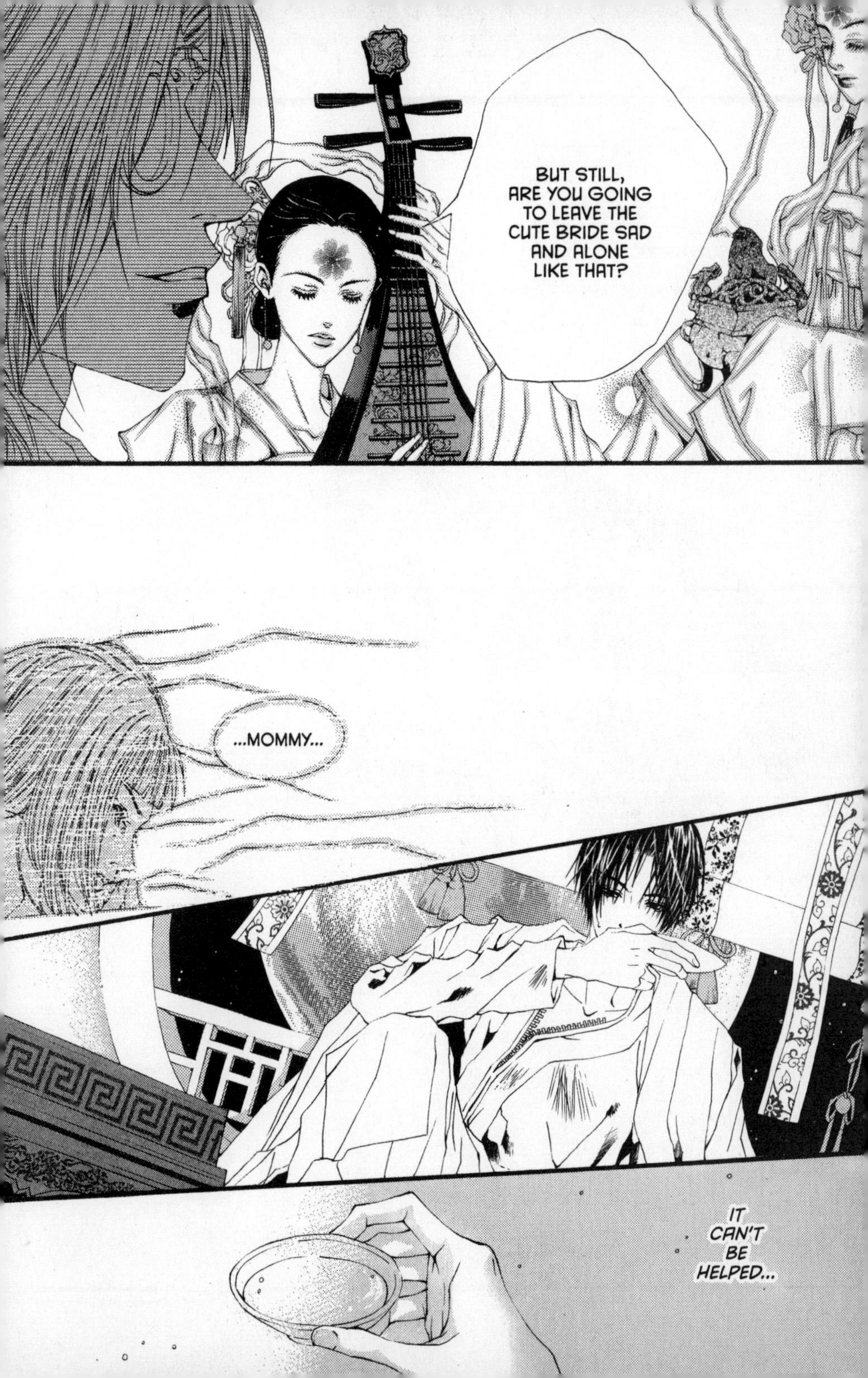
BUT STILL, ARE YOU GOING TO LEAVE THE CUTE BRIDE SAD AND ALONE LIKE THAT?
...MOMMY...
IT CAN'T BE HELPED...

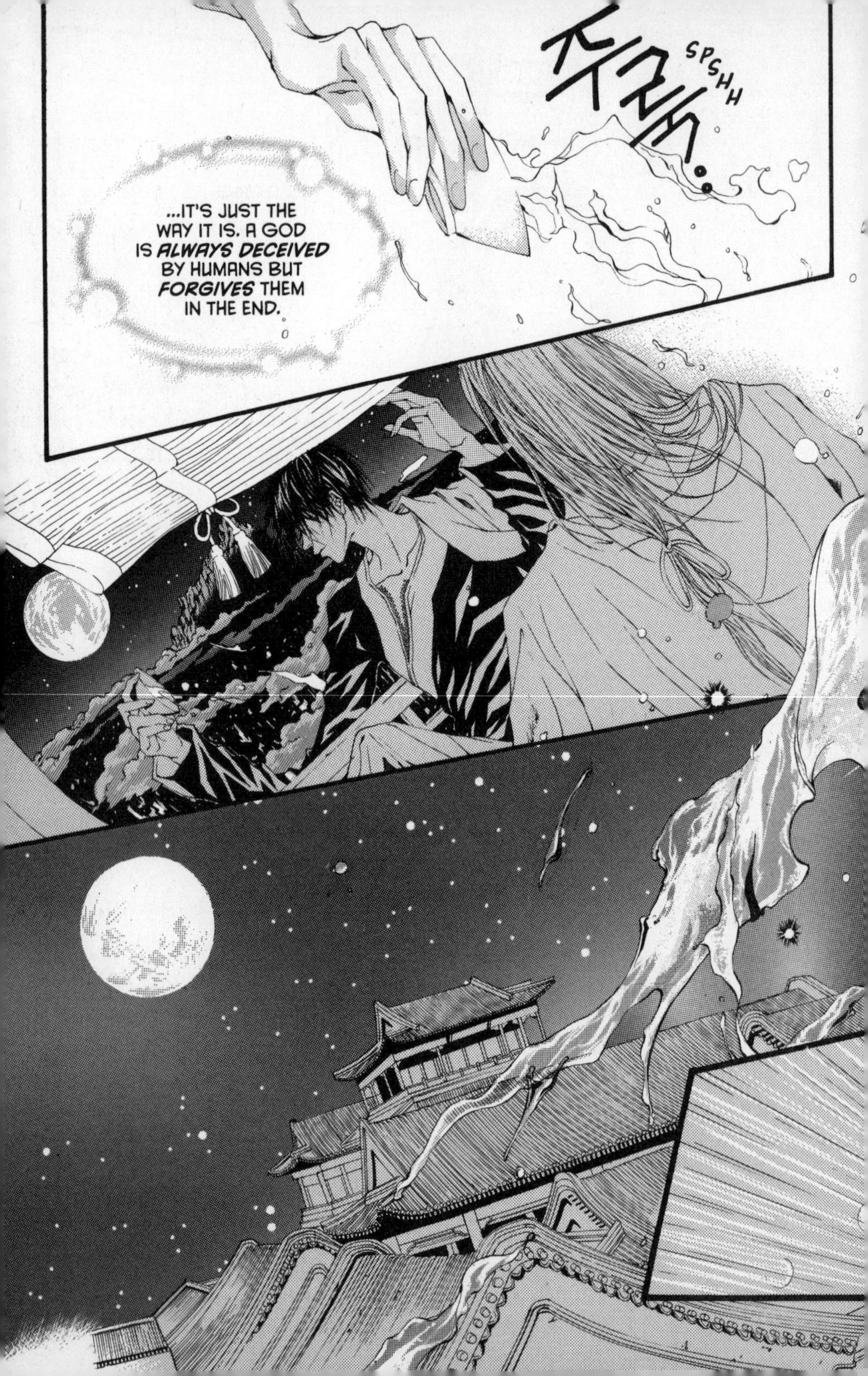
SPSHH
...IT'S JUST THE WAY IT IS. A GOD IS *ALWAYS DECEIVED* BY HUMANS BUT *FORGIVES* THEM IN THE END.

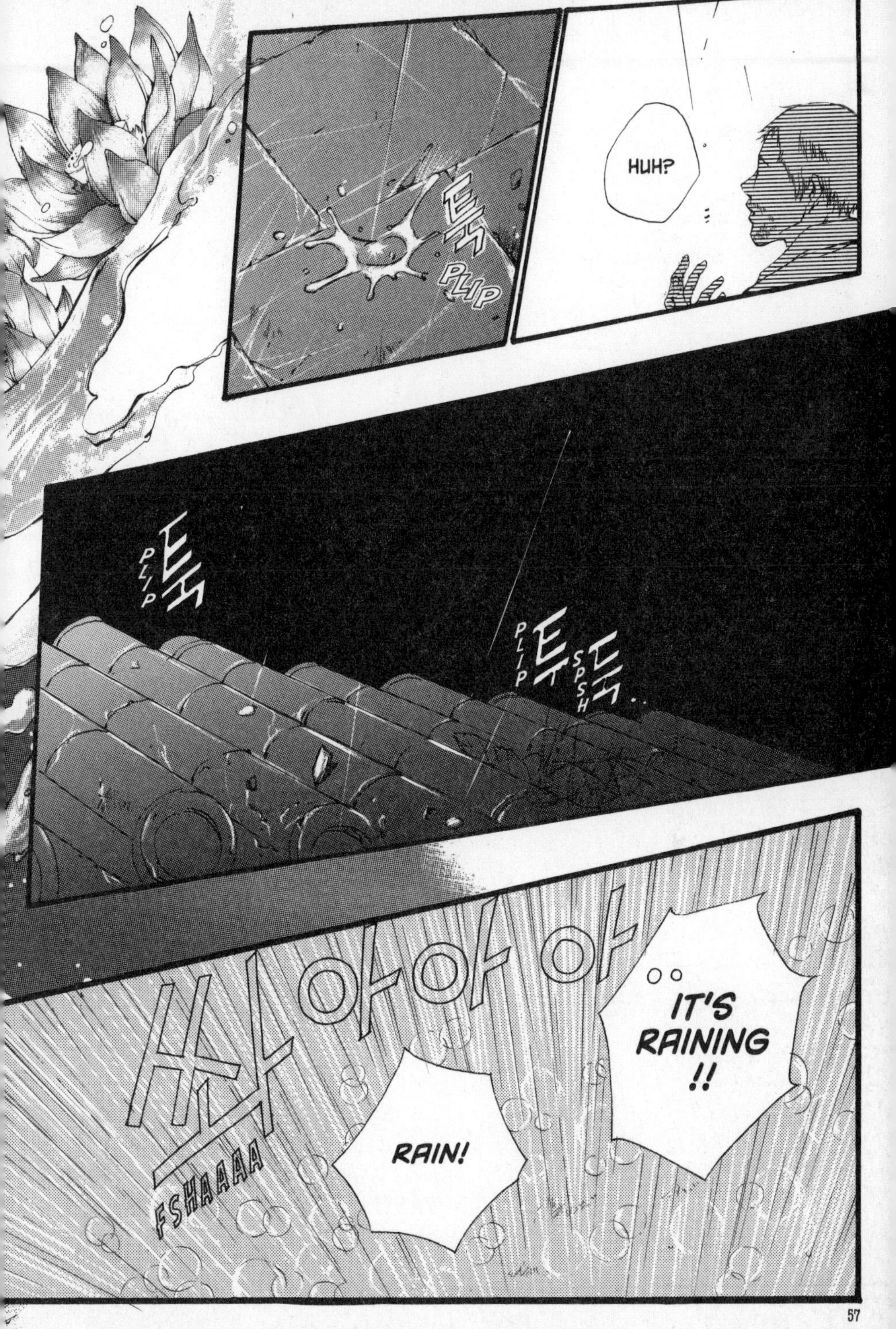
HUH?
PLIP
PLIP
PLIP
SPSH
IT'S RAINING !!
RAIN!
FSHAAAA

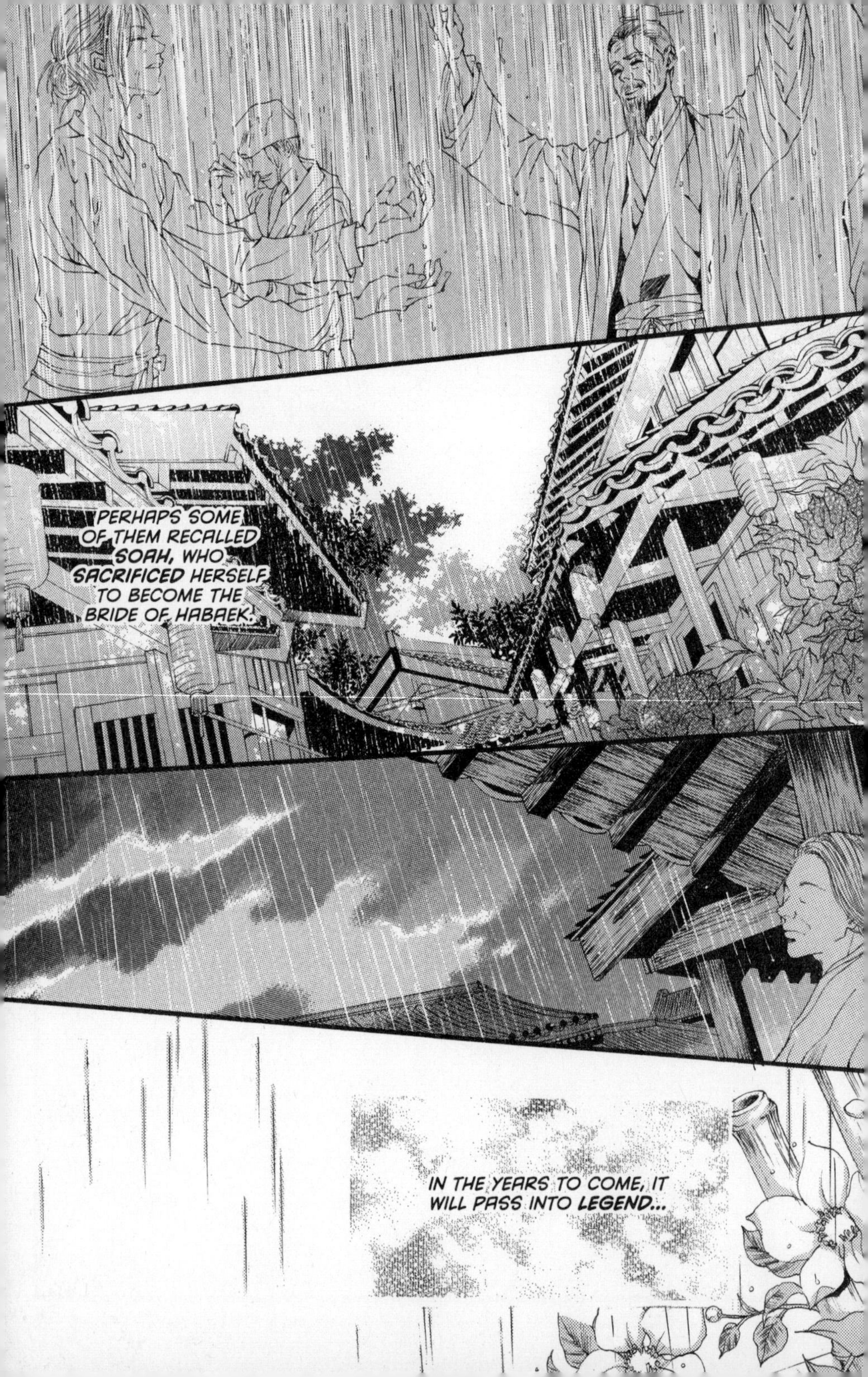
PERHAPS SOME OF THEM RECALLED SOAH, WHO SACRIFICED HERSELF TO BECOME THE BRIDE OF HABAEK.
IN THE YEARS TO COME, IT WILL PASS INTO LEGEND...

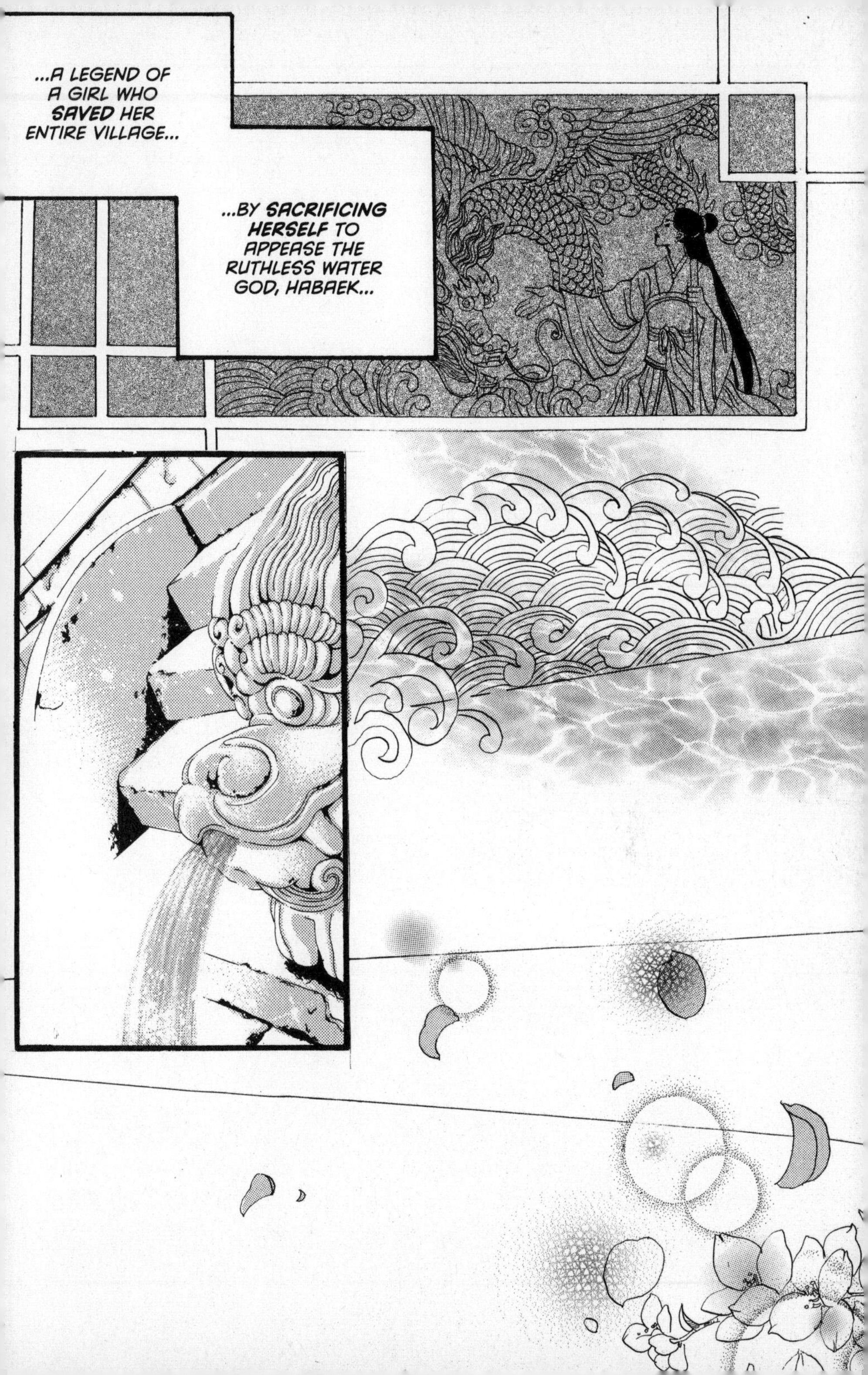
...A LEGEND OF A GIRL WHO SAVED HER ENTIRE VILLAGE...
...BY SACRIFICING HERSELF TO APPEASE THE RUTHLESS WATER GOD, HABAEK...

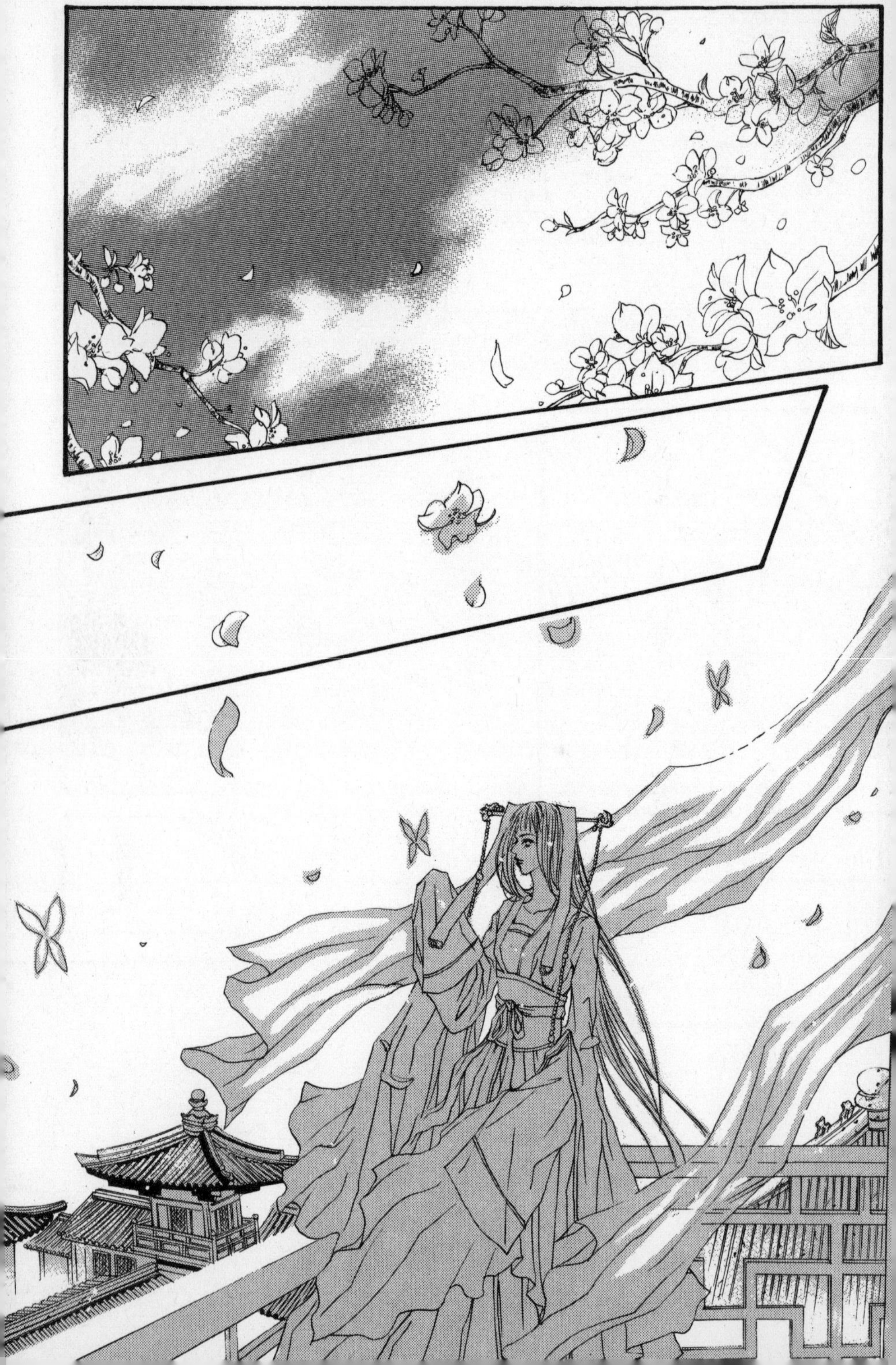

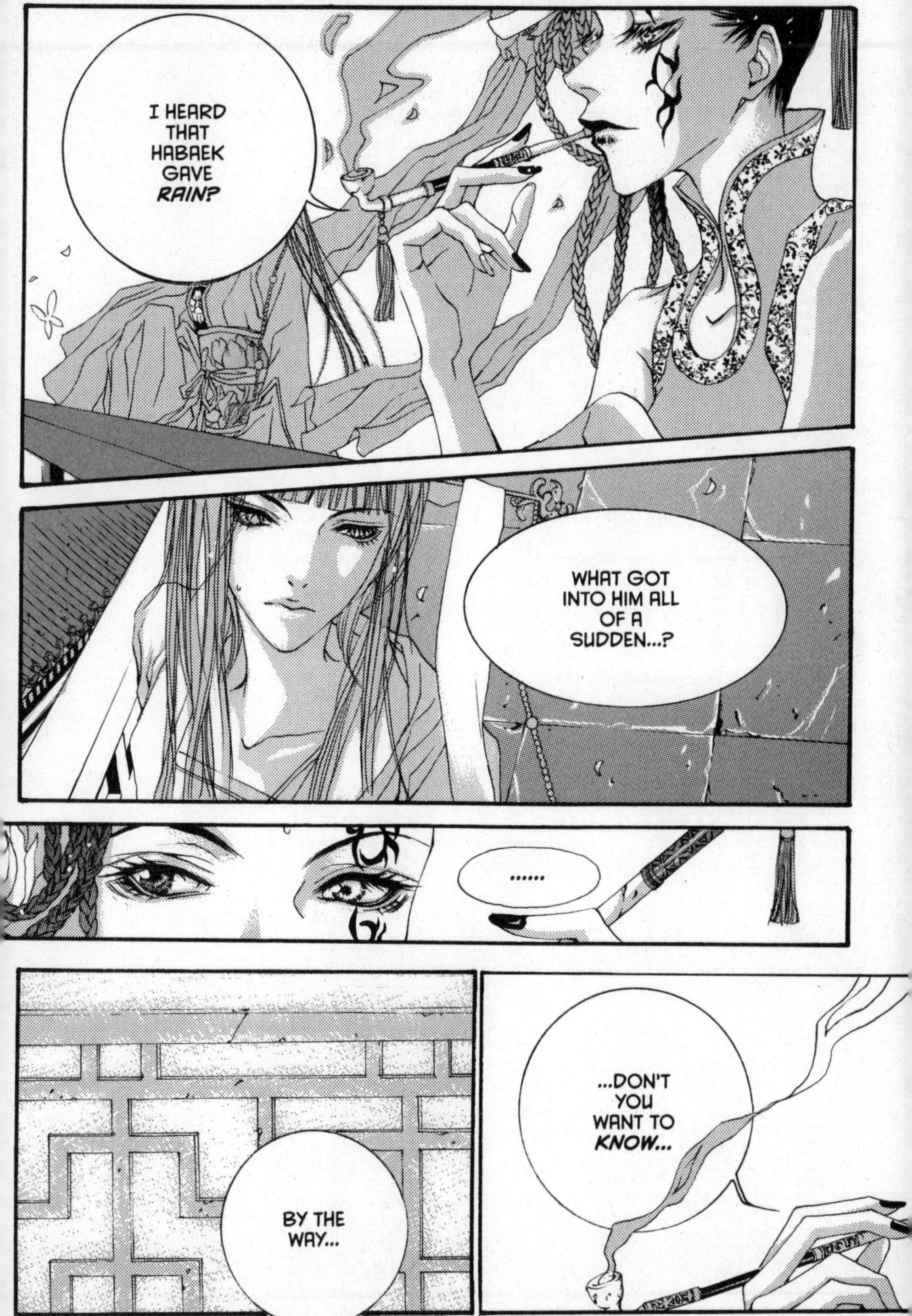
I HEARD THAT HABAEK GAVE *RAIN?*
WHAT GOT INTO HIM ALL OF A SUDDEN...?
......
...DON'T YOU WANT TO *KNOW*...
BY THE WAY...

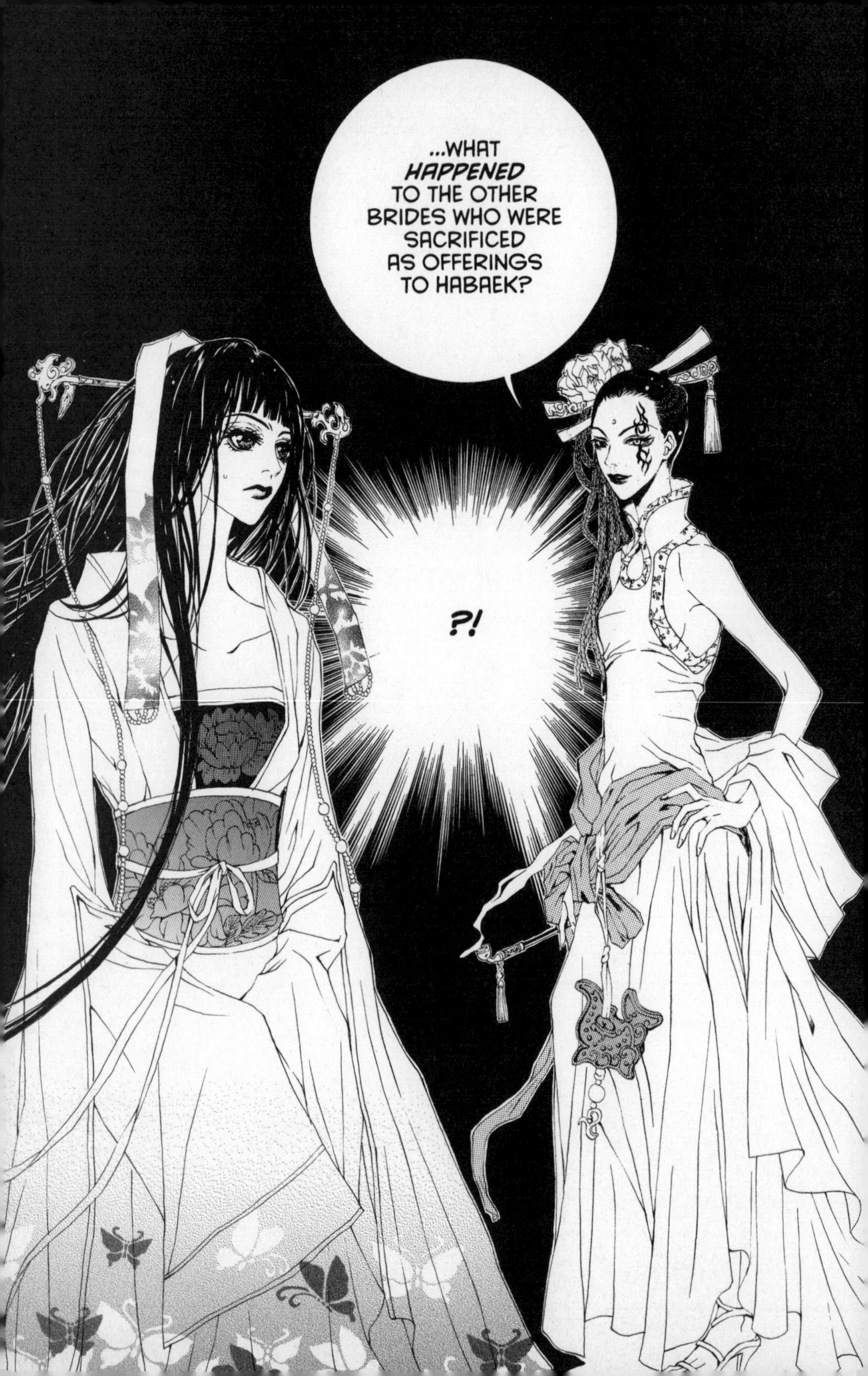
...WHAT *HAPPENED* TO THE OTHER BRIDES WHO WERE SACRIFICED AS OFFERINGS TO HABAEK?
?!

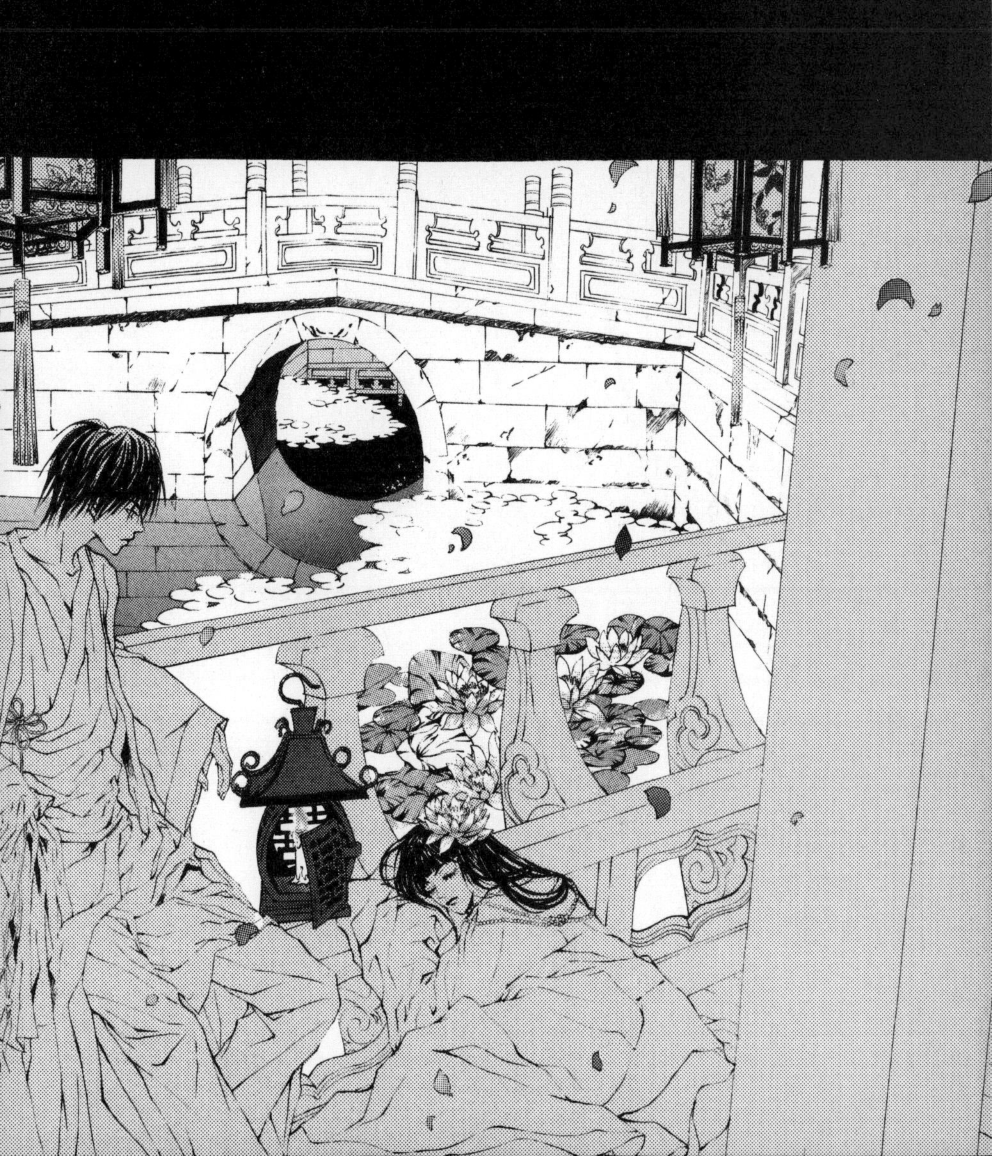

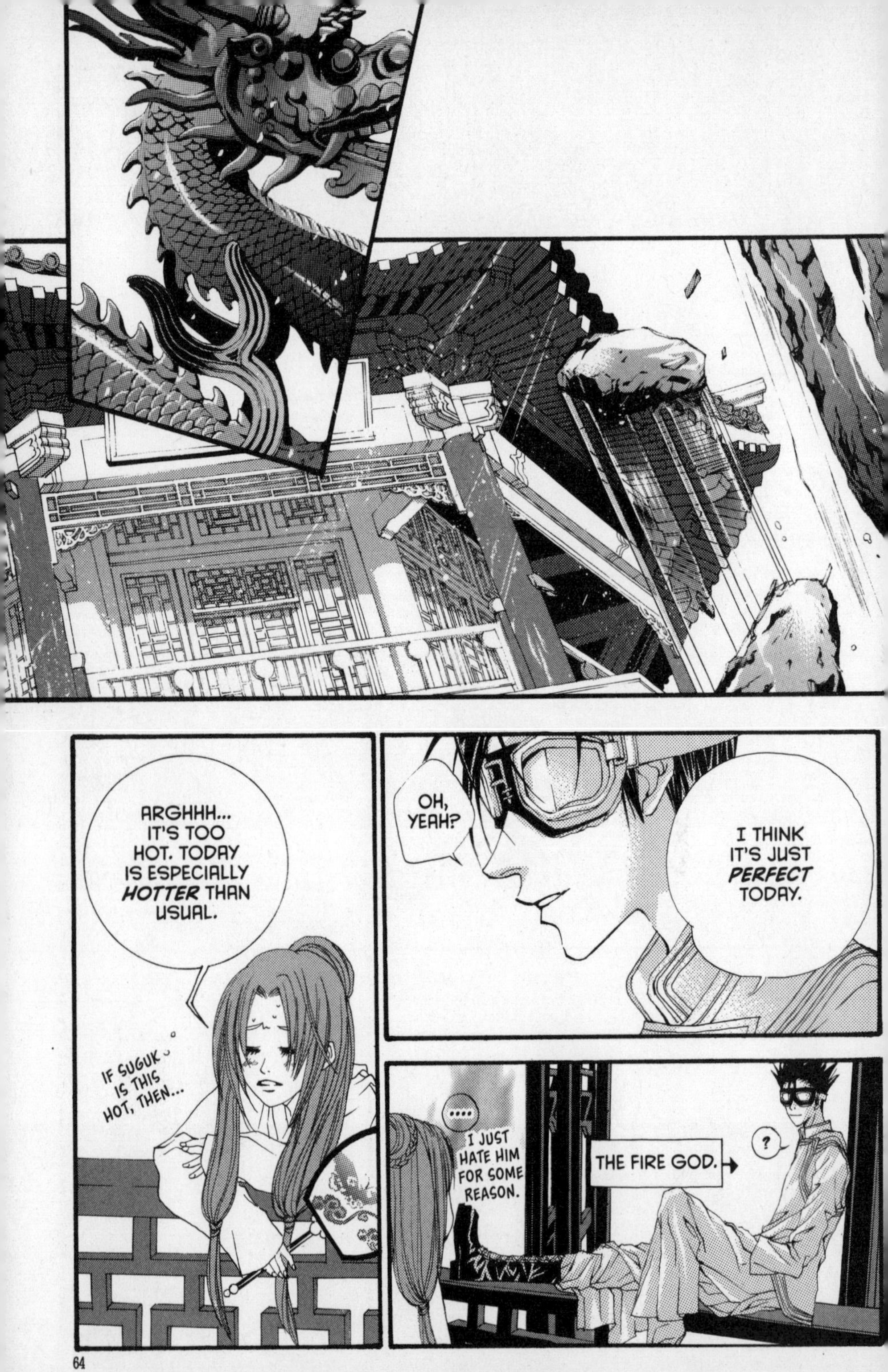
ARGHHH... IT'S TOO HOT. TODAY IS ESPECIALLY HOTTER THAN USUAL.
I THINK IT'S JUST PERFECT TODAY.
OH, YEAH?
IF SUGUK IS THIS HOT, THEN...
THE FIRE GOD.
....
I JUST HATE HIM FOR SOME REASON.
?

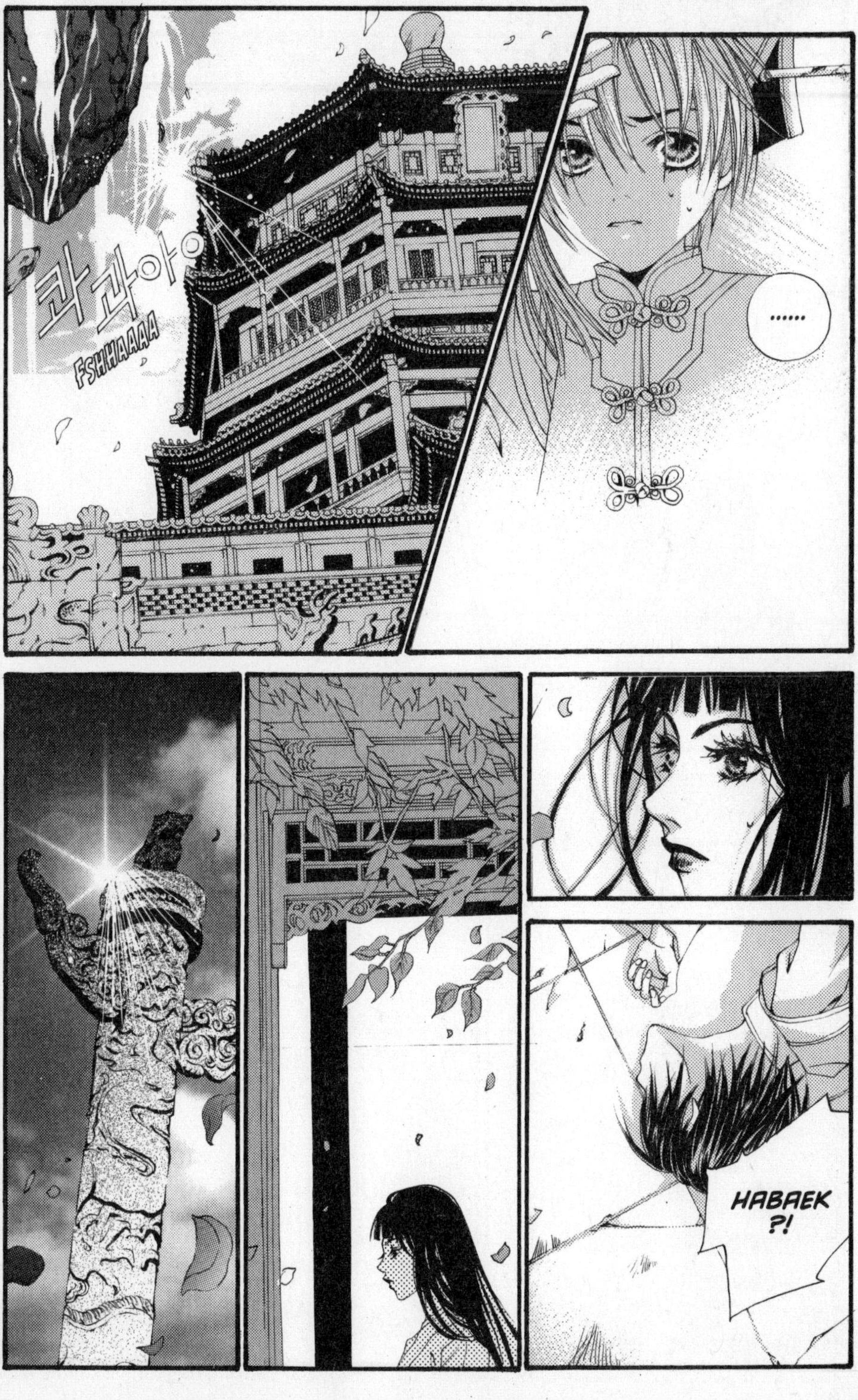

콰콰아아
FSHHAAAA
......
HABAEK ?!

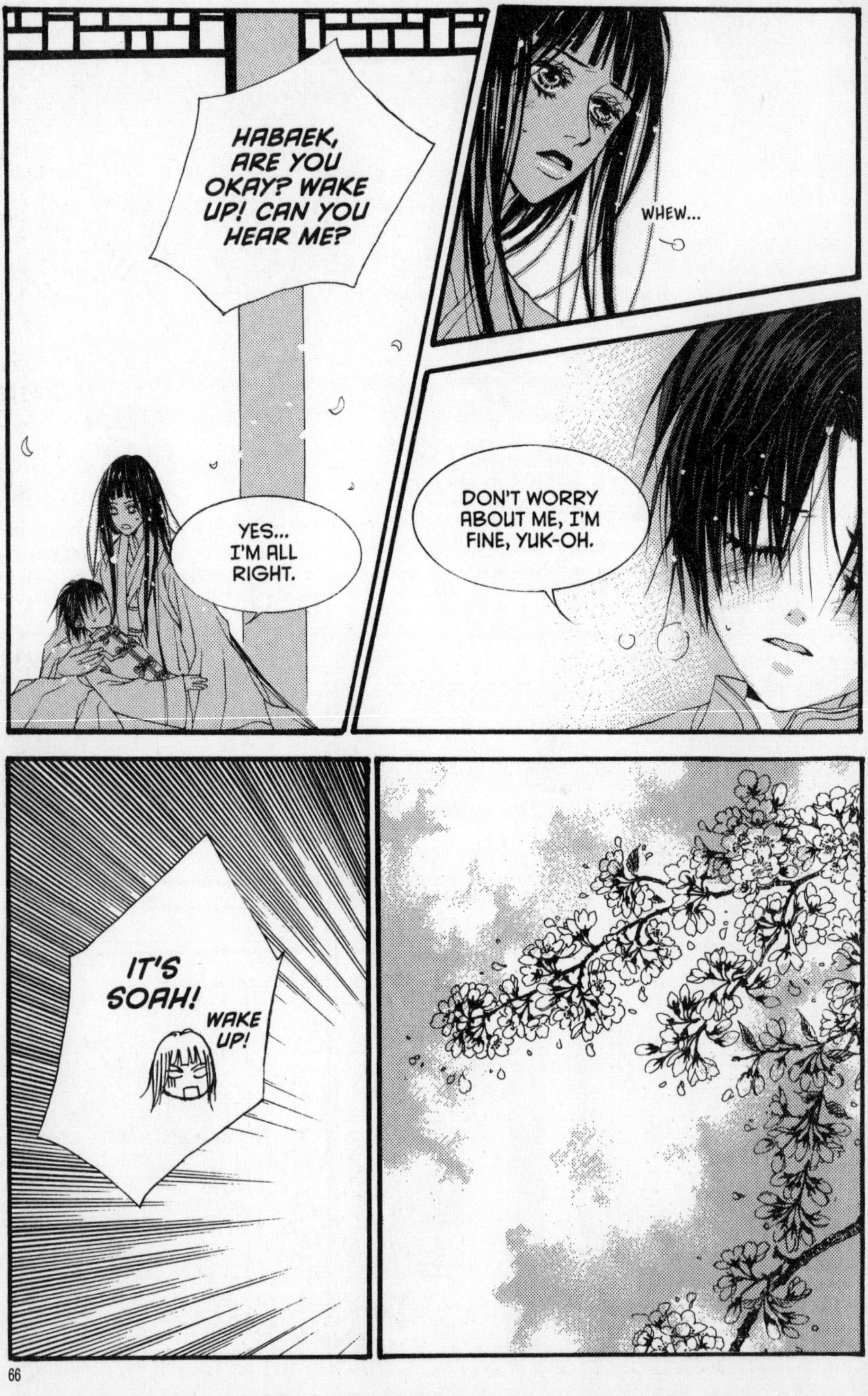
HABAEK, ARE YOU OKAY? WAKE UP! CAN YOU HEAR ME?
WHEW...
YES... I'M ALL RIGHT.
DON'T WORRY ABOUT ME, I'M FINE, YUK-OH.
IT'S SOAH!
WAKE UP!

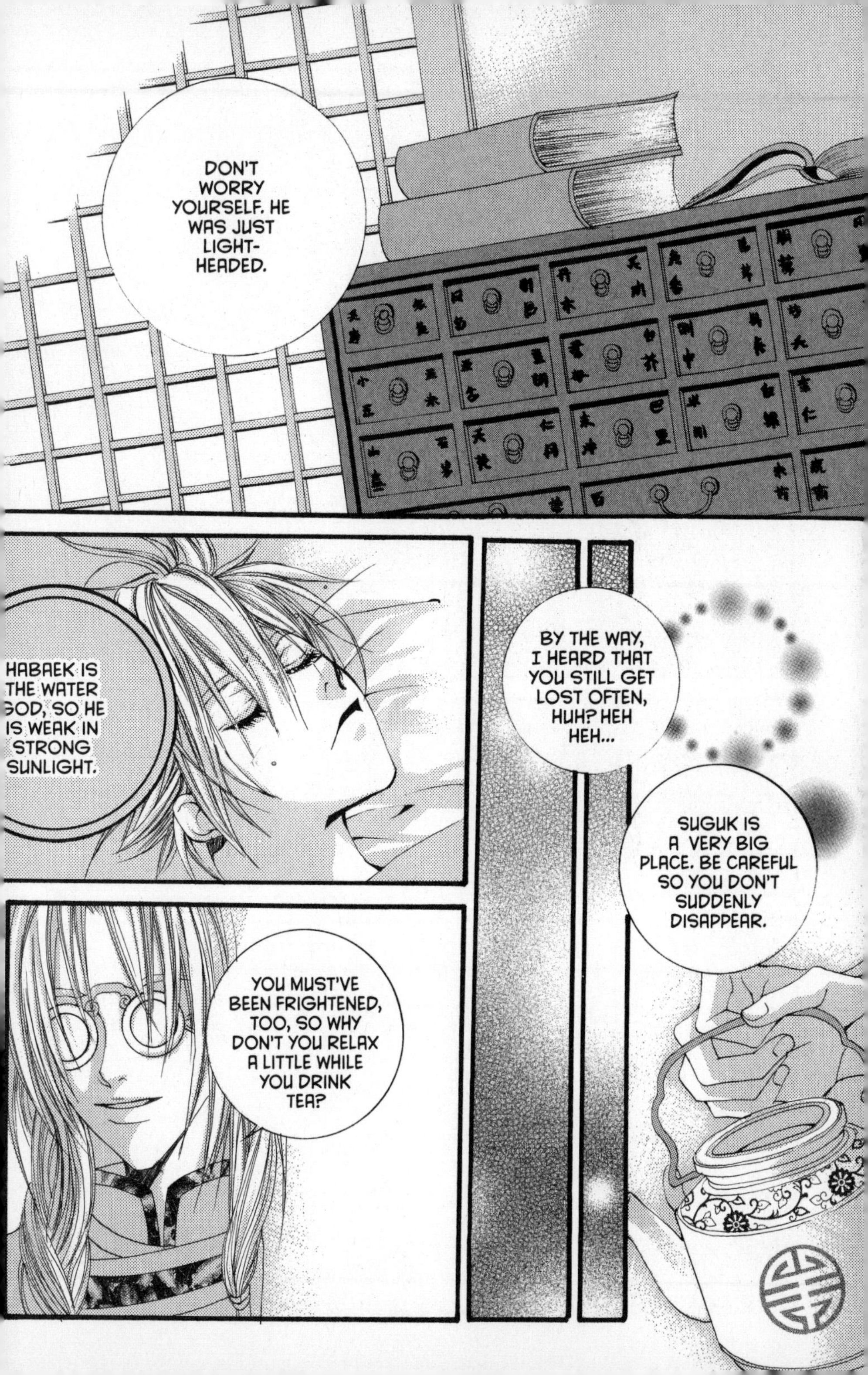
DON'T WORRY YOURSELF. HE WAS JUST LIGHT-HEADED.
HABAEK IS THE WATER GOD, SO HE IS WEAK IN STRONG SUNLIGHT.
BY THE WAY, I HEARD THAT YOU STILL GET LOST OFTEN, HUH? HEH HEH...
SUGUK IS A VERY BIG PLACE. BE CAREFUL SO YOU DON'T SUDDENLY DISAPPEAR.
YOU MUST'VE BEEN FRIGHTENED, TOO, SO WHY DON'T YOU RELAX A LITTLE WHILE YOU DRINK TEA?

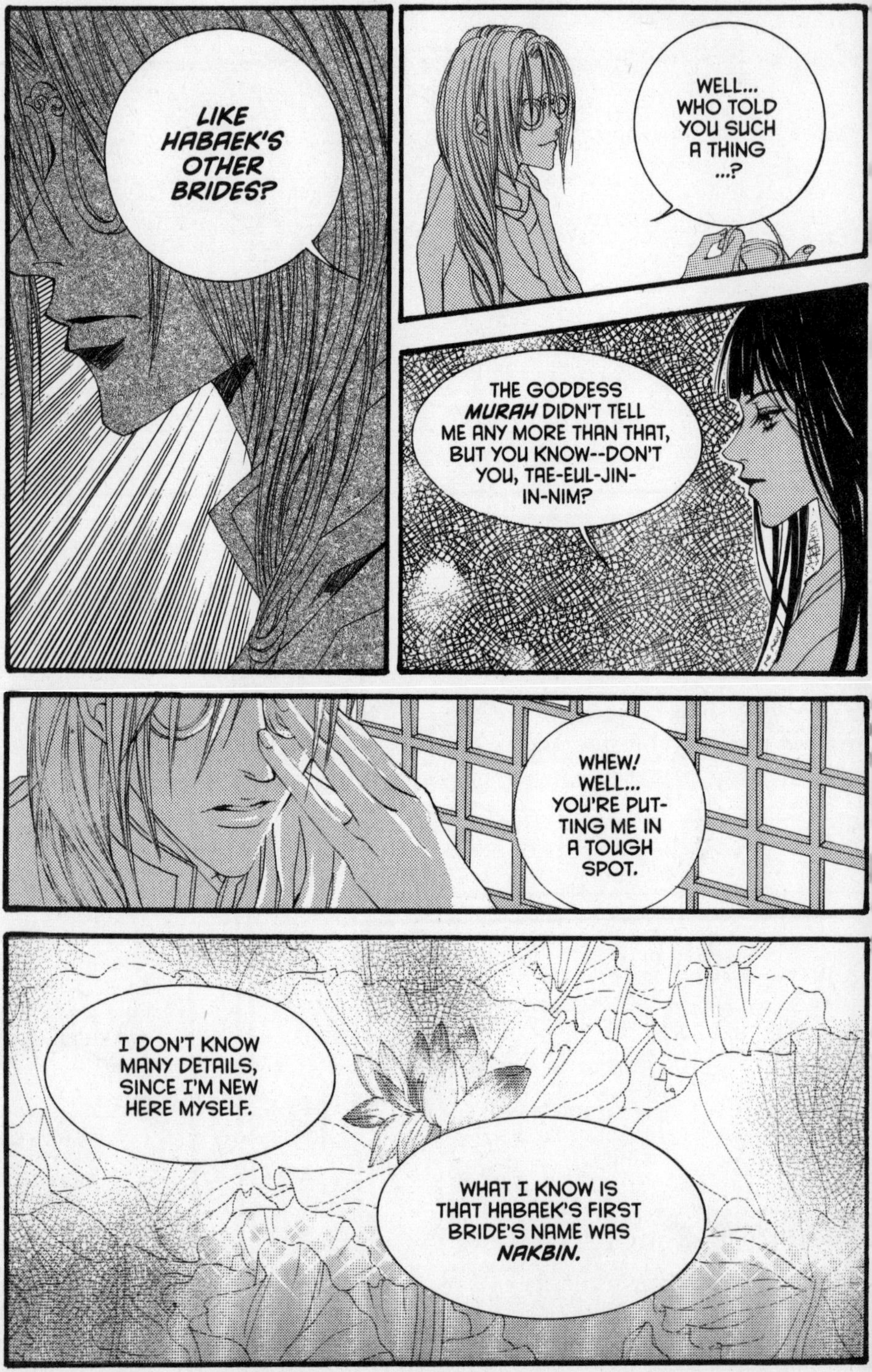
LIKE HABAEK'S OTHER BRIDES?
WELL... WHO TOLD YOU SUCH A THING ...?
THE GODDESS MURAH DIDN'T TELL ME ANY MORE THAN THAT, BUT YOU KNOW--DON'T YOU, TAE-EUL-JIN-IN-NIM?
WHEW! WELL... YOU'RE PUTTING ME IN A TOUGH SPOT.
I DON'T KNOW MANY DETAILS, SINCE I'M NEW HERE MYSELF.
WHAT I KNOW IS THAT HABAEK'S FIRST BRIDE'S NAME WAS NAKBIN.

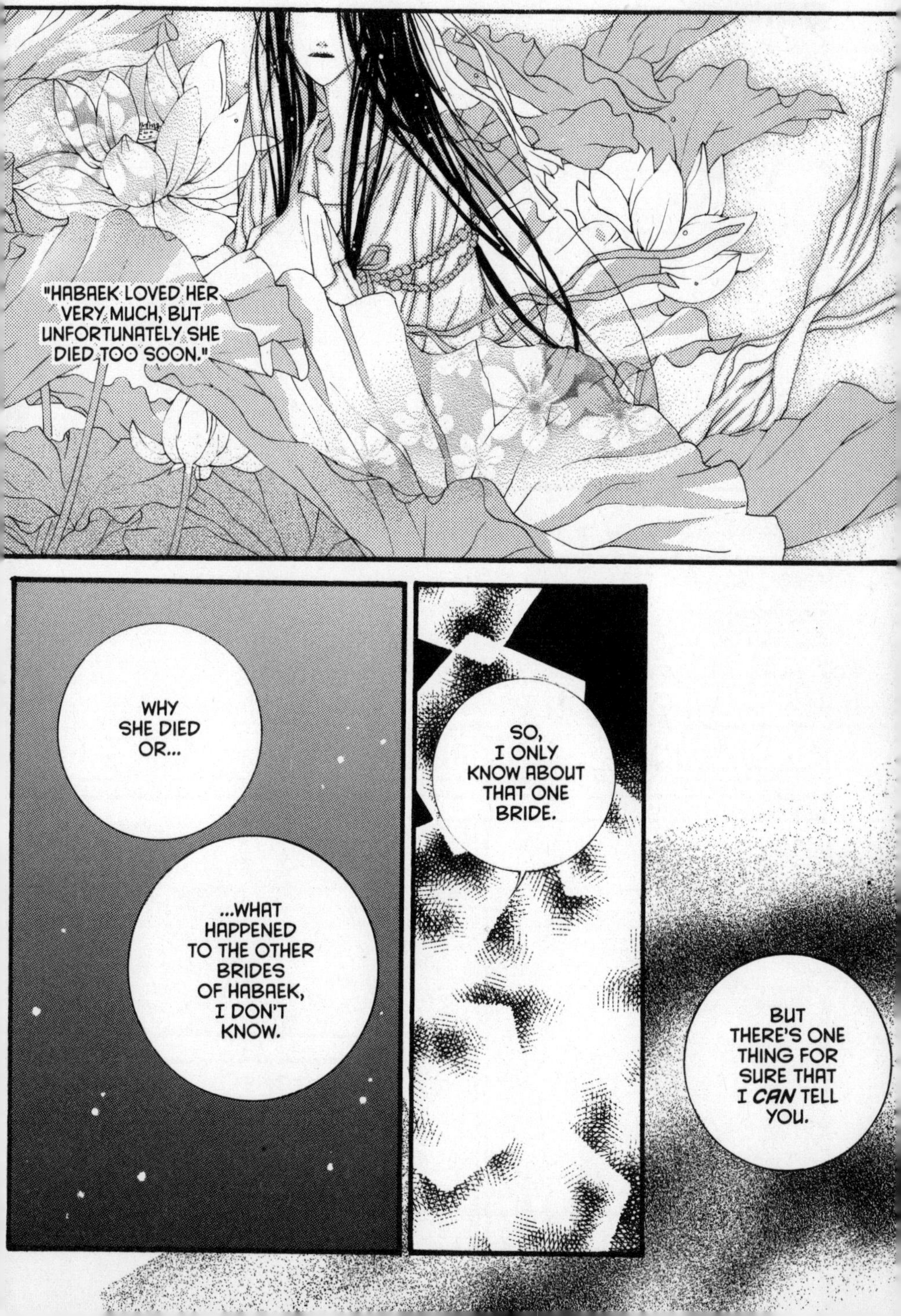
"HABAEK LOVED HER VERY MUCH, BUT UNFORTUNATELY SHE DIED TOO SOON."
WHY SHE DIED OR...
...WHAT HAPPENED TO THE OTHER BRIDES OF HABAEK, I DON'T KNOW.
SO, I ONLY KNOW ABOUT THAT ONE BRIDE.
BUT THERE'S ONE THING FOR SURE THAT I *CAN* TELL YOU.

MANY MIS-UNDERSTAND HIM SINCE HE'S SO IRRITABLE...

...BUT HABAEK IS NOT A *BAD GUY.* SO YOU DON'T NEED TO FEEL UNSAFE.

WELL... I'M ALREADY AWARE OF THAT.

HE GAVE US *RAIN...* BUT...

IF YOU ARE *STILL* NOT SURE, I CAN HAVE A LOOK AT YOUR PALM LINE.

MAYBE YOU WILL FEEL SAFER IF YOU KNOW YOUR FUTURE.

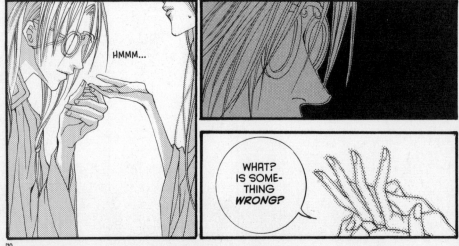

HMMM...

WHAT? IS SOME-THING *WRONG?*

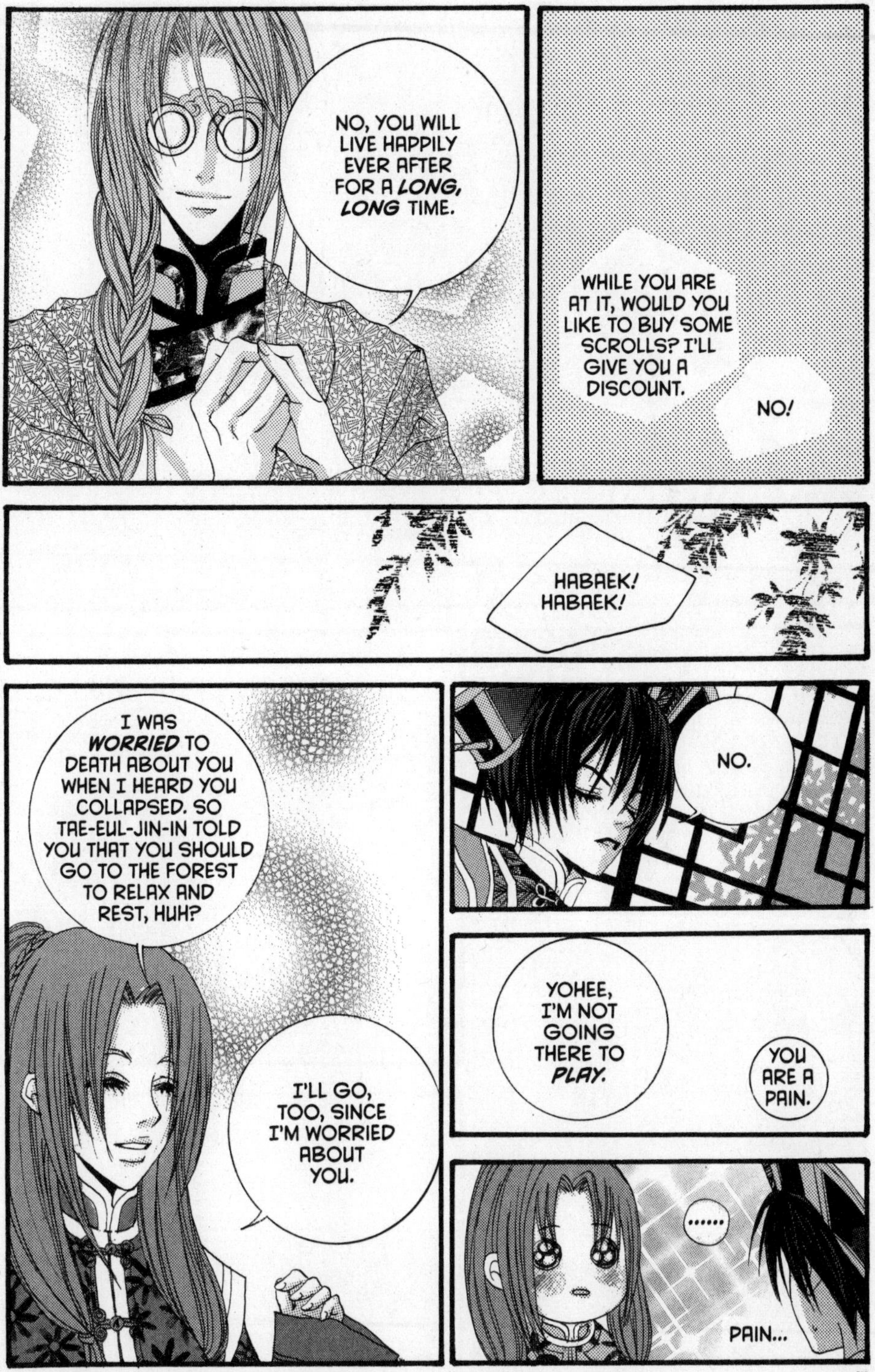
NO, YOU WILL LIVE HAPPILY EVER AFTER FOR A *LONG, LONG* TIME.
WHILE YOU ARE AT IT, WOULD YOU LIKE TO BUY SOME SCROLLS? I'LL GIVE YOU A DISCOUNT.
NO!
HABAEK! HABAEK!
I WAS *WORRIED* TO DEATH ABOUT YOU WHEN I HEARD YOU COLLAPSED. SO TAE-EUL-JIN-IN TOLD YOU THAT YOU SHOULD GO TO THE FOREST TO RELAX AND REST, HUH?
NO.
I'LL GO, TOO, SINCE I'M WORRIED ABOUT YOU.
YOHEE, I'M NOT GOING THERE TO *PLAY*.
YOU ARE A PAIN.
......
PAIN...

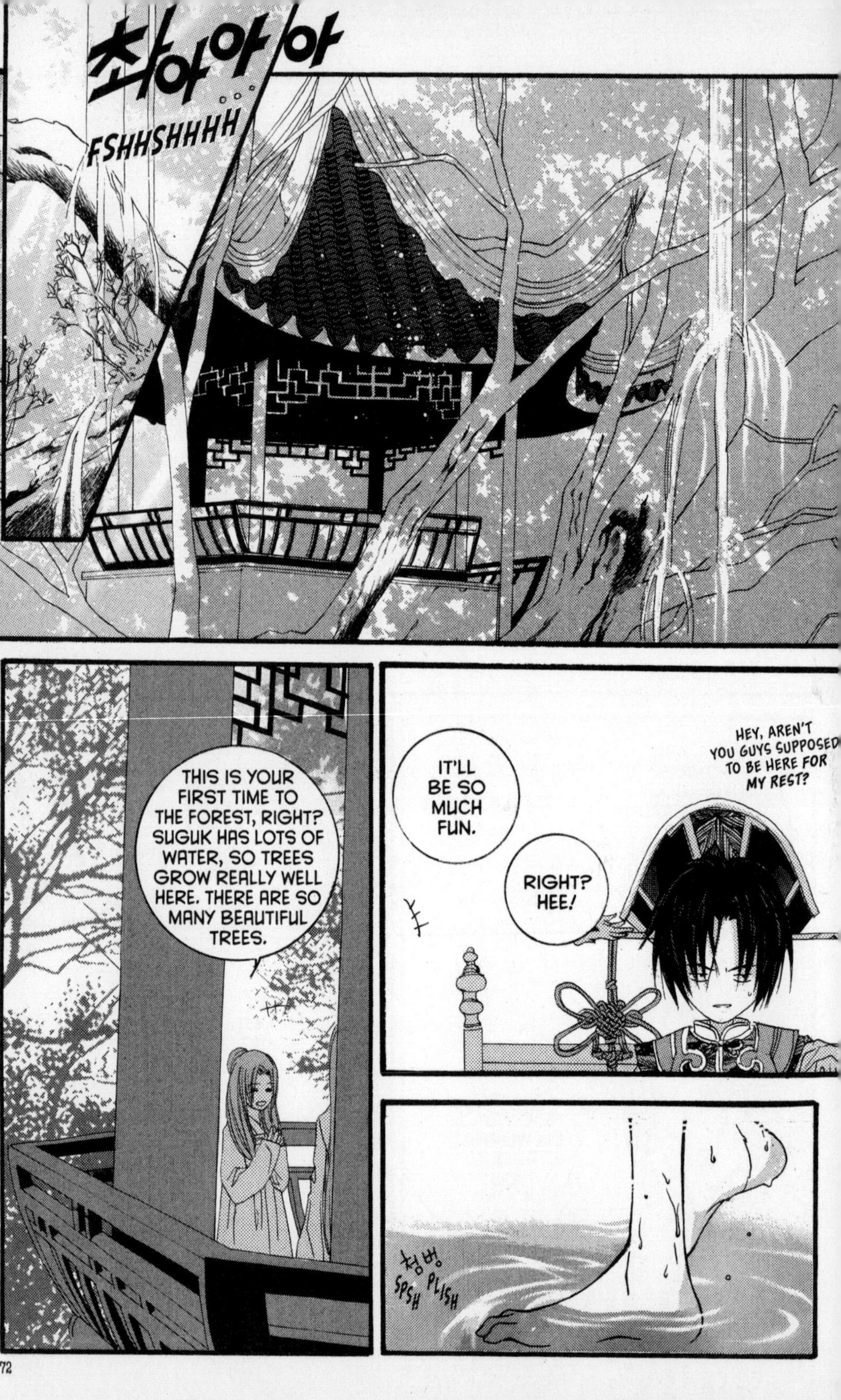
촤아아아
FSHHSHHHH
THIS IS YOUR FIRST TIME TO THE FOREST, RIGHT? SUGUK HAS LOTS OF WATER, SO TREES GROW REALLY WELL HERE. THERE ARE SO MANY BEAUTIFUL TREES.
IT'LL BE SO MUCH FUN.
RIGHT? HEE!
HEY, AREN'T YOU GUYS SUPPOSED TO BE HERE FOR MY REST?
첨벙
SPSH PLISH

PLANTS ARE VERY HONEST... THEY DON'T LIE, AND THEY RETURN AS MUCH LOVE AS THEY RECEIVE.

BEAUTIFUL...

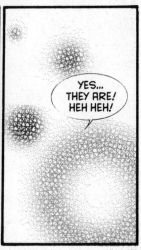

YES... THEY ARE! HEH HEH!

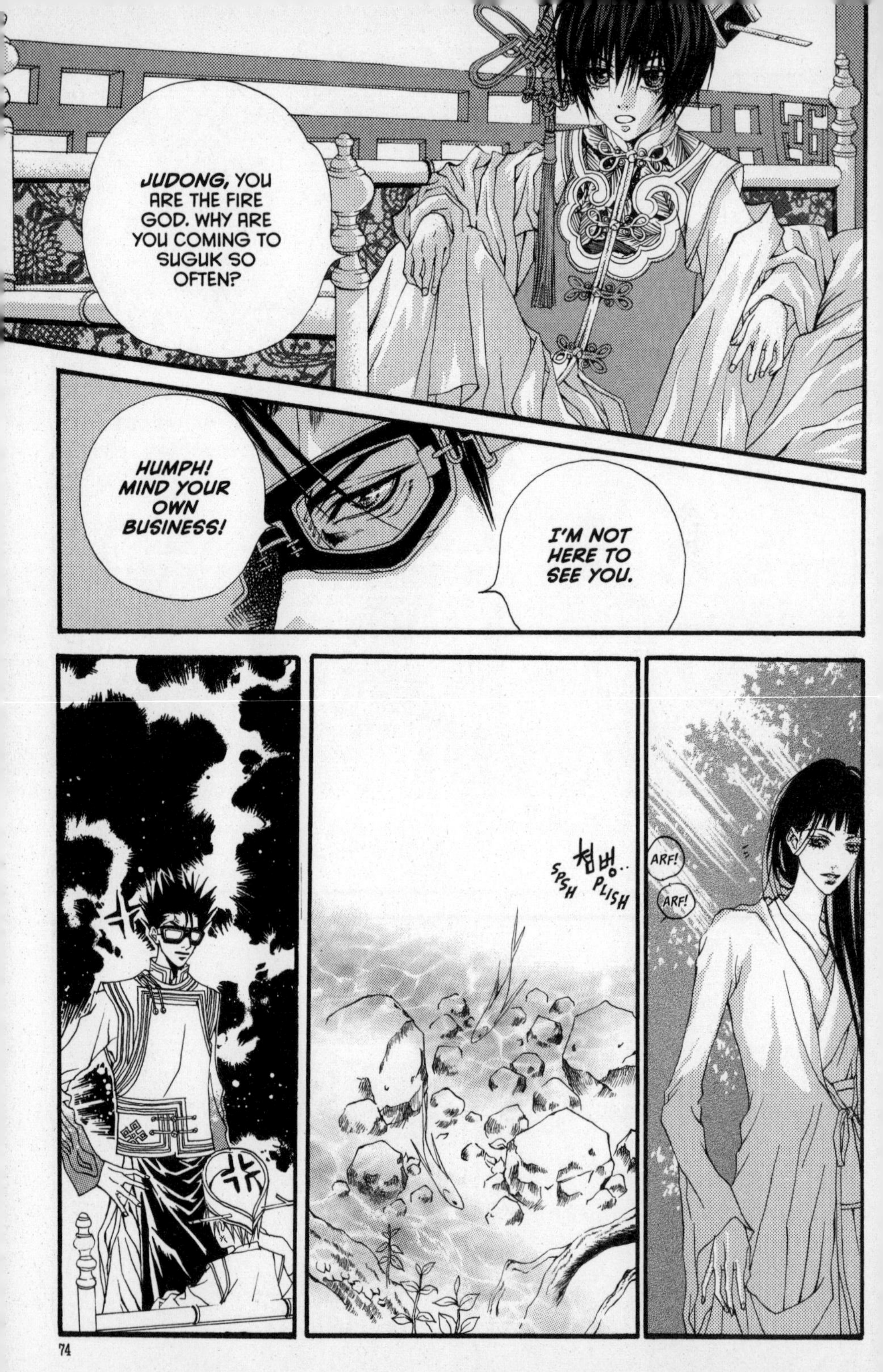

JUDONG, YOU ARE THE FIRE GOD. WHY ARE YOU COMING TO SUGUK SO OFTEN?
HUMPH! MIND YOUR OWN BUSINESS!
I'M NOT HERE TO SEE YOU.
첨벙..
SPSH PLISH
ARF!
ARF!

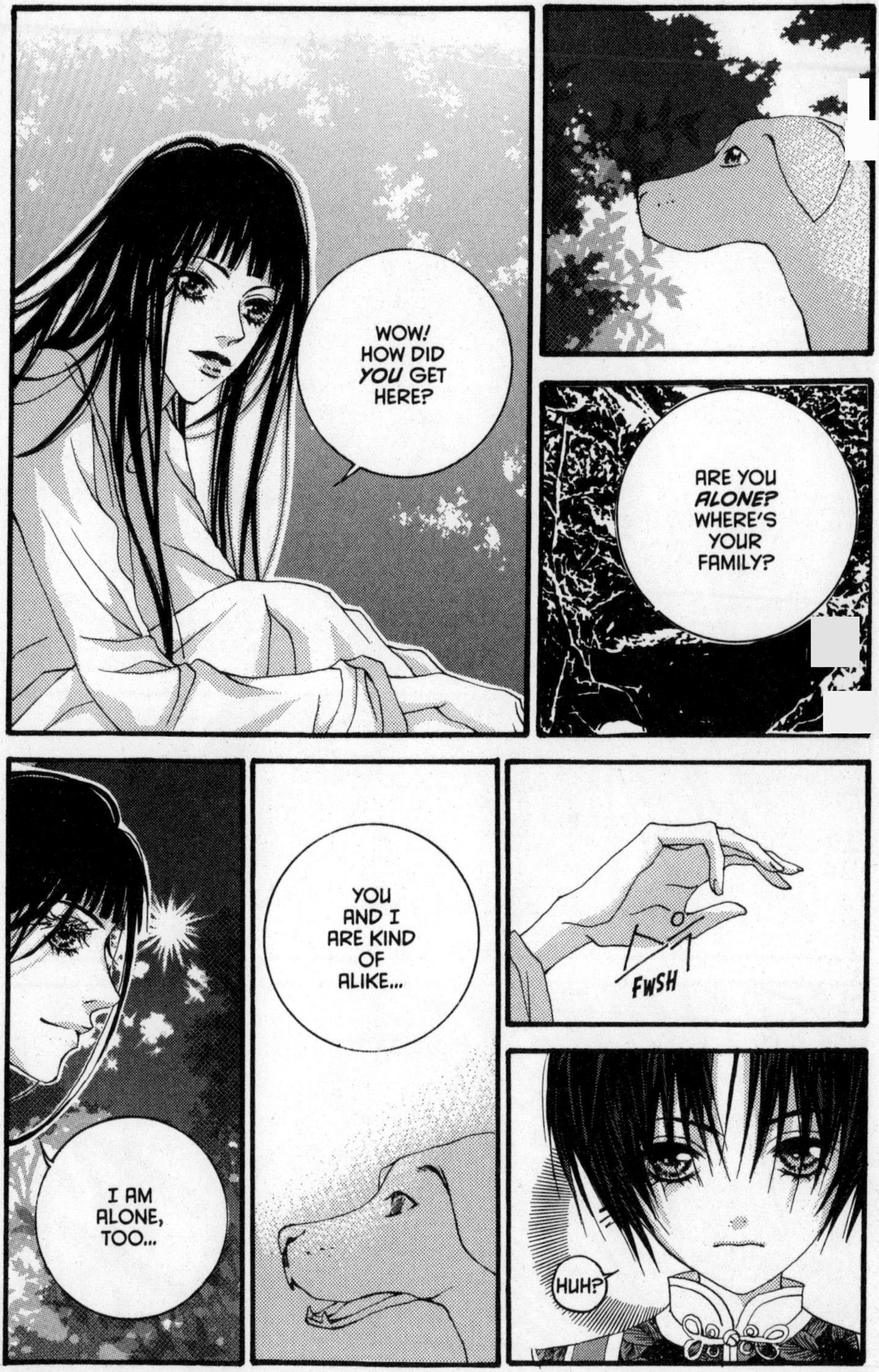
WOW! HOW DID *YOU* GET HERE?
ARE YOU *ALONE?* WHERE'S YOUR FAMILY?
YOU AND I ARE KIND OF ALIKE...
I AM ALONE, TOO...
FWSH
HUH?

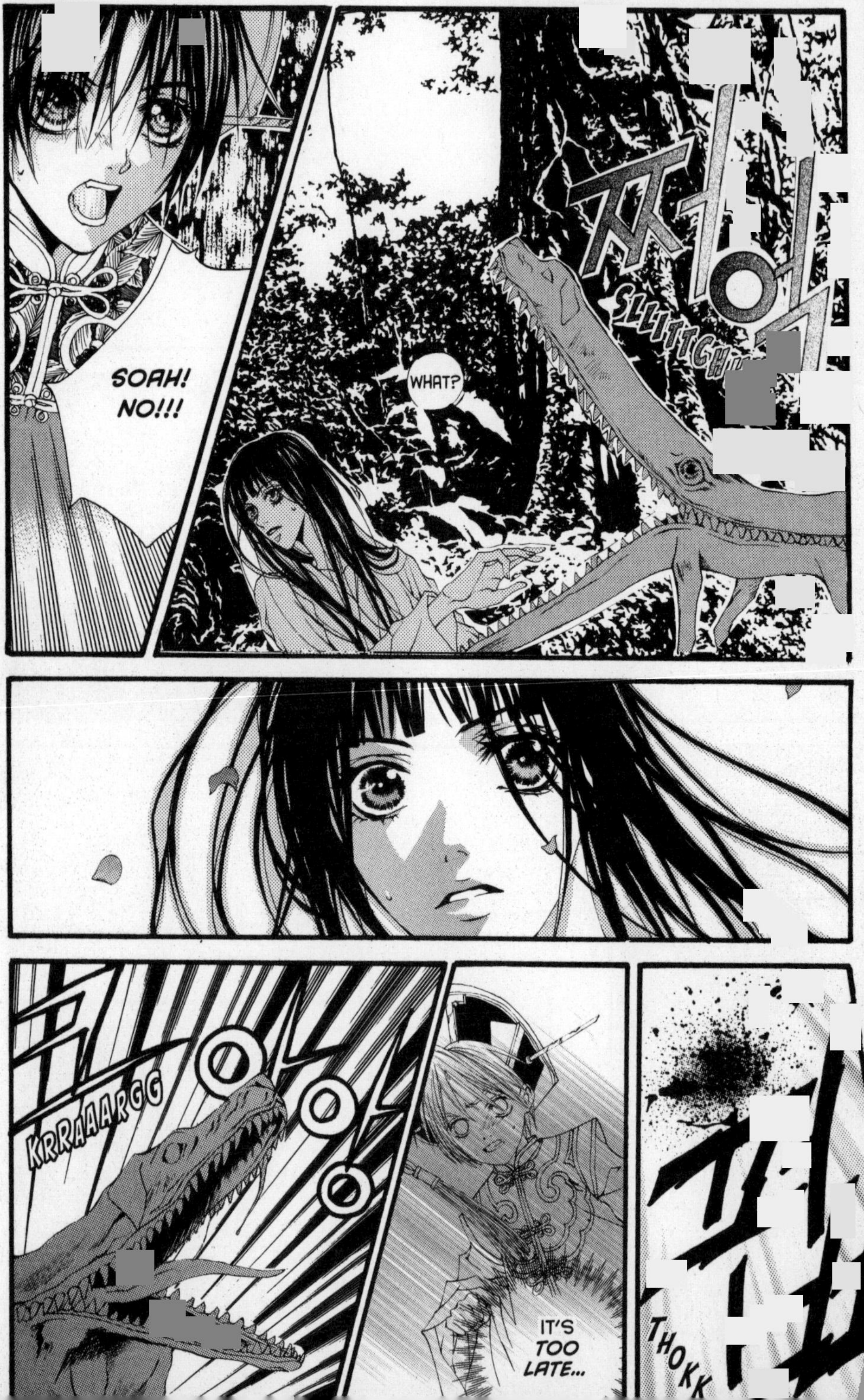
SLLITTCH
WHAT?
SOAH! NO!!!
THOKK
IT'S TOO LATE...
KRRAAARGG

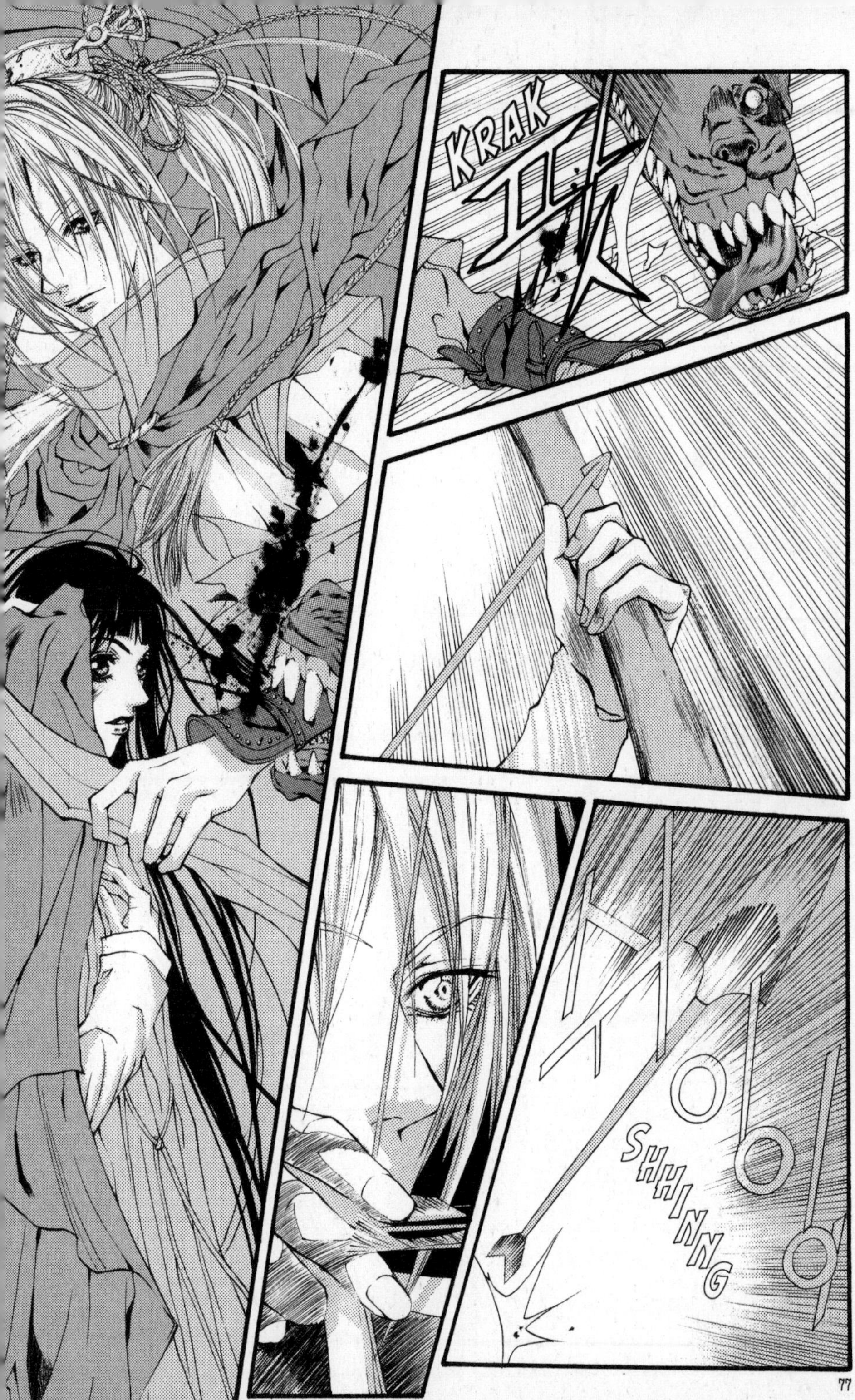
KRAK
SHHINNG

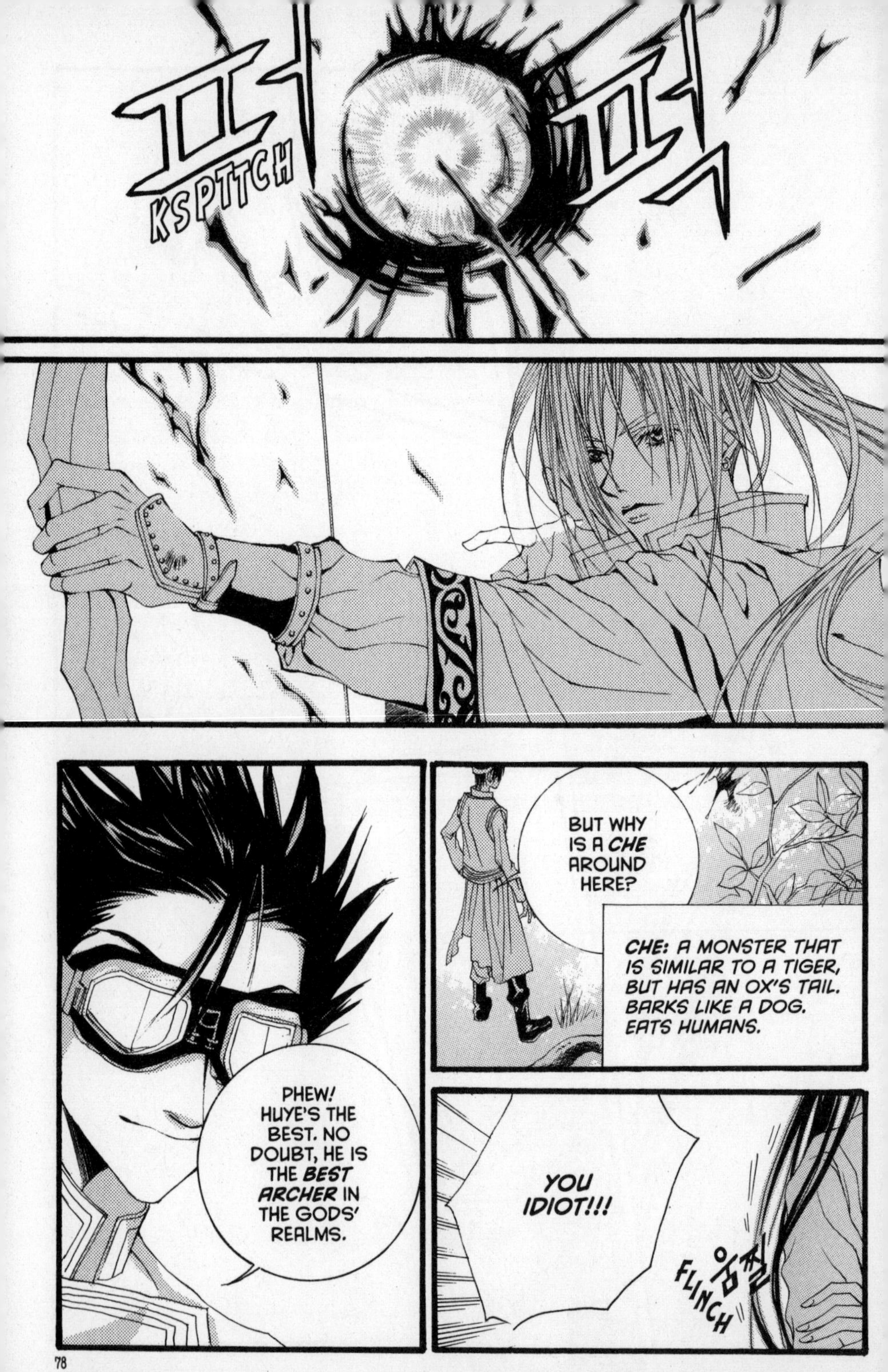
KSPTTCH
PHEW! HUYE'S THE BEST. NO DOUBT, HE IS THE *BEST ARCHER* IN THE GODS' REALMS.
BUT WHY IS A *CHE* AROUND HERE?
CHE: A MONSTER THAT IS SIMILAR TO A TIGER, BUT HAS AN OX'S TAIL. BARKS LIKE A DOG. EATS HUMANS.
YOU IDIOT!!!
FLINCH

ARE YOU GOING TO GROW BRAINS AFTER YOU DIE? WHY AREN'T YOU MORE CAREFUL?!

ARGH!

人으 FWSH

FOO! HE DIDN'T EVEN HELP, BUT NOW HE'S *ALL TALK...*

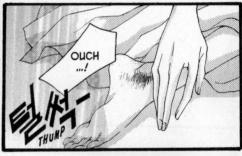

OUCH ...!

틘넋ㅓ-
THUMP

WHAT SHOULD WE DO? I THINK SHE SPRAINED HER ANKLE. WE DON'T EVEN HAVE TAE-EUL-JIN-IN WITH US...

AH, I'LL--

I'LL CARRY HER.

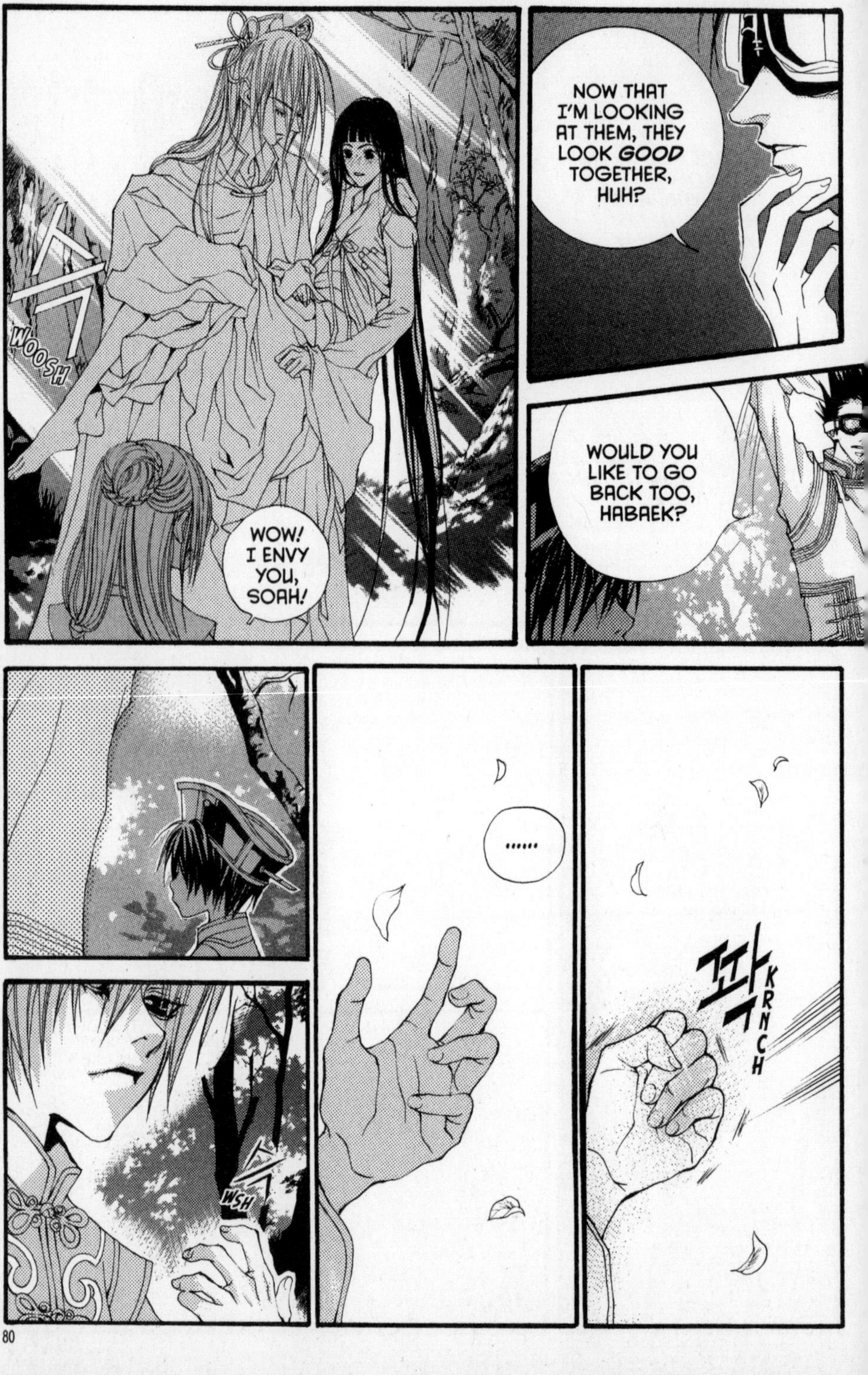
WOOSH
WOW! I ENVY YOU, SOAH!
NOW THAT I'M LOOKING AT THEM, THEY LOOK *GOOD* TOGETHER, HUH?
WOULD YOU LIKE TO GO BACK TOO, HABAEK?
WSH
......
KRNCH

I JUST...
CAN'T
SLEEP.

FLICKER

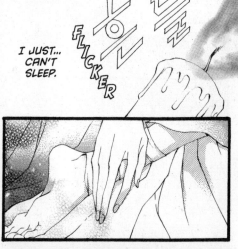

WHERE IS
HABAEK,
ANYWAY?

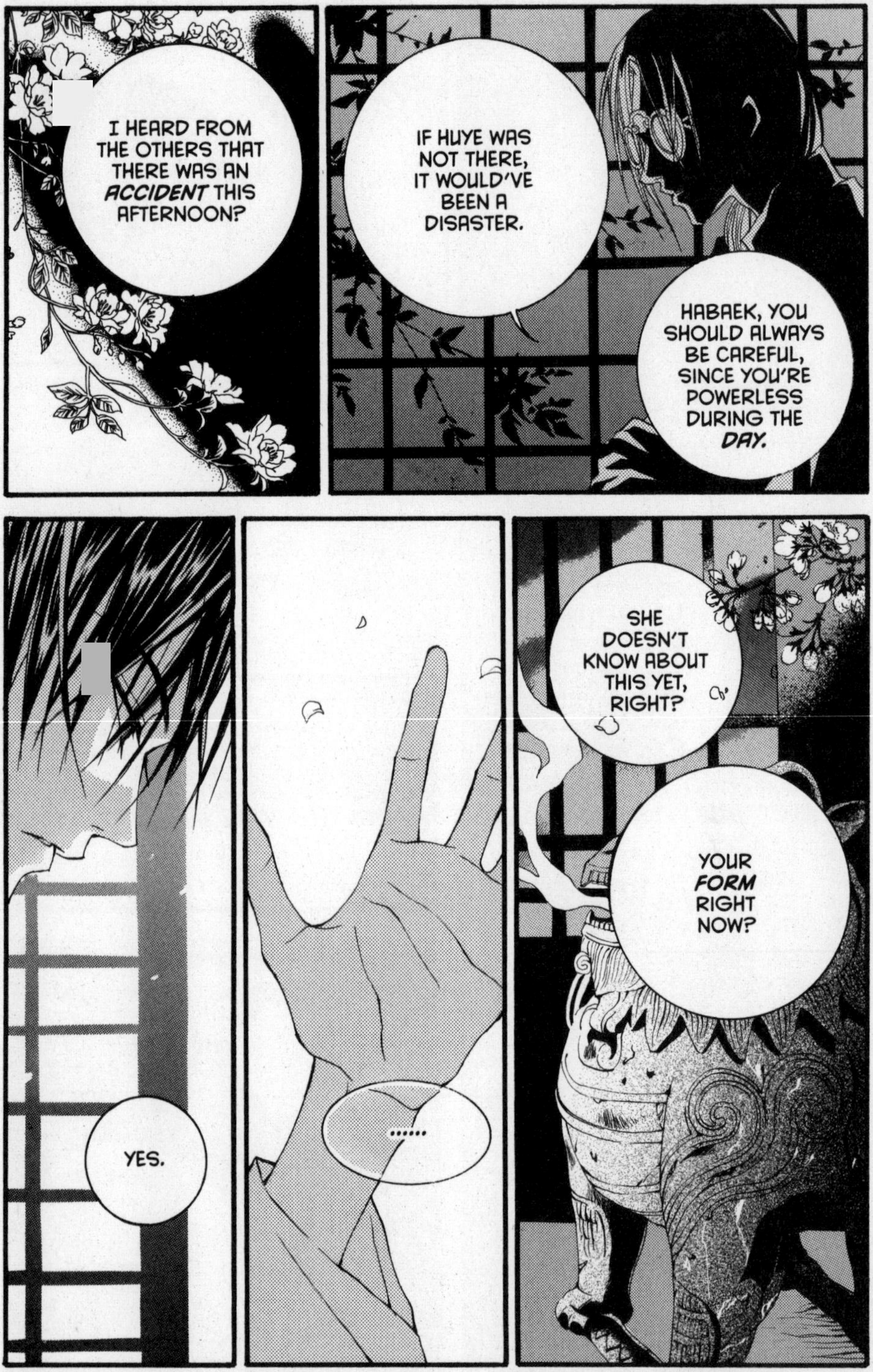
I HEARD FROM THE OTHERS THAT THERE WAS AN ACCIDENT THIS AFTERNOON?
IF HUYE WAS NOT THERE, IT WOULD'VE BEEN A DISASTER.
HABAEK, YOU SHOULD ALWAYS BE CAREFUL, SINCE YOU'RE POWERLESS DURING THE DAY.
YES.
......
SHE DOESN'T KNOW ABOUT THIS YET, RIGHT?
YOUR FORM RIGHT NOW?

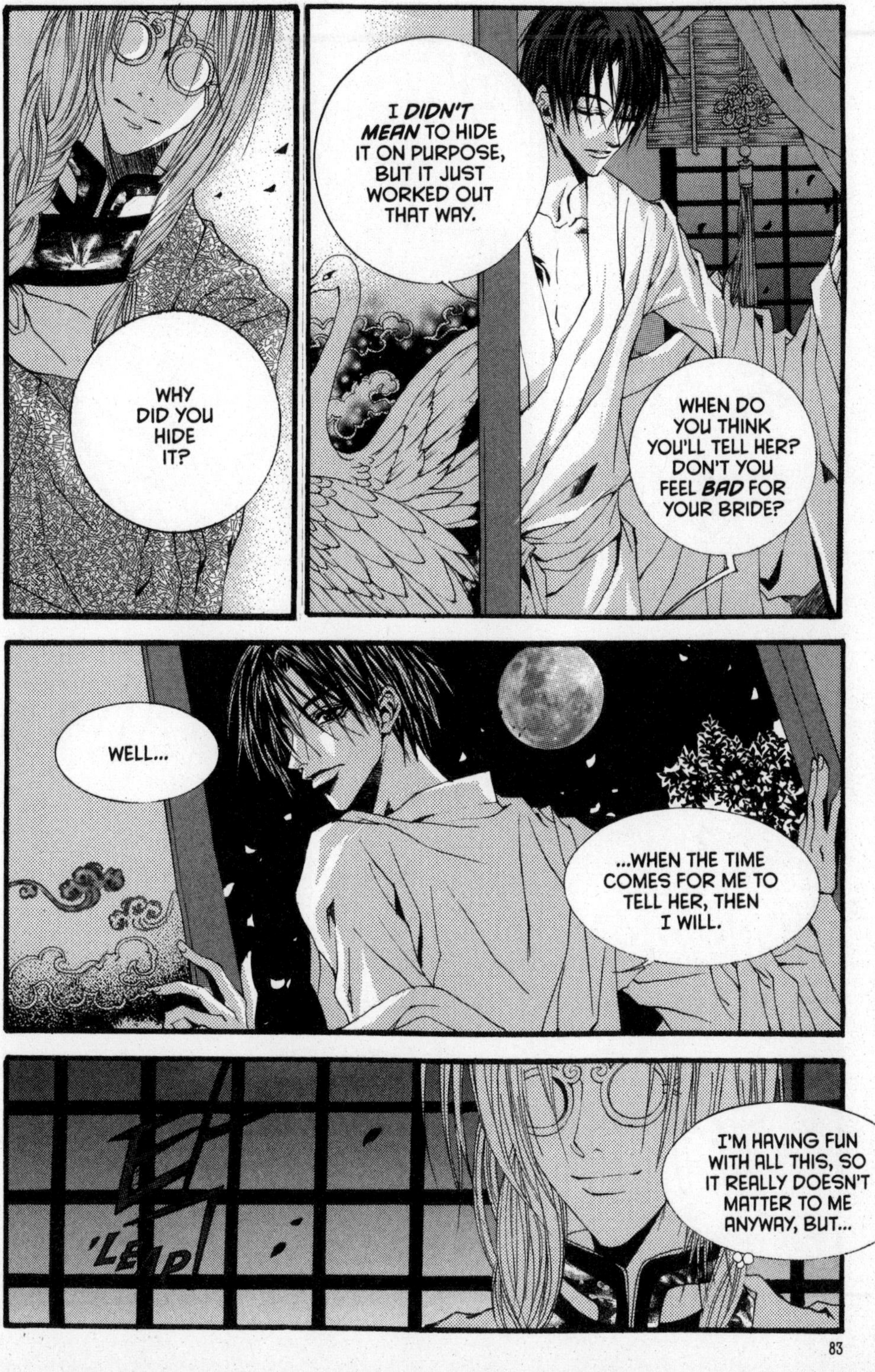
I DIDN'T MEAN TO HIDE IT ON PURPOSE, BUT IT JUST WORKED OUT THAT WAY.
WHY DID YOU HIDE IT?
WHEN DO YOU THINK YOU'LL TELL HER? DON'T YOU FEEL BAD FOR YOUR BRIDE?
WELL...
...WHEN THE TIME COMES FOR ME TO TELL HER, THEN I WILL.
I'M HAVING FUN WITH ALL THIS, SO IT REALLY DOESN'T MATTER TO ME ANYWAY, BUT...
'LEAP

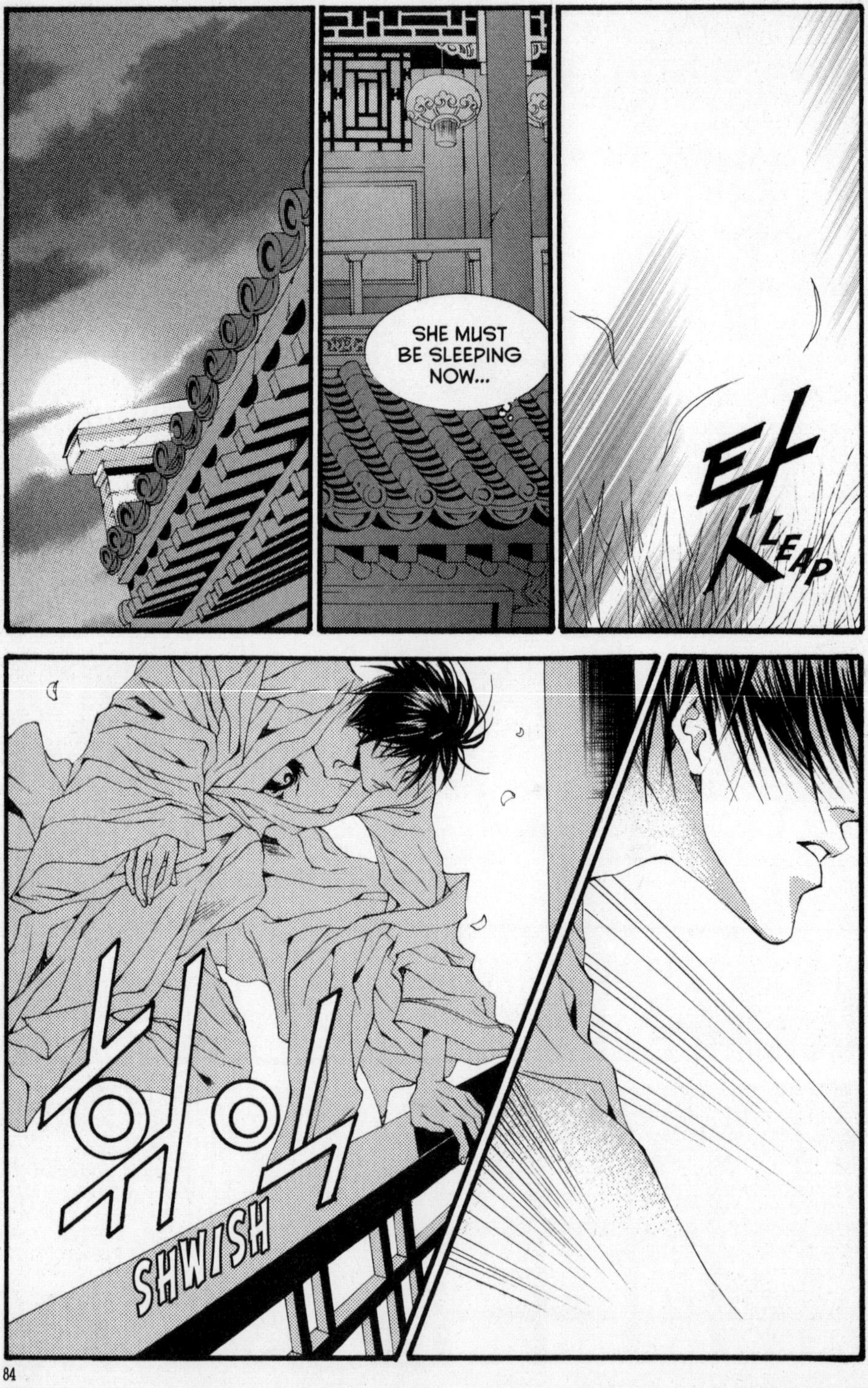
SHE MUST BE SLEEPING NOW...
LEAP
SHWISH

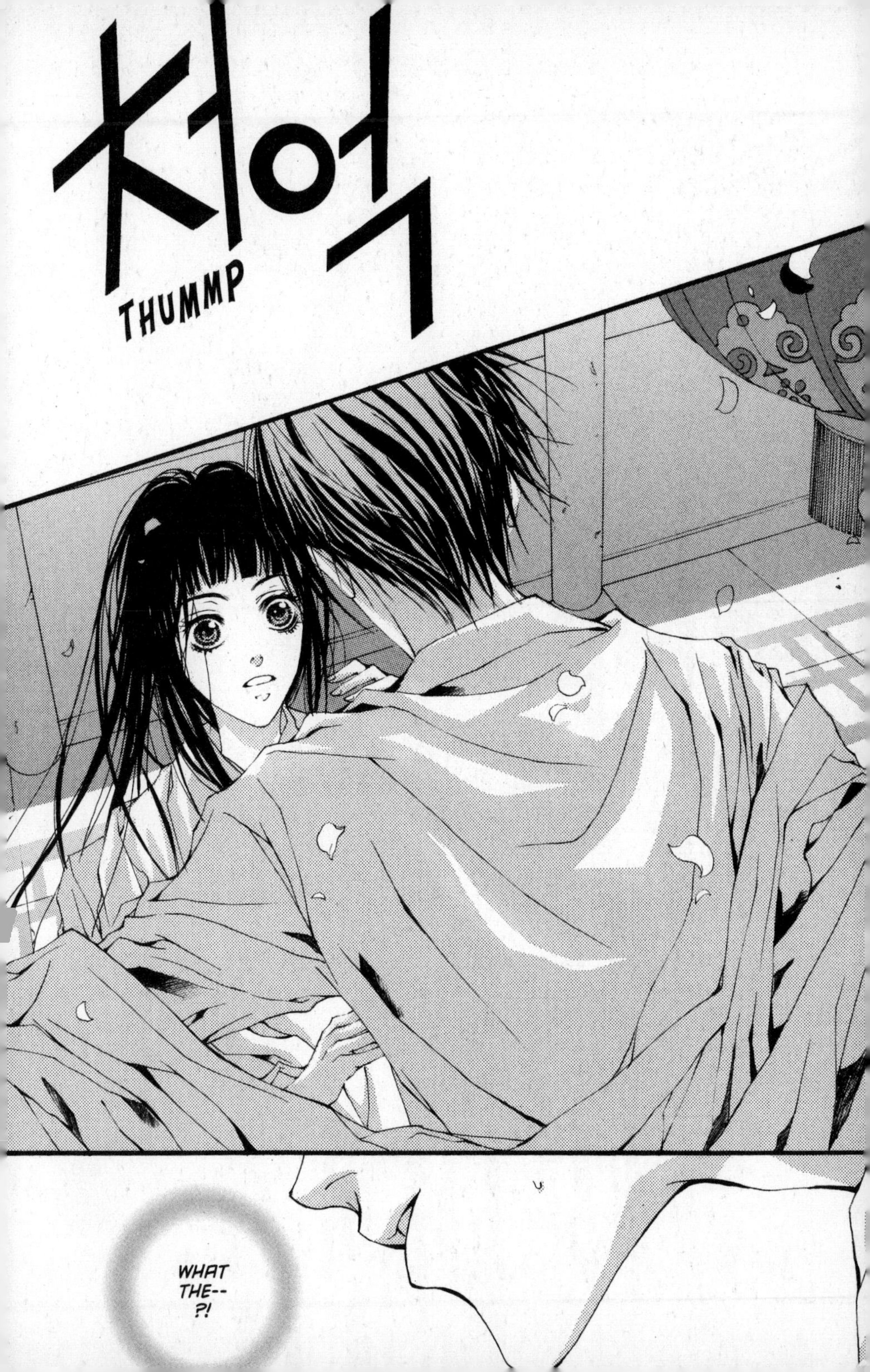

철썩
THUMMP
WHAT THE-- ?!

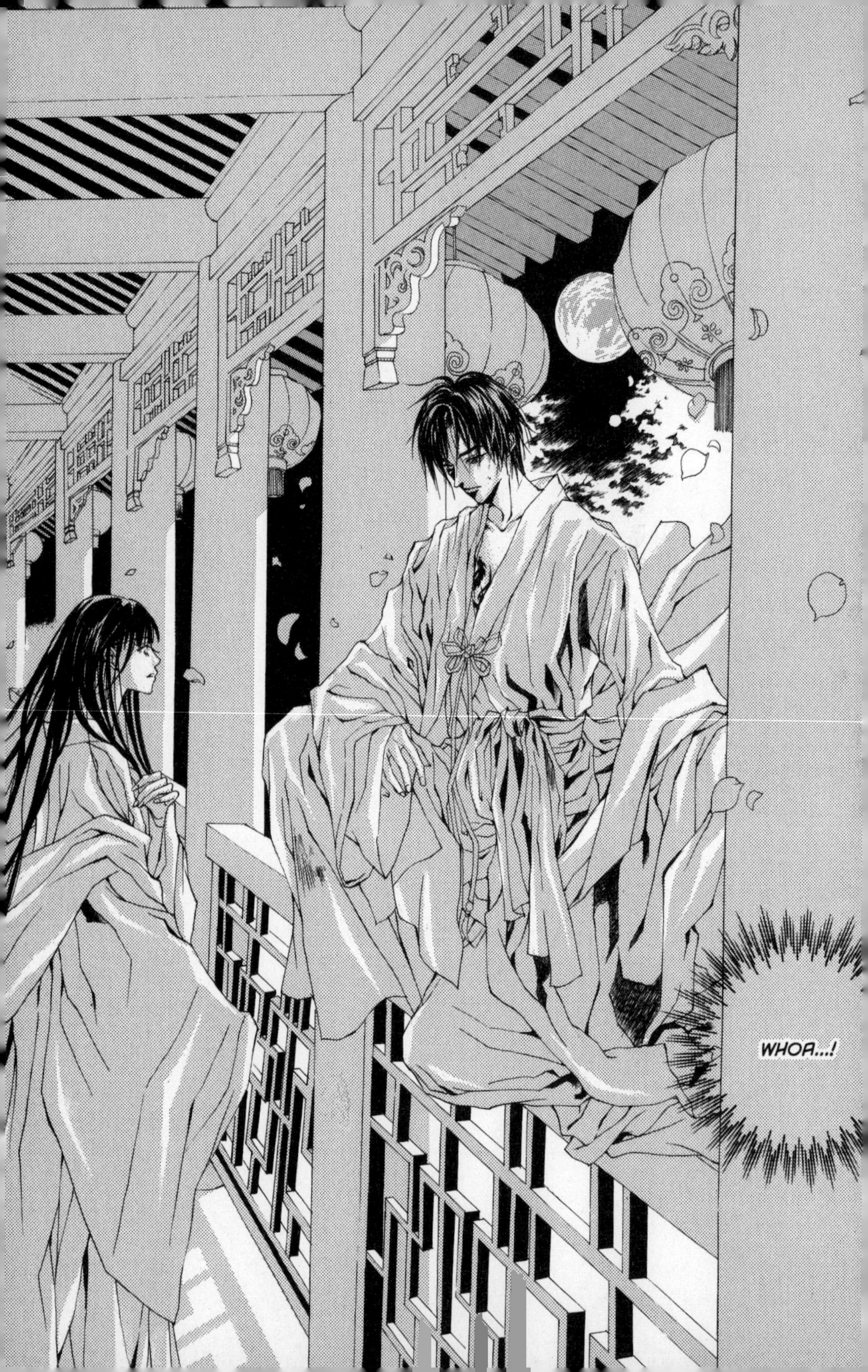
WHOA...!

BRIDE of the WATER GOD

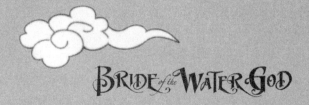

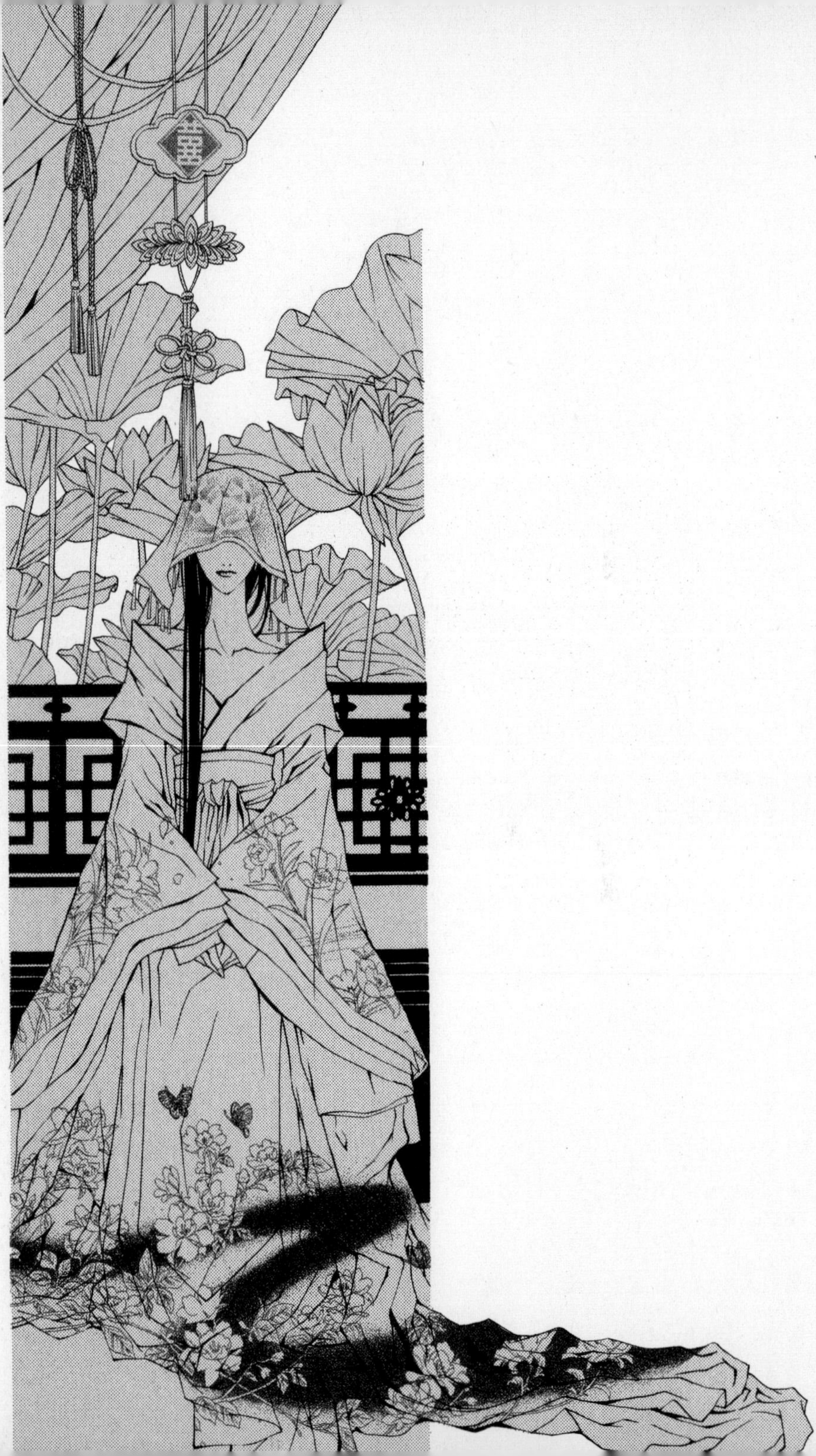

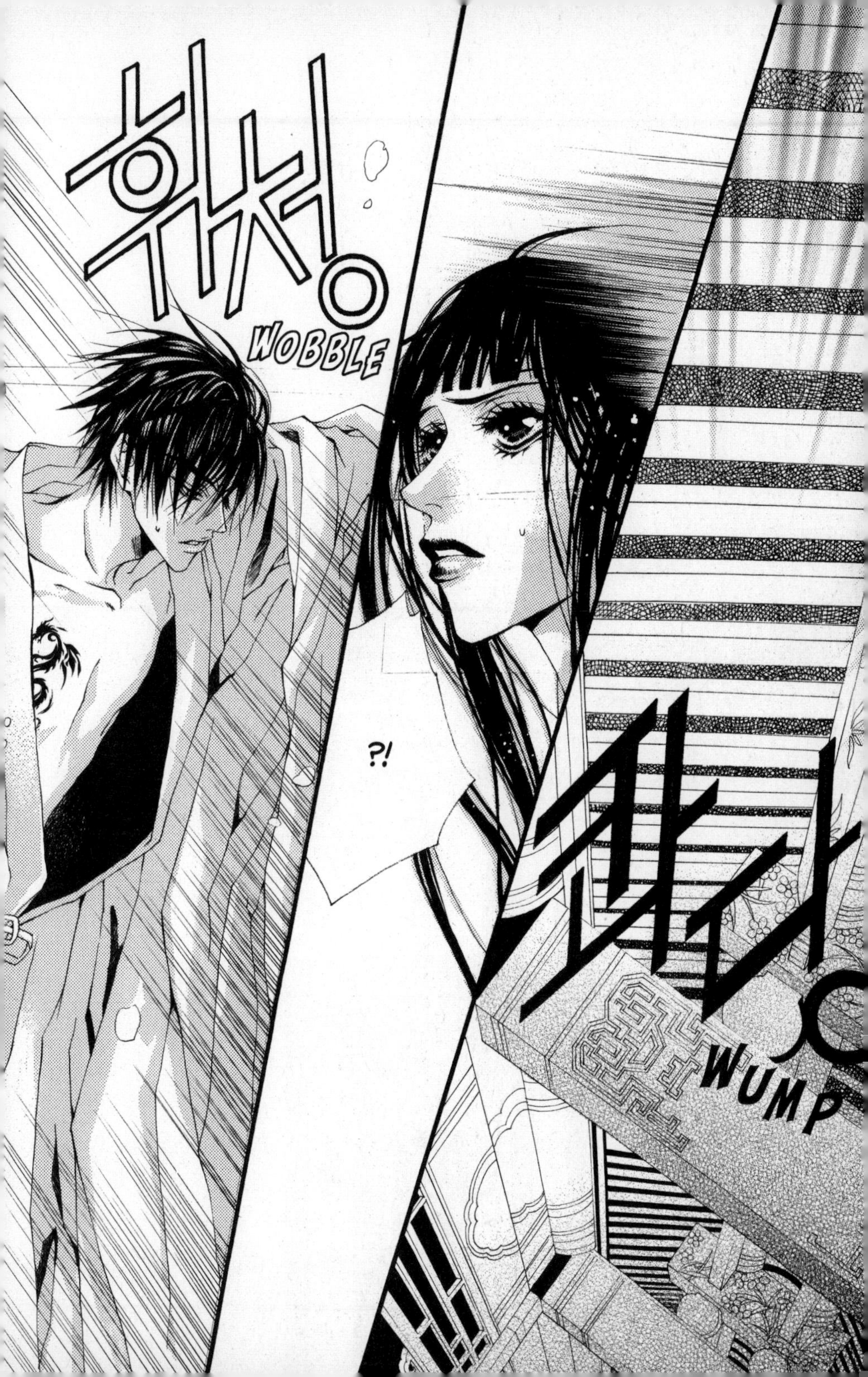
휘청
WOBBLE
?!
WUMP

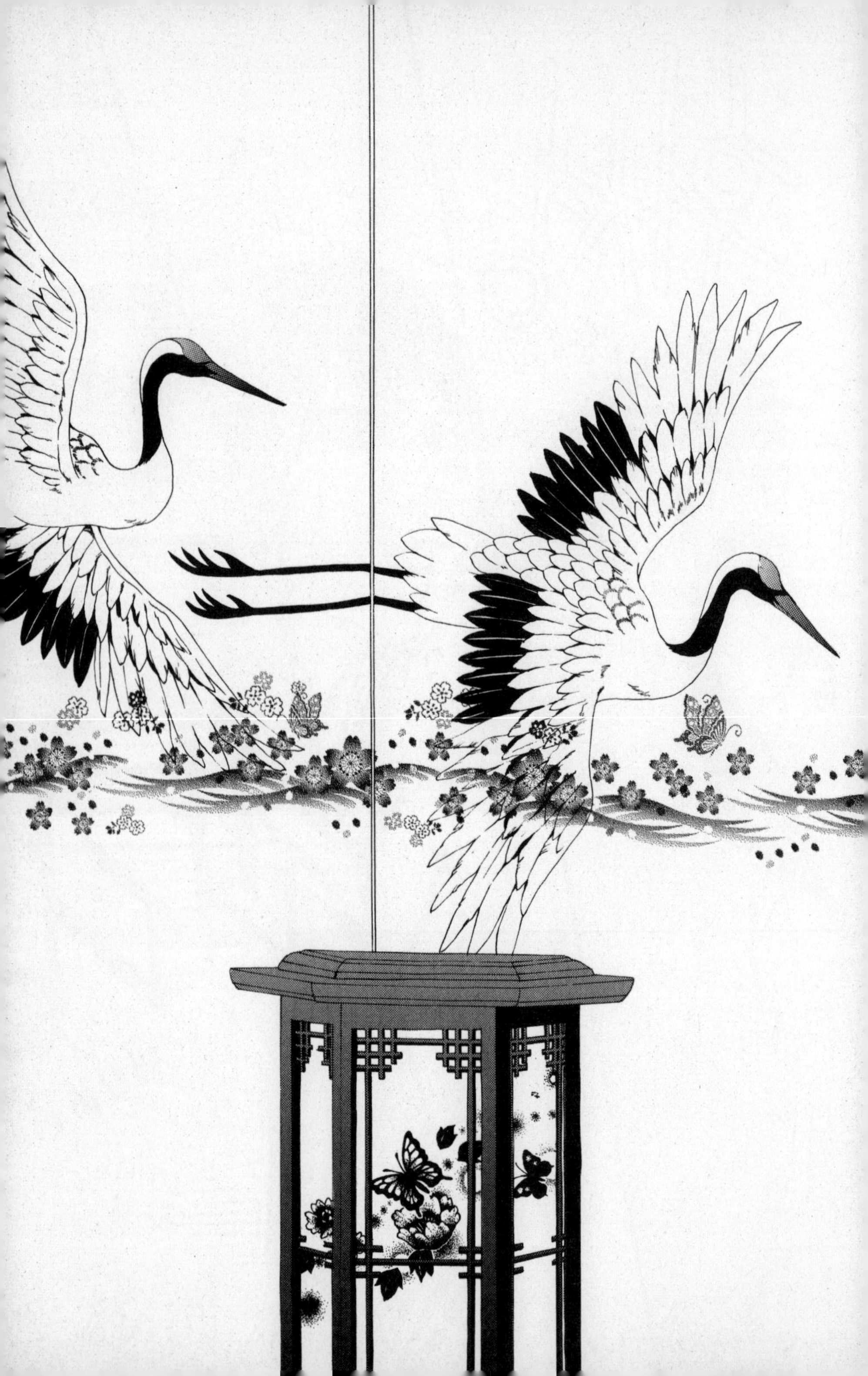

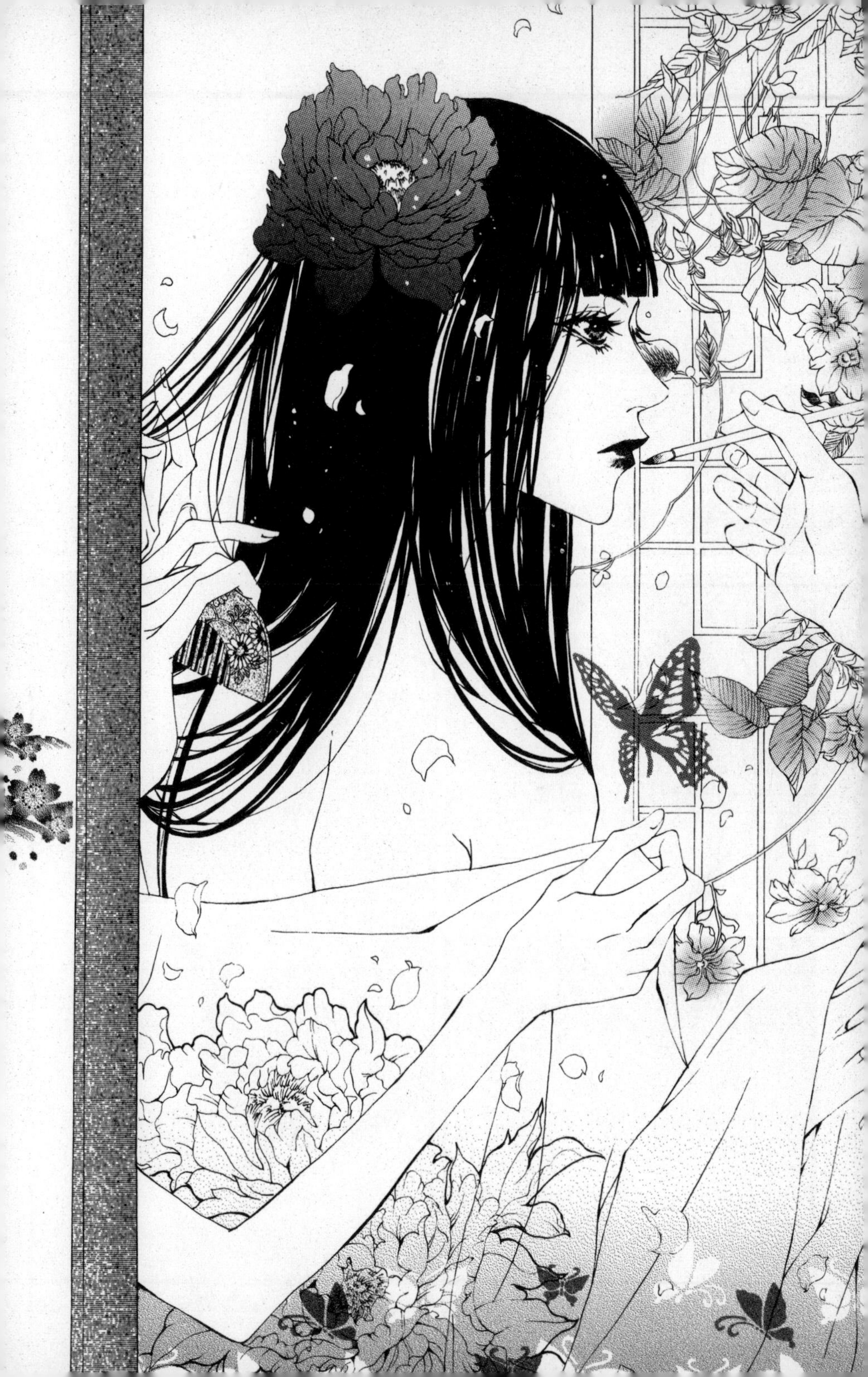

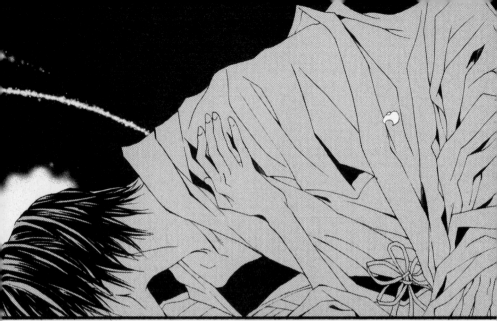

ARGHH...

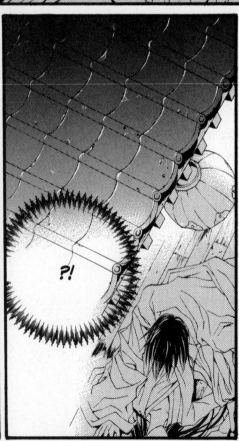

?!

OUCH...

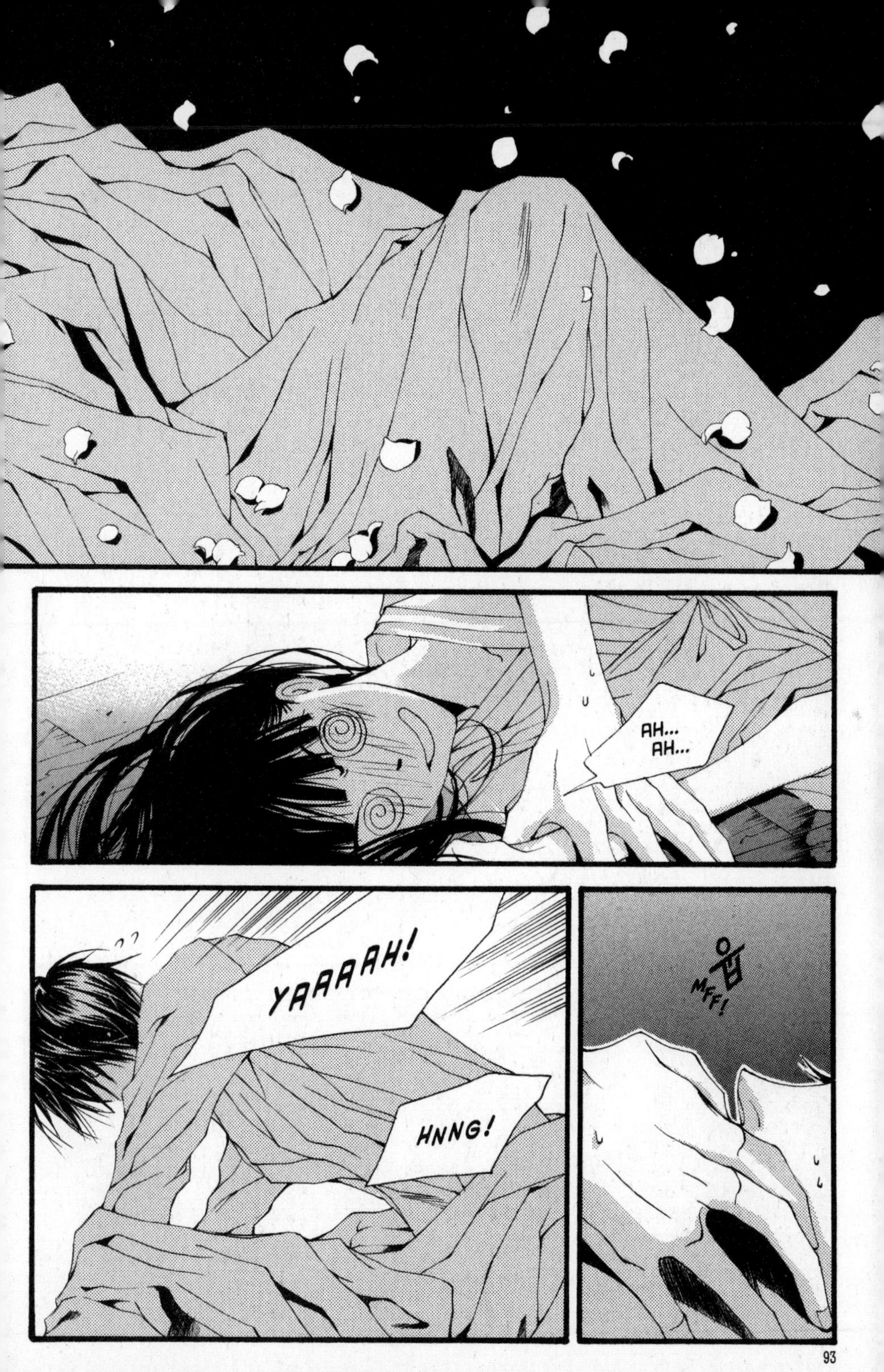
AH... AH...
YAAAAH!
HNNG!
MFF!

I DON'T WANT TO MAKE A BIG FUSS, SO IF YOU *PROMISE* ME THAT YOU WON'T SCREAM, I WILL LET YOU GO.

PROMISE?

NOD NOD NOD NOD

WELL, NOT THAT YOU LOOK REALLY TRUSTWORTHY, BUT...

WSH

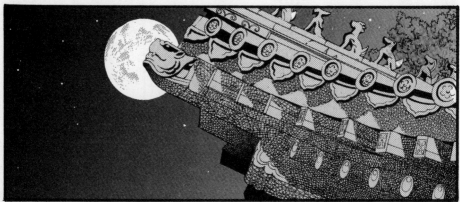

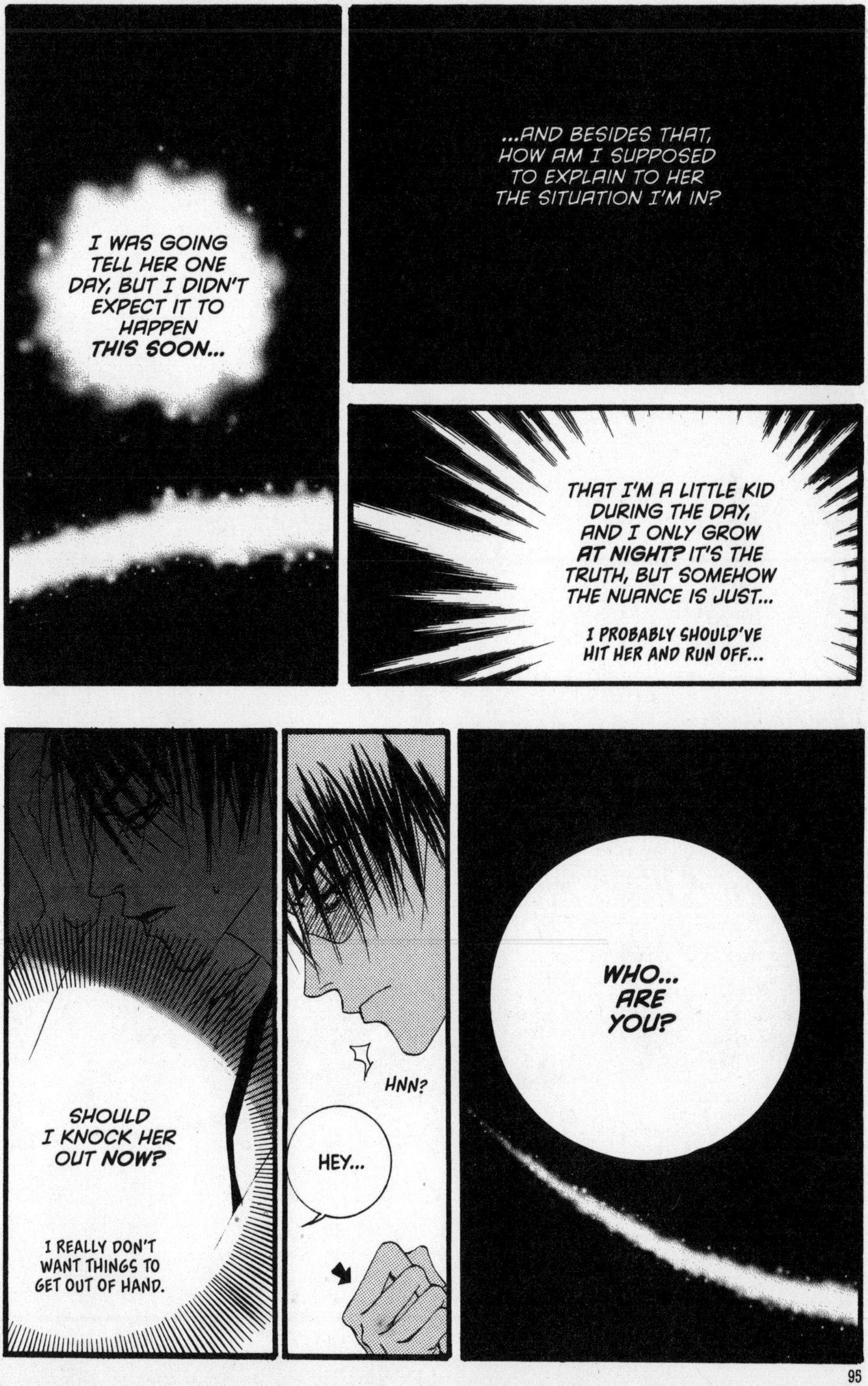
...AND BESIDES THAT, HOW AM I SUPPOSED TO EXPLAIN TO HER THE SITUATION I'M IN?
I WAS GOING TELL HER ONE DAY, BUT I DIDN'T EXPECT IT TO HAPPEN THIS SOON...
THAT I'M A LITTLE KID DURING THE DAY, AND I ONLY GROW AT NIGHT? IT'S THE TRUTH, BUT SOMEHOW THE NUANCE IS JUST...
I PROBABLY SHOULD'VE HIT HER AND RUN OFF...
WHO... ARE YOU?
HNN?
HEY...
SHOULD I KNOCK HER OUT NOW?
I REALLY DON'T WANT THINGS TO GET OUT OF HAND.

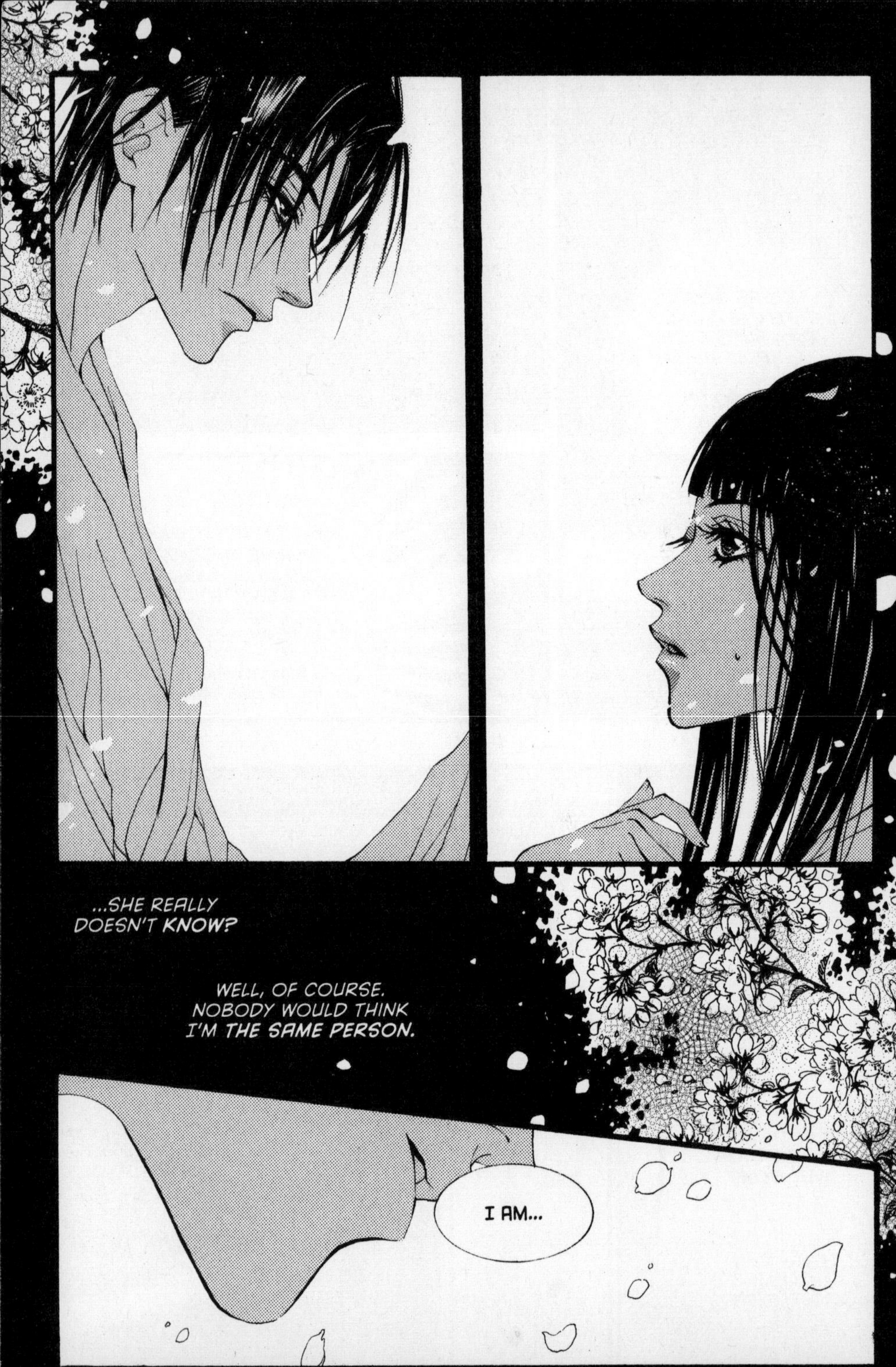
...SHE REALLY
DOESN'T KNOW?
WELL, OF COURSE.
NOBODY WOULD THINK
I'M THE SAME PERSON.
I AM...

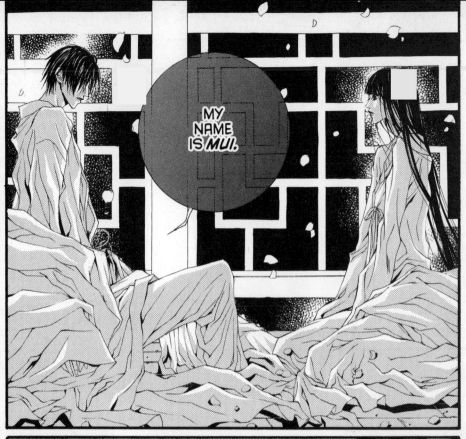

MY NAME IS *MUI.*

MUI...

SO, LIKE...

...YOU'RE HABAEK'S COUSIN, RIGHT?

GUESS YOU'RE A FAR REMOVED COUSIN. YOU GUYS DON'T LOOK ALIKE AT ALL...

I'M MYSELF.

I LIED IN THE HEAT OF THE MOMENT, BUT IT'LL BE BETTER TO KEEP THE SITUATION LIKE THIS.

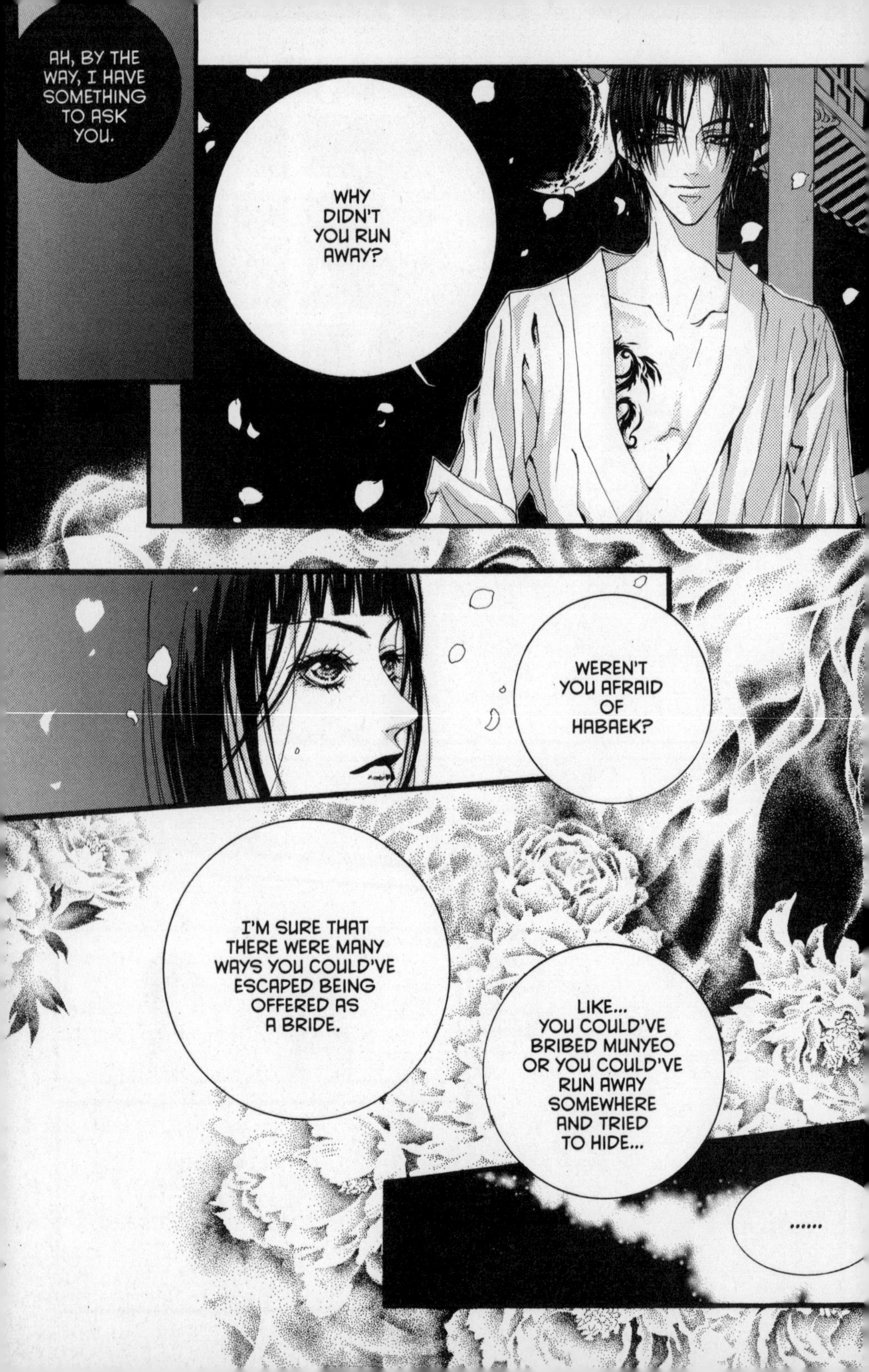
AH, BY THE WAY, I HAVE SOMETHING TO ASK YOU.
WHY DIDN'T YOU RUN AWAY?
WEREN'T YOU AFRAID OF HABAEK?
I'M SURE THAT THERE WERE MANY WAYS YOU COULD'VE ESCAPED BEING OFFERED AS A BRIDE.
LIKE... YOU COULD'VE BRIBED MUNYEO OR YOU COULD'VE RUN AWAY SOMEWHERE AND TRIED TO HIDE...
......

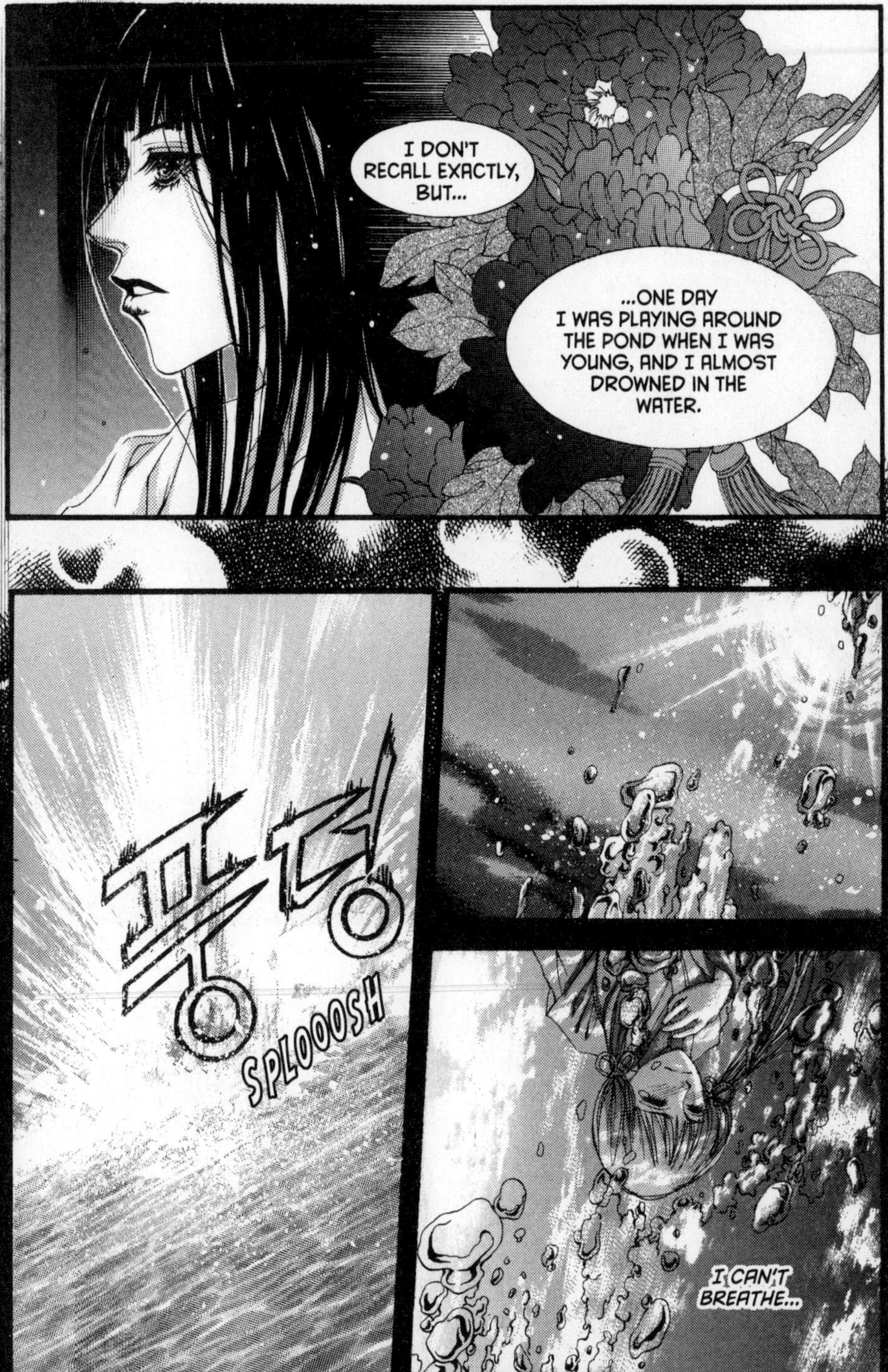
I DON'T RECALL EXACTLY, BUT...
...ONE DAY I WAS PLAYING AROUND THE POND WHEN I WAS YOUNG, AND I ALMOST DROWNED IN THE WATER.
풍덩
SPLOOOSH
I CAN'T BREATHE...

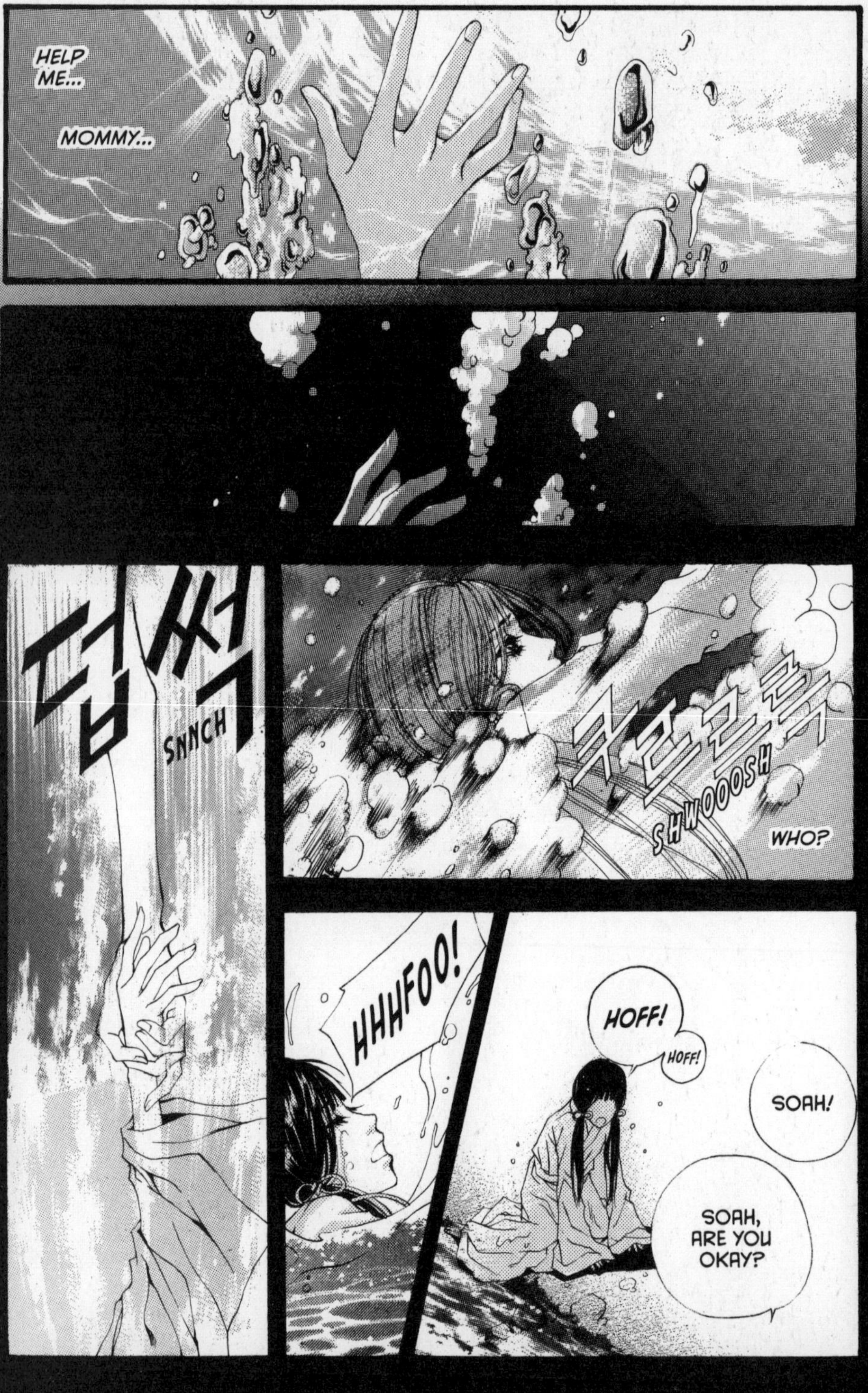
HELP ME...
MOMMY...
덥썩
SNNCH
SHWOOOSH
WHO?
HHHFOO!
HOFF!
HOFF!
SOAH!
SOAH, ARE YOU OKAY?

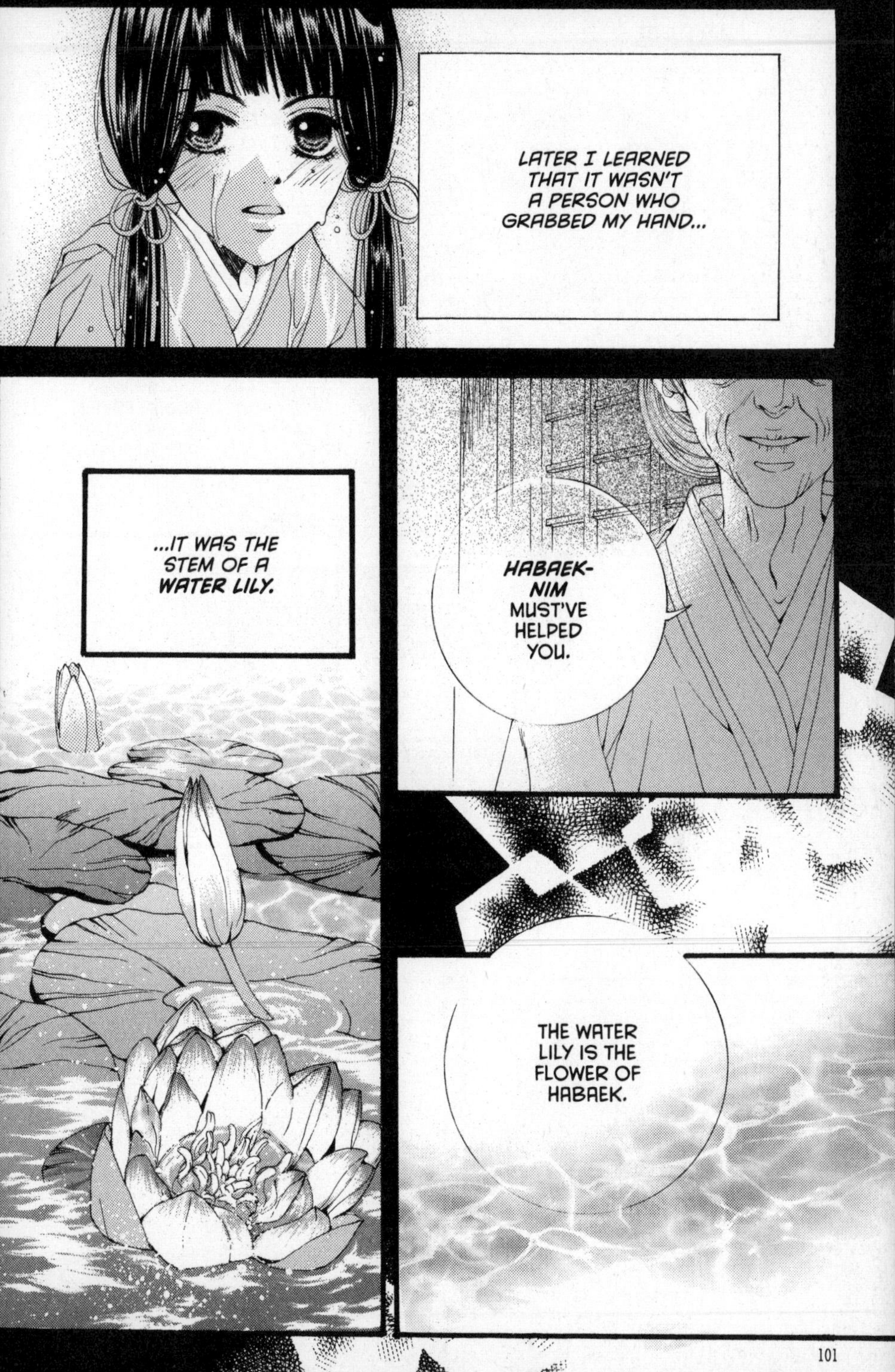
LATER I LEARNED THAT IT WASN'T A PERSON WHO GRABBED MY HAND...
...IT WAS THE STEM OF A WATER LILY.
HABAEK-NIM MUST'VE HELPED YOU.
THE WATER LILY IS THE FLOWER OF HABAEK.

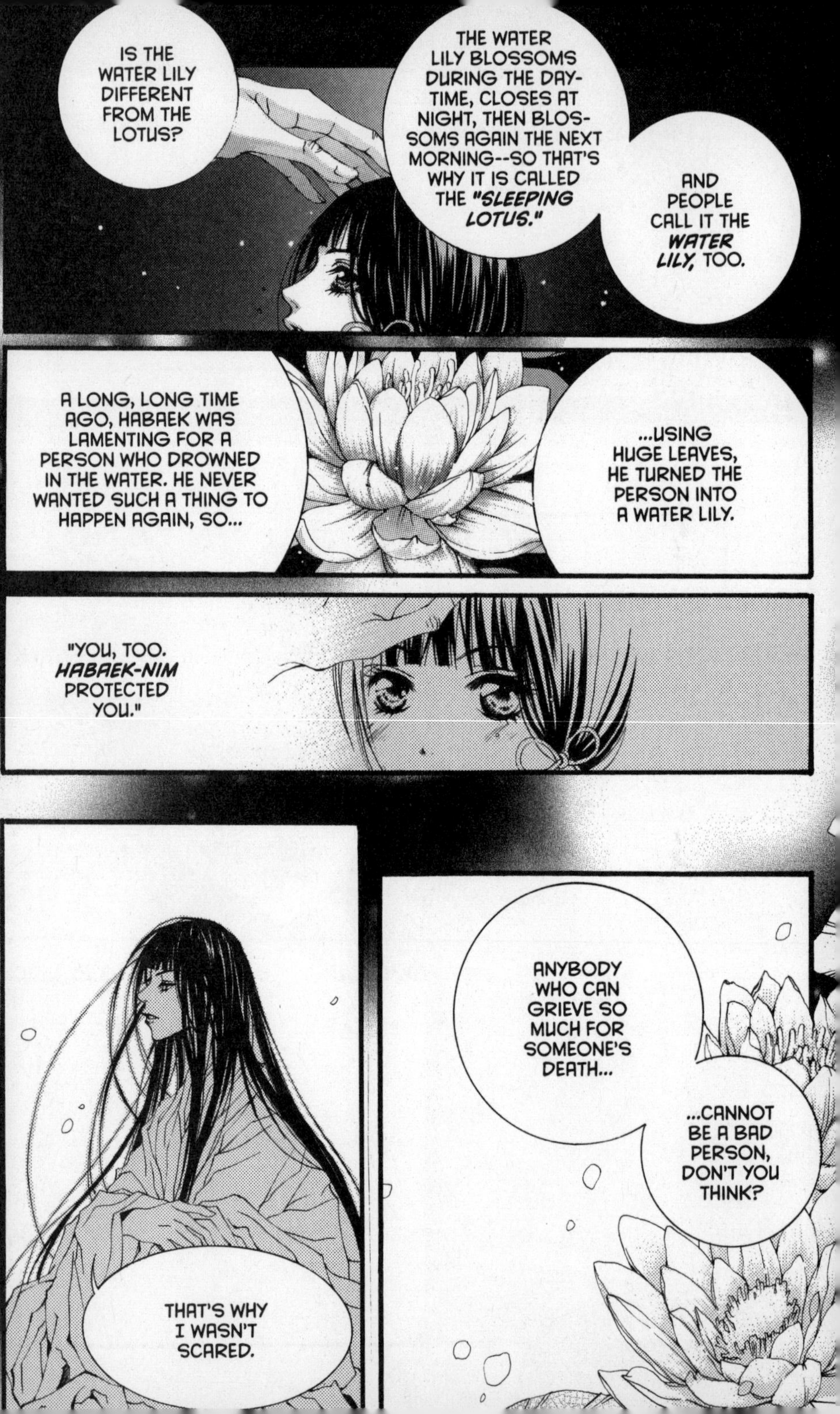

THE WATER LILY BLOSSOMS DURING THE DAY-TIME, CLOSES AT NIGHT, THEN BLOS-SOMS AGAIN THE NEXT MORNING--SO THAT'S WHY IT IS CALLED THE "SLEEPING LOTUS."
IS THE WATER LILY DIFFERENT FROM THE LOTUS?
AND PEOPLE CALL IT THE WATER LILY, TOO.
...USING HUGE LEAVES, HE TURNED THE PERSON INTO A WATER LILY.
A LONG, LONG TIME AGO, HABAEK WAS LAMENTING FOR A PERSON WHO DROWNED IN THE WATER. HE NEVER WANTED SUCH A THING TO HAPPEN AGAIN, SO...
"YOU, TOO. HABAEK-NIM PROTECTED YOU."
ANYBODY WHO CAN GRIEVE SO MUCH FOR SOMEONE'S DEATH...
...CANNOT BE A BAD PERSON, DON'T YOU THINK?
THAT'S WHY I WASN'T SCARED.

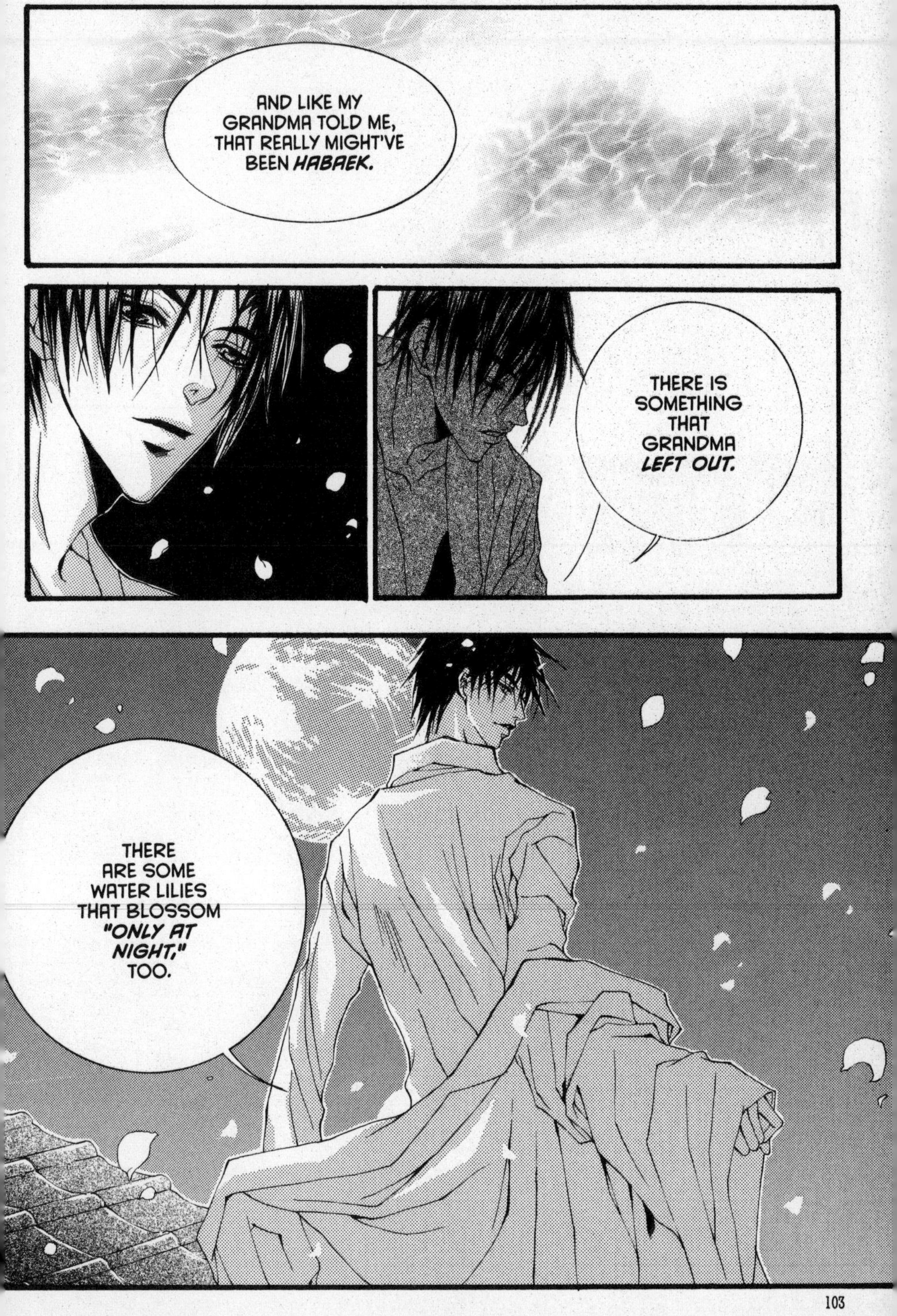
AND LIKE MY GRANDMA TOLD ME, THAT REALLY MIGHT'VE BEEN *HABAEK.*
THERE IS SOMETHING THAT GRANDMA *LEFT OUT.*
THERE ARE SOME WATER LILIES THAT BLOSSOM *"ONLY AT NIGHT,"* TOO.

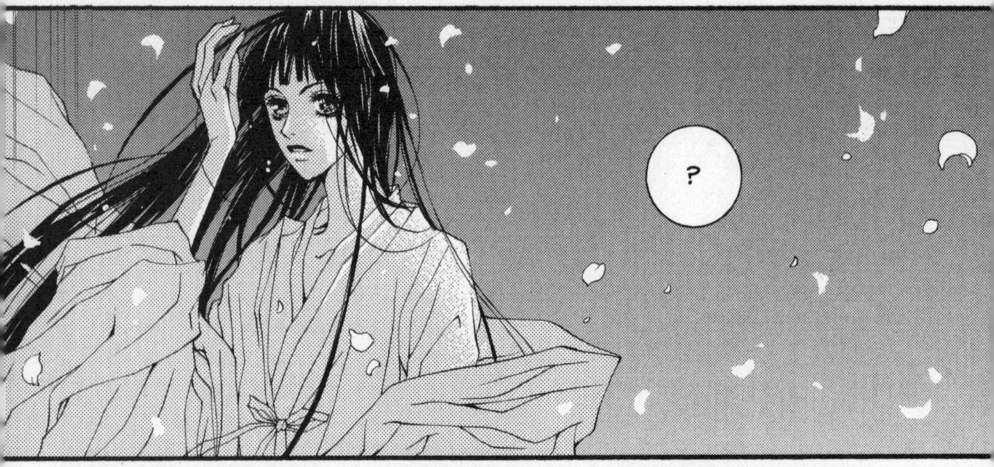
?

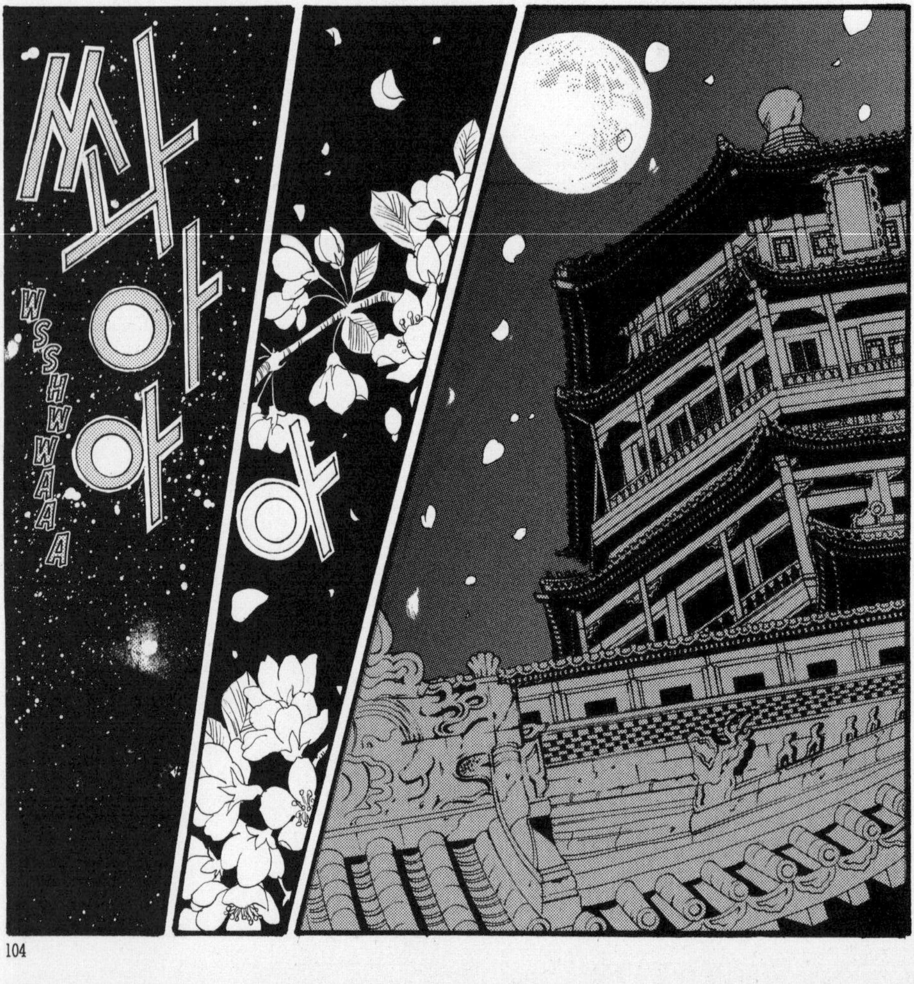
쏴아아아
WSSHWWAAAA

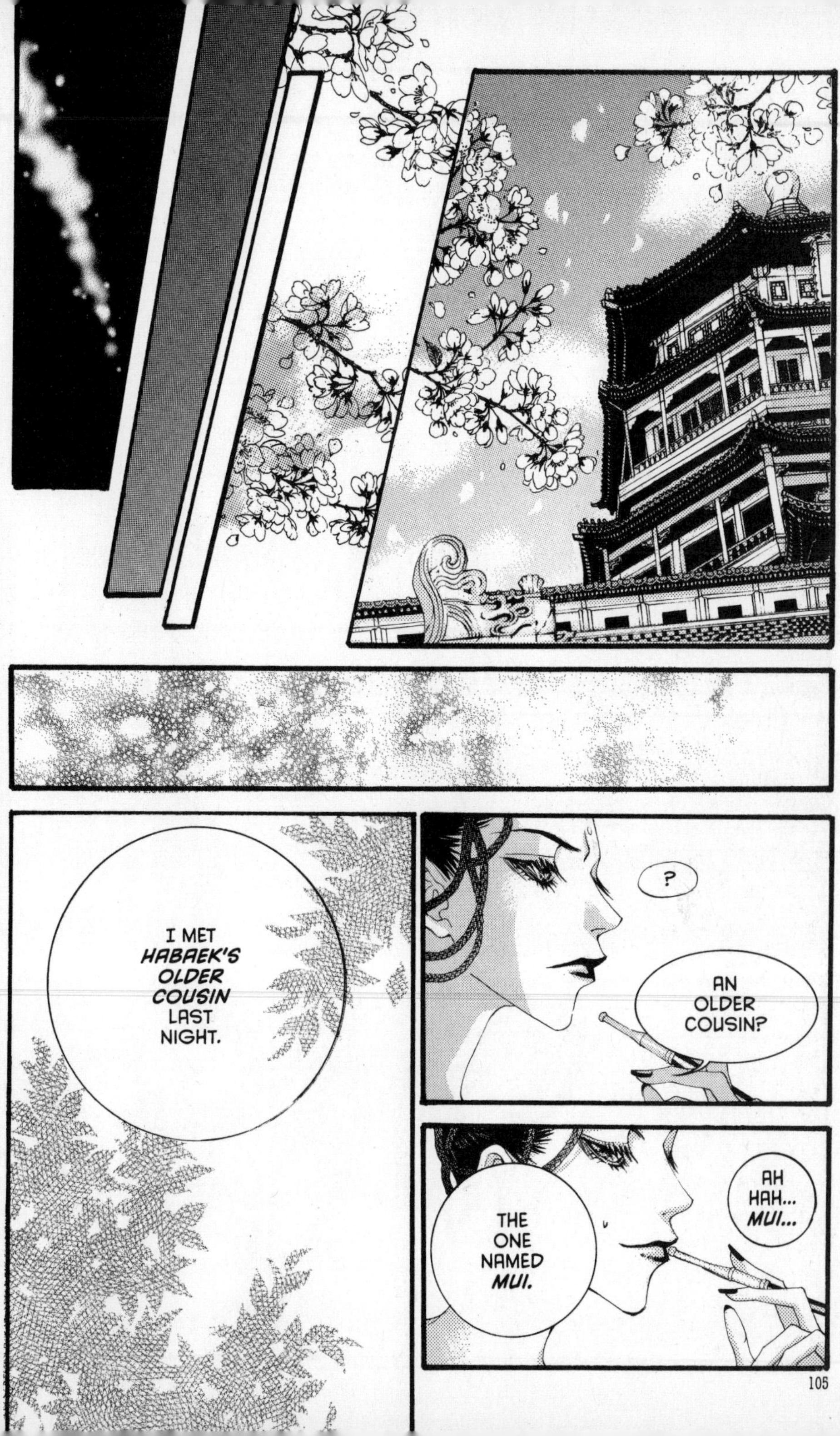
I MET *HABAEK'S OLDER COUSIN* LAST NIGHT.
?
AN OLDER COUSIN?
THE ONE NAMED *MUI.*
AH HAH... *MUI...*

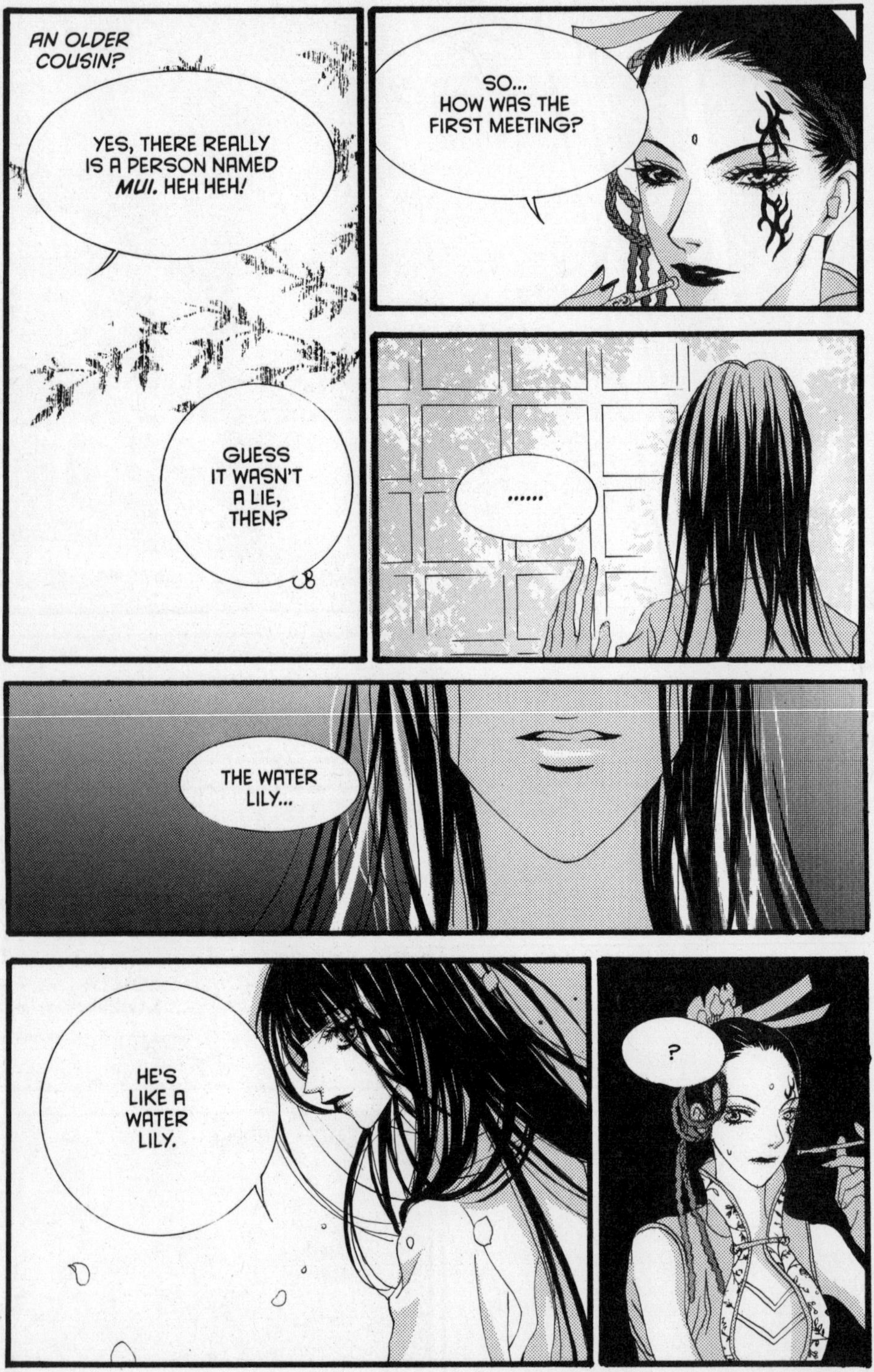
AN OLDER COUSIN?
YES, THERE REALLY IS A PERSON NAMED MUI. HEH HEH!
SO... HOW WAS THE FIRST MEETING?
GUESS IT WASN'T A LIE, THEN?
......
THE WATER LILY...
HE'S LIKE A WATER LILY.
?

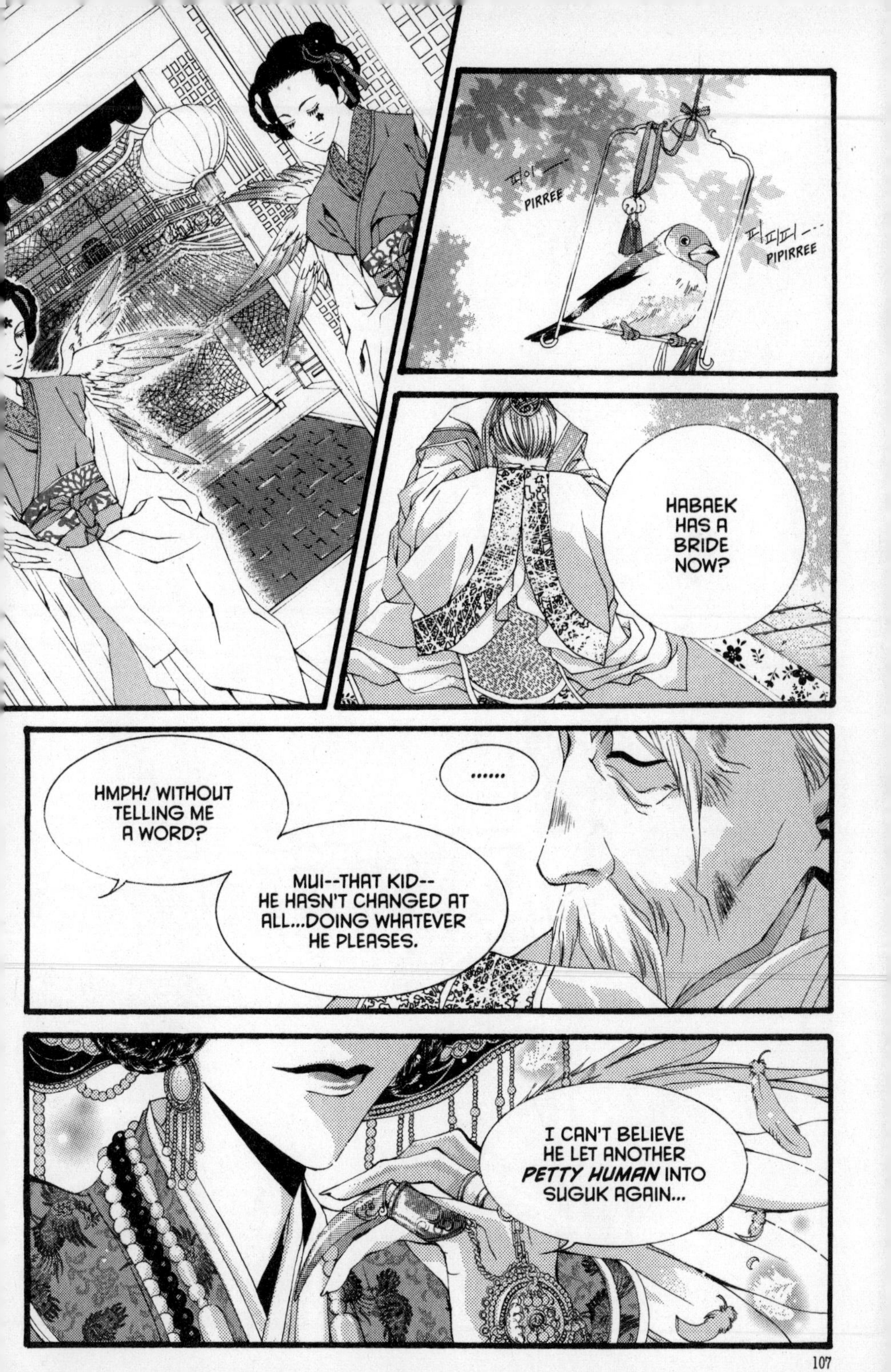

삐이---
PIRREE
삐삐삐---
PIPIRREE
HABAEK HAS A BRIDE NOW?
......
HMPH! WITHOUT TELLING ME A WORD?
MUI--THAT KID-- HE HASN'T CHANGED AT ALL...DOING WHATEVER HE PLEASES.
I CAN'T BELIEVE HE LET ANOTHER *PETTY HUMAN* INTO SUGUK AGAIN...

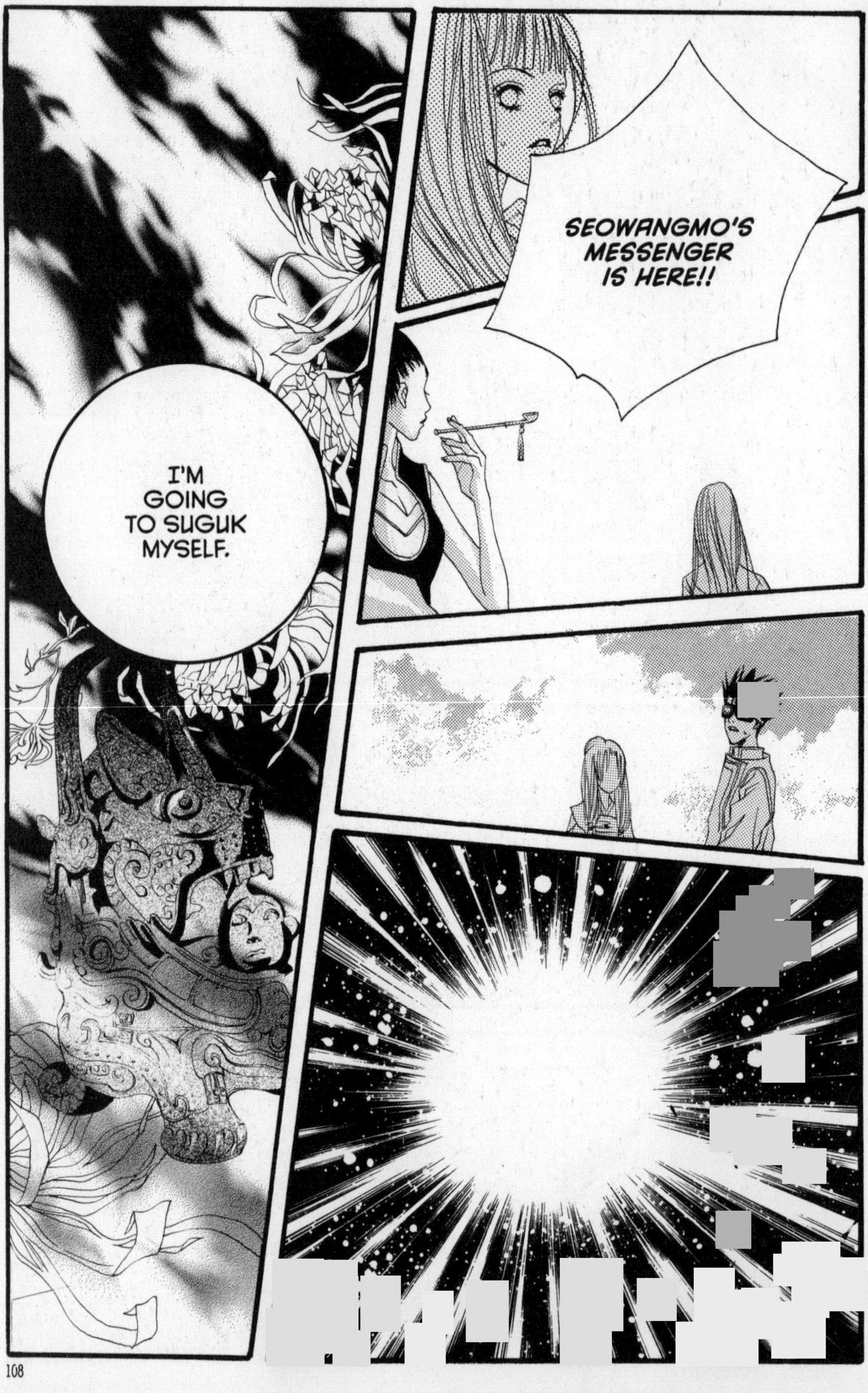
SEOWANGMO'S MESSENGER IS HERE!!
I'M GOING TO SUGUK MYSELF.

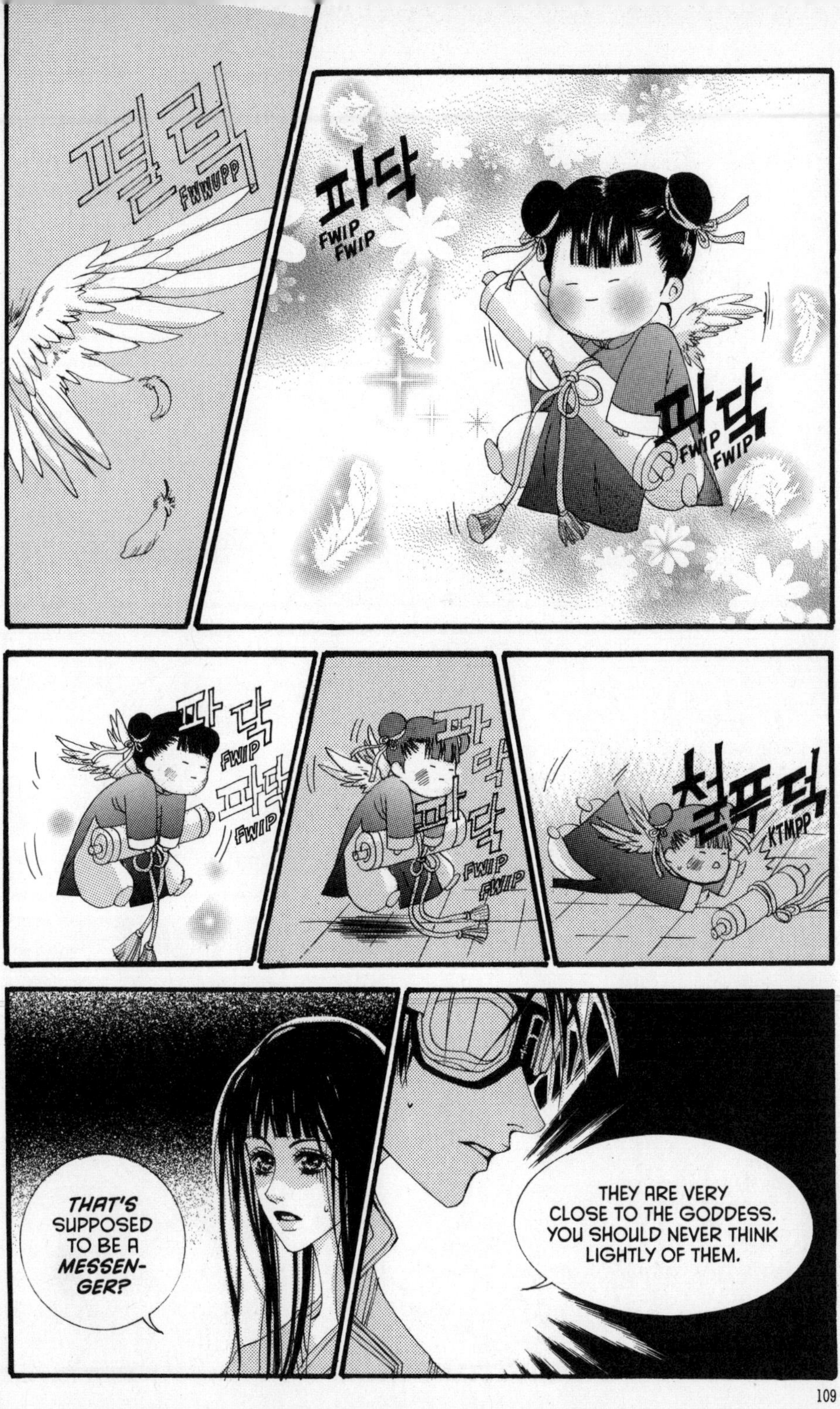
펄럭
FWWUPP
파닥
FWIP FWIP
파닥
FWIP FWIP
파닥
FWIP
파닥
FWIP
파닥
파닥
FWIP FWIP
철푸덕
KTMPP
THAT'S SUPPOSED TO BE A MESSENGER?
THEY ARE VERY CLOSE TO THE GODDESS. YOU SHOULD NEVER THINK LIGHTLY OF THEM.

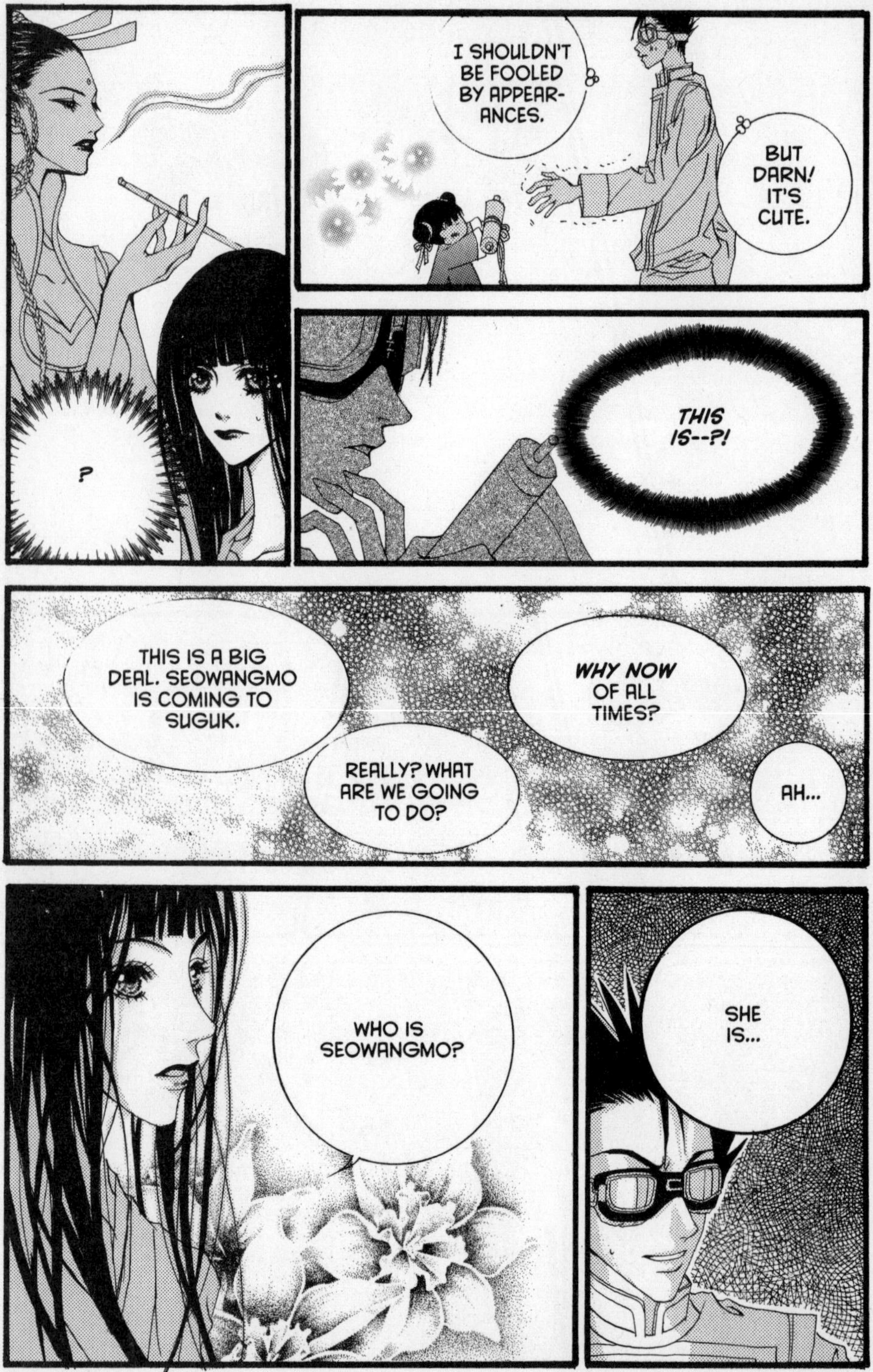
I SHOULDN'T BE FOOLED BY APPEAR-ANCES.
BUT DARN! IT'S CUTE.
?
THIS IS--?!
THIS IS A BIG DEAL. SEOWANGMO IS COMING TO SUGUK.
REALLY? WHAT ARE WE GOING TO DO?
WHY NOW OF ALL TIMES?
AH...
WHO IS SEOWANGMO?
SHE IS...

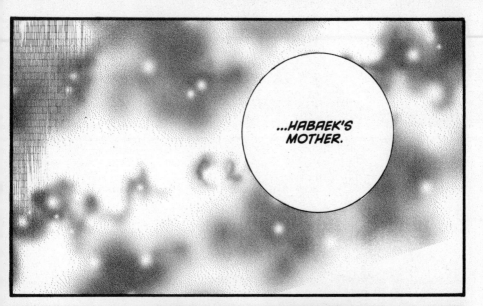

...HABAEK'S MOTHER.

I GUESS SHE IS VERY STRICT?

IT SEEMS LIKE EVERYBODY'S SCARED OF HER...

IT'S NOT THAT SHE'S MERELY STRICT...

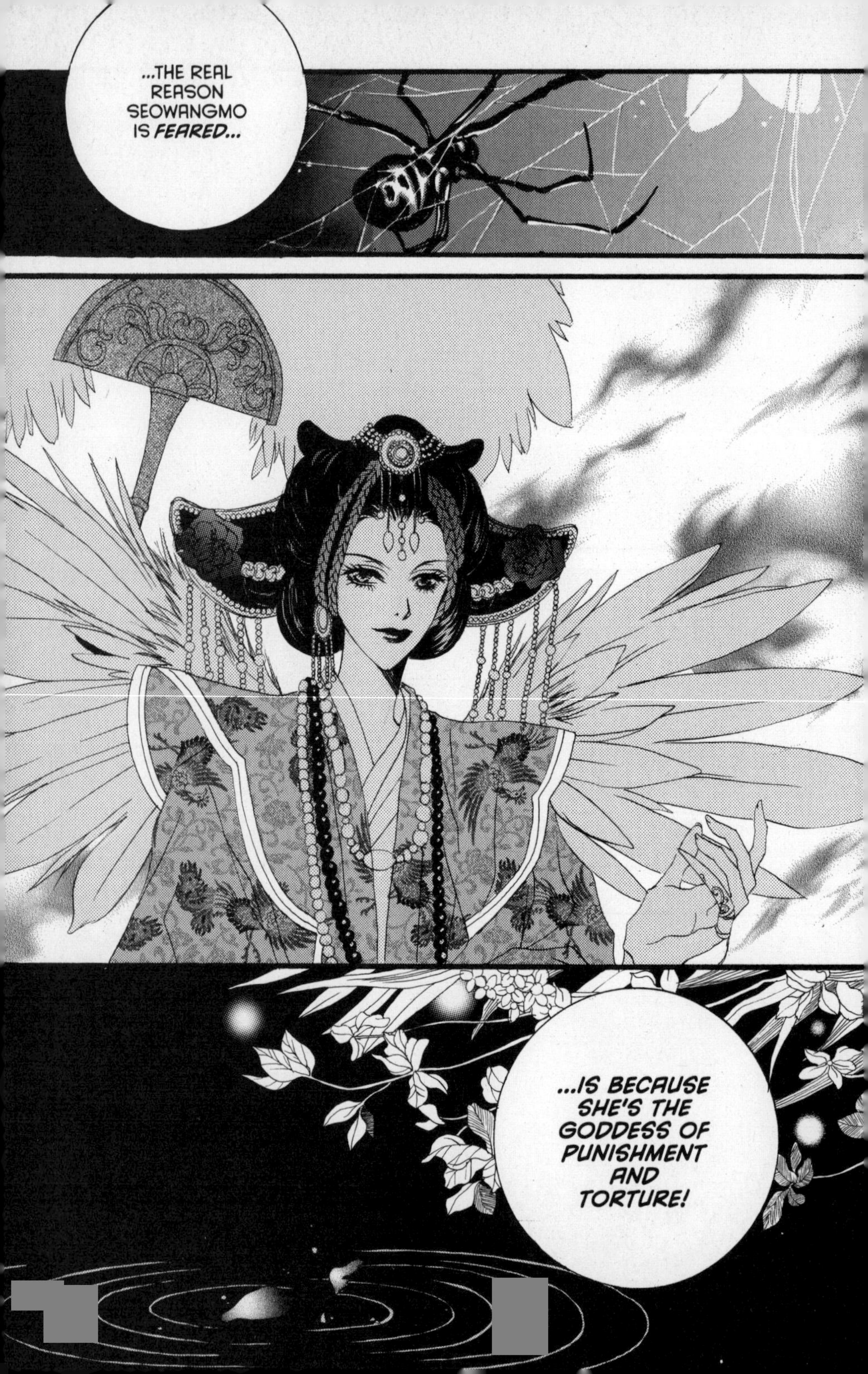
...THE REAL REASON SEOWANGMO IS *FEARED*...
...IS BECAUSE SHE'S THE GODDESS OF PUNISHMENT AND TORTURE!

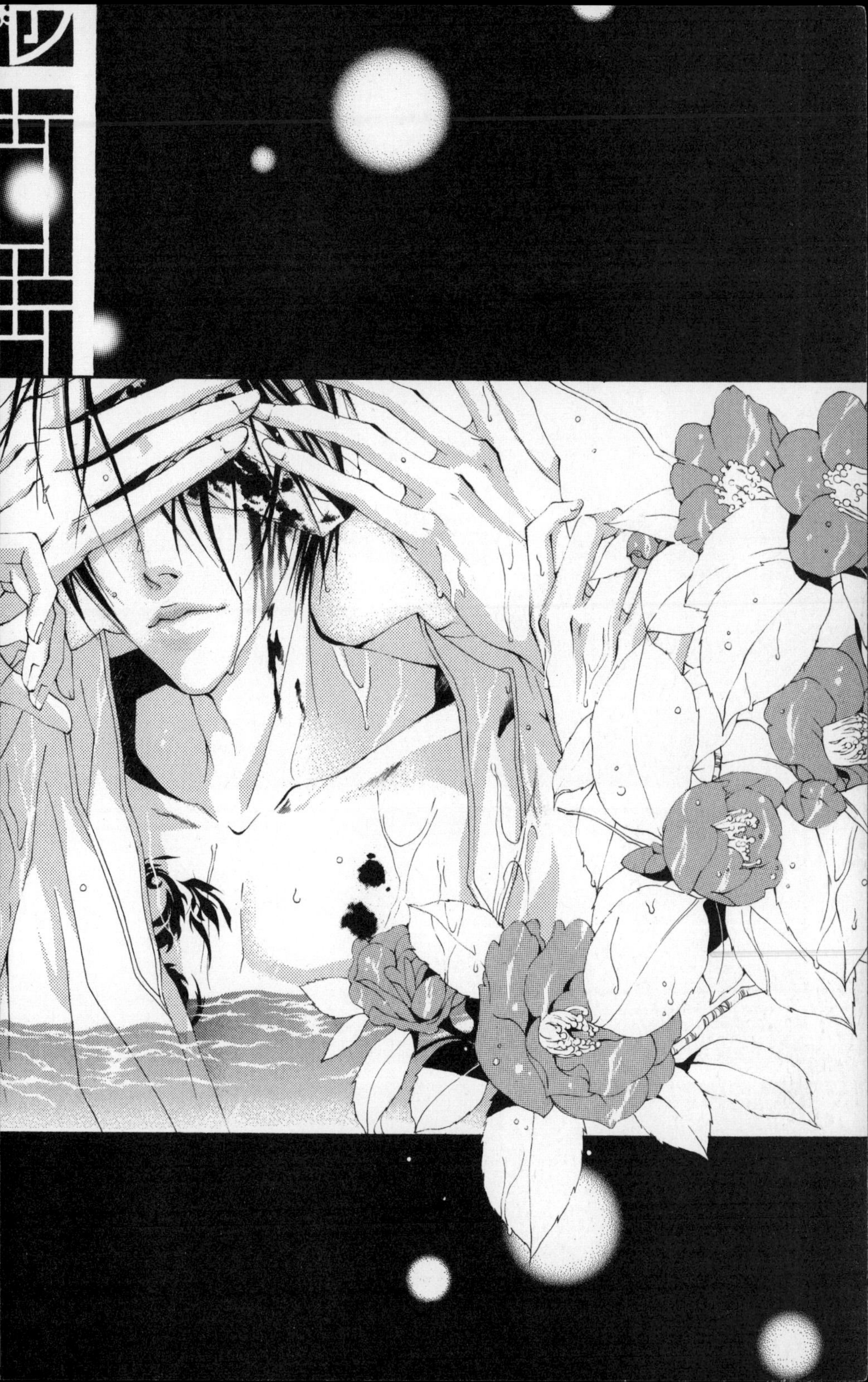

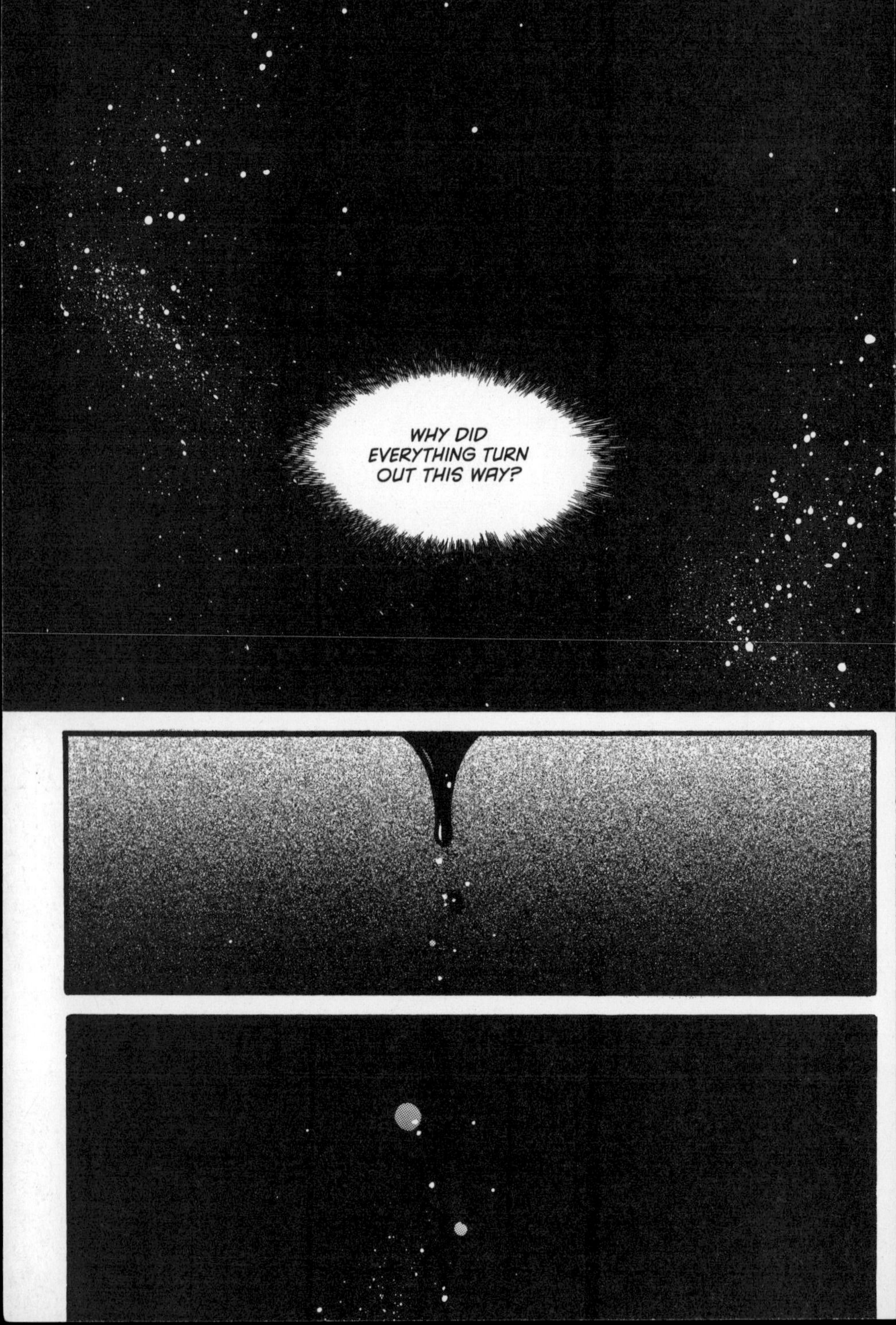
WHY DID EVERYTHING TURN OUT THIS WAY?

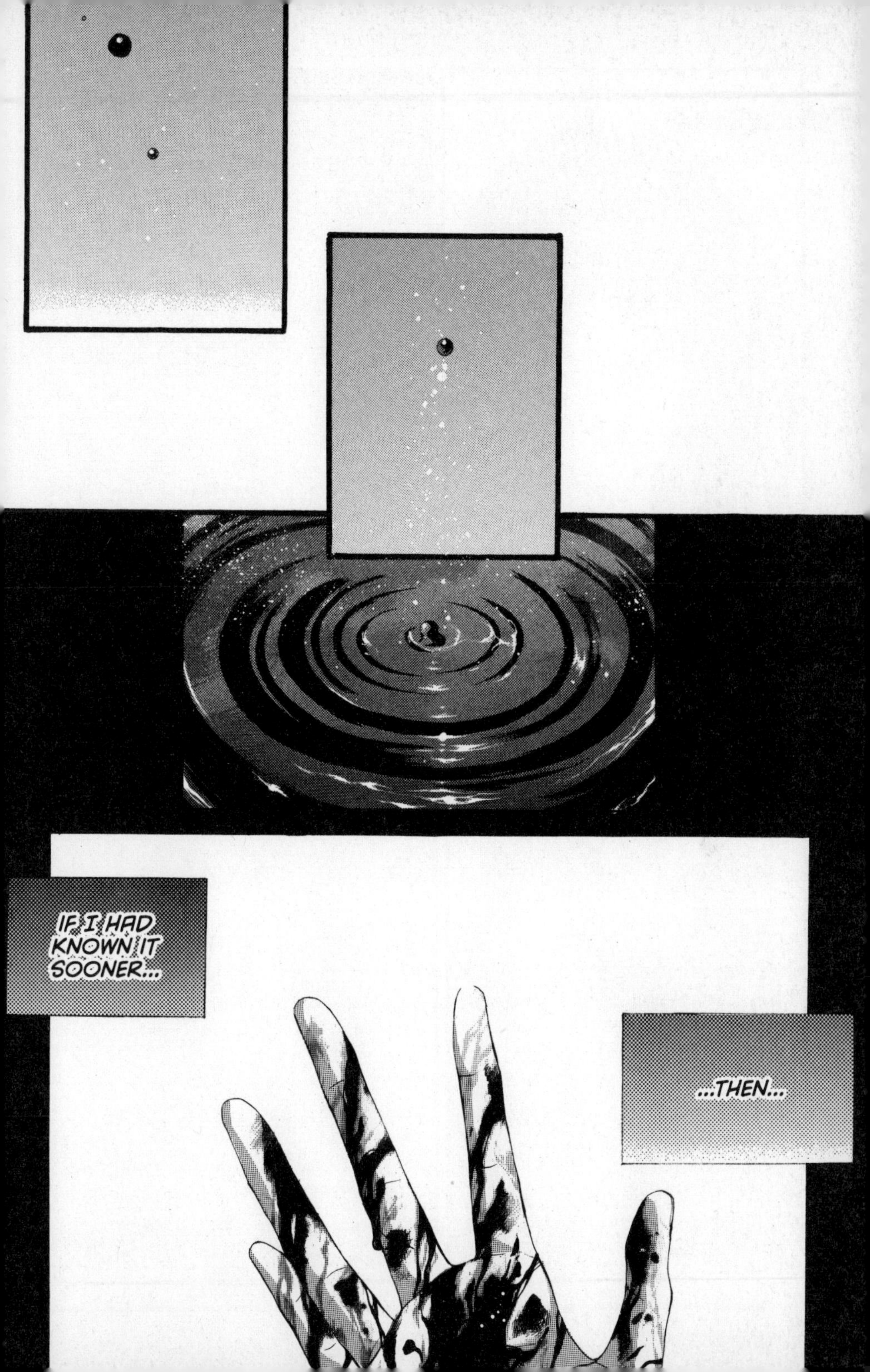
IF I HAD KNOWN IT SOONER...
...THEN...

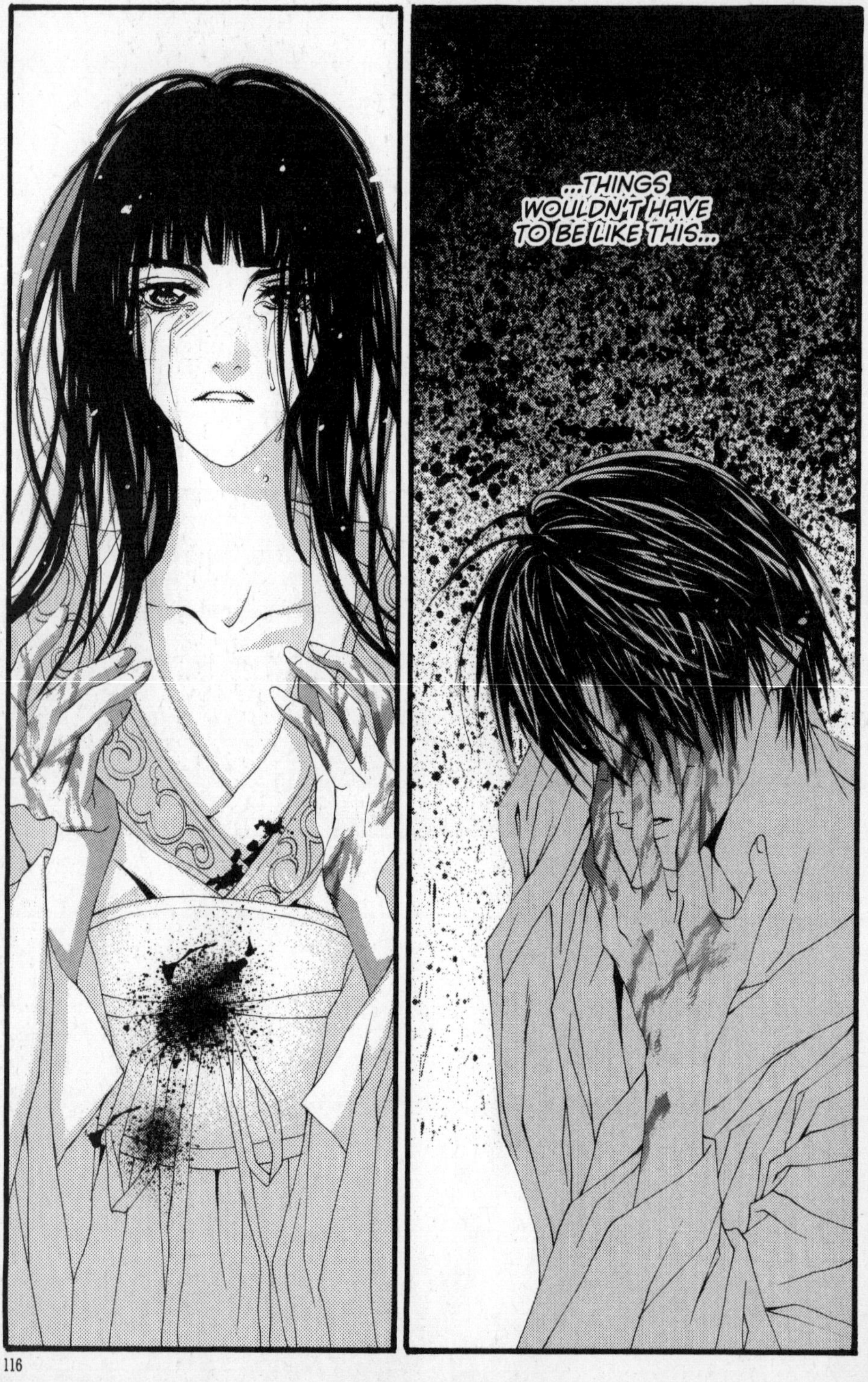
...THINGS WOULDN'T HAVE TO BE LIKE THIS...

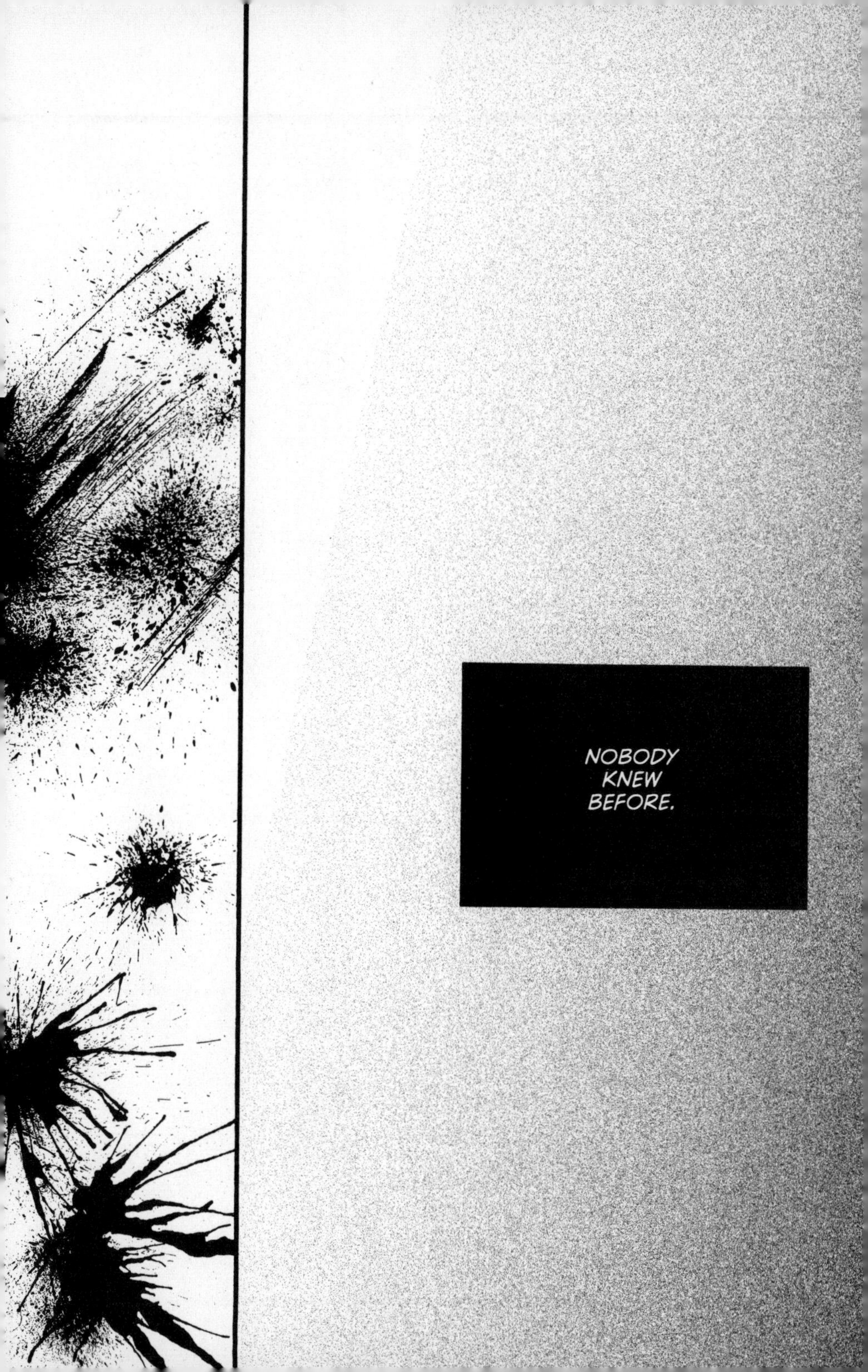
NOBODY KNEW BEFORE.

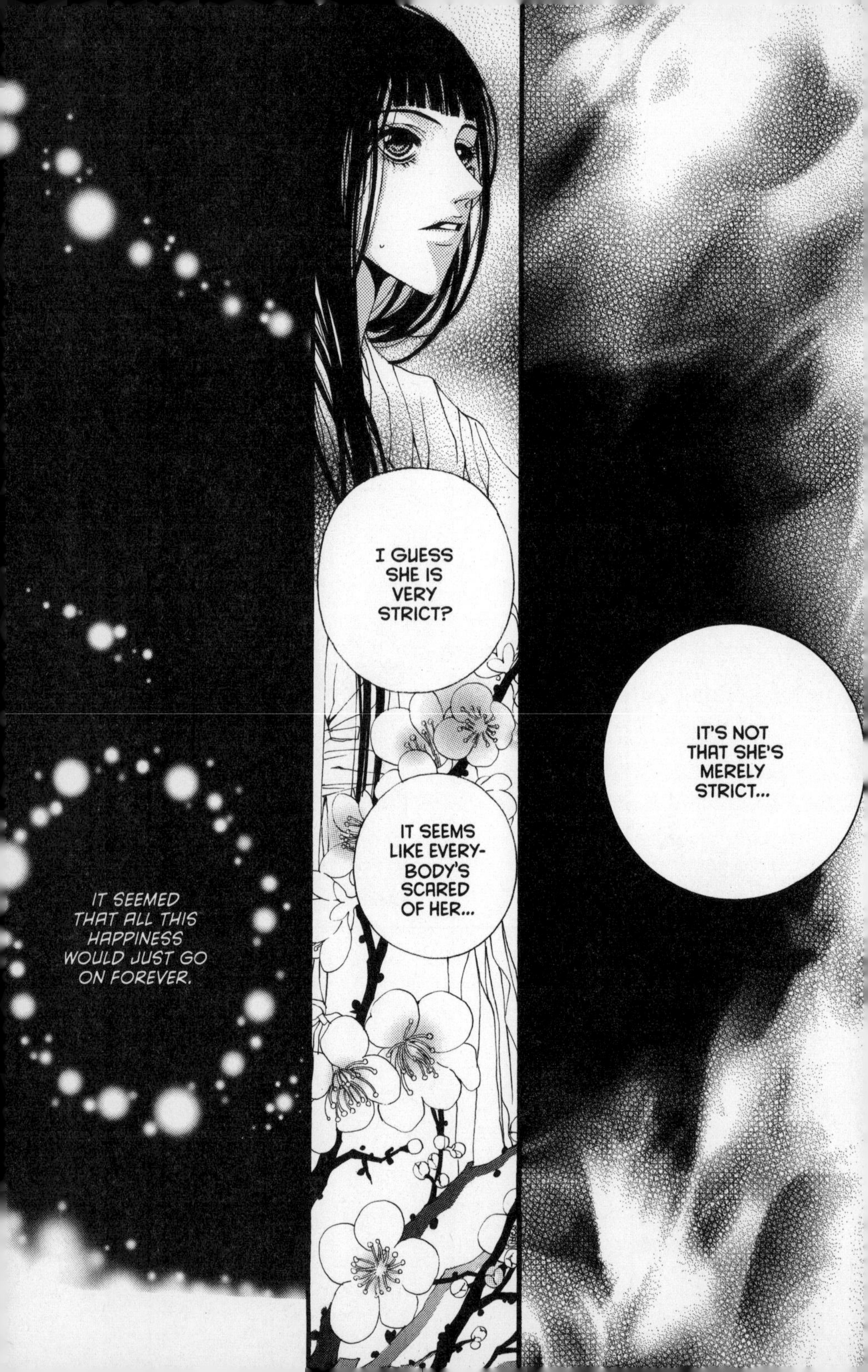
IT'S NOT THAT SHE'S MERELY STRICT...
I GUESS SHE IS VERY STRICT?
IT SEEMS LIKE EVERY-BODY'S SCARED OF HER...
IT SEEMED THAT ALL THIS HAPPINESS WOULD JUST GO ON FOREVER.

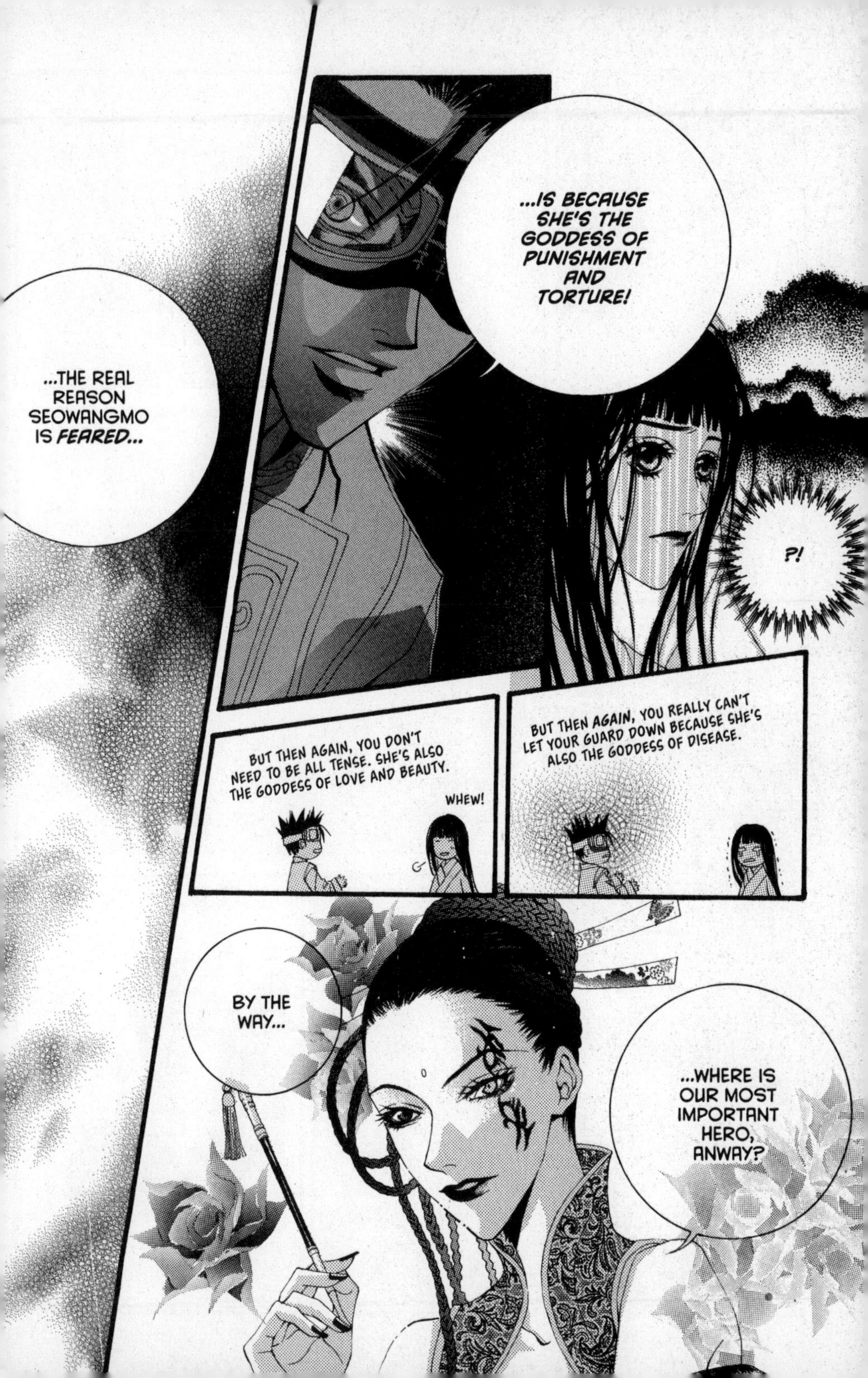
...THE REAL REASON SEOWANGMO IS FEARED...
...IS BECAUSE SHE'S THE GODDESS OF PUNISHMENT AND TORTURE!
?!
BUT THEN AGAIN, YOU DON'T NEED TO BE ALL TENSE. SHE'S ALSO THE GODDESS OF LOVE AND BEAUTY.
WHEW!
BUT THEN AGAIN, YOU REALLY CAN'T LET YOUR GUARD DOWN BECAUSE SHE'S ALSO THE GODDESS OF DISEASE.
BY THE WAY...
...WHERE IS OUR MOST IMPORTANT HERO, ANWAY?

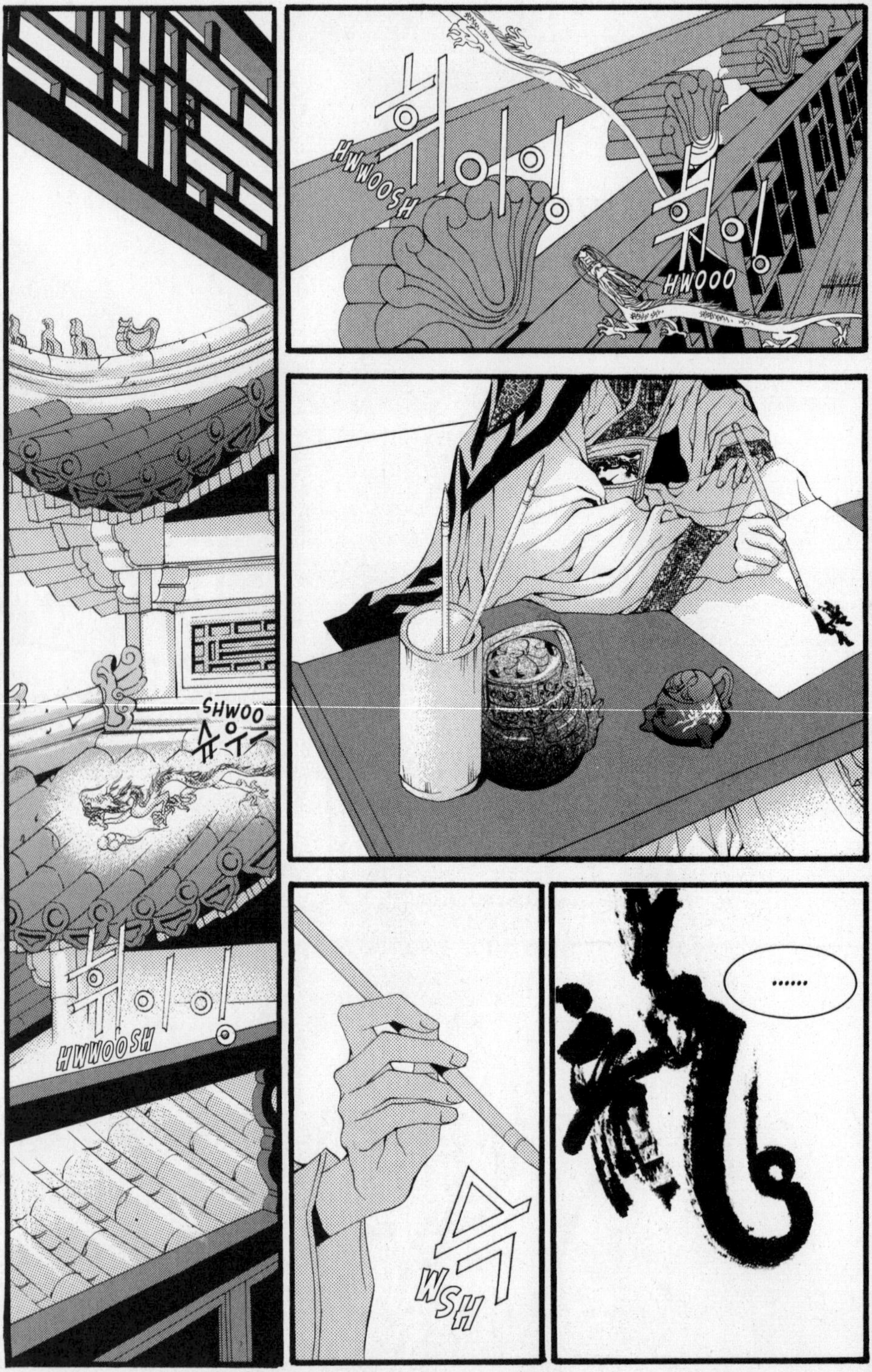

휘이잉!
HWWOOSH
휘잉!
HWOOO
슈이—
SHWOO
휘이잉!
HWWOOSH
슥
WSH
......

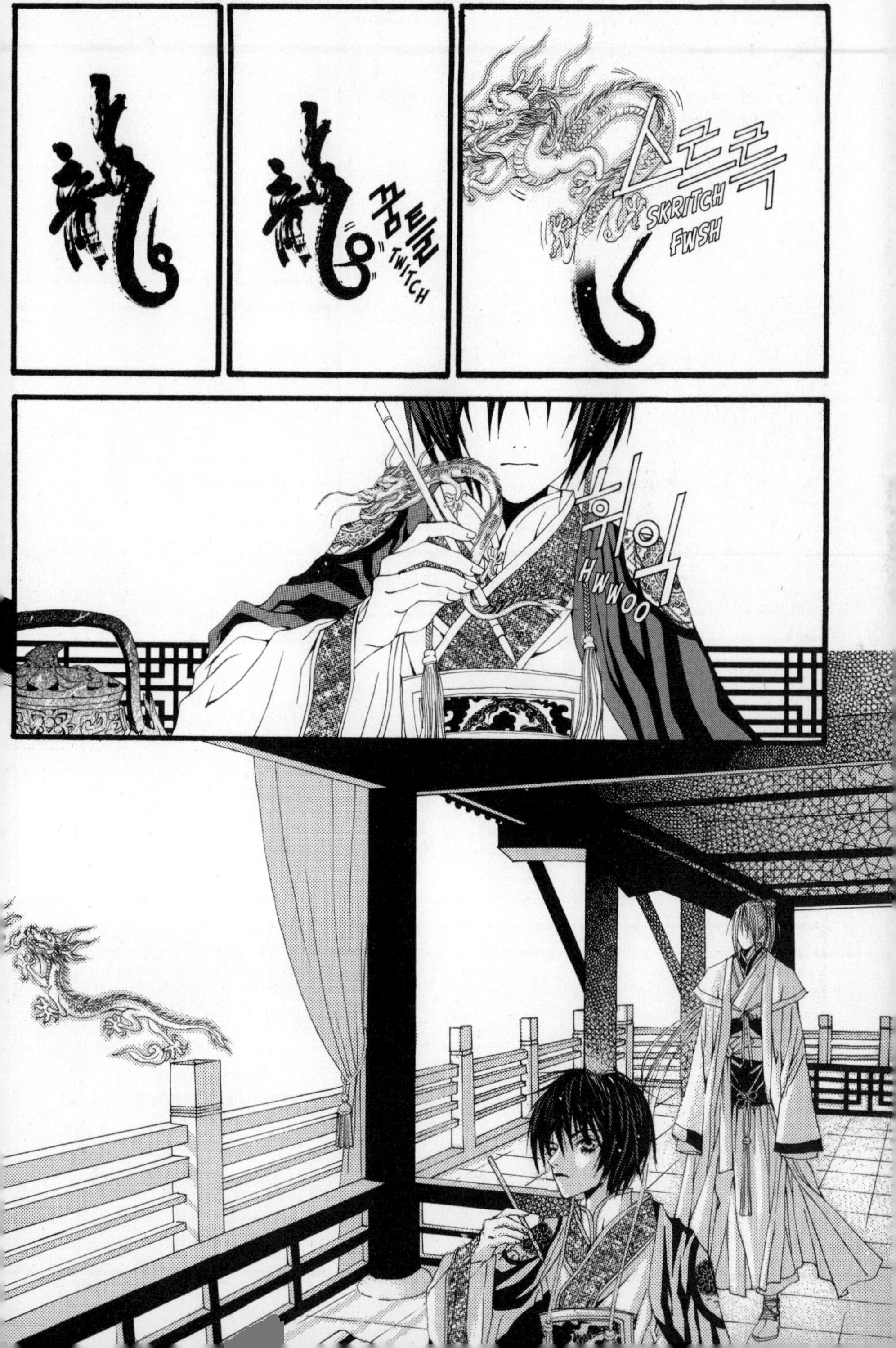
꿈틀
TWITCH
스르륵
SKRITCH
FWSH
휘이잉
HWWOO

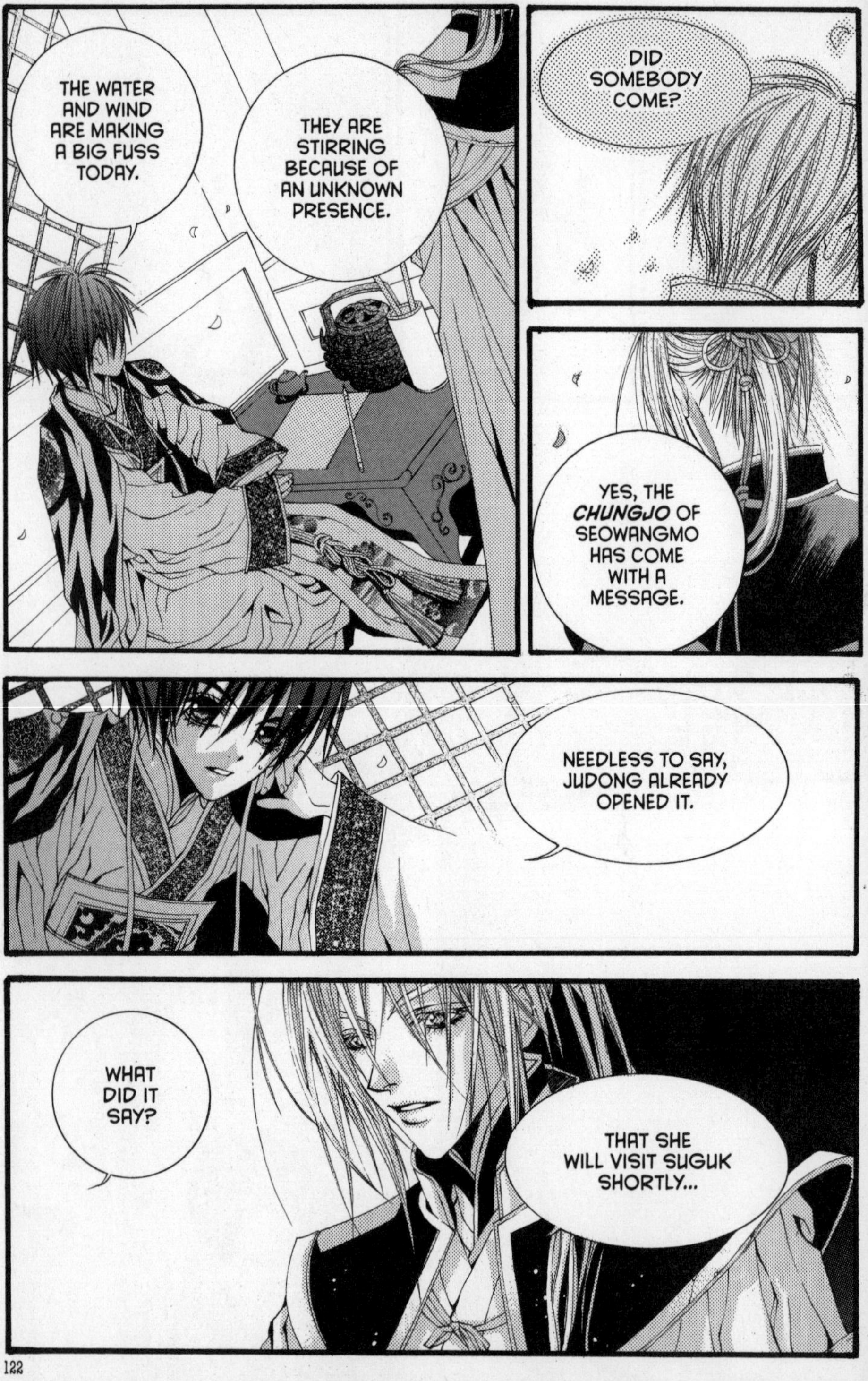
THE WATER AND WIND ARE MAKING A BIG FUSS TODAY.
THEY ARE STIRRING BECAUSE OF AN UNKNOWN PRESENCE.
DID SOMEBODY COME?
YES, THE *CHUNGJO* OF SEOWANGMO HAS COME WITH A MESSAGE.
NEEDLESS TO SAY, JUDONG ALREADY OPENED IT.
WHAT DID IT SAY?
THAT SHE WILL VISIT SUGUK SHORTLY...

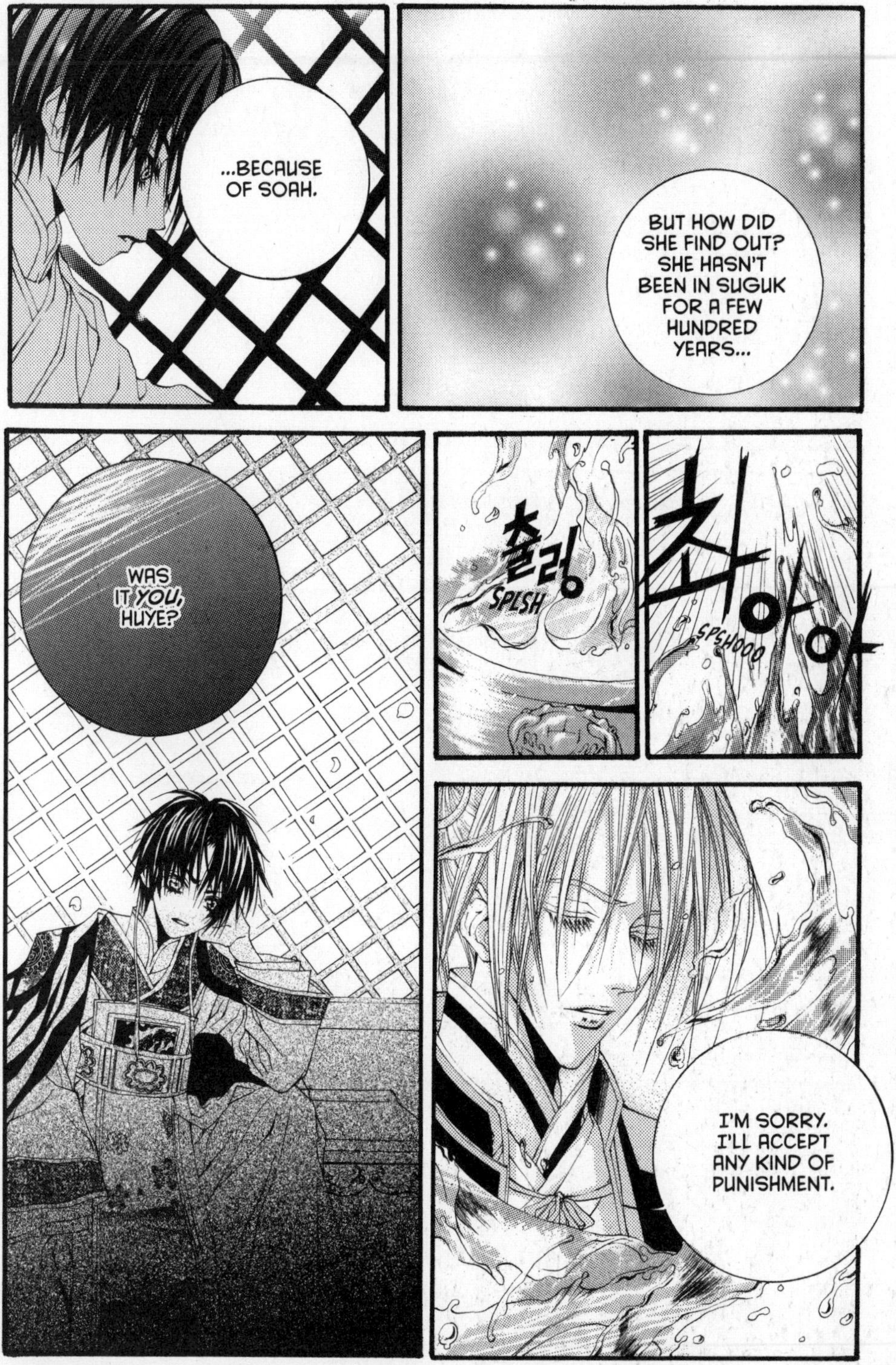

...BECAUSE OF SOAH.
BUT HOW DID SHE FIND OUT? SHE HASN'T BEEN IN SUGUK FOR A FEW HUNDRED YEARS...
WAS IT *YOU*, HUYE?
출렁
SPLSH
촤아악
SPSHOOO
I'M SORRY. I'LL ACCEPT ANY KIND OF PUNISHMENT.

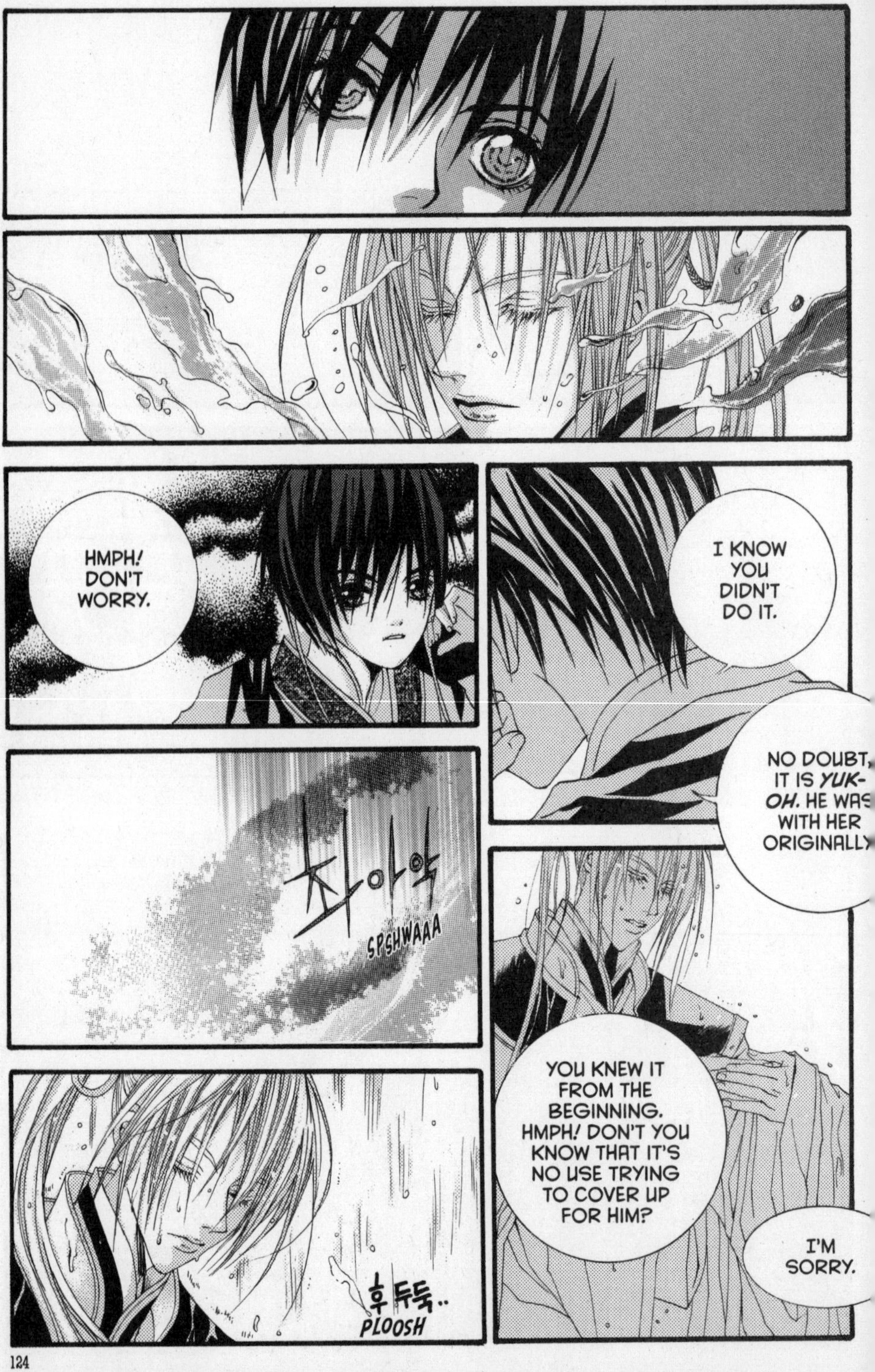
HMPH! DON'T WORRY.
I KNOW YOU DIDN'T DO IT.
NO DOUBT, IT IS *YUK-OH*. HE WAS WITH HER ORIGINALLY
SPSHWAAA
YOU KNEW IT FROM THE BEGINNING. HMPH! DON'T YOU KNOW THAT IT'S NO USE TRYING TO COVER UP FOR HIM?
I'M SORRY.
후두둑..
PLOOSH

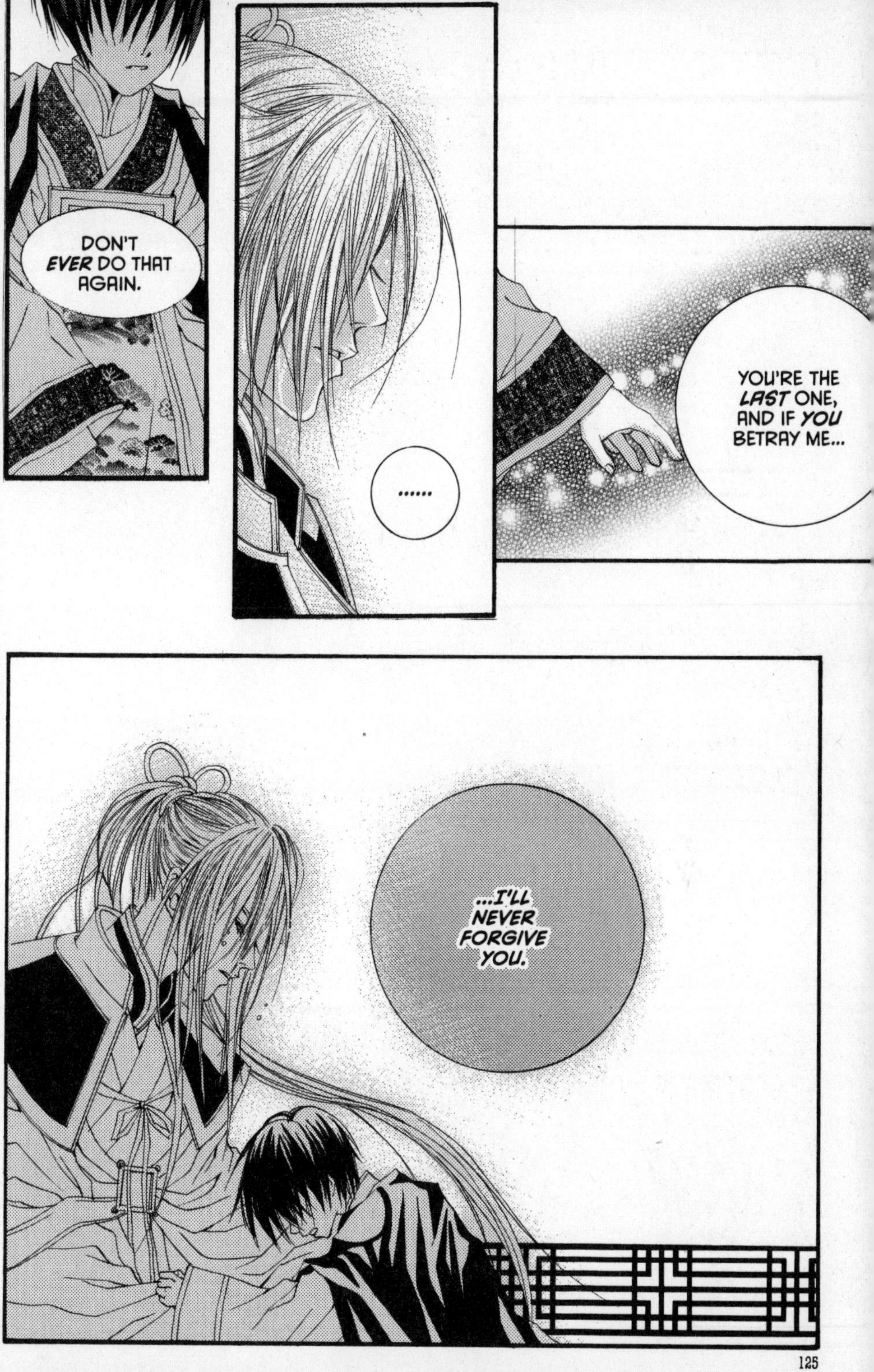
DON'T
EVER DO THAT
AGAIN.
......
YOU'RE THE
LAST ONE,
AND IF YOU
BETRAY ME...
...I'LL
NEVER
FORGIVE
YOU.

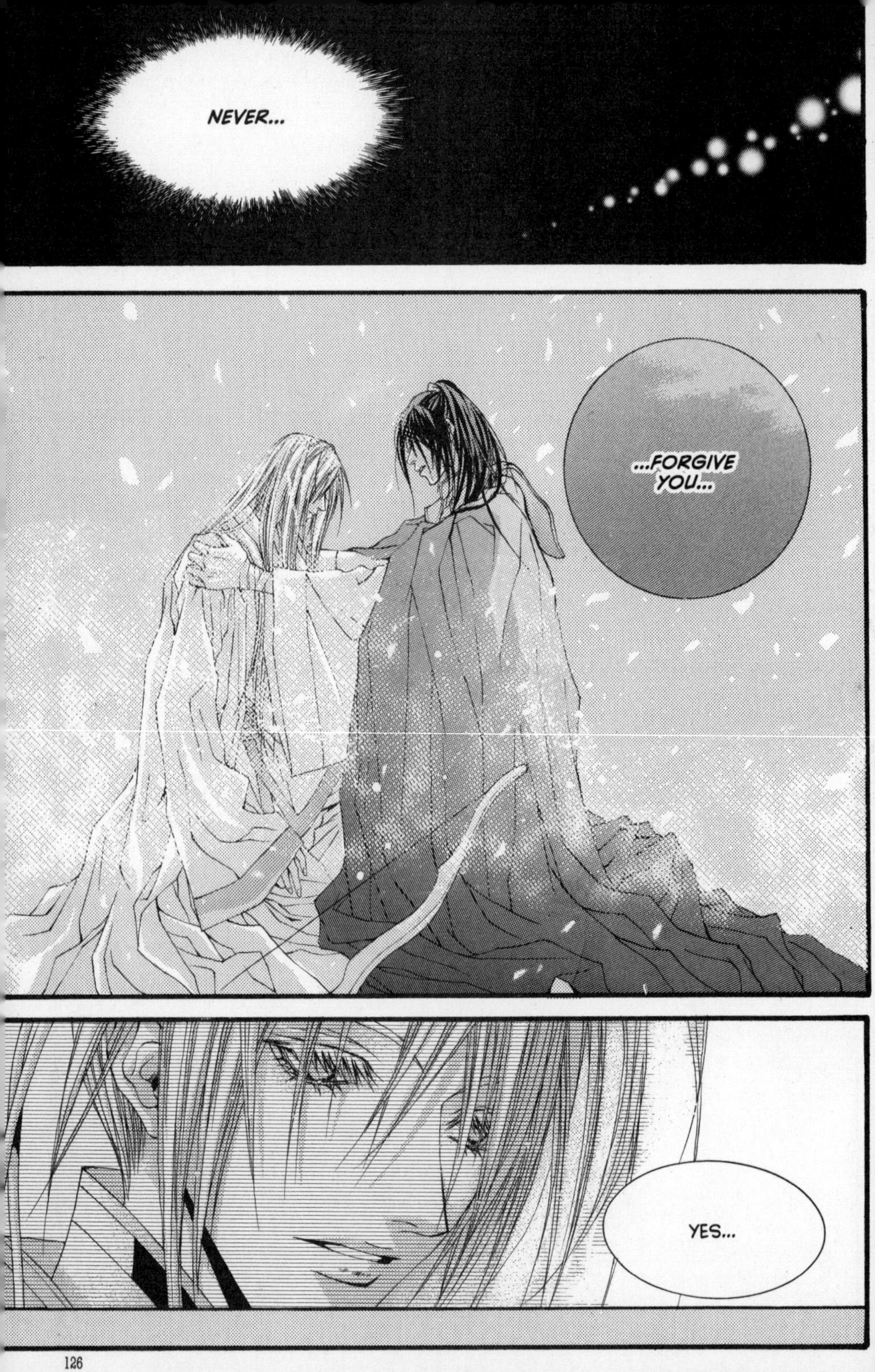
NEVER...
...FORGIVE YOU...
YES...

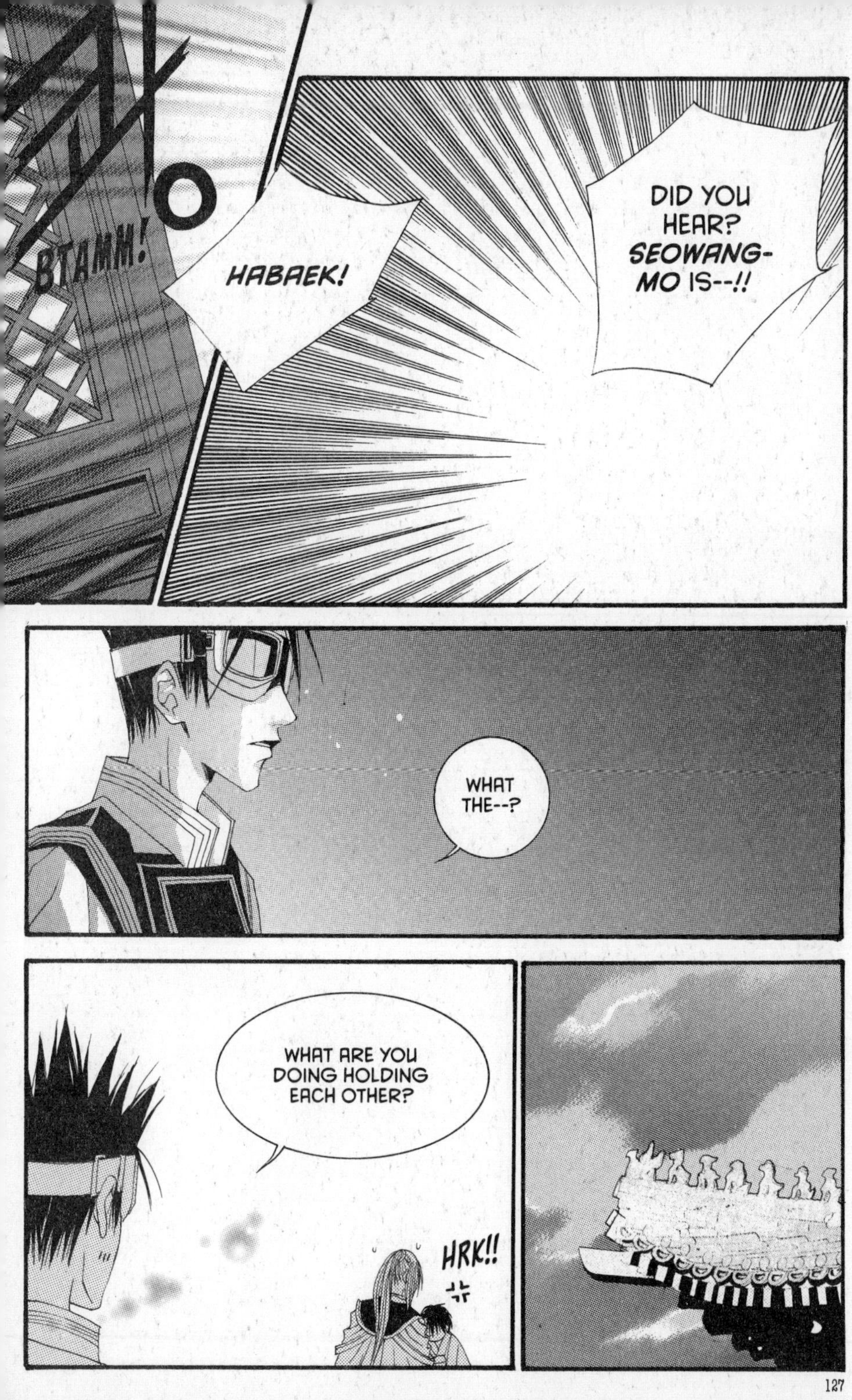
BTAMM!
DID YOU HEAR? SEOWANG-MO IS--!!
HABAEK!
WHAT THE--?
WHAT ARE YOU DOING HOLDING EACH OTHER?
HRK!!

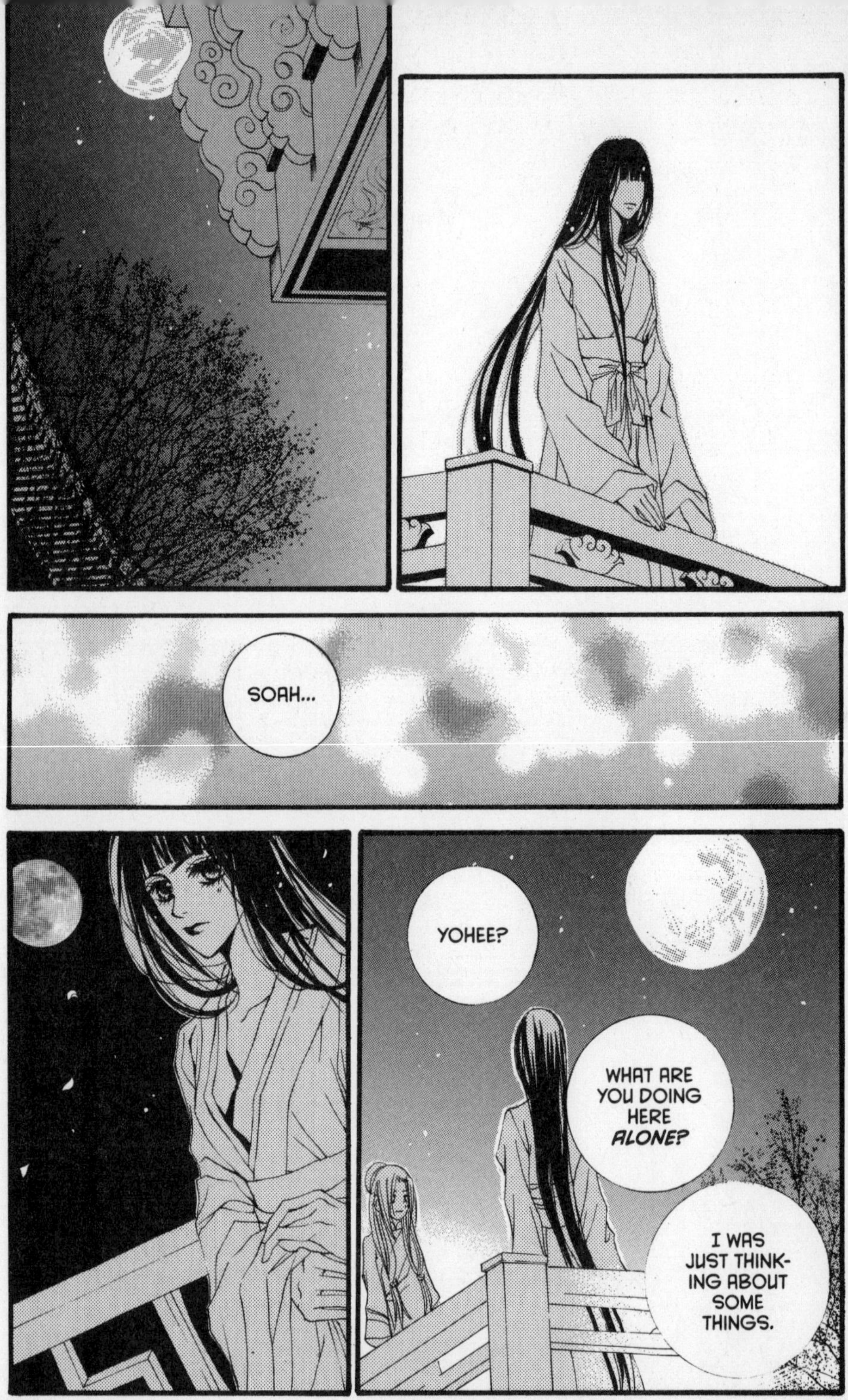
SOAH...
YOHEE?
WHAT ARE YOU DOING HERE *ALONE?*
I WAS JUST THINKING ABOUT SOME THINGS.

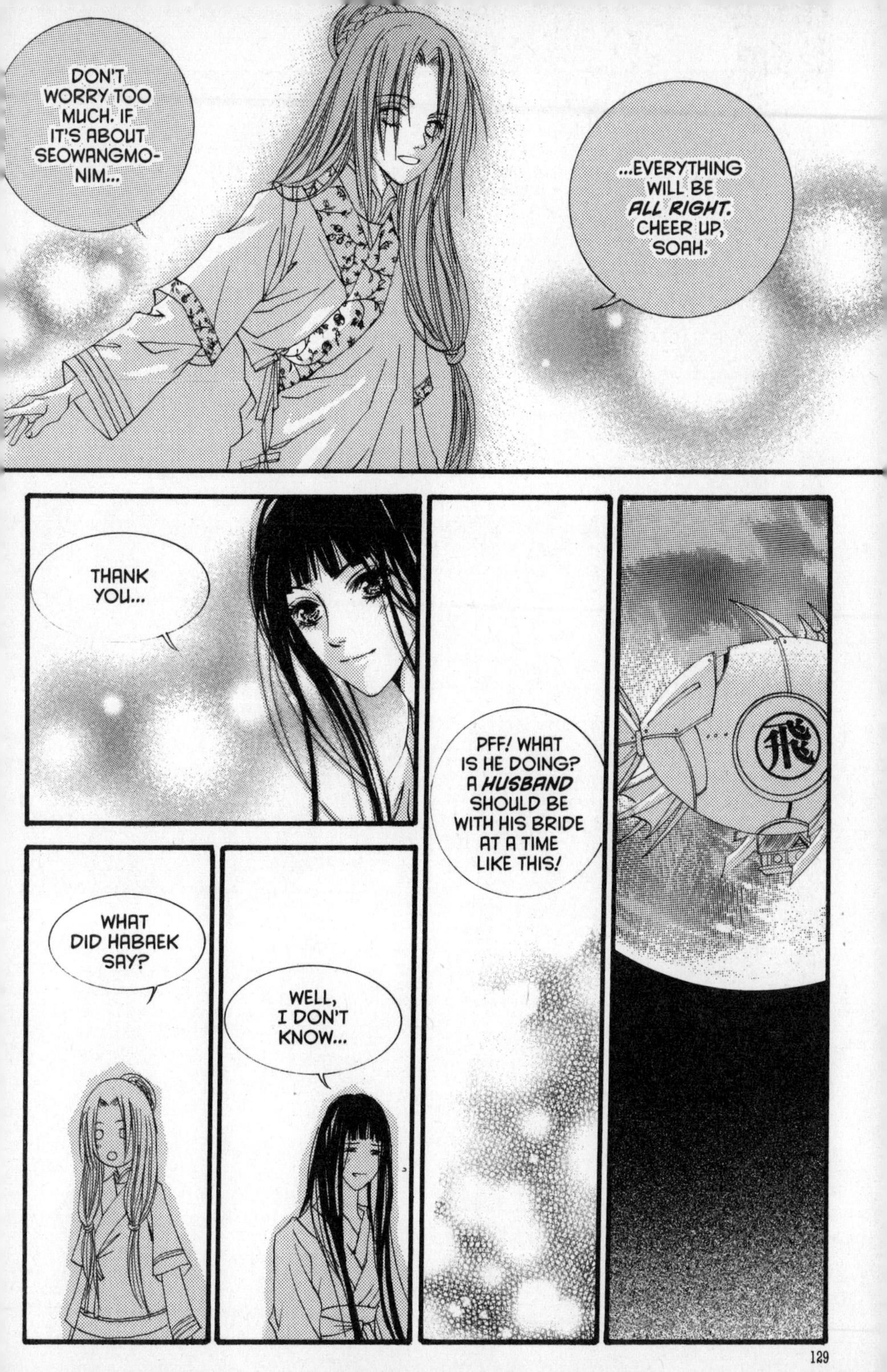
DON'T WORRY TOO MUCH. IF IT'S ABOUT SEOWANGMO-NIM...
...EVERYTHING WILL BE ALL RIGHT. CHEER UP, SOAH.
THANK YOU...
PFF! WHAT IS HE DOING? A HUSBAND SHOULD BE WITH HIS BRIDE AT A TIME LIKE THIS!
飛
WHAT DID HABAEK SAY?
WELL, I DON'T KNOW...

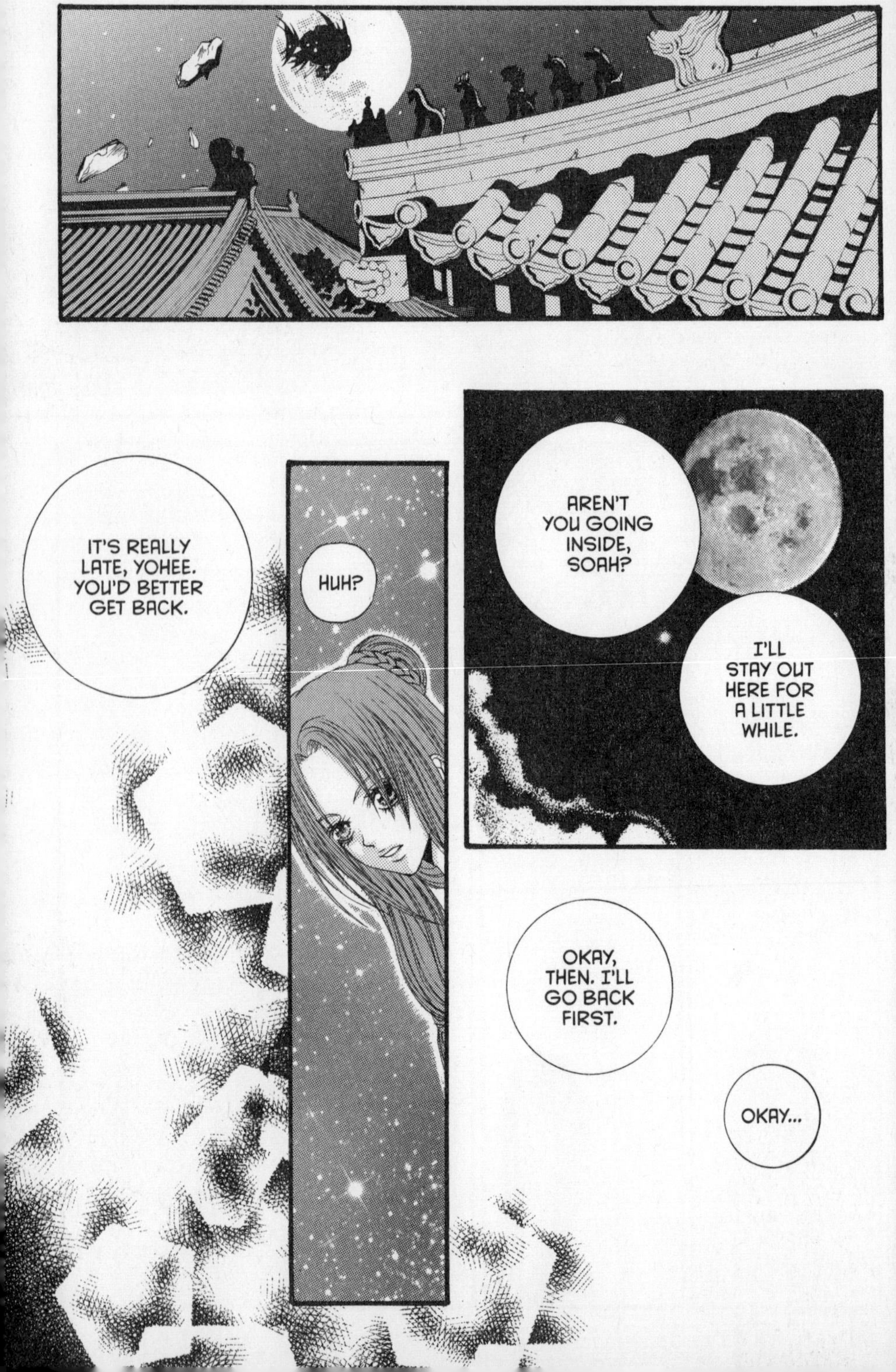
AREN'T YOU GOING INSIDE, SOAH?
I'LL STAY OUT HERE FOR A LITTLE WHILE.
IT'S REALLY LATE, YOHEE. YOU'D BETTER GET BACK.
HUH?
OKAY, THEN. I'LL GO BACK FIRST.
OKAY...

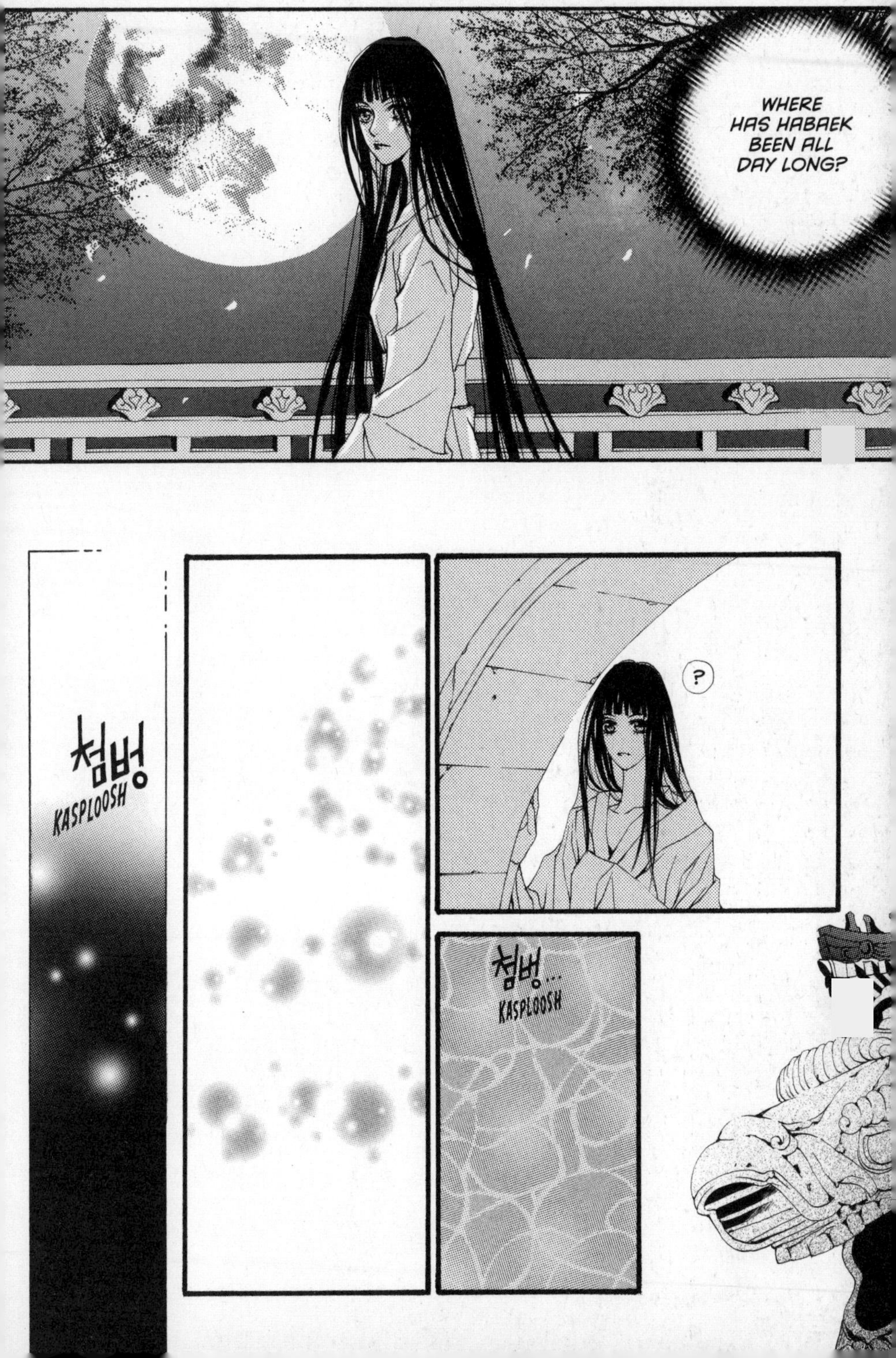
WHERE HAS HABAEK BEEN ALL DAY LONG?
?
첨벙...
KASPLOOSH
첨벙
KASPLOOSH

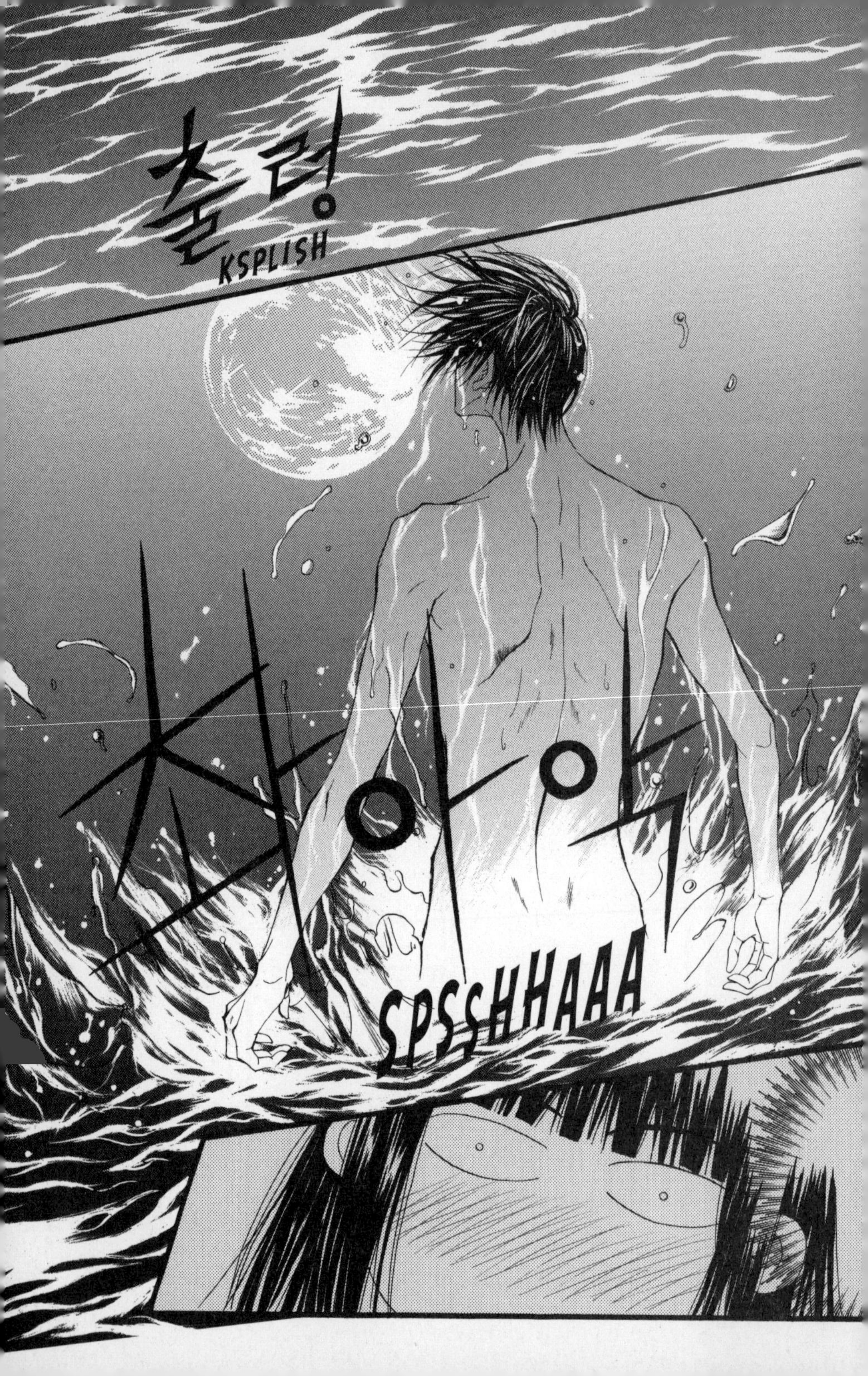
출렁
KSPLISH
쏴아아
SPSSHHAAA

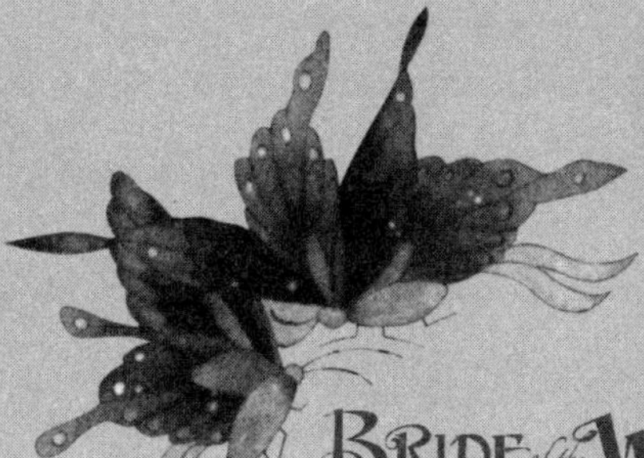

BRIDE of the WATER GOD

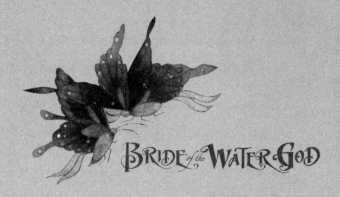

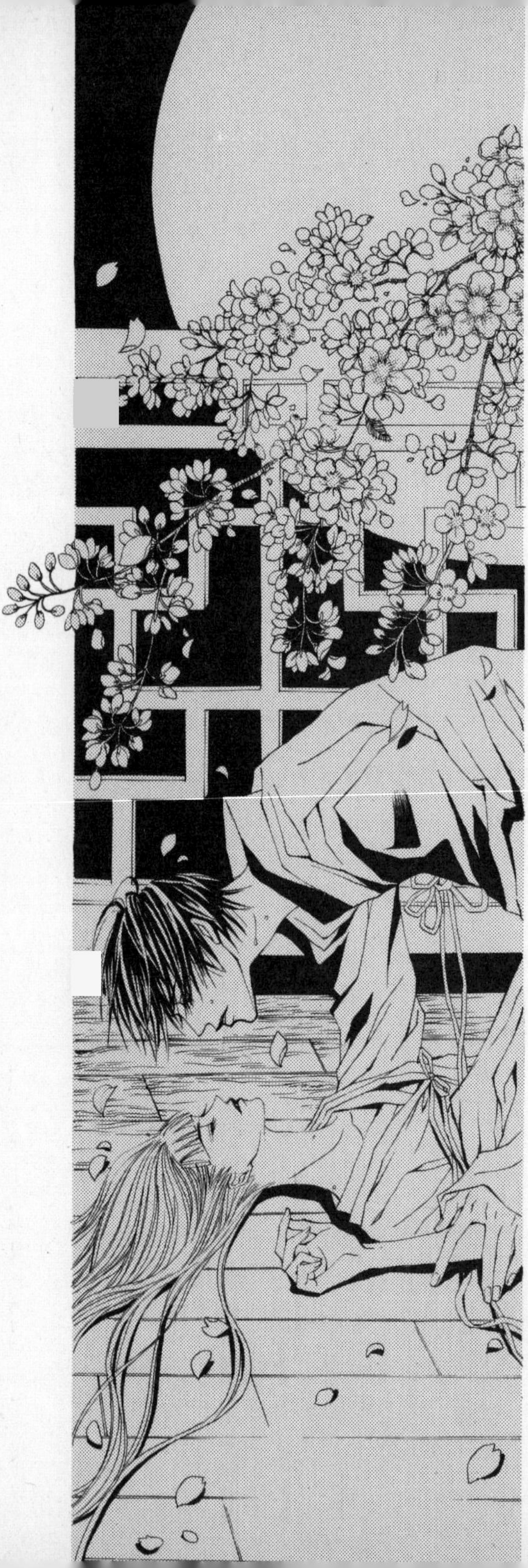

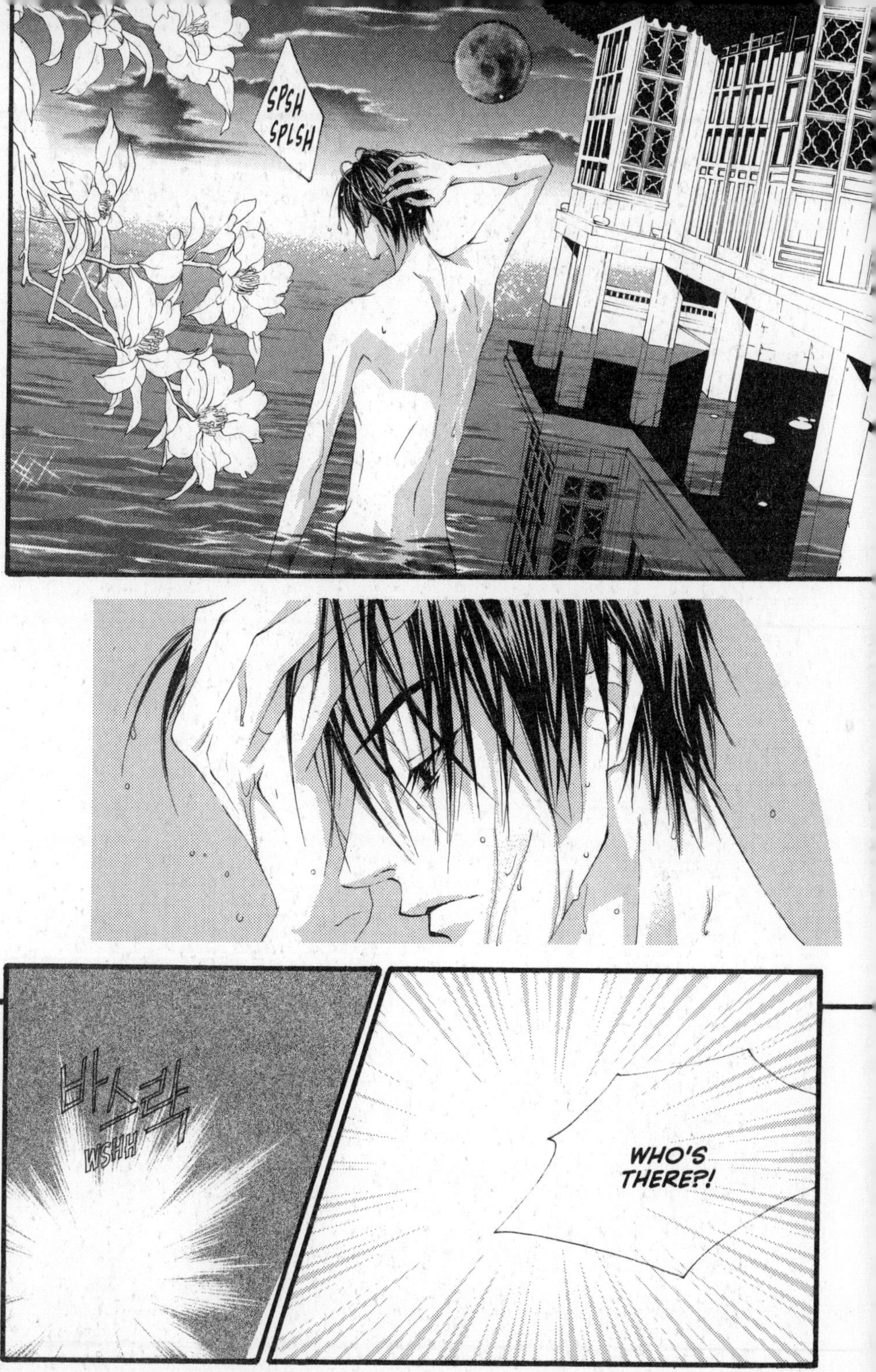
SPSH SPLSH
바스락
WSHH
WHO'S THERE?!

AROUND GUHA WE WANDER ABOUT
THE WIND RISES TO CROSS THE WAVE
WITHIN THIS WAGON OF WATER, HOW CAN I TAKE SHELTER
WHILE RIDING THE TWO DRAGONS THAT FOLLOW ANOTHER?
--FROM "THE POEM OF HABAEK"
 (GUGA POEM / CHOSA STYLE)

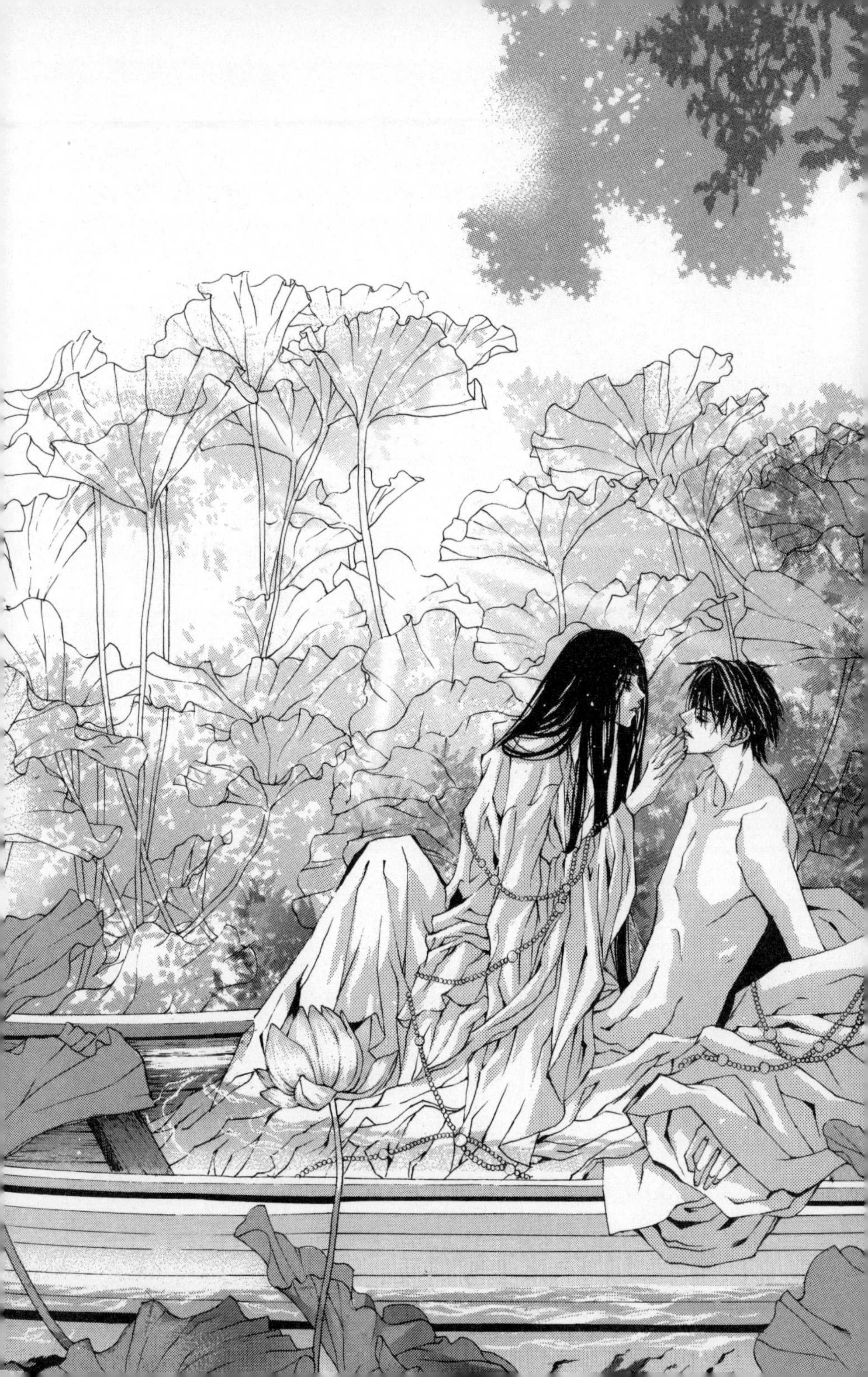

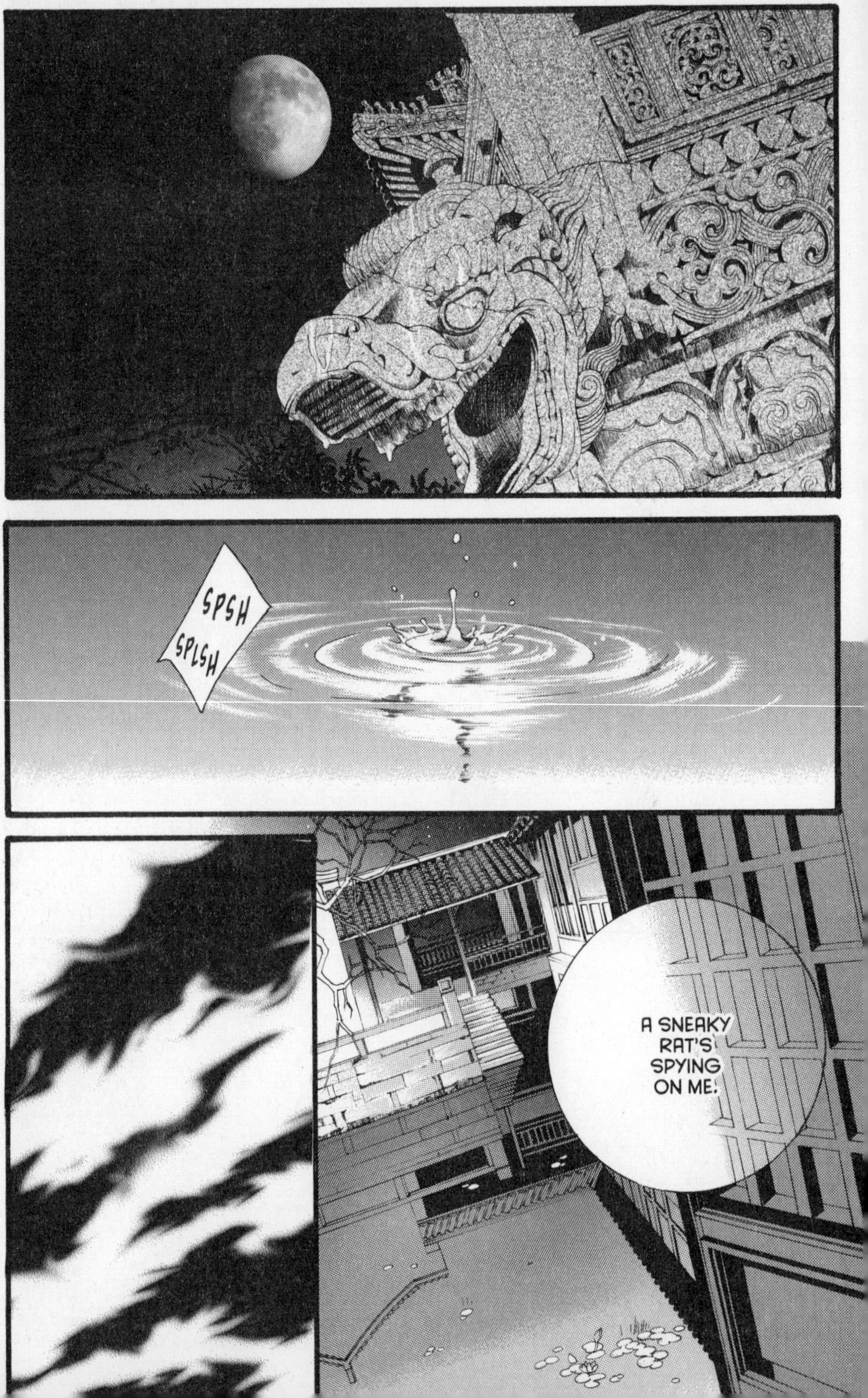
SPSH
SPLSH
A SNEAKY RAT'S SPYING ON ME.

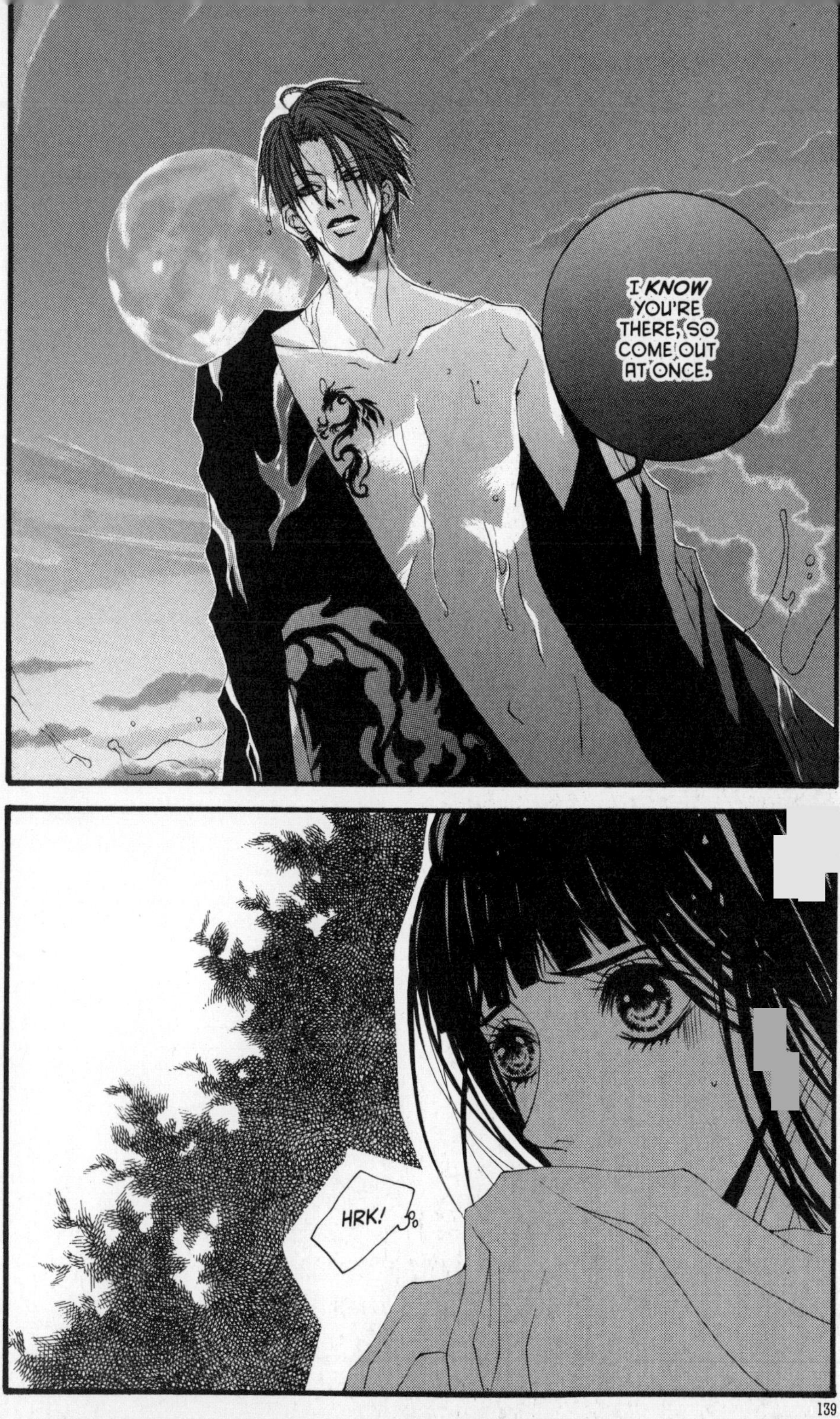
I KNOW YOU'RE THERE, SO COME OUT AT ONCE.
HRK!

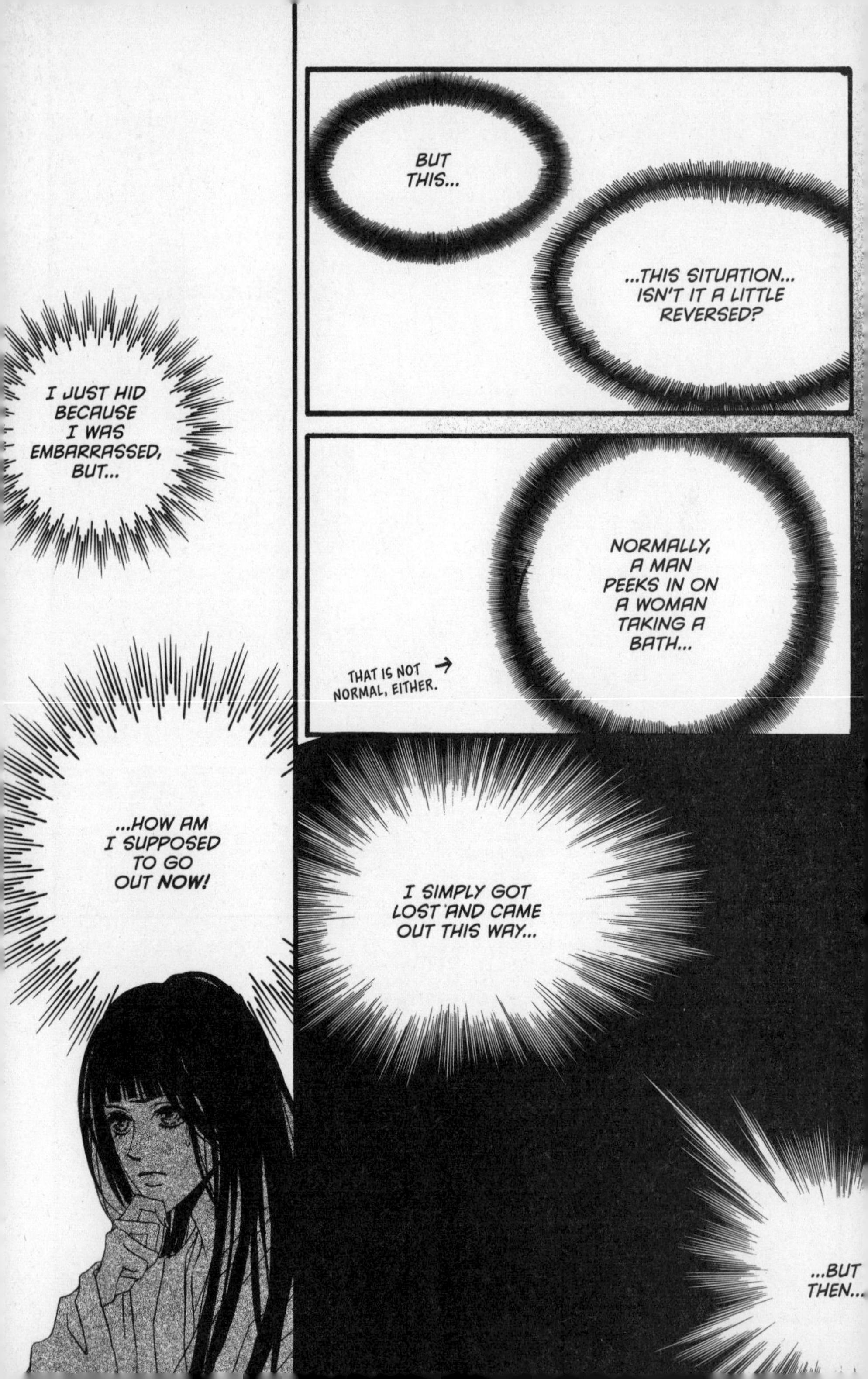
BUT THIS...
...THIS SITUATION... ISN'T IT A LITTLE REVERSED?
NORMALLY, A MAN PEEKS IN ON A WOMAN TAKING A BATH...
THAT IS NOT NORMAL, EITHER.
I SIMPLY GOT LOST AND CAME OUT THIS WAY...
...BUT THEN...
I JUST HID BECAUSE I WAS EMBARRASSED, BUT...
...HOW AM I SUPPOSED TO GO OUT NOW!

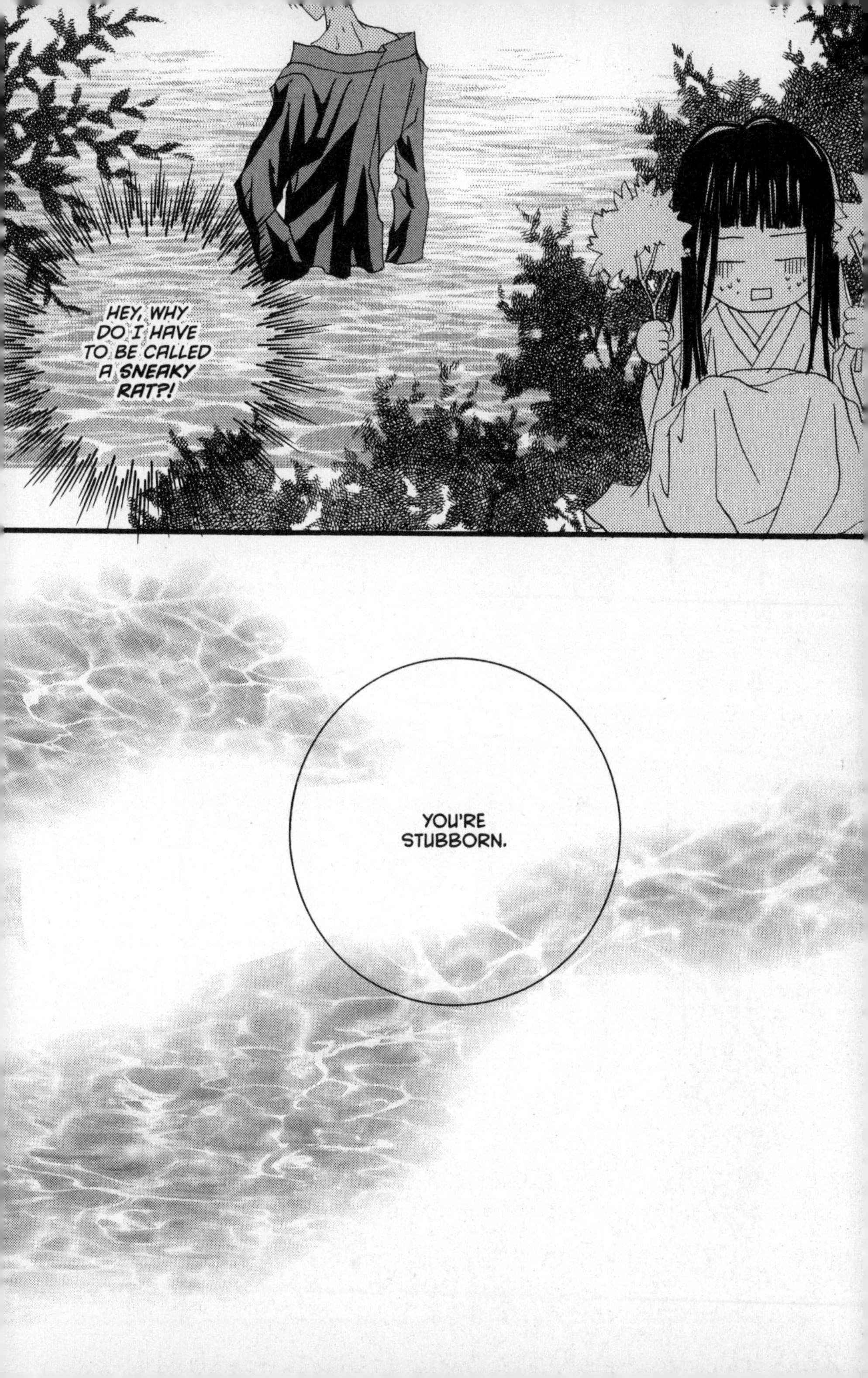
HEY, WHY DO I HAVE TO BE CALLED A SNEAKY RAT?!
YOU'RE STUBBORN.

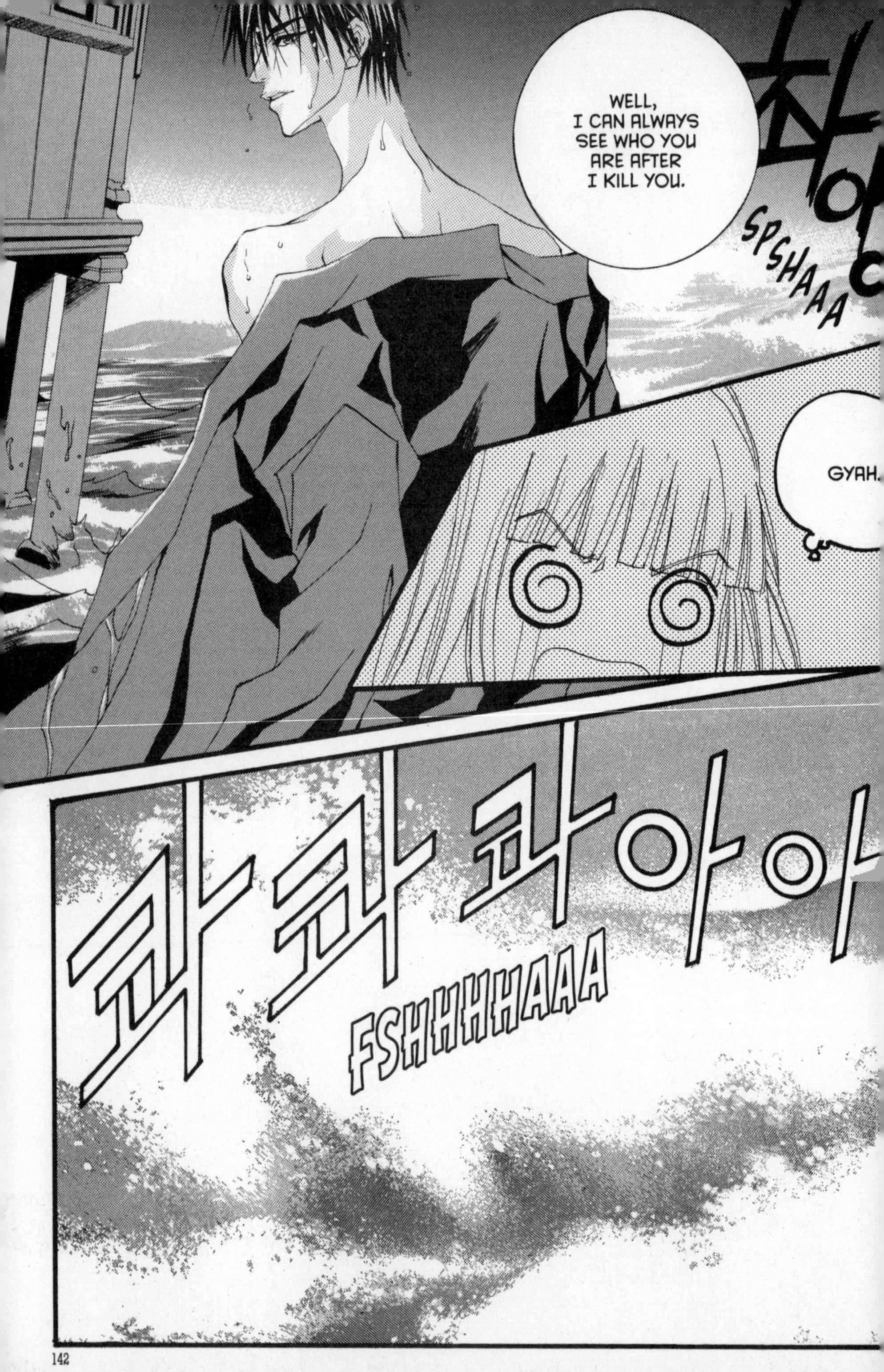
WELL, I CAN ALWAYS SEE WHO YOU ARE AFTER I KILL YOU.
SPSHAAA
GYAH.
콰콰콰아아
FSHHHHAAA

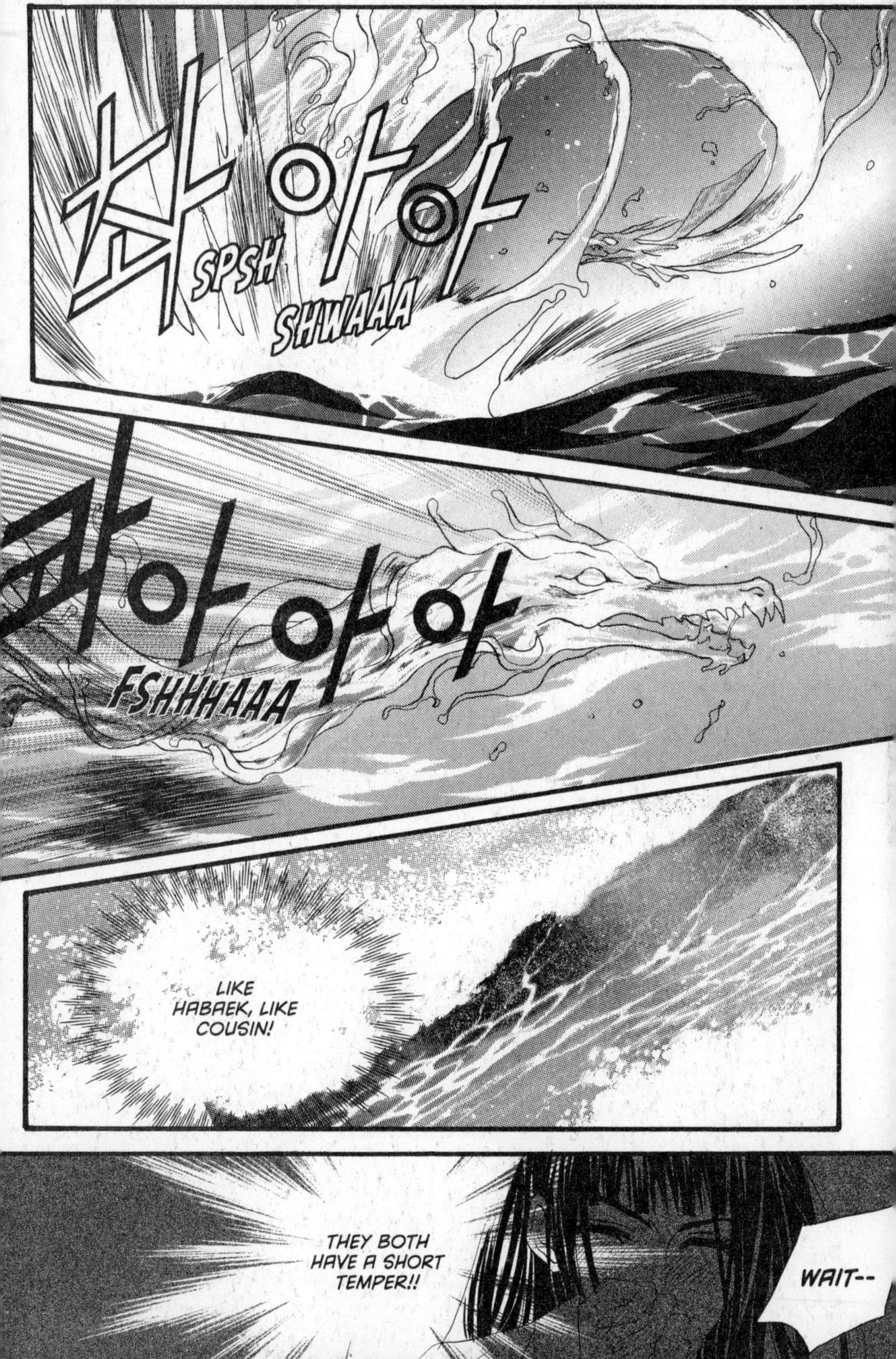
SPSH
SHWAAA
FSHHHAAA
LIKE HABAEK, LIKE COUSIN!
THEY BOTH HAVE A SHORT TEMPER!!
WAIT--

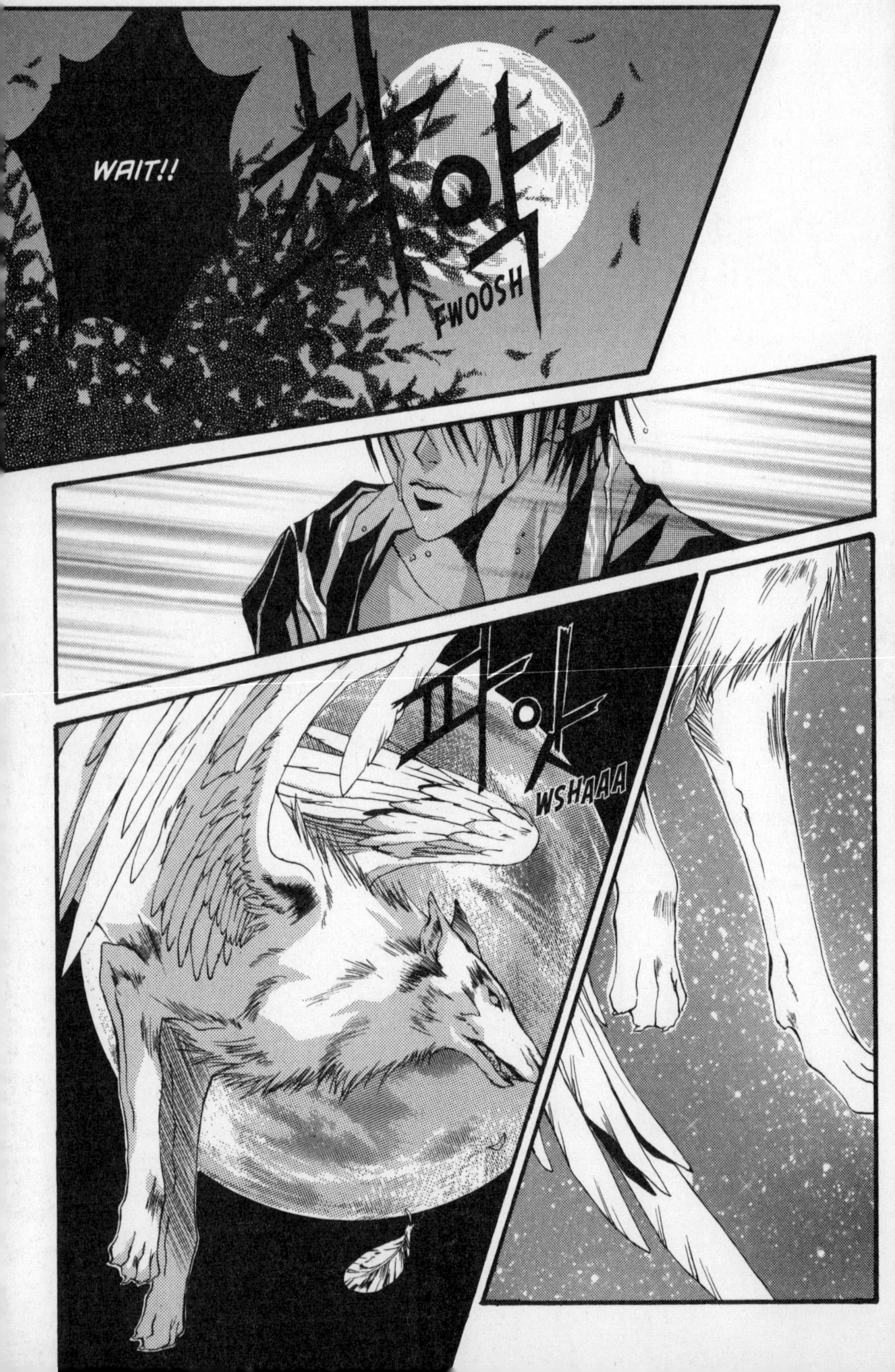
WAIT!!
FWOOSH
WSHAAA

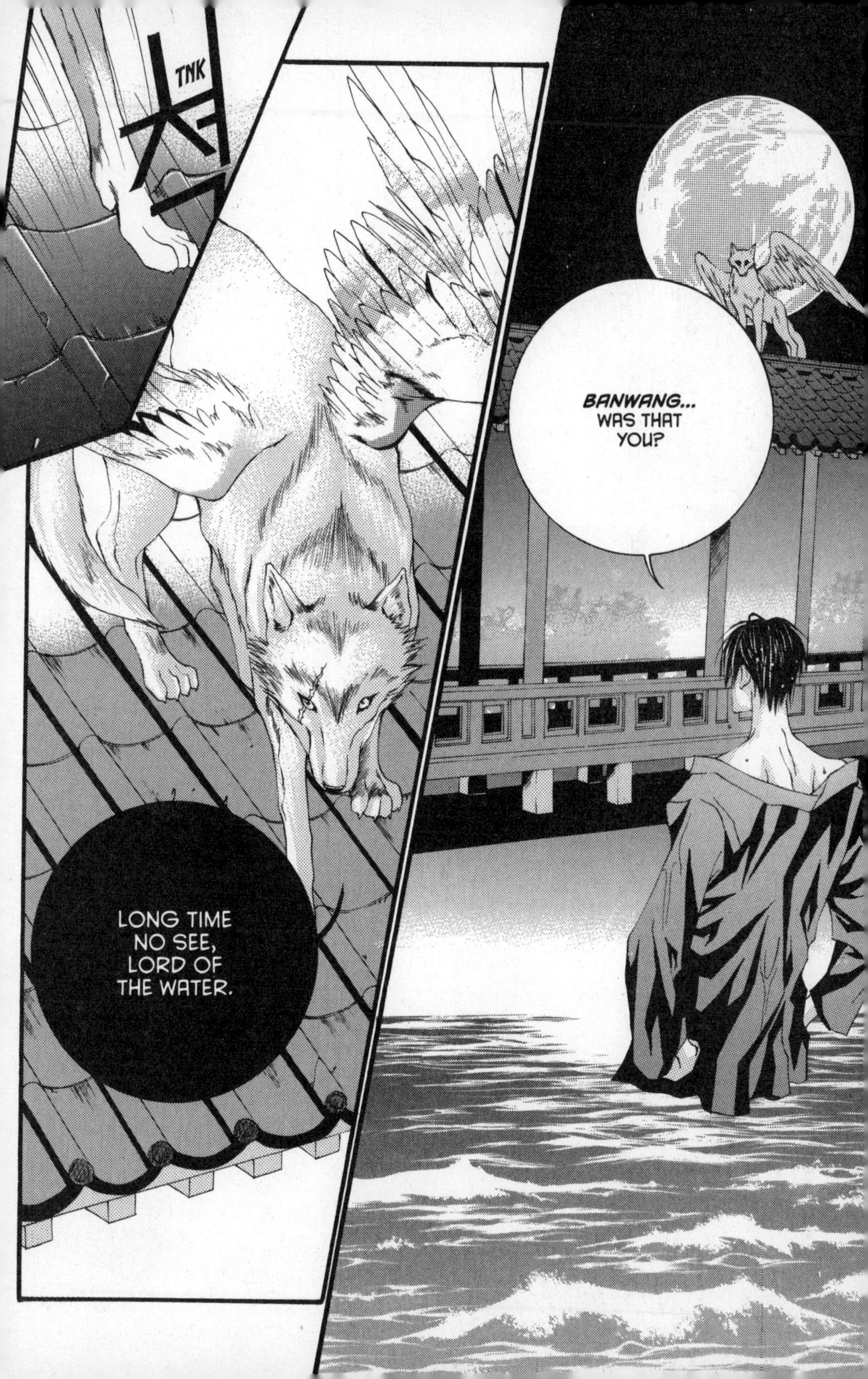

BANWANG...
WAS THAT
YOU?
TNK
LONG TIME
NO SEE,
LORD OF
THE WATER.

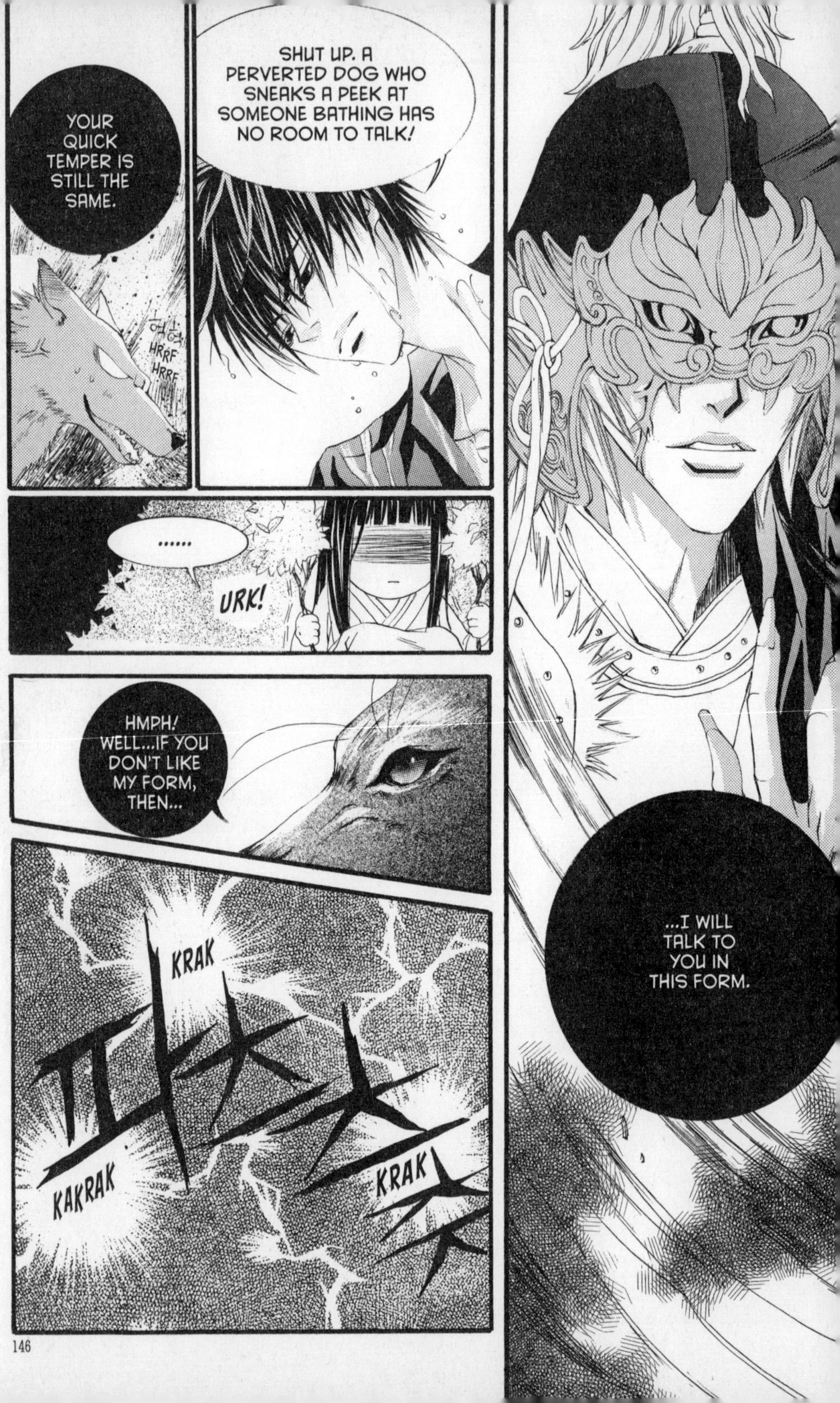
YOUR QUICK TEMPER IS STILL THE SAME.
SHUT UP. A PERVERTED DOG WHO SNEAKS A PEEK AT SOMEONE BATHING HAS NO ROOM TO TALK!
HRRF HRRF
......
URK!
HMPH! WELL...IF YOU DON'T LIKE MY FORM, THEN...
KRAK
KAKRAK
KRAK
...I WILL TALK TO YOU IN THIS FORM.

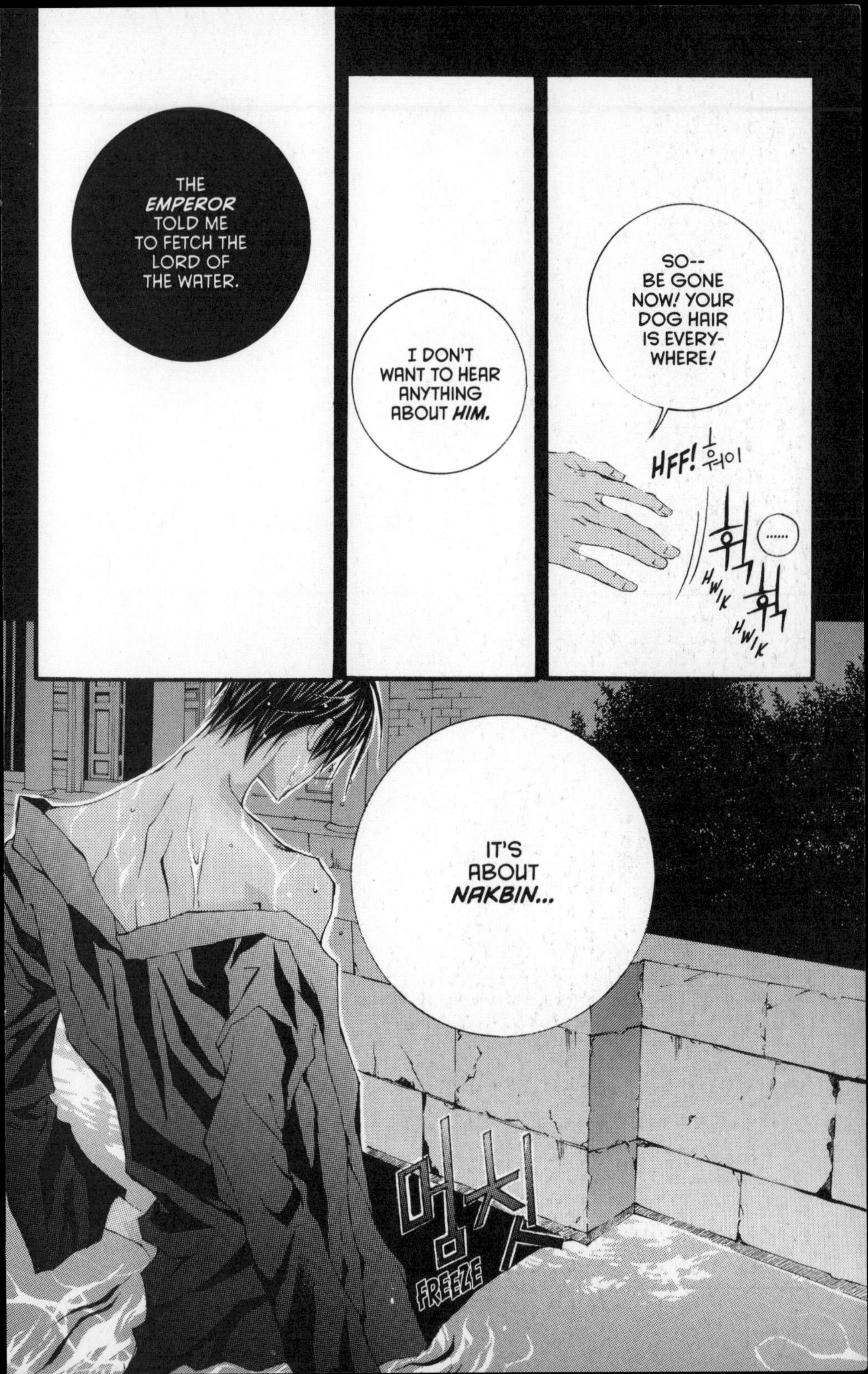

THE EMPEROR TOLD ME TO FETCH THE LORD OF THE WATER.
I DON'T WANT TO HEAR ANYTHING ABOUT HIM.
SO-- BE GONE NOW! YOUR DOG HAIR IS EVERY-WHERE!
HFF! 휘이
......
휙 HWIK
휙 HWIK
IT'S ABOUT NAKBIN...
멈칫
FREEZE

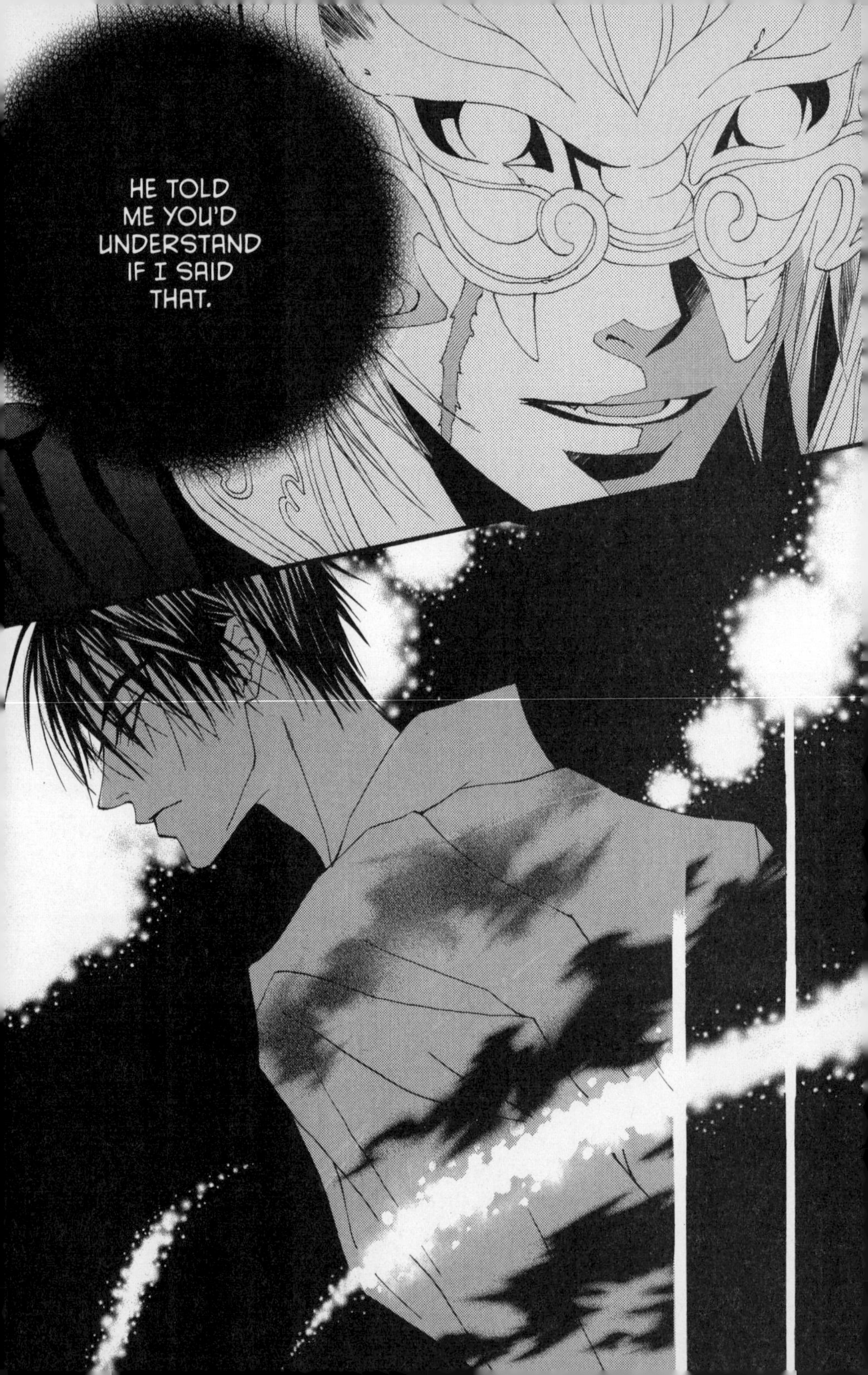
HE TOLD ME YOU'D UNDERSTAND IF I SAID THAT.

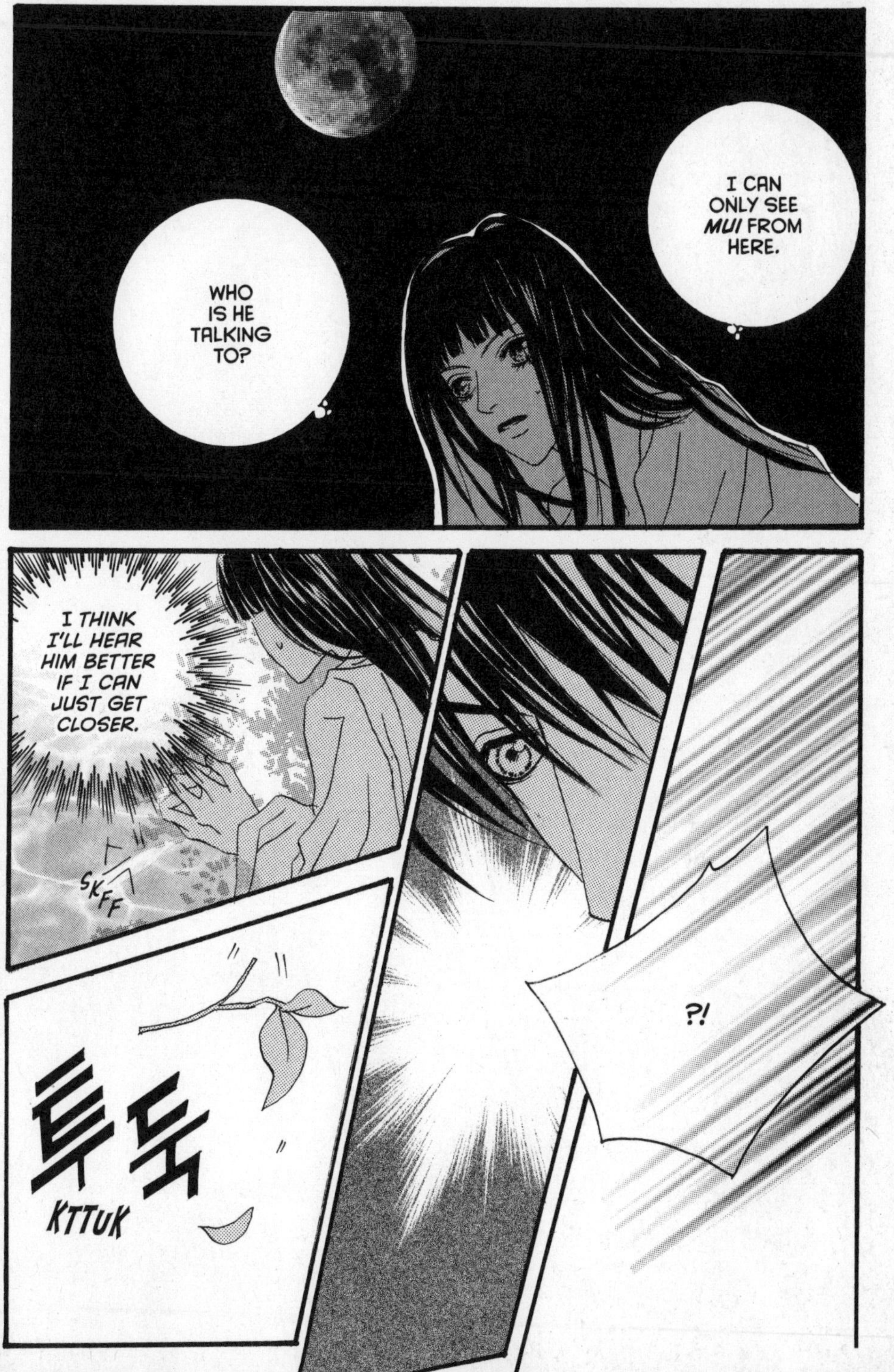
I CAN ONLY SEE MUI FROM HERE.
WHO IS HE TALKING TO?
I THINK I'LL HEAR HIM BETTER IF I CAN JUST GET CLOSER.
SKFF
?!
투둑
KTTUK

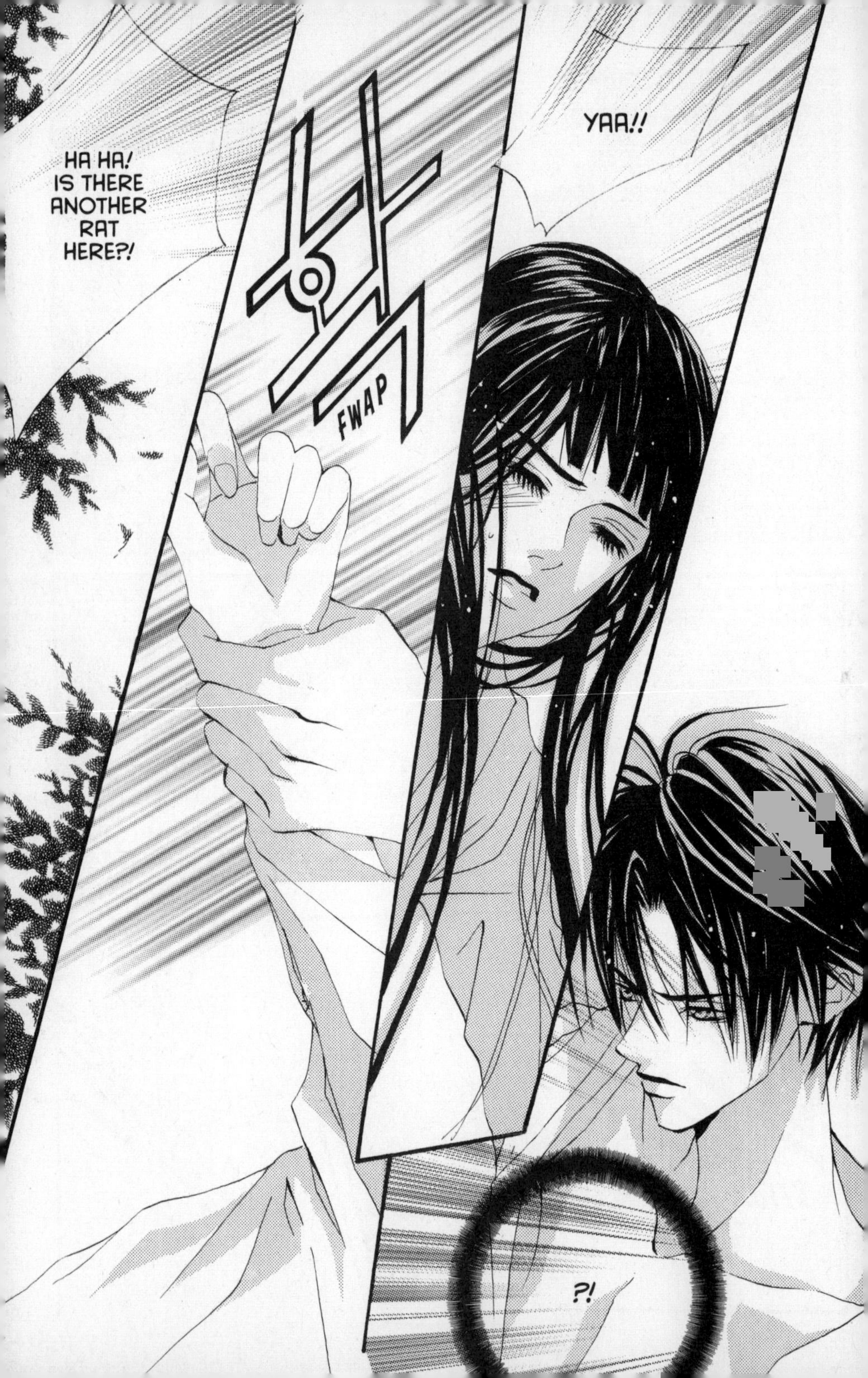
YAA!!
HA HA! IS THERE ANOTHER RAT HERE?!
FWAP
?!

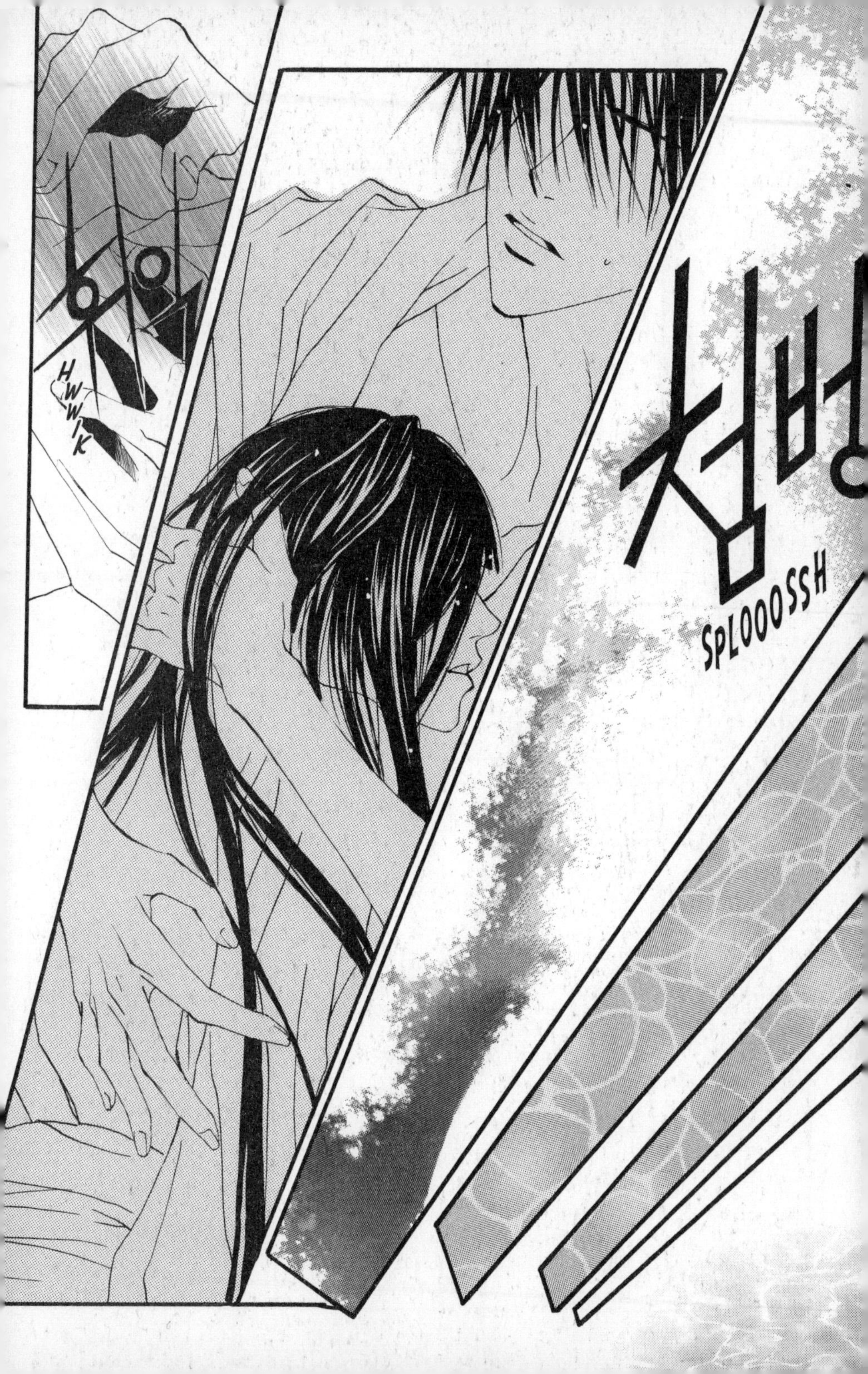

HWWIK
첨벙
SPLOOOSSH

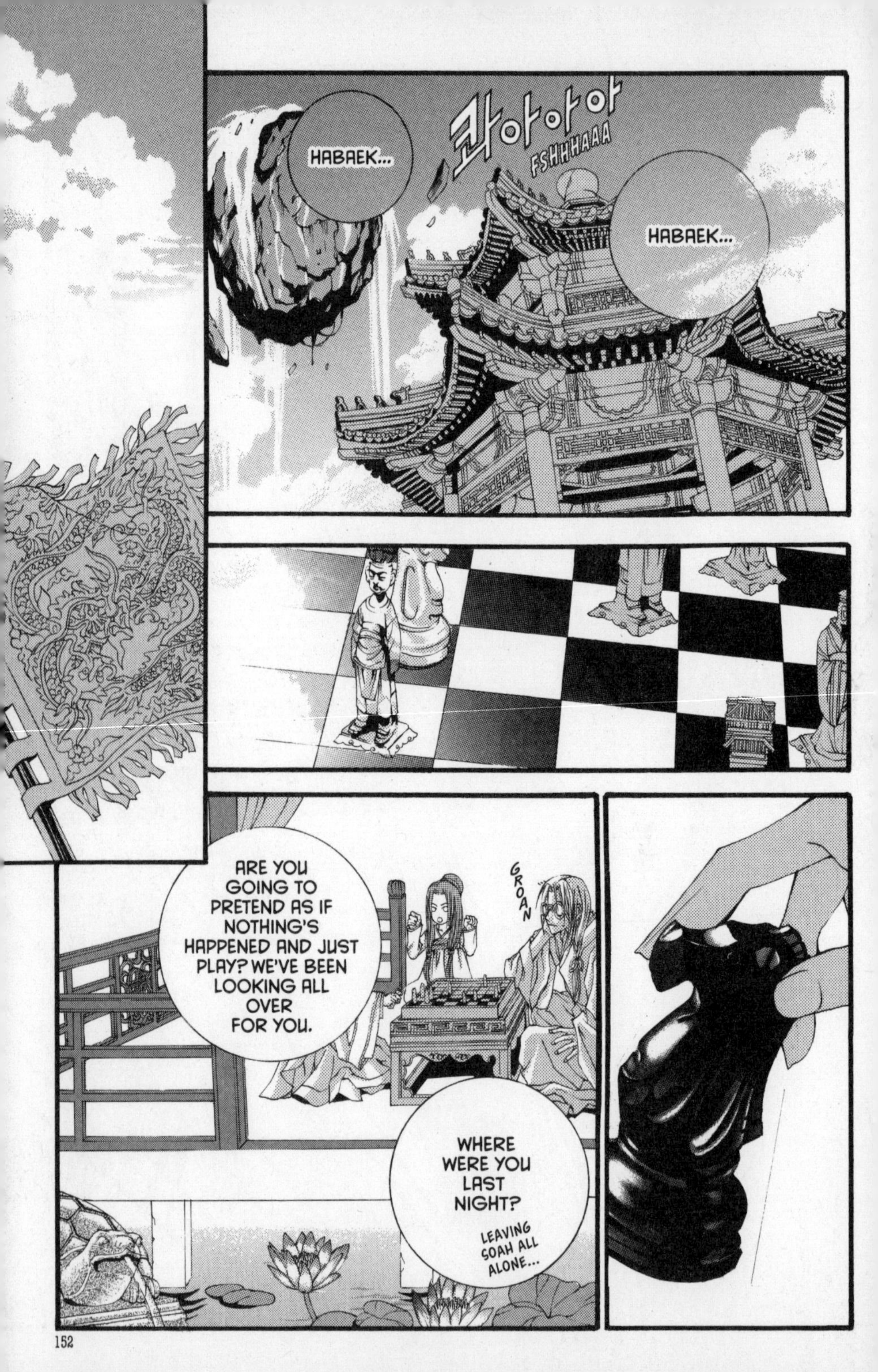

HABAEK...
콰아아아
FSHHHAAA
HABAEK...
ARE YOU GOING TO PRETEND AS IF NOTHING'S HAPPENED AND JUST PLAY? WE'VE BEEN LOOKING ALL OVER FOR YOU.
GROAN
WHERE WERE YOU LAST NIGHT?
LEAVING SOAH ALL ALONE...

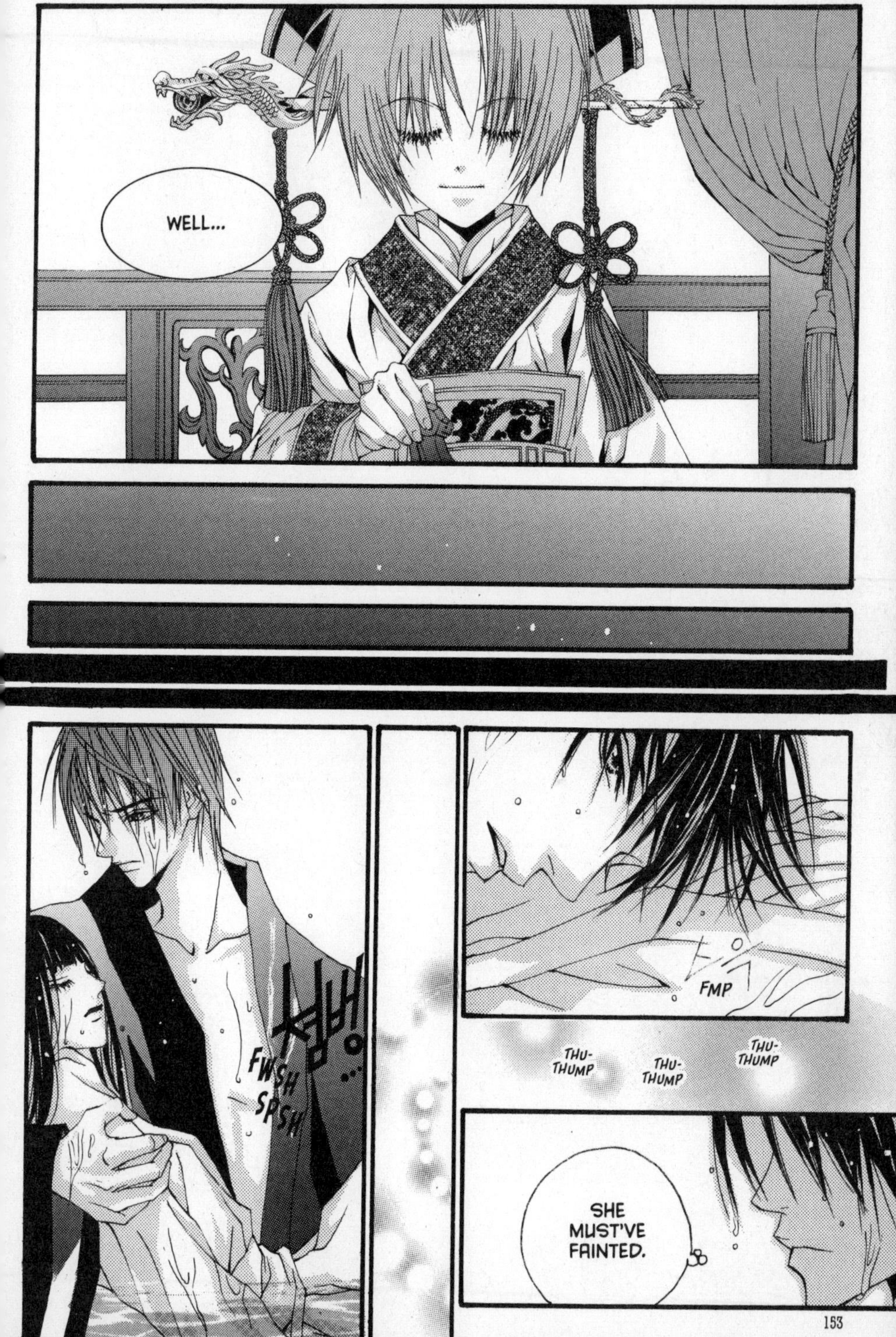
WELL...
FWSH SPSH!
FMP
THU-THUMP
THU-THUMP
THU-THUMP
SHE MUST'VE FAINTED.

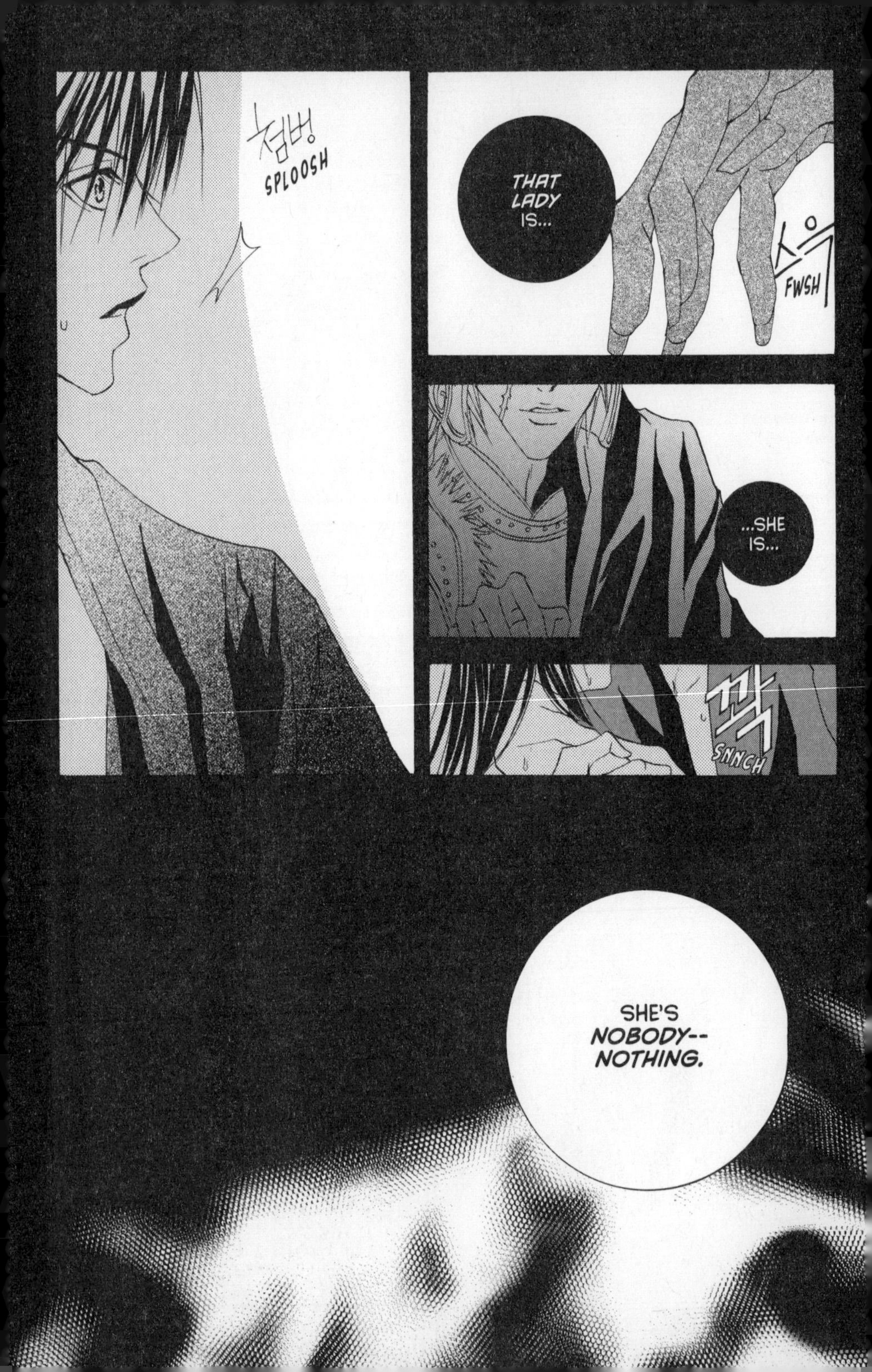
첨벙
SPLOOSH
THAT LADY IS...
스윽
FWSH
...SHE IS...
SNNCH
SHE'S *NOBODY--NOTHING.*

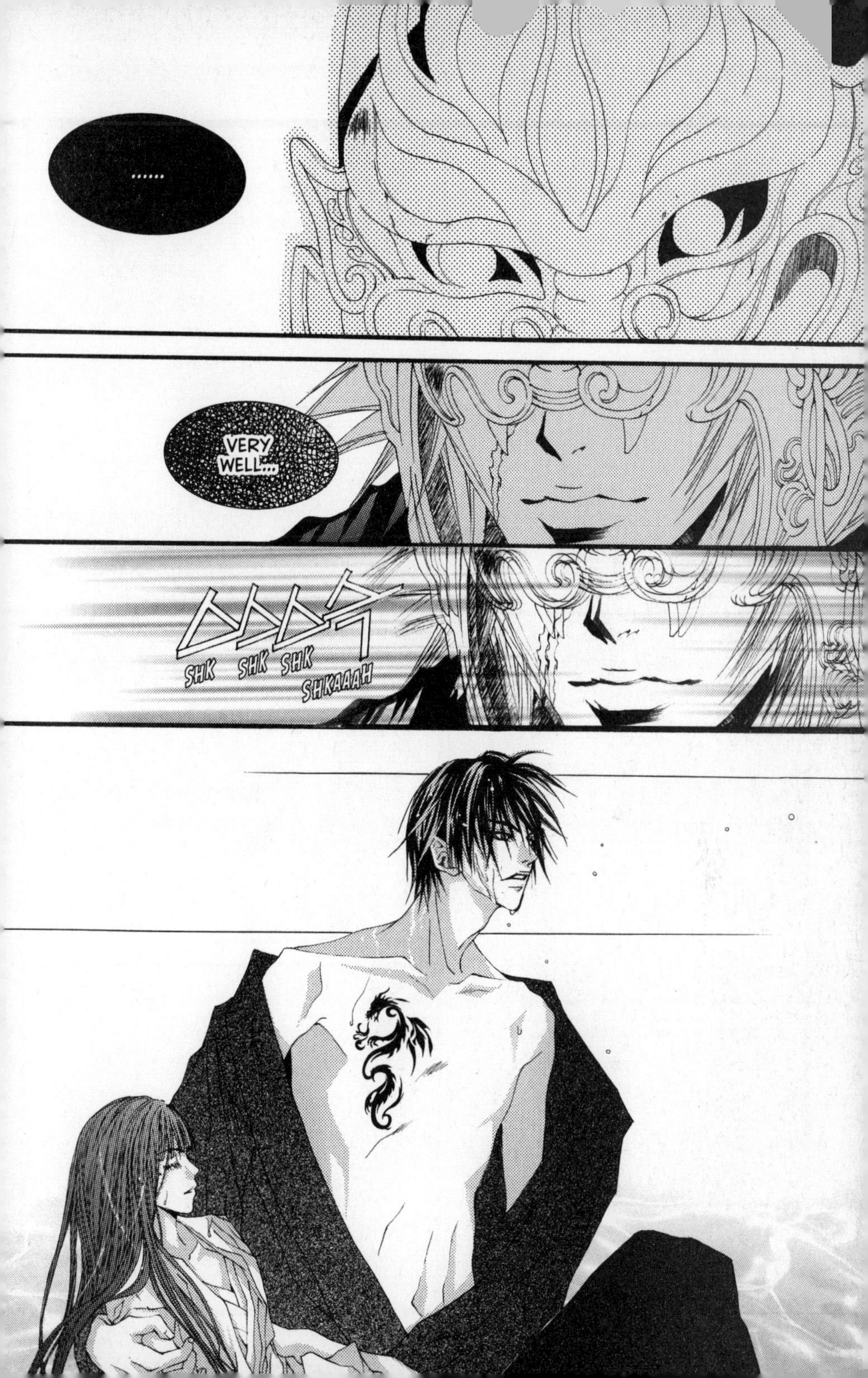
……
VERY WELL…
SHK SHK SHK SHKAAAH

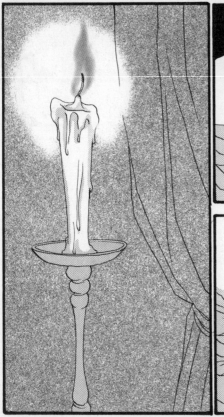

WHO IS THIS?

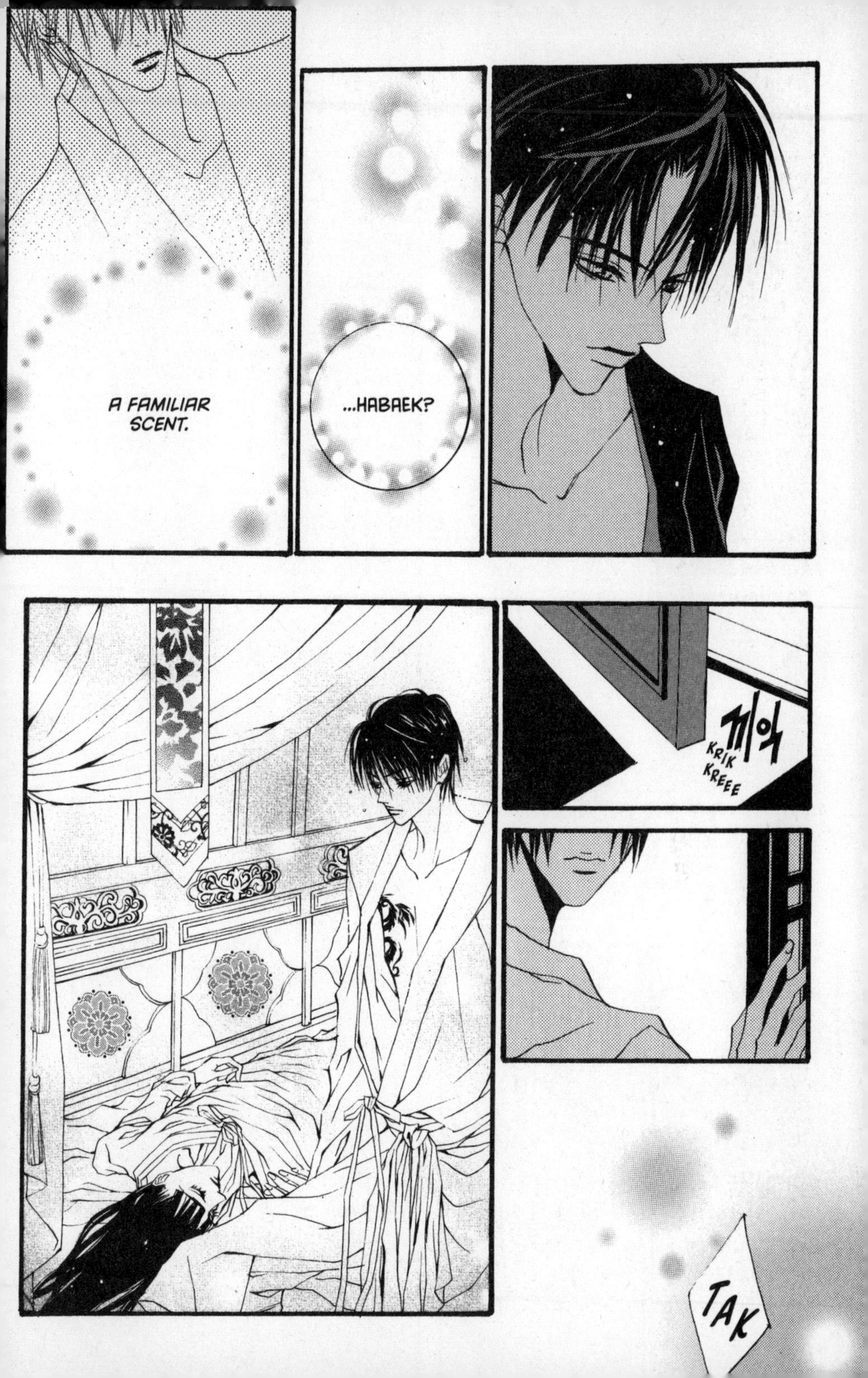
A FAMILIAR SCENT.
...HABAEK?
끼익
KRIK KREEE
TAK

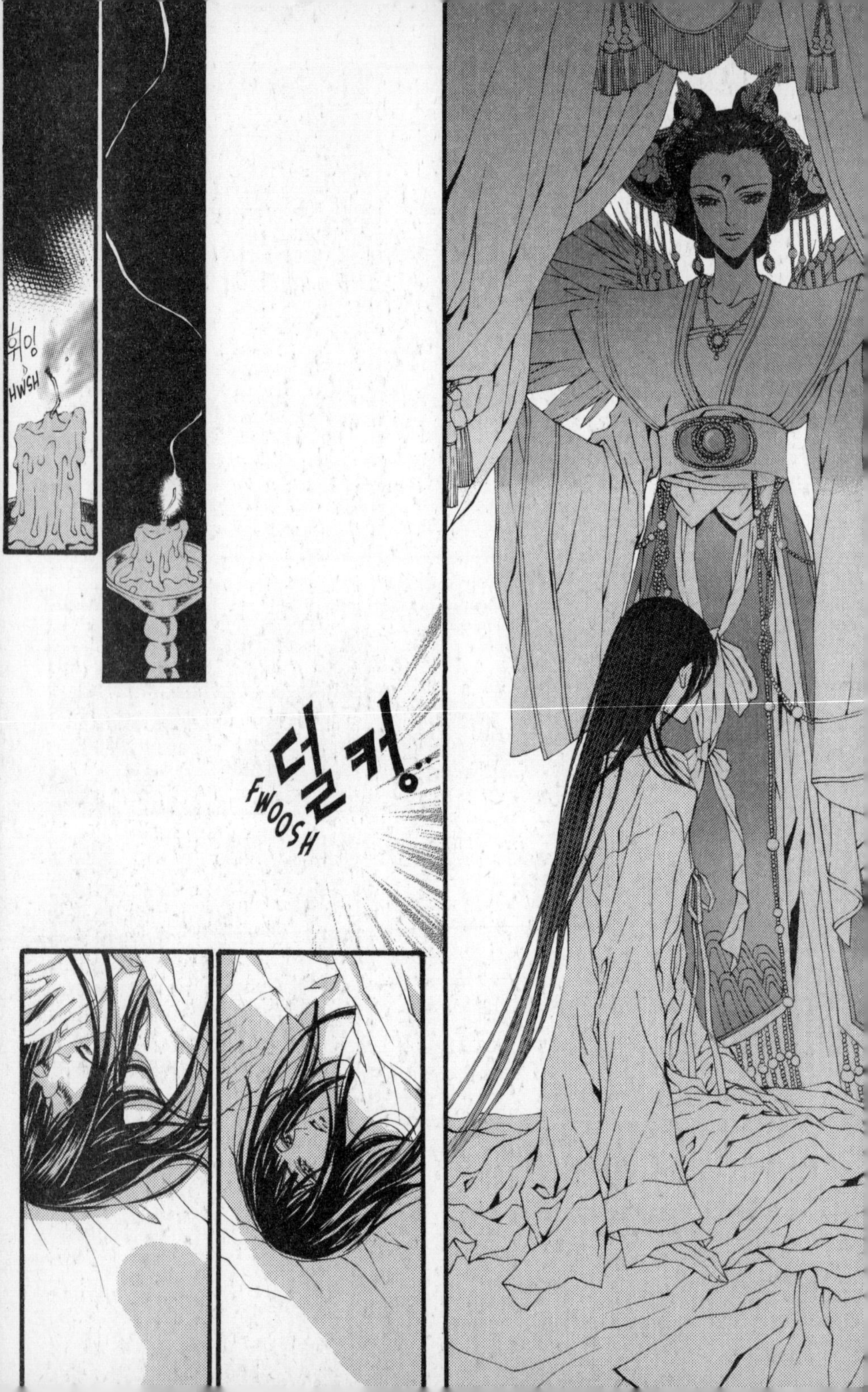
휘잉
HWSH
덜컥
FWOOSH

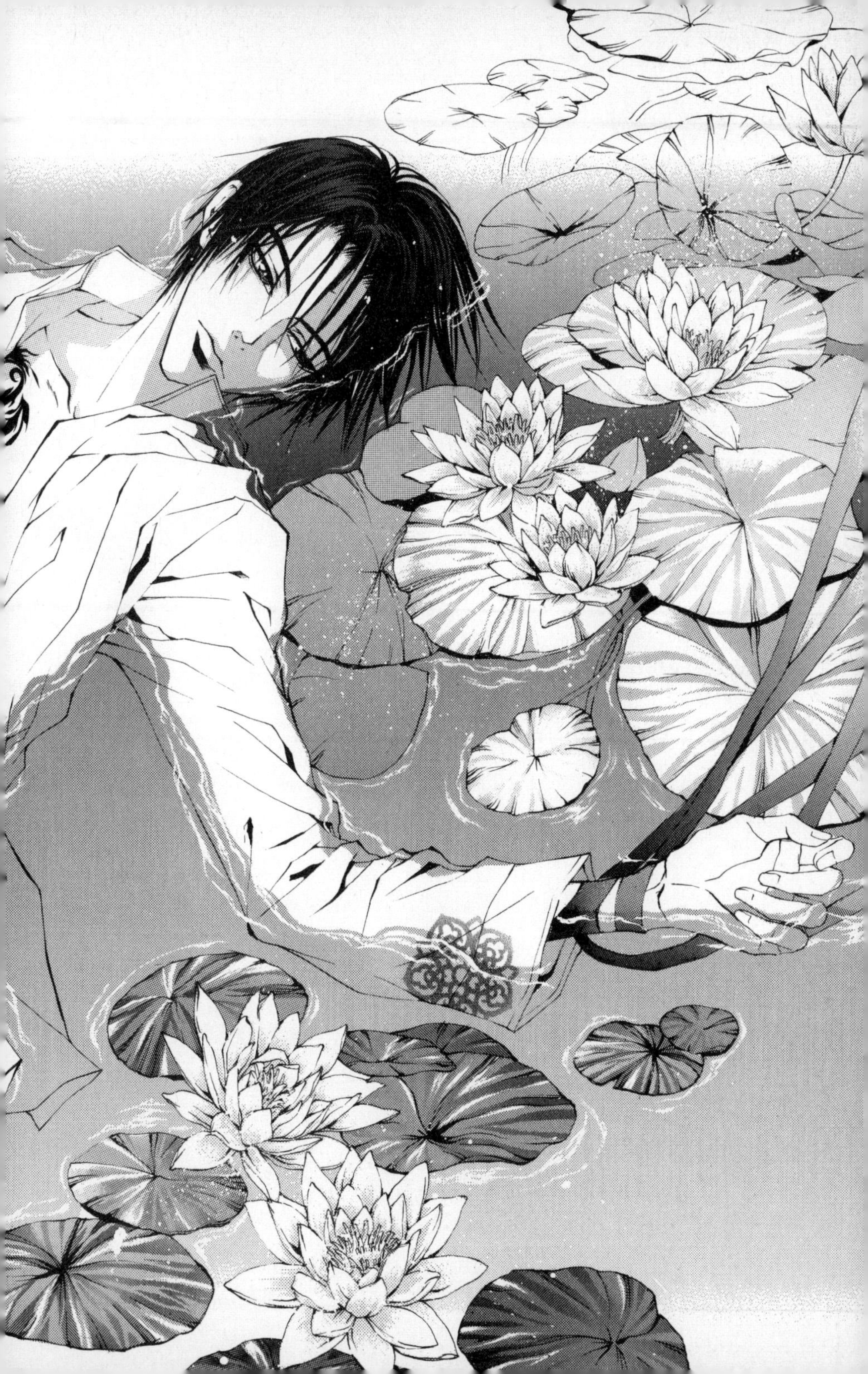

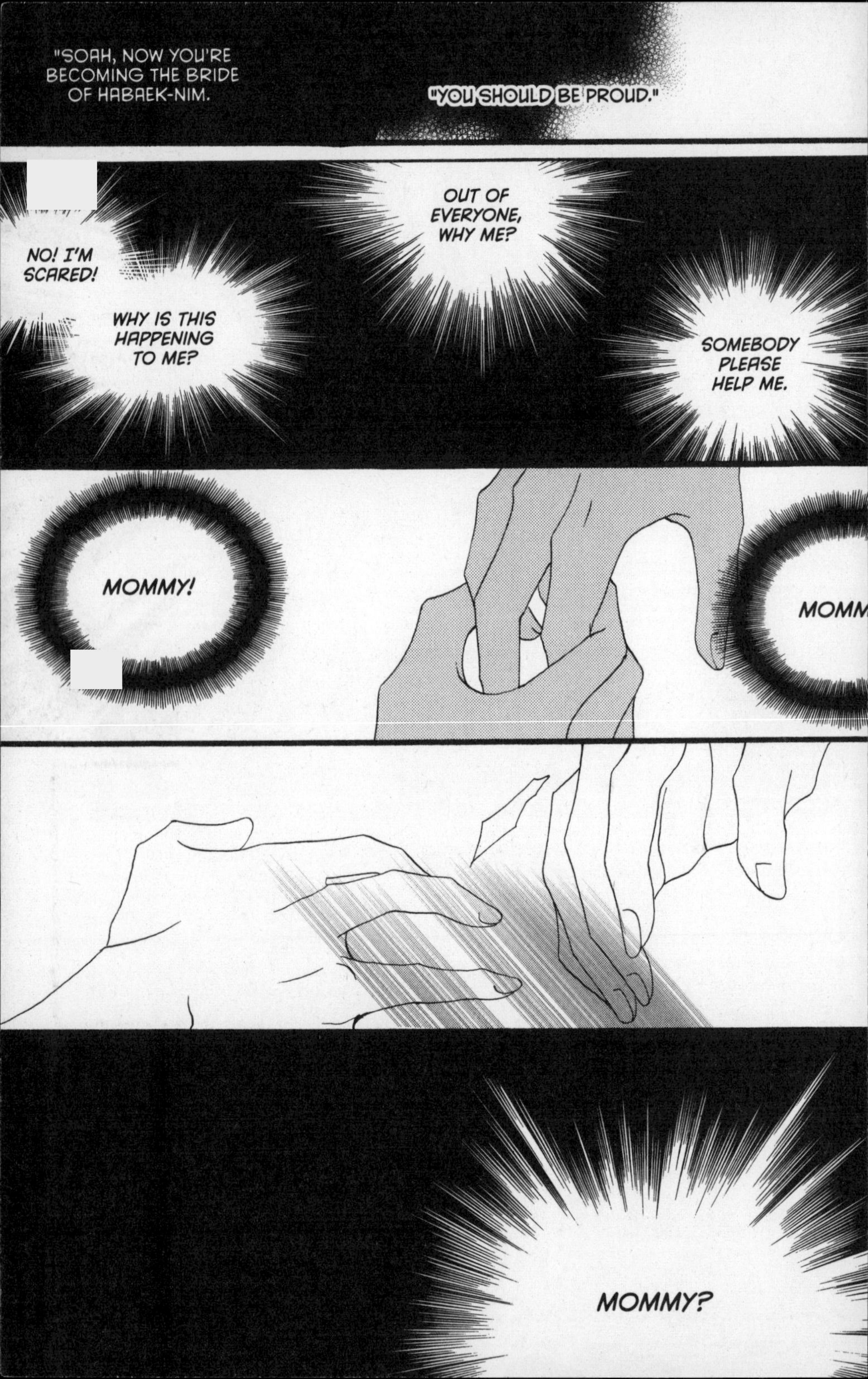
"SOAH, NOW YOU'RE BECOMING THE BRIDE OF HABAEK-NIM.
"YOU SHOULD BE PROUD."
NO! I'M SCARED!
WHY IS THIS HAPPENING TO ME?
OUT OF EVERYONE, WHY ME?
SOMEBODY PLEASE HELP ME.
MOMMY!
MOMMY?

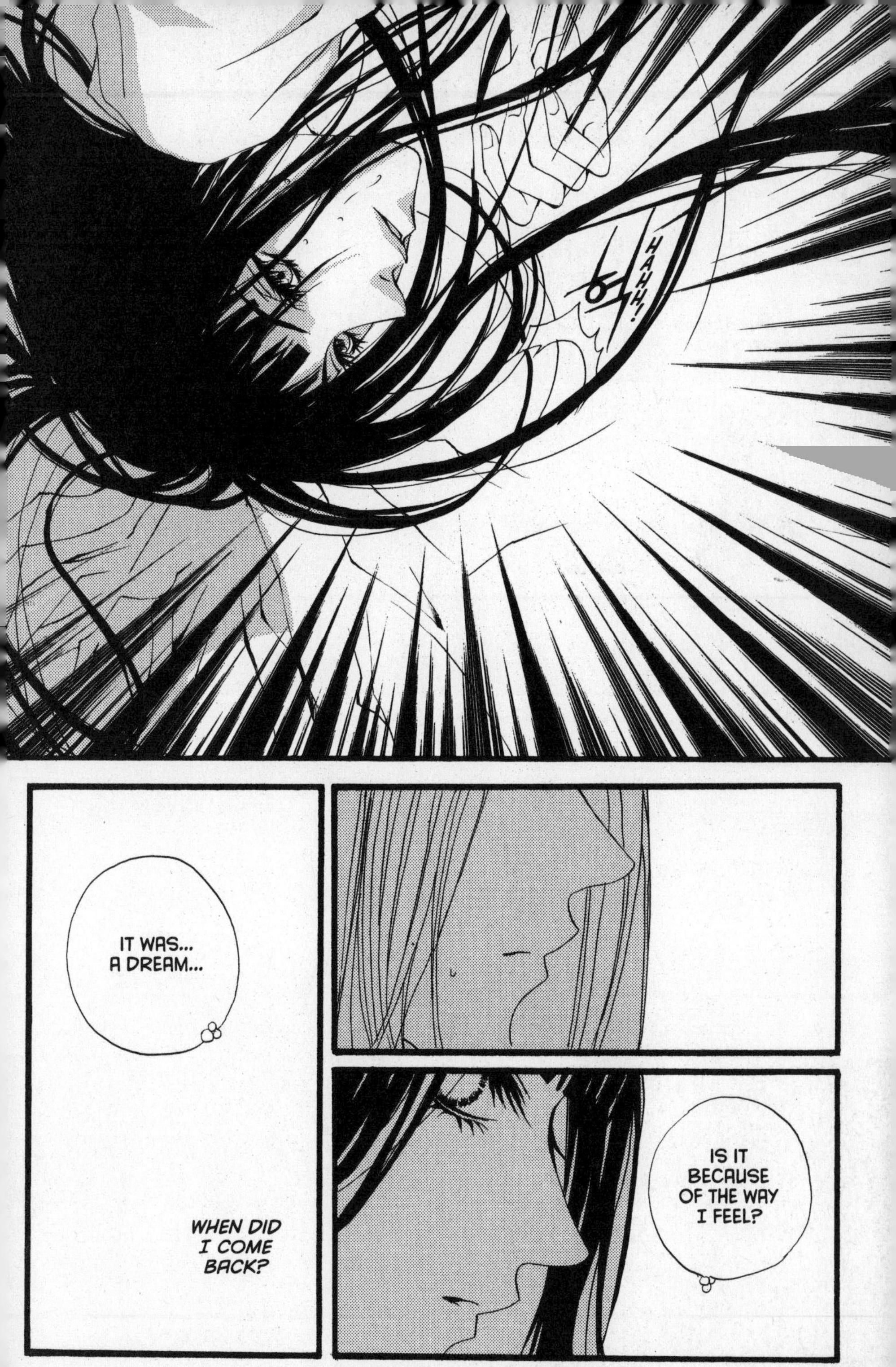
HAHH!
IT WAS... A DREAM...
WHEN DID I COME BACK?
IS IT BECAUSE OF THE WAY I FEEL?

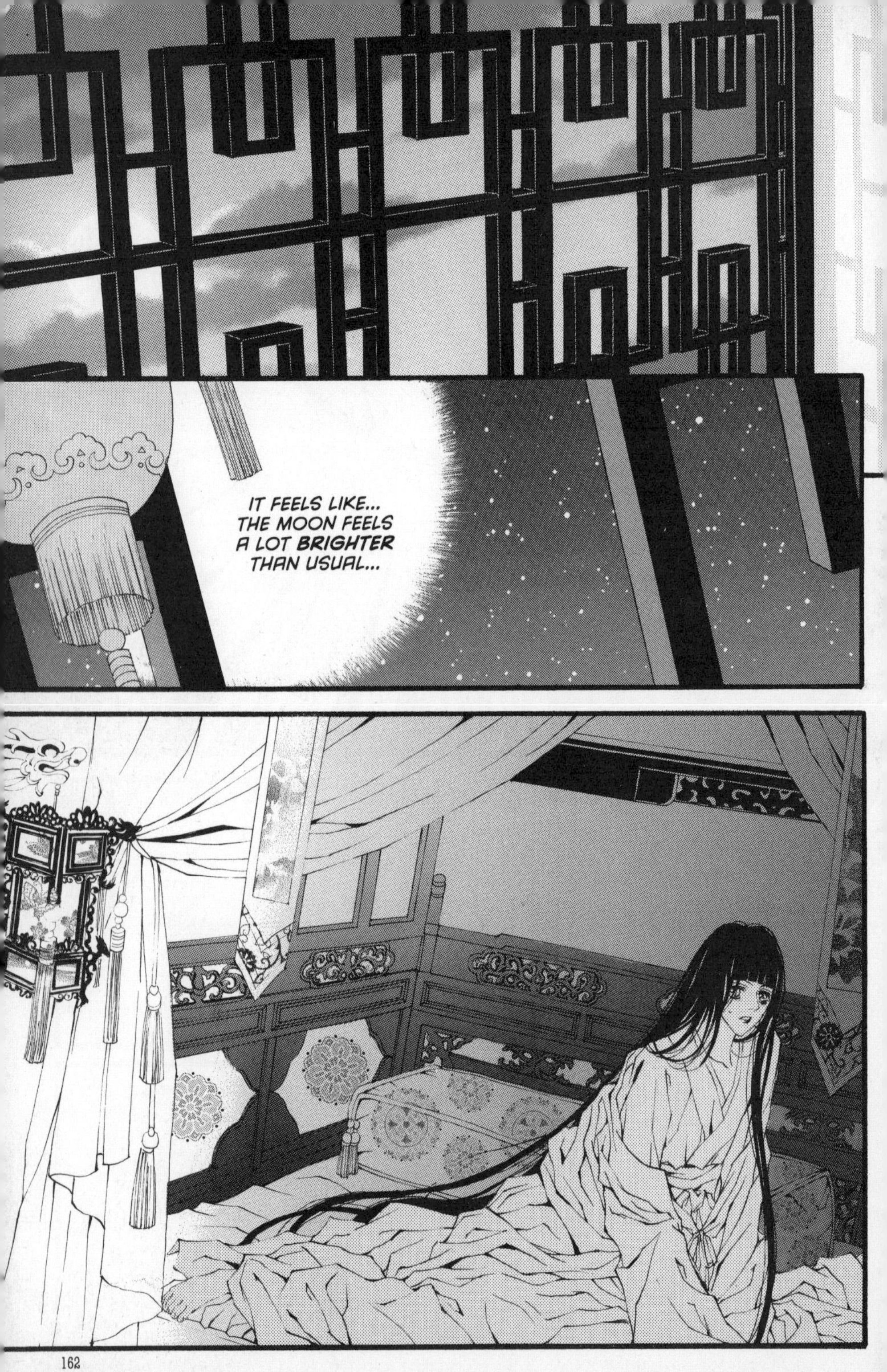
IT FEELS LIKE... THE MOON FEELS A LOT BRIGHTER THAN USUAL...

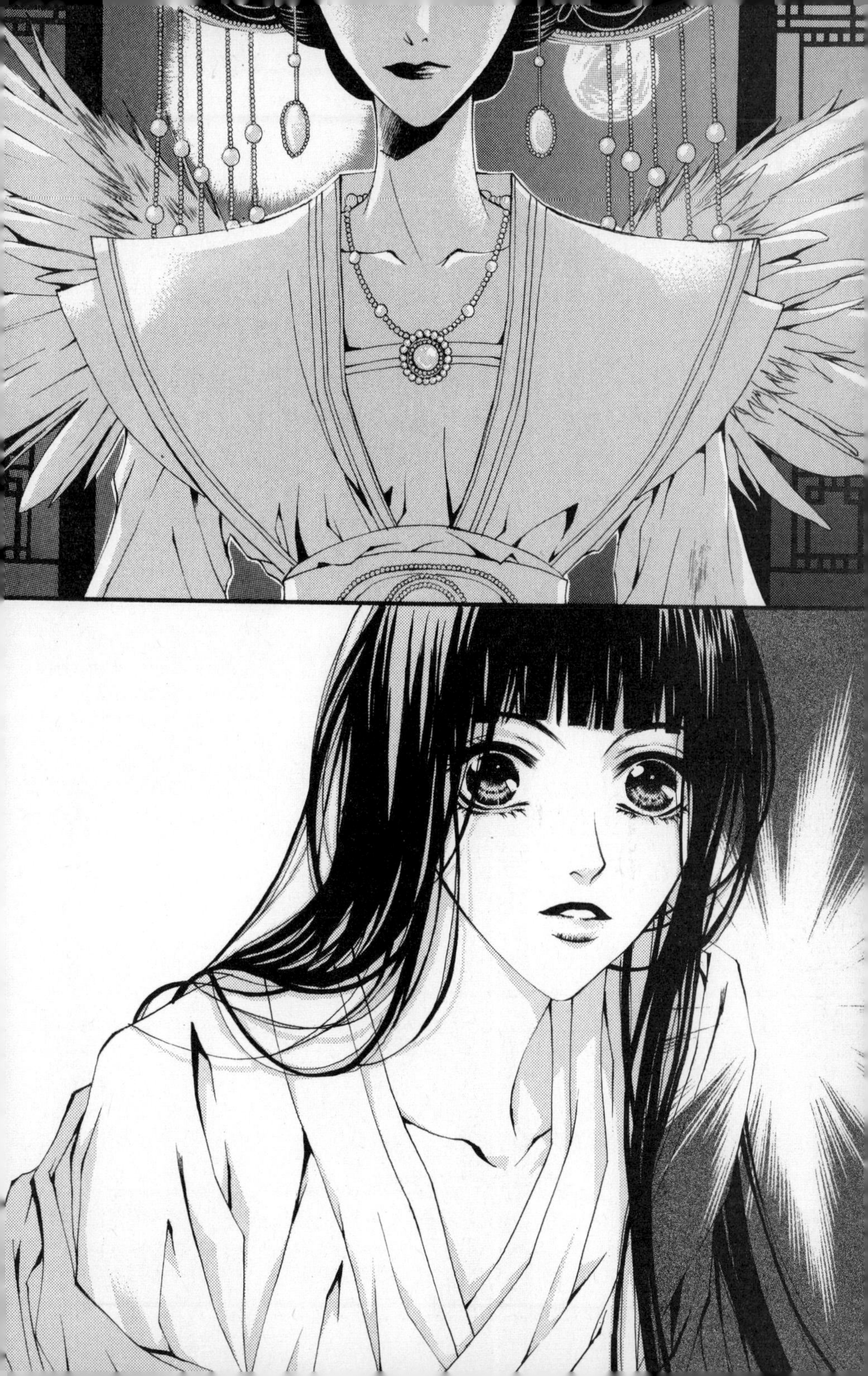

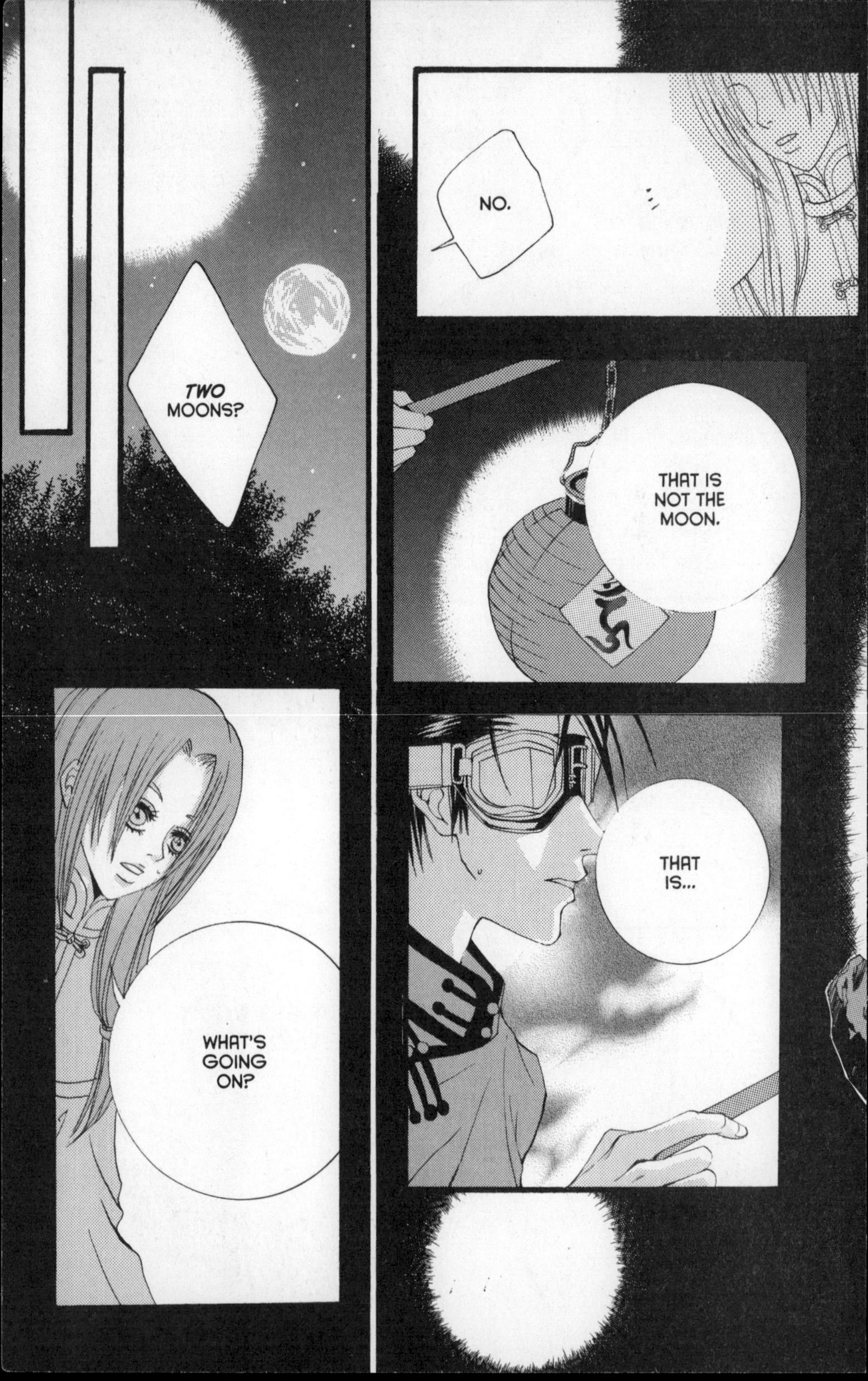
NO.
...
TWO MOONS?
THAT IS NOT THE MOON.
THAT IS...
WHAT'S GOING ON?

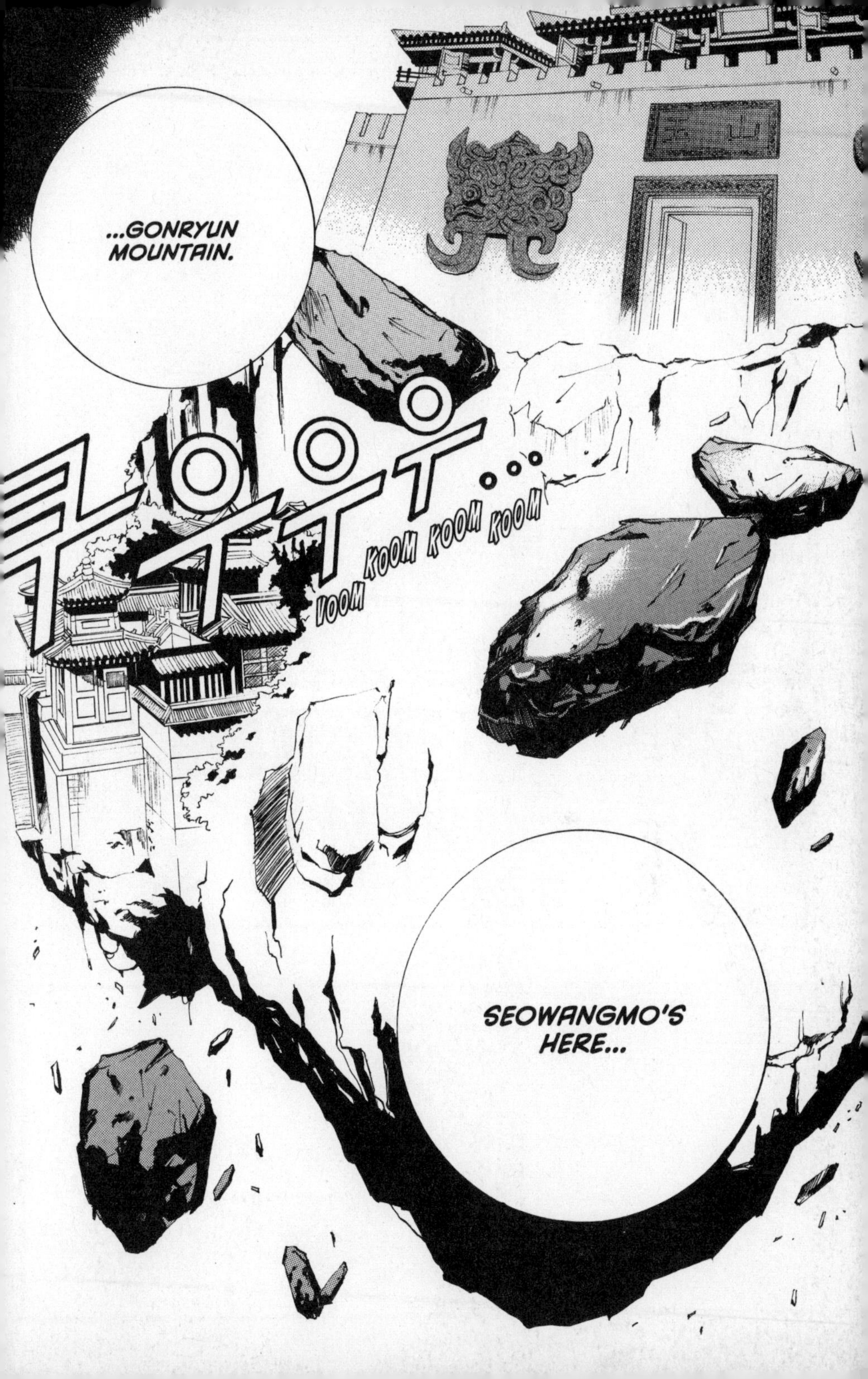

...GONRYUN MOUNTAIN.
VOOM KOOM KOOM KOOM
SEOWANGMO'S HERE...

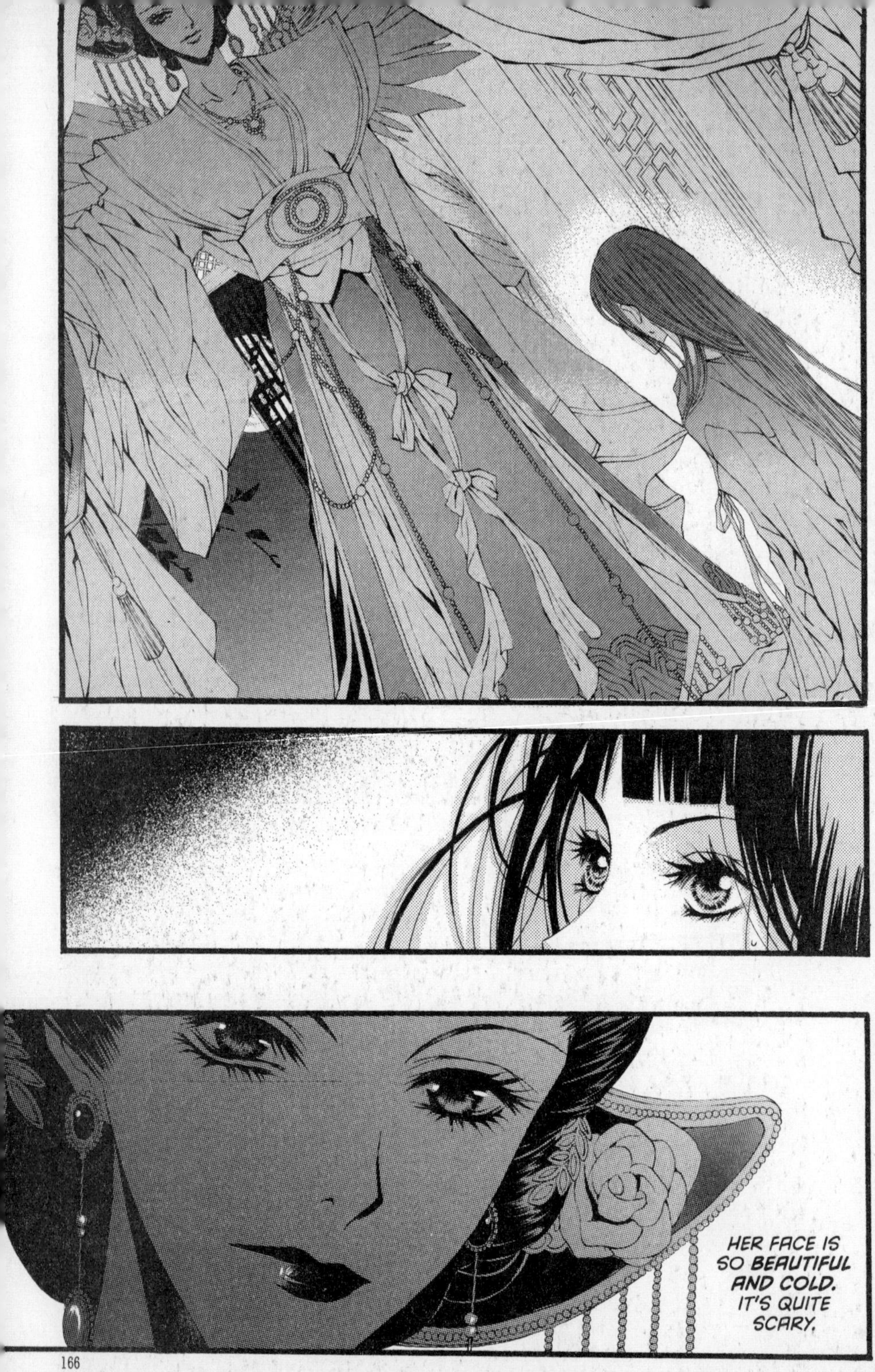
HER FACE IS SO BEAUTIFUL AND COLD. IT'S QUITE SCARY.

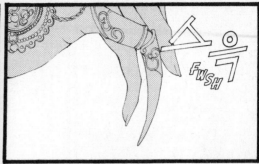

I CAN TELL
WHO THIS IS
WITHOUT ASKING
ANYTHING...

FWSH

움찔
FLINCH

SO THIS IS
THE *HUMAN GIRL*
WHO IS SUPPOSED
TO BE THE
BRIDE...

SHE IS...

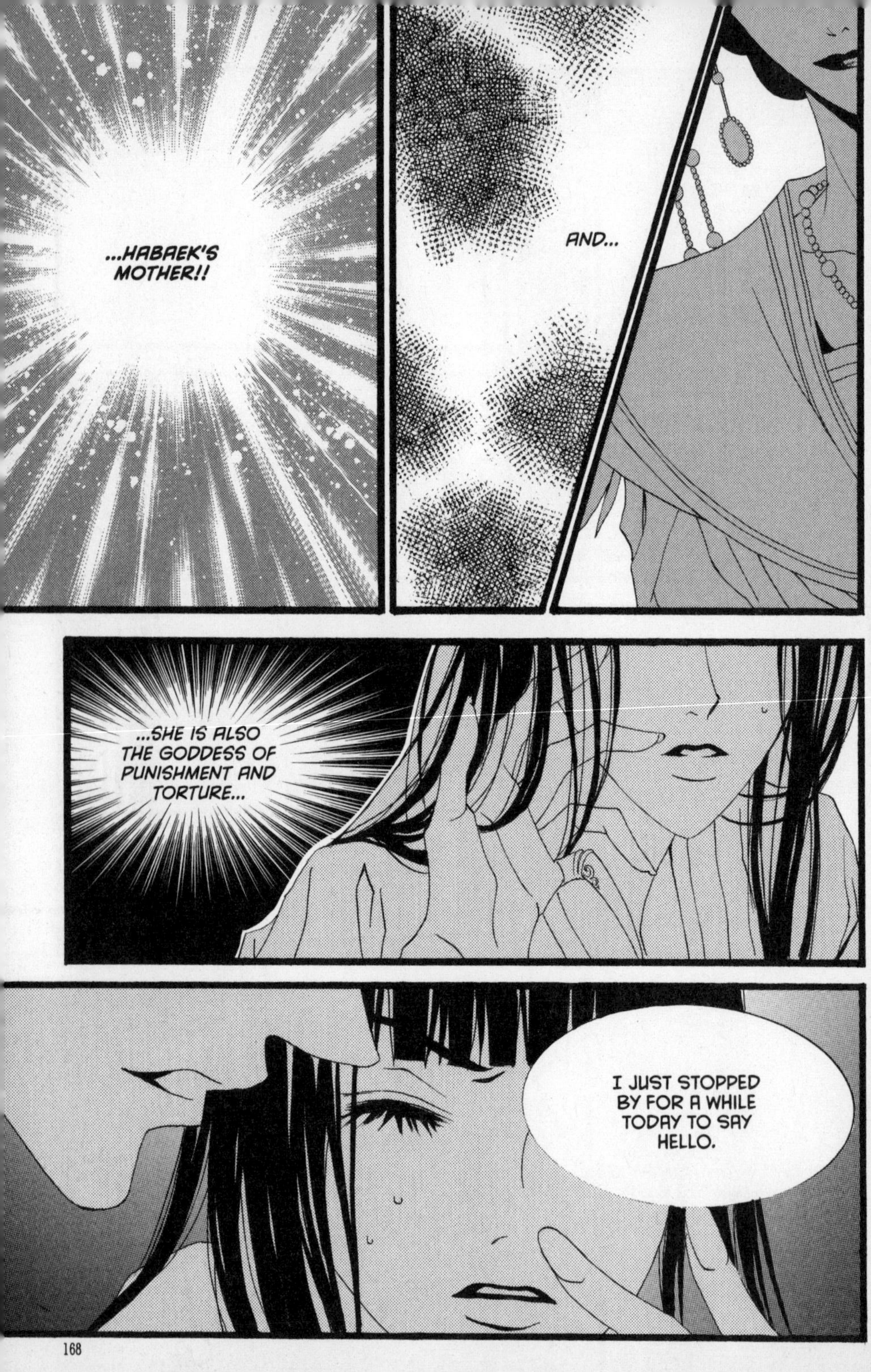

...HABAEK'S MOTHER!!
AND...
...SHE IS ALSO THE GODDESS OF PUNISHMENT AND TORTURE...
I JUST STOPPED BY FOR A WHILE TODAY TO SAY HELLO.

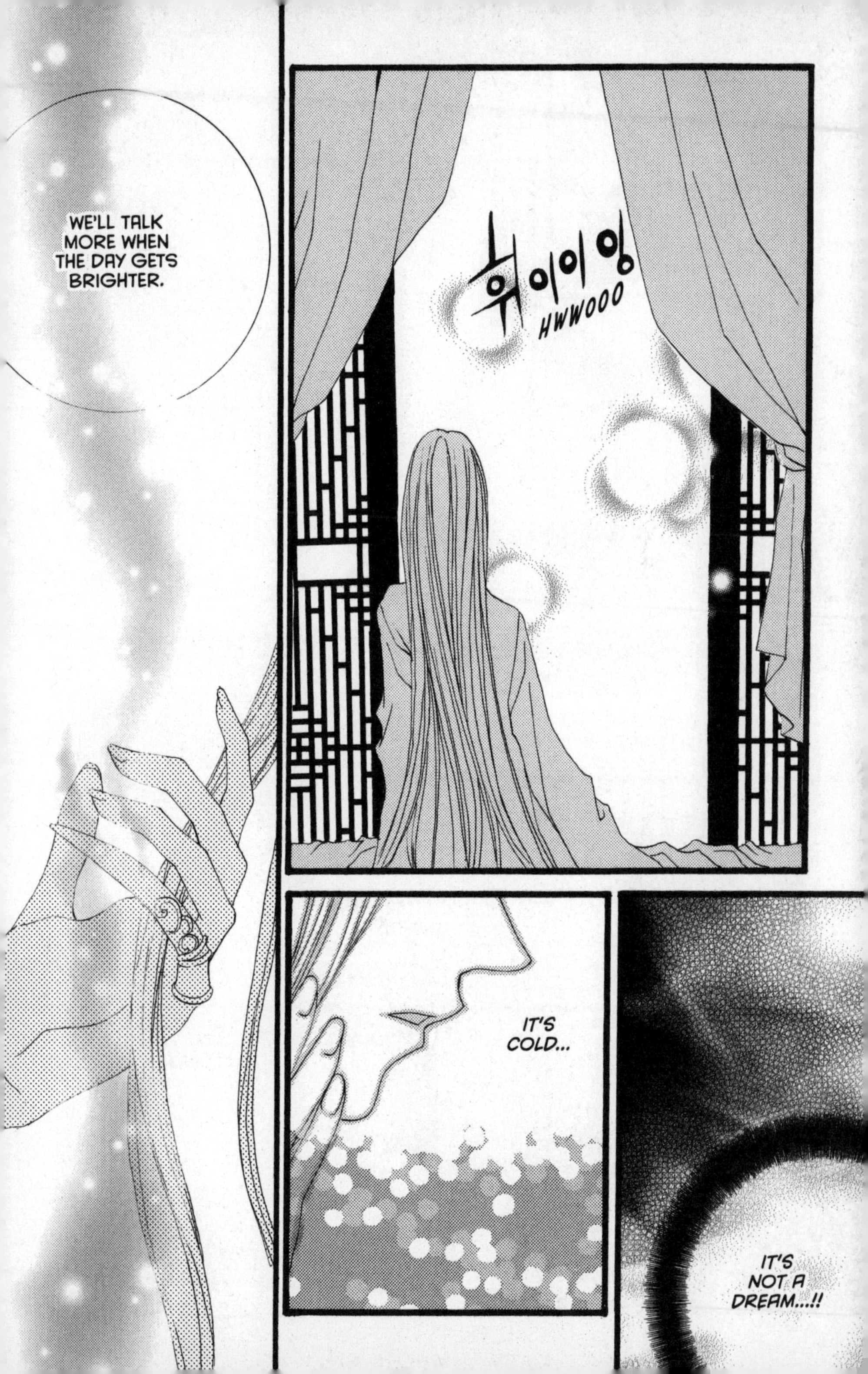
WE'LL TALK MORE WHEN THE DAY GETS BRIGHTER.
휘이이 잉
HWWOOO
IT'S COLD...
IT'S NOT A DREAM...!!

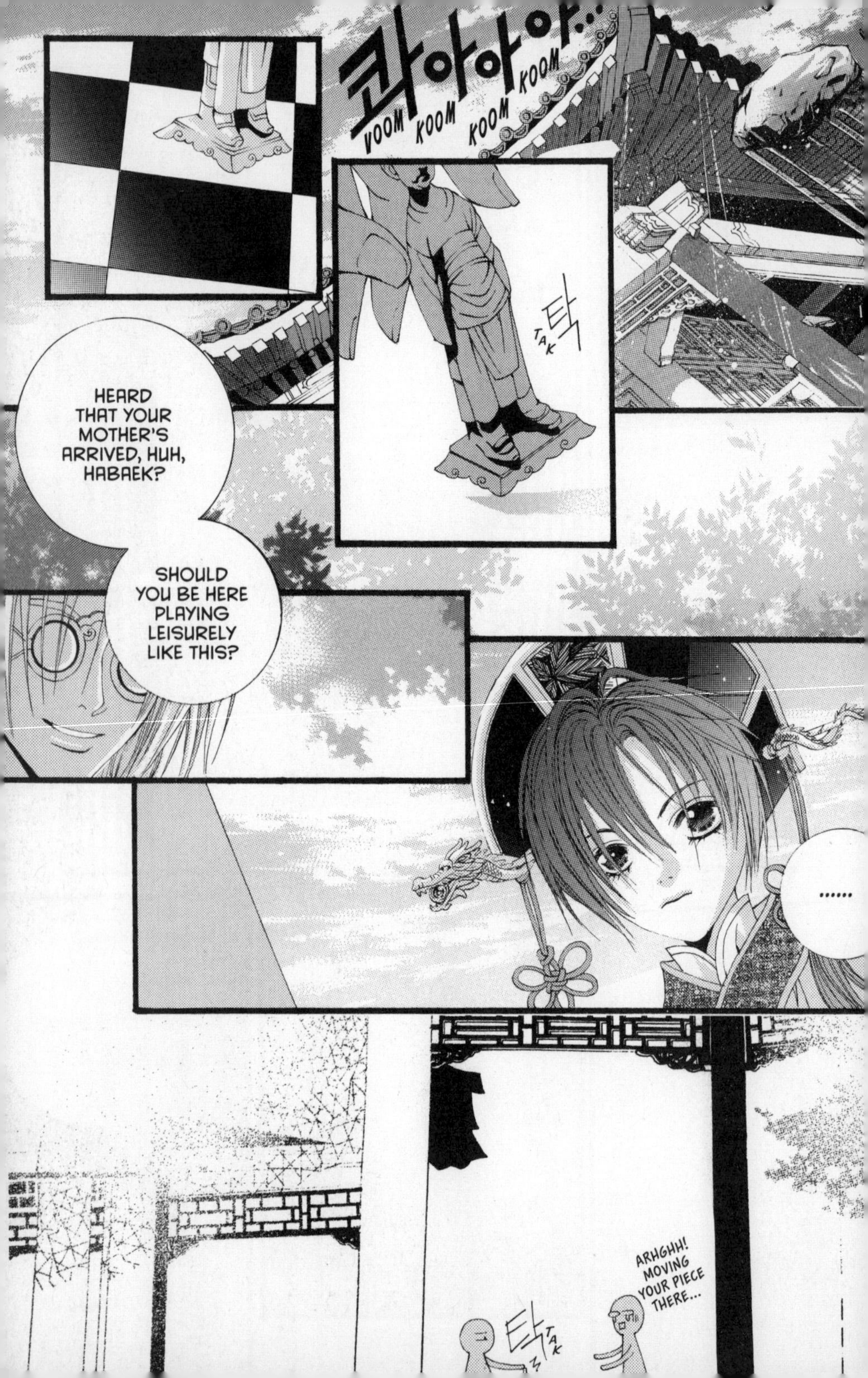

콰아아아...
VOOM KOOM KOOM KOOM
탁
TAK
HEARD THAT YOUR MOTHER'S ARRIVED, HUH, HABAEK?
SHOULD YOU BE HERE PLAYING LEISURELY LIKE THIS?
......
ARHGHH! MOVING YOUR PIECE THERE...
탁
TAK

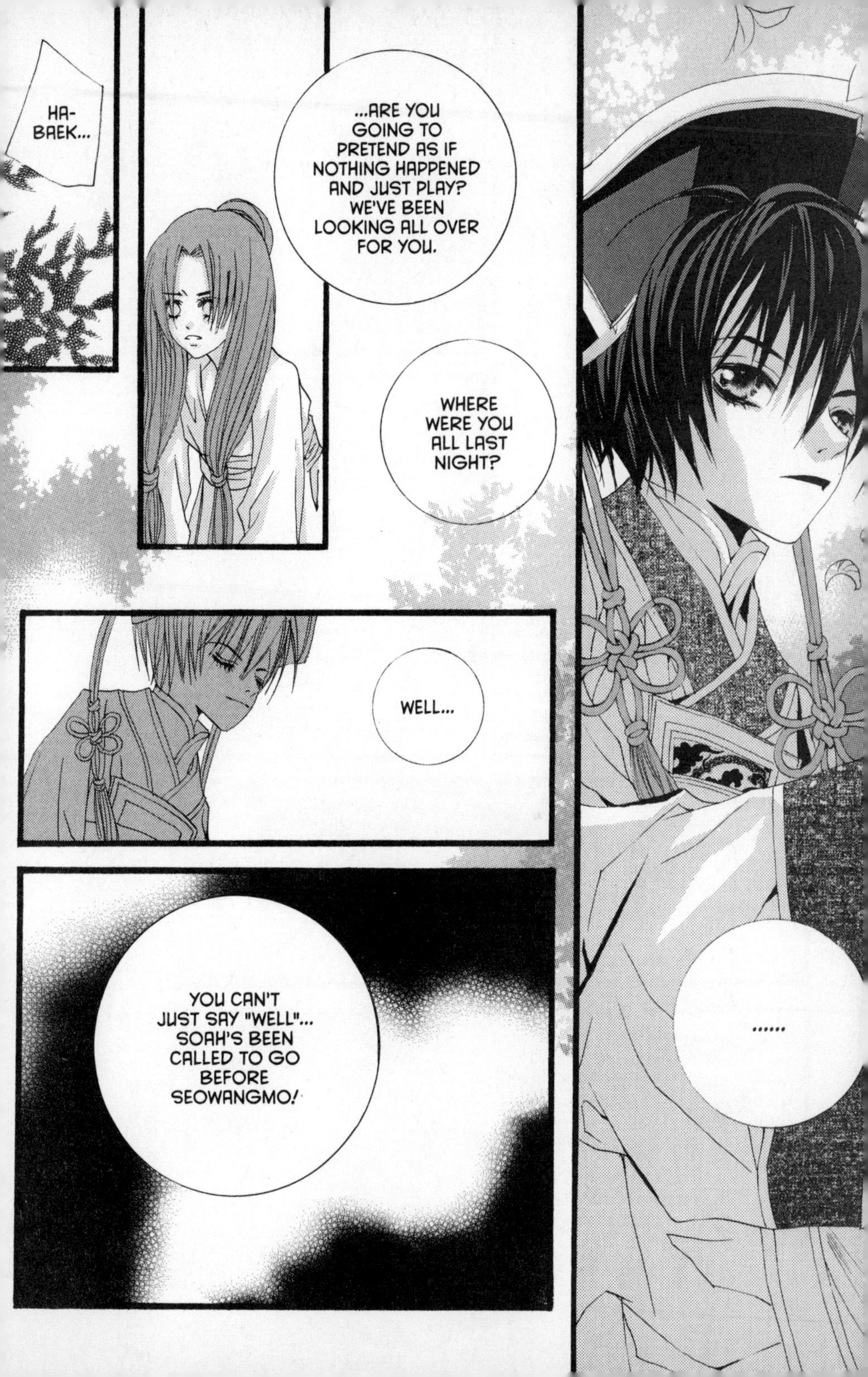
HA-BAEK...
...ARE YOU GOING TO PRETEND AS IF NOTHING HAPPENED AND JUST PLAY? WE'VE BEEN LOOKING ALL OVER FOR YOU.
WHERE WERE YOU ALL LAST NIGHT?
WELL...
......
YOU CAN'T JUST SAY "WELL"... SOAH'S BEEN CALLED TO GO BEFORE SEOWANGMO!

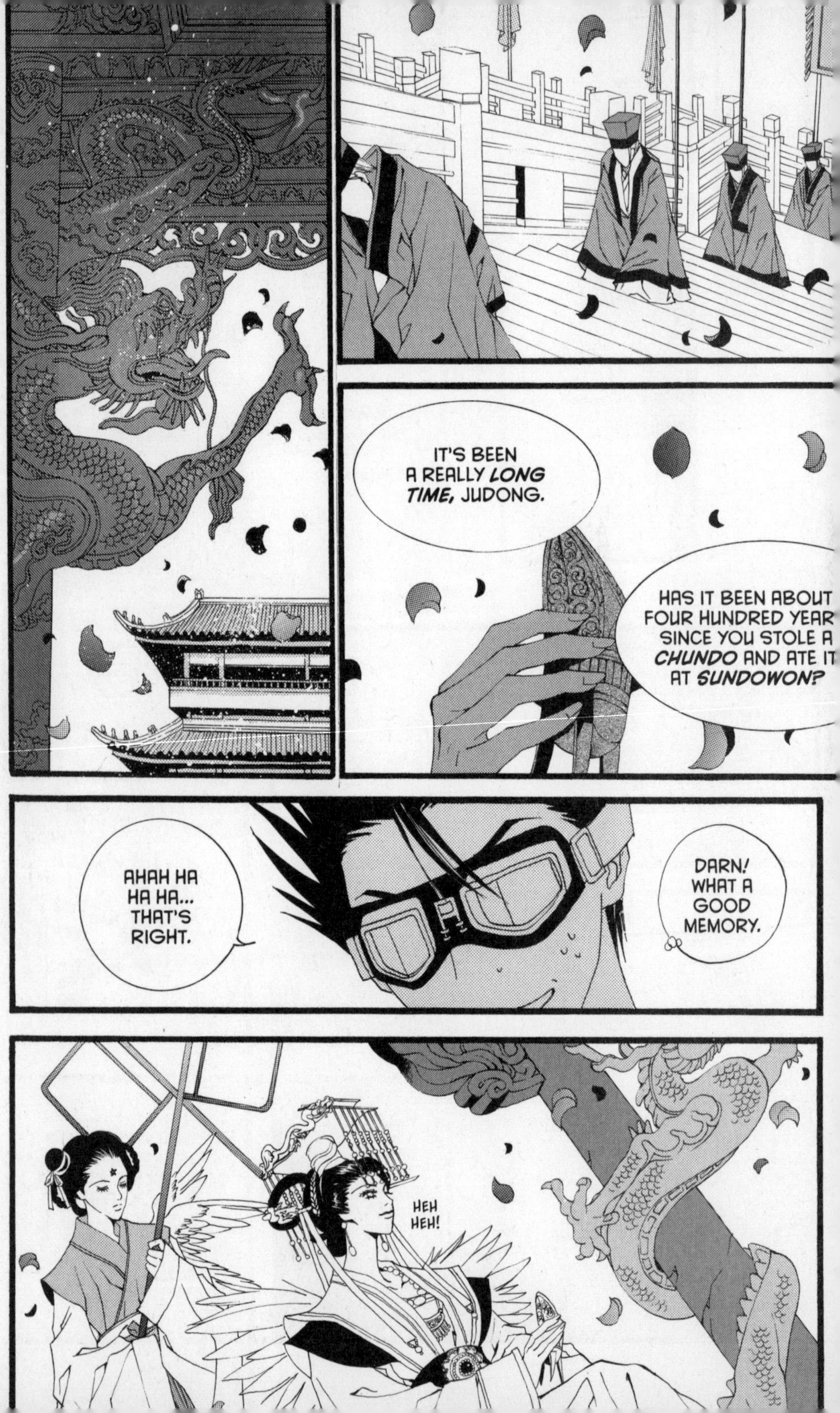
IT'S BEEN A REALLY *LONG TIME,* JUDONG.
HAS IT BEEN ABOUT FOUR HUNDRED YEAR SINCE YOU STOLE A *CHUNDO* AND ATE IT AT *SUNDOWON?*
AHAH HA HA HA... THAT'S RIGHT.
DARN! WHAT A GOOD MEMORY.
HEH HEH!

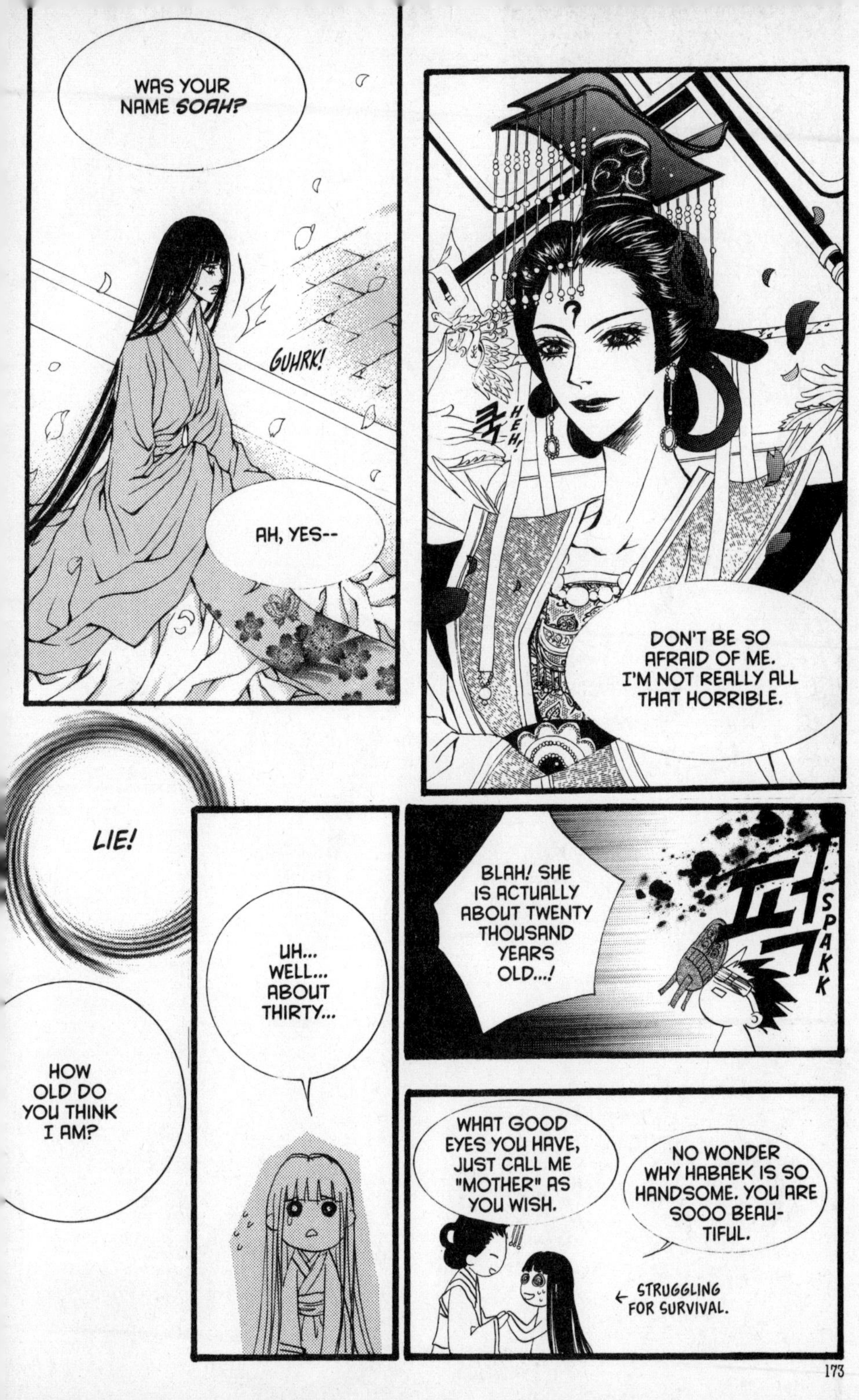
WAS YOUR NAME SOAH?
GUHRK!
AH, YES--
HEH HEH!
DON'T BE SO AFRAID OF ME. I'M NOT REALLY ALL THAT HORRIBLE.
LIE!
HOW OLD DO YOU THINK I AM?
UH... WELL... ABOUT THIRTY...
BLAH! SHE IS ACTUALLY ABOUT TWENTY THOUSAND YEARS OLD...!
SPAKK
WHAT GOOD EYES YOU HAVE, JUST CALL ME "MOTHER" AS YOU WISH.
NO WONDER WHY HABAEK IS SO HANDSOME. YOU ARE SOOO BEAU-TIFUL.
← STRUGGLING FOR SURVIVAL.

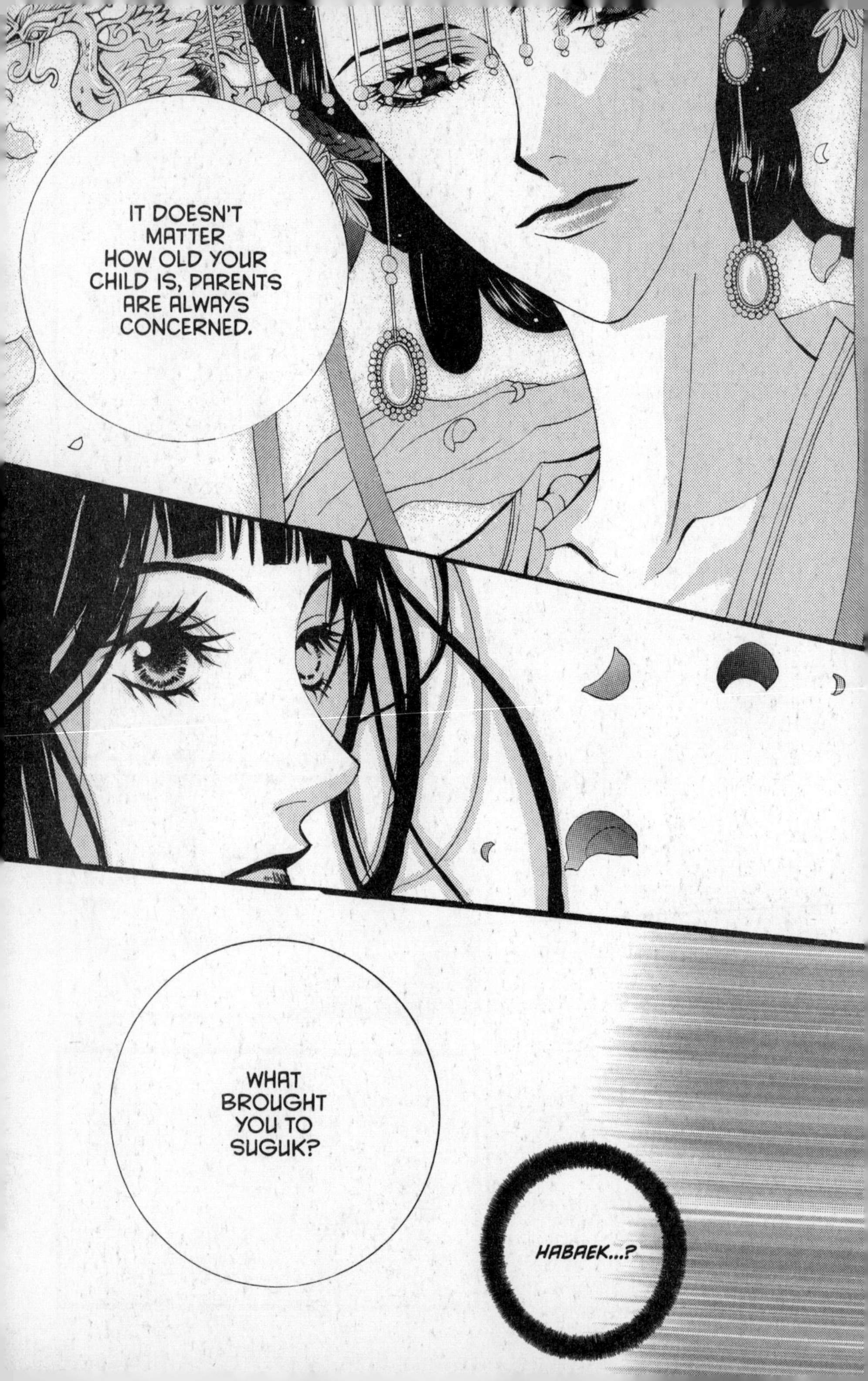
IT DOESN'T MATTER HOW OLD YOUR CHILD IS, PARENTS ARE ALWAYS CONCERNED.
WHAT BROUGHT YOU TO SUGUK?
HABAEK...?

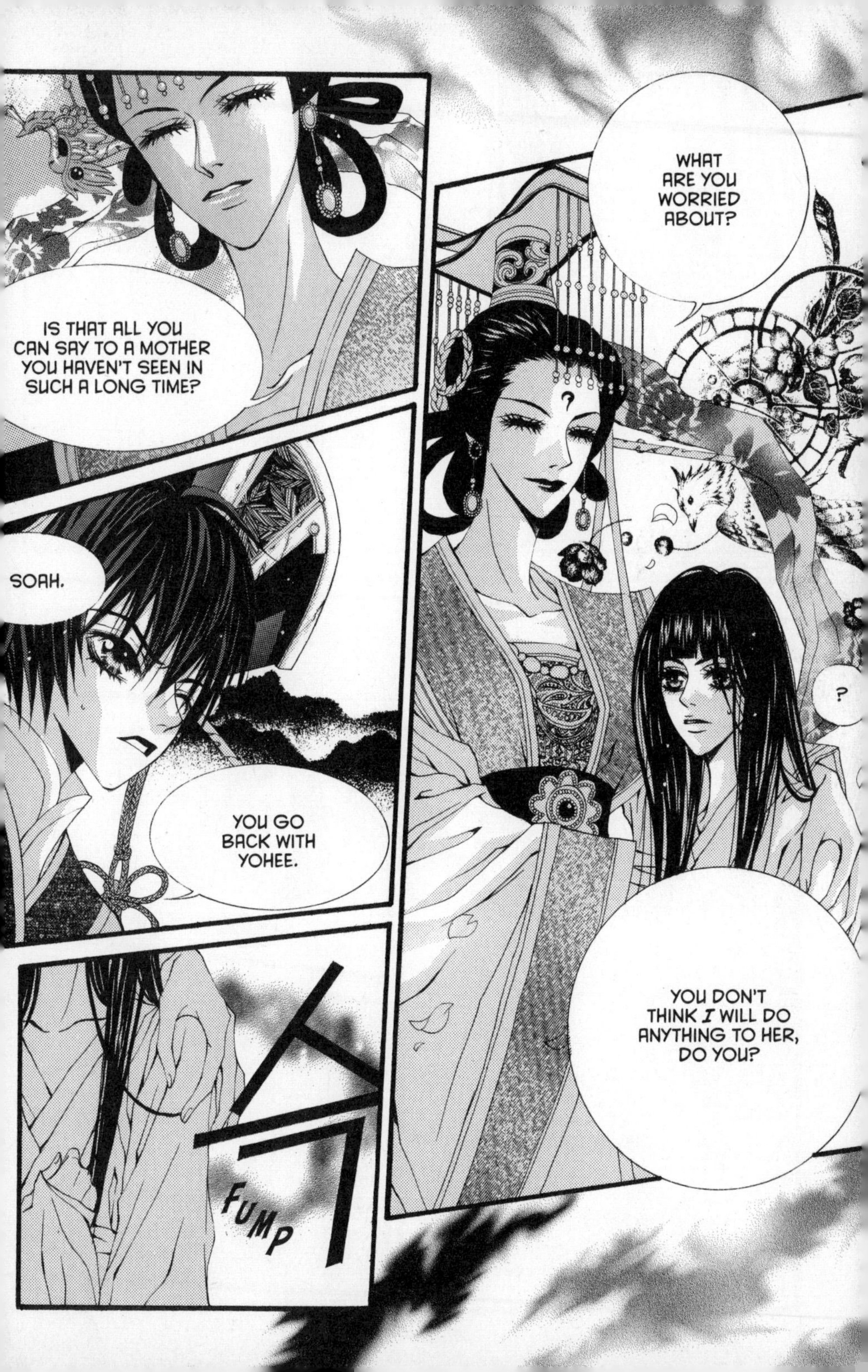
IS THAT ALL YOU CAN SAY TO A MOTHER YOU HAVEN'T SEEN IN SUCH A LONG TIME?
SOAH.
YOU GO BACK WITH YOHEE.
FUMP
WHAT ARE YOU WORRIED ABOUT?
?
YOU DON'T THINK *I* WILL DO ANYTHING TO HER, DO YOU?

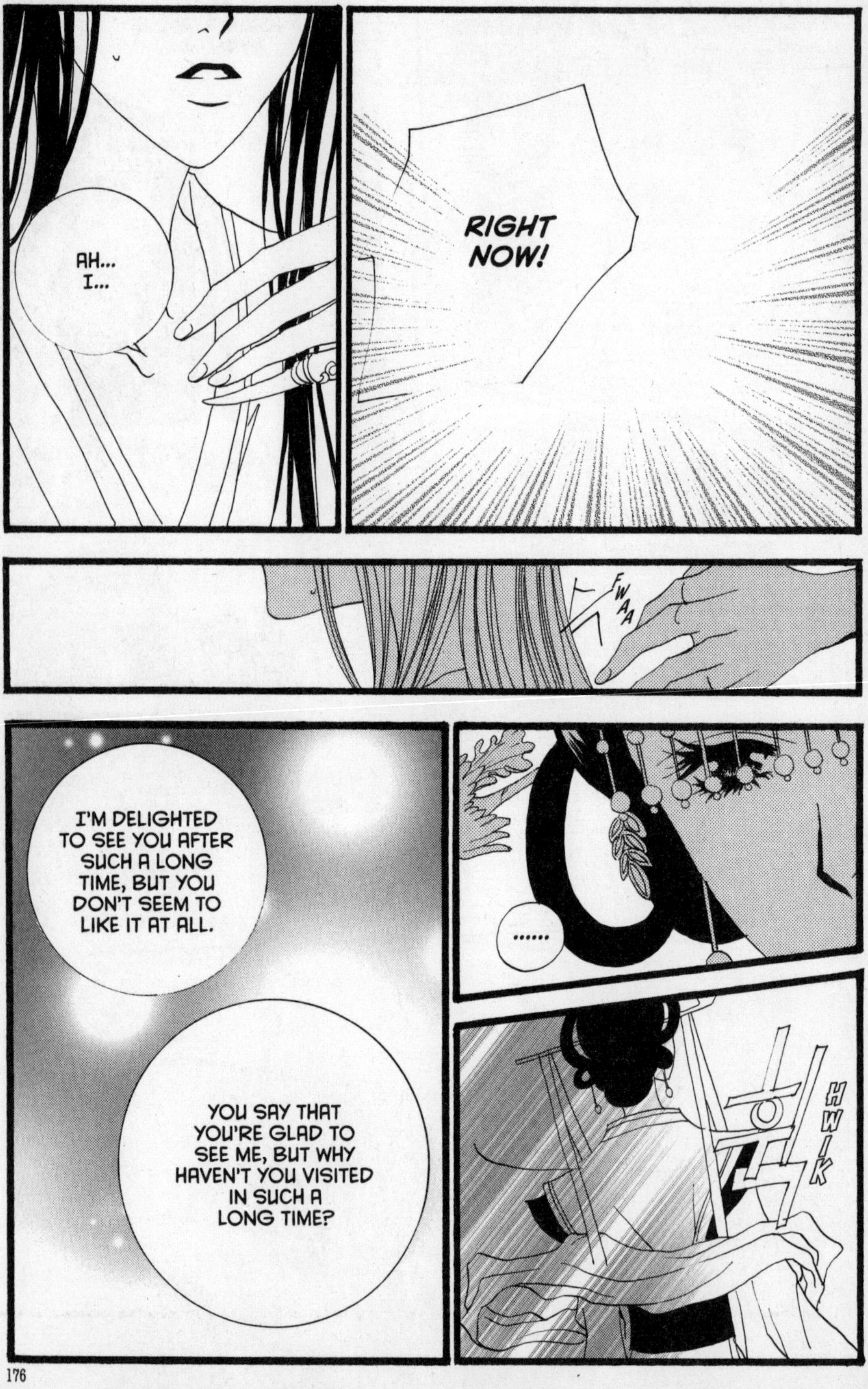
RIGHT NOW!
AH... I...
FWAA
......
I'M DELIGHTED TO SEE YOU AFTER SUCH A LONG TIME, BUT YOU DON'T SEEM TO LIKE IT AT ALL.
HWIK
YOU SAY THAT YOU'RE GLAD TO SEE ME, BUT WHY HAVEN'T YOU VISITED IN SUCH A LONG TIME?

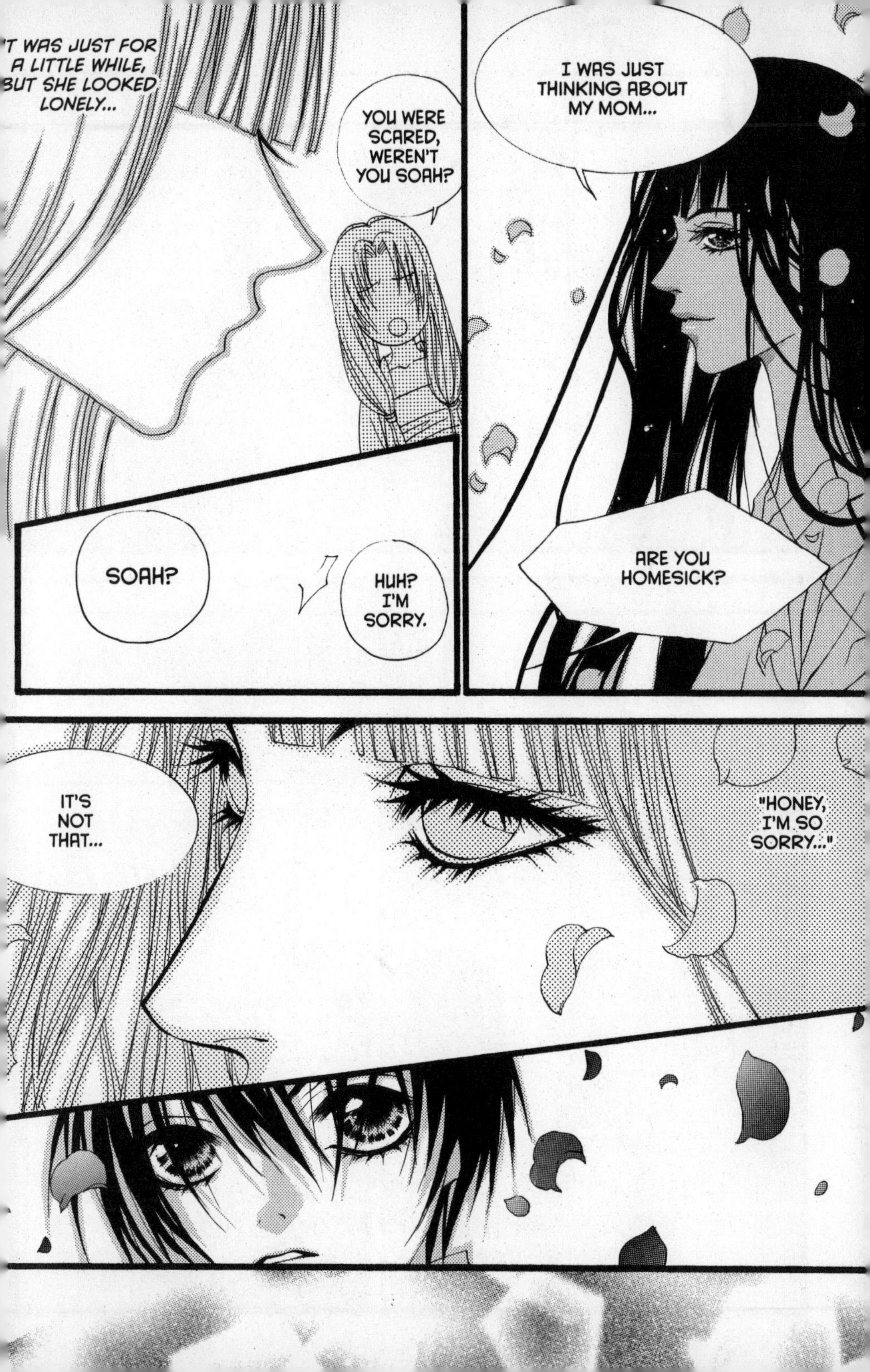
'T WAS JUST FOR A LITTLE WHILE, BUT SHE LOOKED LONELY...
YOU WERE SCARED, WEREN'T YOU SOAH?
I WAS JUST THINKING ABOUT MY MOM...
SOAH?
HUH? I'M SORRY.
ARE YOU HOMESICK?
IT'S NOT THAT...
"HONEY, I'M SO SORRY..."

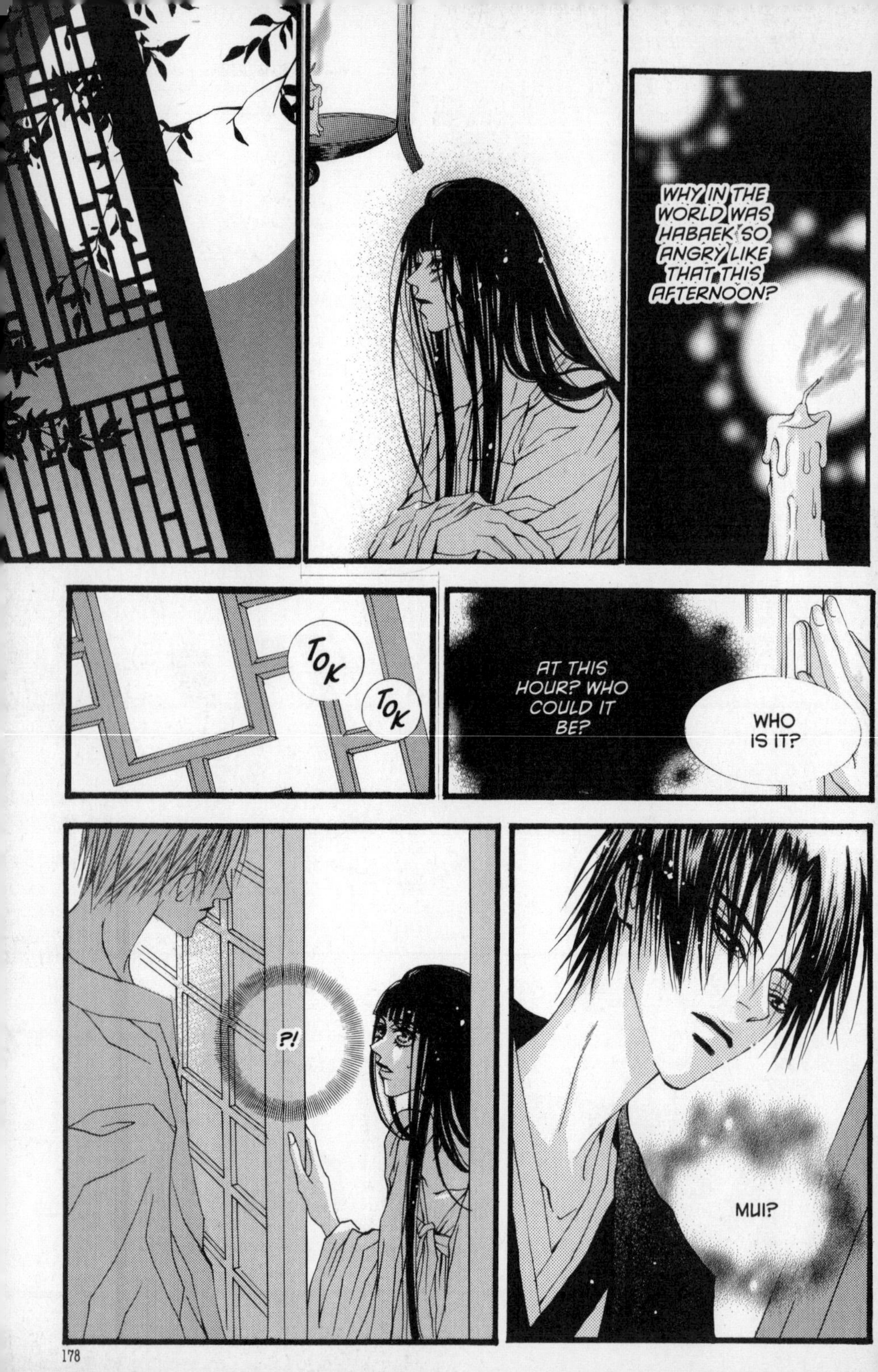
WHY IN THE WORLD WAS HABAEK SO ANGRY LIKE THAT THIS AFTERNOON?
TOK
TOK
AT THIS HOUR? WHO COULD IT BE?
WHO IS IT?
?!
MUI?

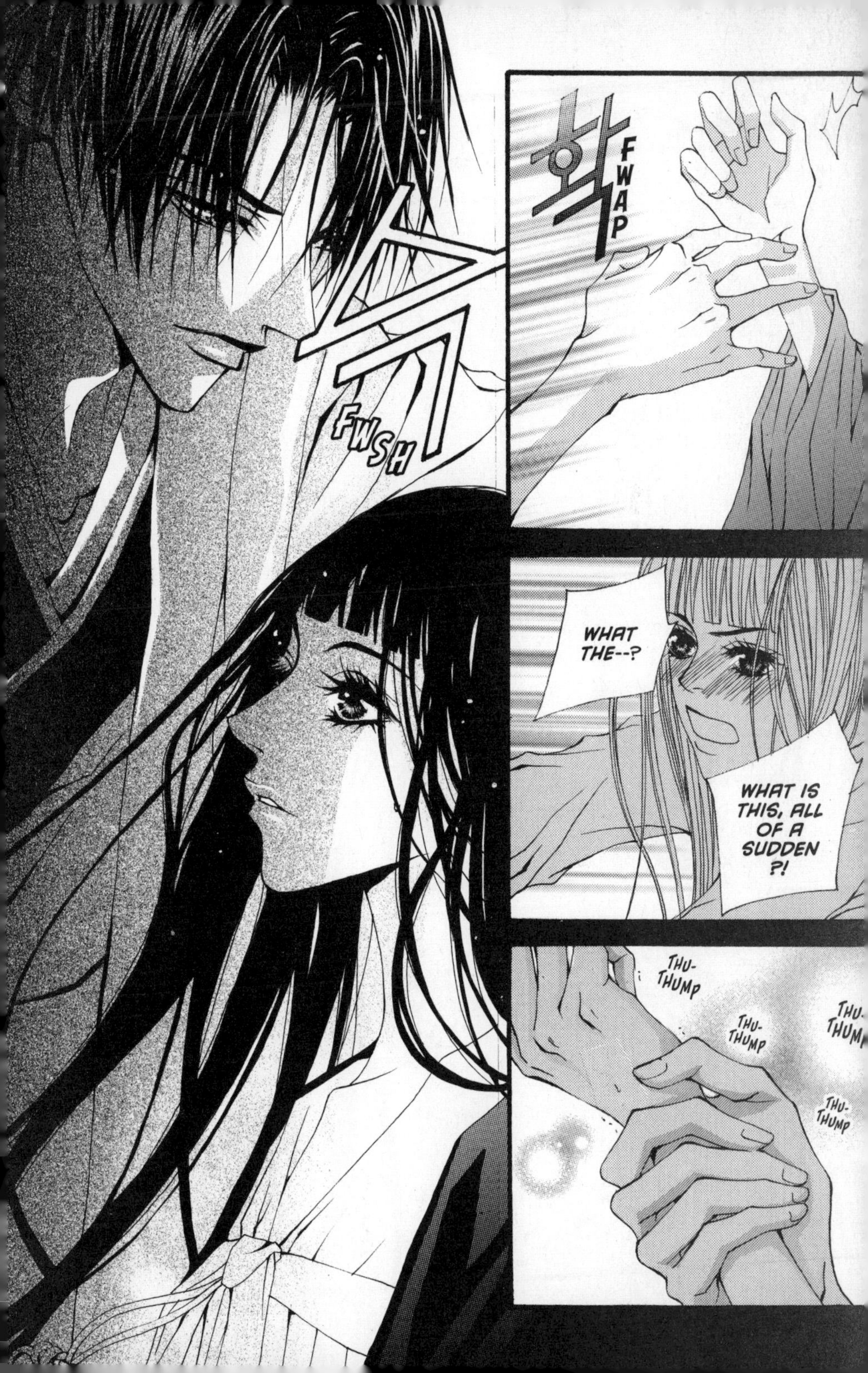

FWAP
WHAT THE--?
WHAT IS THIS, ALL OF A SUDDEN ?!
THU-THUMP
THU-THUMP
THU-THUMP
THU-THUMP
FWSH

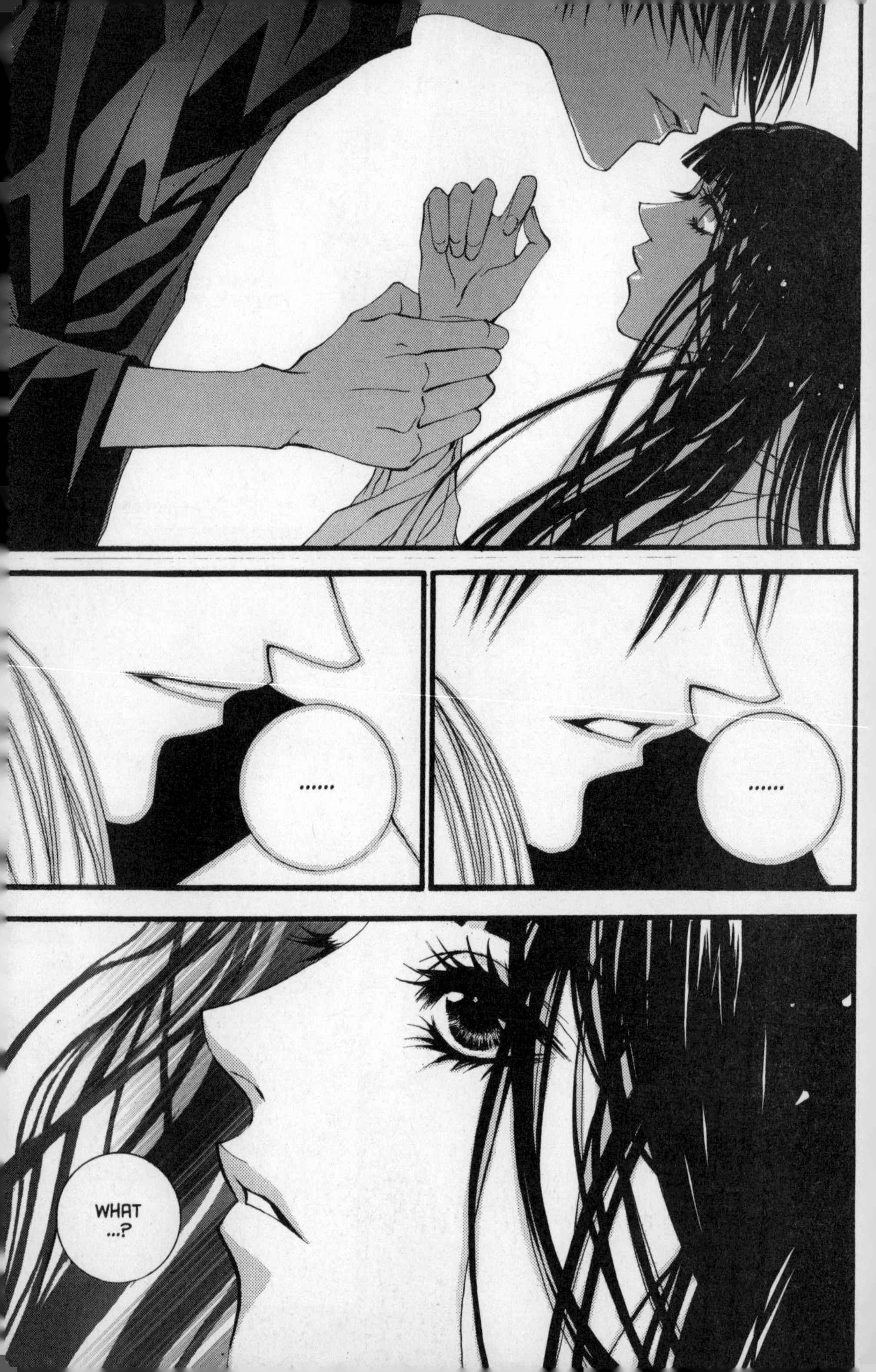
......
......
WHAT
...?

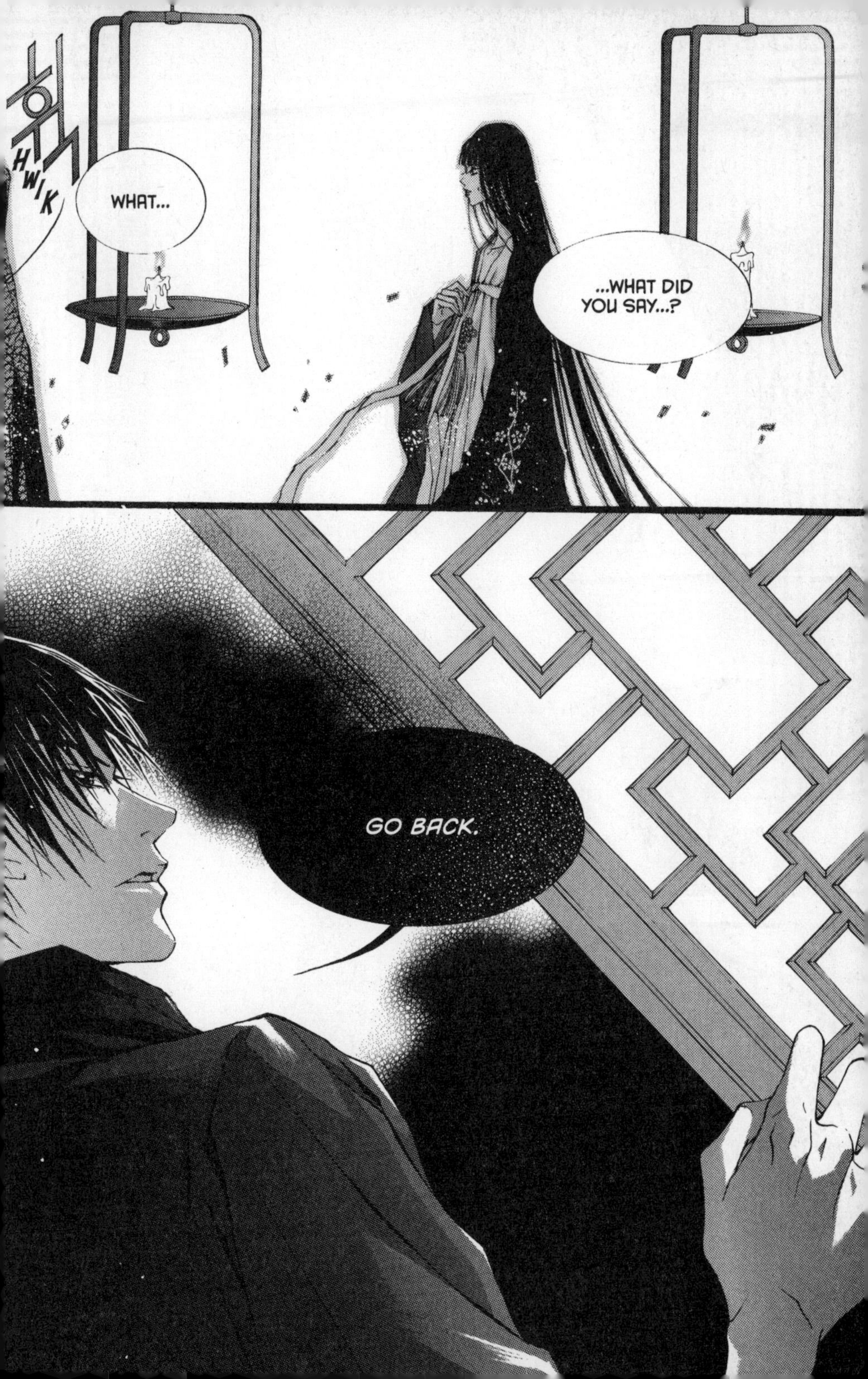
HWIK
WHAT...
...WHAT DID YOU SAY...?
GO BACK.

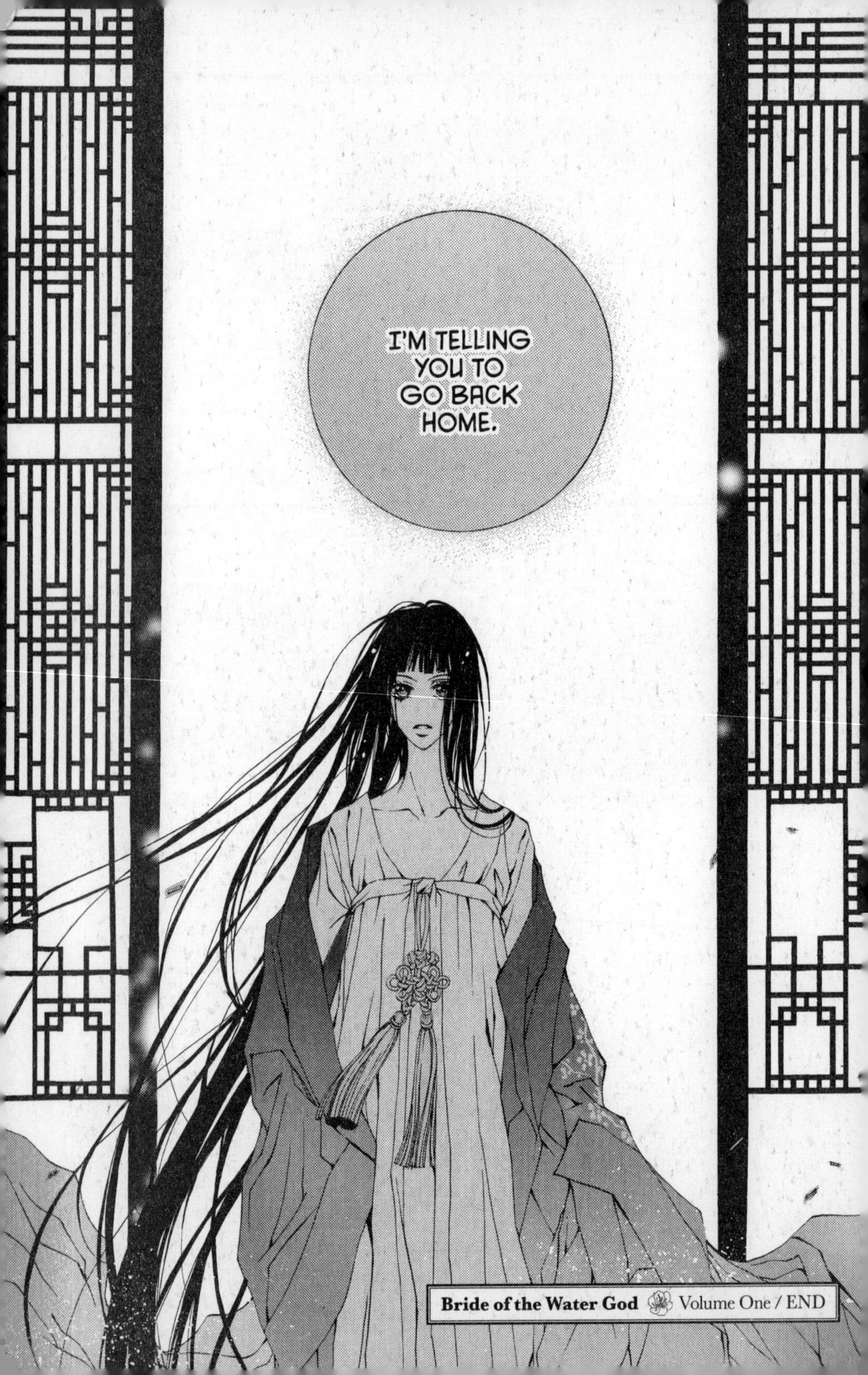
I'M TELLING YOU TO GO BACK HOME.
Bride of the Water God Volume One / END

EPILOGUE

THANK YOU SO MUCH FOR READING ALL THE WAY UP TO THIS POINT.

ACTUALLY, I'M REALLY SHY ABOUT TELLING MY STORIES TO OTHERS.

BLUSH

SO...WHEN I WAS YOUNG, I USED TO WRITE MY STORIES DOWN, FOLDING THE SHEETS OF PAPER ABOUT TWENTY-SEVEN TIMES. THEN I HID THEM SO THAT NOBODY COULD SEE THEM.

FOLD
FOLD

SO "BRIDE OF THE WATER GOD" IS THE FIRST STORY I EVER TOLD TO OTHERS.

YOU ACTUALLY CANNOT FOLD PAPER MORE THAN ABOUT TEN TIMES.

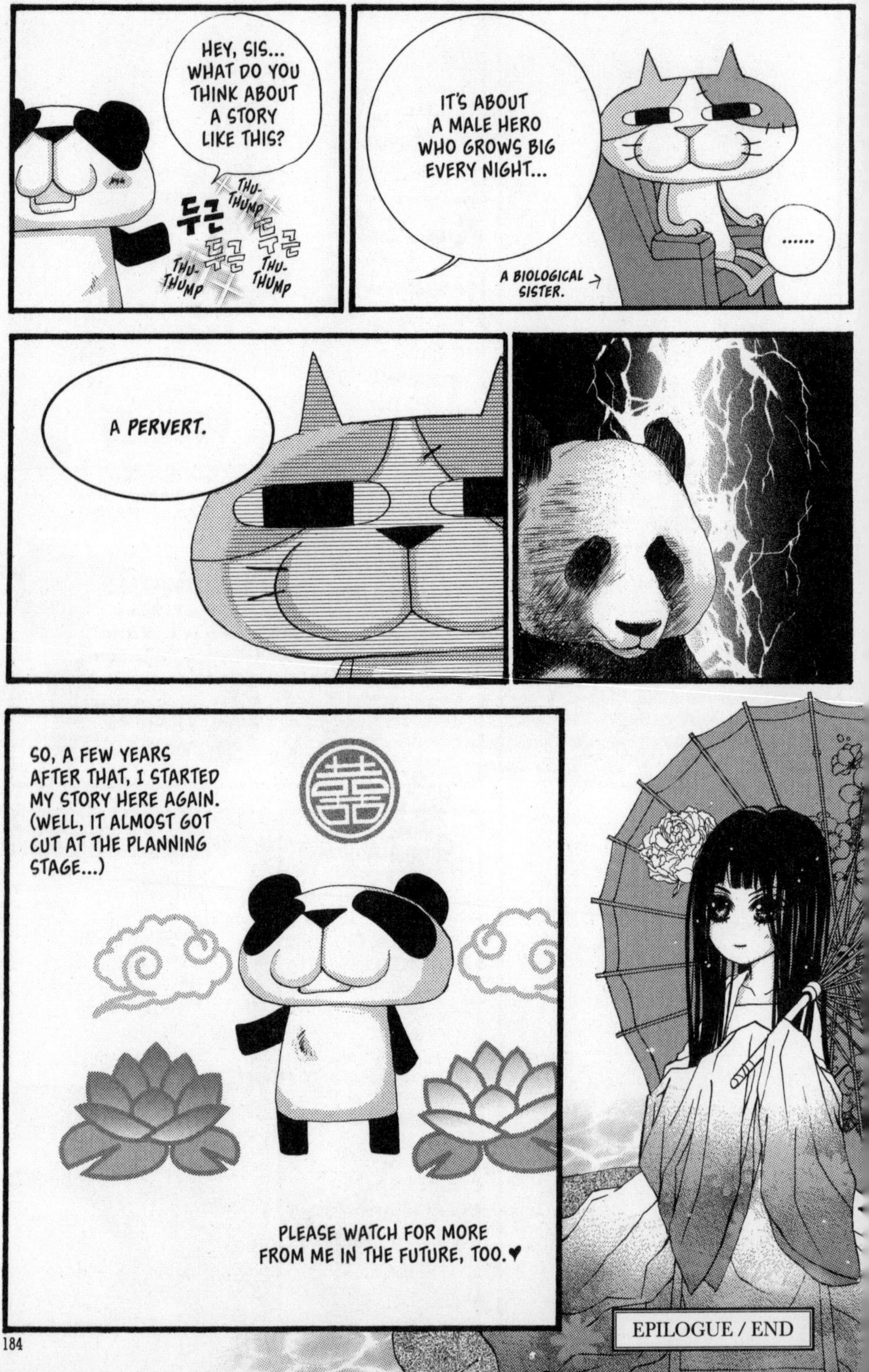
HEY, SIS... WHAT DO YOU THINK ABOUT A STORY LIKE THIS?
두근
THU-THUMP
두근
THU-THUMP
두근
THU-THUMP
IT'S ABOUT A MALE HERO WHO GROWS BIG EVERY NIGHT...
A BIOLOGICAL SISTER.
......
A PERVERT.
SO, A FEW YEARS AFTER THAT, I STARTED MY STORY HERE AGAIN. (WELL, IT ALMOST GOT CUT AT THE PLANNING STAGE...)
PLEASE WATCH FOR MORE FROM ME IN THE FUTURE, TOO.♥
EPILOGUE / END

publisher
Mike Richardson

digital production
Ryan Hill

collection designer
David Nestelle

art director
Lia Ribacchi

Special thanks to Tina Alessi, Davey Estrada, Michael Gombos, Julia Kwon, and Cara Niece.

English-language version produced by DARK HORSE COMICS.

BRIDE OF THE WATER GOD Volume 1
© 2006 Mi-Kyung Yun. All rights reserved. Original Korean edition published by Seoul
Cultural Publishers, Inc. English translation rights arranged with Seoul Cultural Publishers,
Inc. English edition copyright © 2007 Dark Horse Comics, Inc. All rights reserved. Dark Horse
Manhwa™ is a trademark of Dark Horse Comics, Inc. No portion of this publication may be repro-
duced or transmitted, in any form or by any means, without the express written permission of Dark
Horse Comics, Inc. Names, characters, places, and incidents featured in this publication are either
the product of the author's imagination or are used fictitiously. Any resemblance to actual persons
(living or dead), events, institutions, or locales, without satiric intent, is coincidental.

Dark Horse Manhwa
A division of Dark Horse Comics, Inc.
10956 SE Main Street
Milwaukie OR 97222

darkhorse.com

To find a comics shop in your area, call the
Comic Shop Locator Service toll-free at 1-888-266-4226

First edition: October 2007
ISBN: 978-1-59307-849-2

7 9 10 8 6
Printed in the United States of America

People say that one's creation comes to possess their soul when one pours their mind and hope into it.

I thank you so much for reading my stories, although I have a lot to work on. I will keep working harder.

—Mi-Kyung Yun

CREATOR PROFILE

Born on October 14, 1980. Majored in Animation at Mokwon University.

Received the silver medal for Seoul Media Group's "Shin-in-gong-mo-jeon" ("New Artist Debut Competition") for *Na-eu Ji-gu Bang-moon-gi* (*The Journey of My Earth Visit*) in 2003.

Received a "Shin-in-sang" ("Best New Artist") award from the Dokja-manhwa-daesang organization for *Railroad* in 2004.

Currently publishing *Bride of the Water God* serially in the Korean comics magazine *Wink*.

3 1901 04242 4558

STORY NOTE: The poem that appears on page 136 is a Chinese poem. *Chosa* is one of the literary styles developed during China's "Cho" dynasty. Within this style, *guga* poetry was specially dedicated to singing about and worshipping gods such as Habaek (the water god), Judong (the fire god), and others.

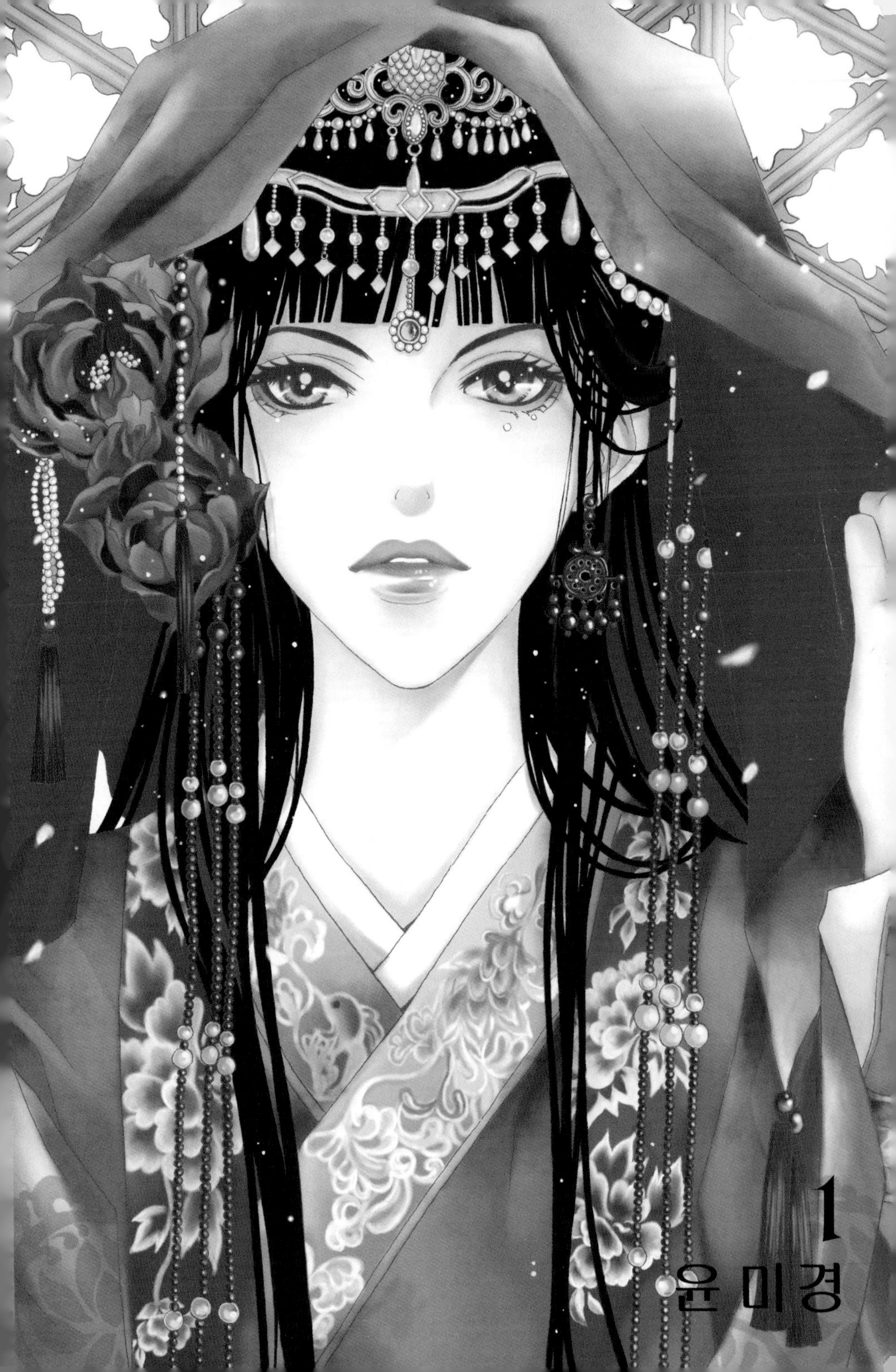
1
윤미경

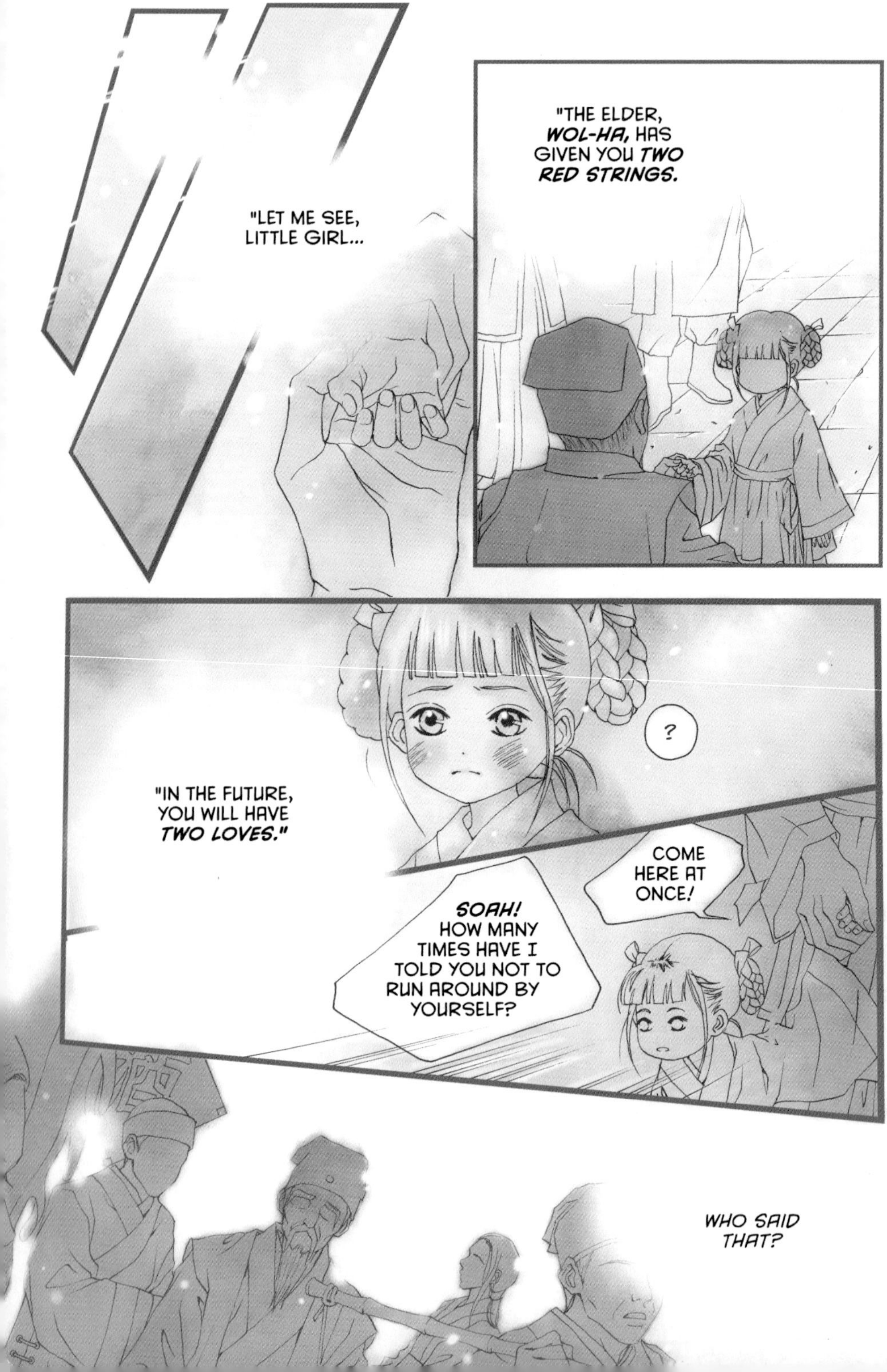
"LET ME SEE, LITTLE GIRL...
"THE ELDER, *WOL-HA,* HAS GIVEN YOU *TWO RED STRINGS.*
?
"IN THE FUTURE, YOU WILL HAVE *TWO LOVES."*
COME HERE AT ONCE!
SOAH! HOW MANY TIMES HAVE I TOLD YOU NOT TO RUN AROUND BY YOURSELF?
WHO SAID THAT?